T0340133

Productivity Accounting

The Economics of Business Performance

The productivity of a business exerts a significant influence on its financial performance. A similar influence exists for industries and economies: those with superior productivity performance thrive at the expense of others. Productivity performance helps explain the growth and demise of businesses and the relative prosperity of nations. *Productivity Accounting: The Economics of Business Performance* offers an in-depth analysis of variation in business performance, providing the reader with an analytical framework within which to account for this variation and its causes and consequences. The primary focus is the individual business, and the principal effect of business productivity performance is on business financial performance. Alternative measures of financial performance are considered, including profit, profitability, cost, unit cost, and return on assets. Combining analytical rigor with empirical illustrations, the analysis draws on wide-ranging literature, both historical and current, from business and economics, and explains how businesses create value and distribute it.

Emili Grifell-Tatjé is currently Professor of Management and Business Economics in the Department of Business at the Universitat Autònoma de Barcelona; formerly he was head of the department and academic director of the doctoral program in Economics, Management, and Organization. He has received research grants from academic and private institutions and has been awarded visiting appointments by various universities around the world. Professor Grifell-Tatjé has published in a wide range of academic journals.

C. A. Knox Lovell is Honorary Professor with the Centre for Efficiency and Productivity Analysis in the School of Economics at the University of Queensland. He served as Editor-in-Chief of the *Journal of Productivity Analysis* for a decade. He has authored several books, including *Production Frontiers* (with Rolf Färe and Shawna Grosskopf) and *Stochastic Frontier Analysis* (with Subal Kumbhakhar) for Cambridge University Press.

Productivity Accounting

The Economics of Business Performance

EMILI GRIFELL-TATJÉ
Universitat Autònoma de Barcelona

C. A. KNOX LOVELL
University of Queensland

CAMBRIDGE
UNIVERSITY PRESS

University Printing House, Cambridge CB2 8BS, United Kingdom

One Liberty Plaza, 20th Floor, New York, NY 10006, USA

477 Williamstown Road, Port Melbourne, VIC 3207, Australia

314-321, 3rd Floor, Plot 3, Splendor Forum, Jasola District Centre, New Delhi - 110025, India

79 Anson Road, #06-04/06, Singapore 079906

Cambridge University Press is part of the University of Cambridge.

It furthers the University's mission by disseminating knowledge in the pursuit of education, learning and research at the highest international levels of excellence.

www.cambridge.org
Information on this title: www.cambridge.org/9780521709873

First published 2015

A catalogue record for this publication is available from the British Library

Library of Congress Cataloging in Publication data
Grifell-Tatjé, E. (Emili)
Productivity accounting : the economics of business performance / Emili Grifell-Tatje,
C.A. Knox Lovell.
pages   cm
Includes bibliographical references and indexes.
ISBN 978-0-521-88353-5 (hardback)
1. Productivity accounting.   2. Industrial productivity – Measurement.   3. Profit.
I. Lovell, C. A. Knox.   II. Title.
HF5686.P86G75   2015
657′.7–dc 3   2014027962

ISBN 978-0-521-88353-5 Hardback
ISBN 978-0-521-70987-3 Paperback

To the Ladies
Mercè, Marta, Julie, Heidi, Claire, Gemma, Sydney, Savannah, Addison, Holly, and Lucinda

Contents

Part I   Productivity and Profitability

Tables

Figures

Preface

We were inspired to write this book by the pioneering works of Hiram S. Davis and John W. Kendrick. Davis, a staff member and Director of the Industrial Research Unit in the Wharton School of Finance and Commerce at the University of Pennsylvania, wrote on prices, wages, and industrial relations, and more extensively on productivity. His work on productivity influenced Kendrick, the foremost productivity expert of our time (and also a reviewer of the prospectus for this book), and Kendrick in turn has influenced a generation of productivity scholars.

Both writers were concerned with productivity growth at the aggregate level. In *The Industrial Study of Economic Progress*, the first of two books devoted to productivity, Davis proposed to investigate productivity at the industry level, and was equally concerned with the sources, both internal and external, of productivity growth and the sharing of the benefits that productivity growth conferred. He claimed that productivity growth constituted one, but not the sole, driver of "economic progress," which is more far-reaching than the more popular concepts of real income or real income per capita. Economic progress also depends on a distribution of the productivity gains in which all members of society benefit, and the ability to address the labor displacement and social costs of industrial development that productivity growth generates.

In his authoritative *Productivity Trends in the United States* Kendrick measured US productivity growth over a half-century, finding that it accounted for three quarters of the increase in real output per capita, a concept less inclusive, and more concrete, than Davis's notion of economic progress. Kendrick then showed that, as a consequence, prices of final goods and services increased less than prices of the factors of production did, and he concluded that this explains how the fruits of productivity growth were distributed to providers of the factor services. This also implies that the measurement of productivity change can be based on price changes, an idea central to the work of the French writer Fourastié that is enjoying a renaissance more than a half-century later.

Both writers were also concerned with productivity growth at the level of the individual business.

In *Productivity Accounting* Davis studied productivity in a business and devoted much of his attention to the relationship between productivity growth and financial performance, a relationship he called "productivity accounting," a term we have borrowed for the title of our book. He also explained the need to convert the accountant's current price accounts to constant price accounts in order to obtain a productivity measure independent of prices. Davis also continued his interest in the distribution of the benefits of productivity growth to consumers, resource suppliers, labor, management, and investors, and the concept of investor input played a central role in his analysis.

In a pair of books devoted to the measurement of business productivity – *Measuring Company Productivity* (with Daniel Creamer) and a subsequent updated version, *Improving Company Productivity* – Kendrick referred explicitly to the influence of Davis. He echoed Davis by emphasizing the necessity of converting current price accounts to constant price accounts in order to measure productivity, and he explored the relationship between productivity change, price change, and profitability change. He devoted considerable attention to measurement problems, partly within the context of several case studies.

In this book we follow Davis and Kendrick by examining productivity dispersion and the determinants of productivity change, by relating productivity change to change in financial performance, and by exploring the distribution of the benefits of productivity change. We do so within an analytical framework, augmented with empirical applications. We have reviewed a wide range of literature, in business and economics, created around the world over a long period of time, in academe, in consultancies, and in government agencies. We have learned much about productivity dispersion and its persistence from studies that appeared nearly a century ago in *Monthly Labor Review*, a journal published by the US Bureau of Labor Statistics. We have gained valuable insights into the relationship between productivity and business financial performance from reading *Productivity*

Measurement Review, a journal published quarterly from 1955 through 1965 by the European Productivity Agency. We have gained additional insights into the distribution of the benefits of productivity change, and to alternative definitions of these benefits, from reading several monographs published under the auspices of the Centre d'Étude des Revenus et des Coûts (CERC) in Paris during the late 1960s and early 1970s. None of these sources occupies a prominent place on the bookshelves of most scholars. We have incurred some debts in the lengthy process of writing this book.

We are indebted to the innovators whose contributions we have absorbed, re-interpreted, and hopefully not distorted. Our primary influences have been the two pioneers, Hiram Davis and John Kendrick. We also have benefited from exposure to the large analytical and empirical body of work produced by André L. A. Vincent, Raymond Courbis, and Philippe Templé (who, while acknowledging the influence of Kendrick, were more interested in the distribution, rather than the generation, of productivity gains) and their colleagues in Paris; Bela Gold, Samuel Eilon, and their colleagues, whose work on integrated managerial control ratios and related matters academics tend to overlook; the detailed business histories of Alfred Chandler and H. Thomas Johnson; Ephraim Sudit and his colleagues, whose business experience has enriched academic discourse; William W. Lewis and a host of writers for the *McKinsey Quarterly* and the McKinsey Global Institute, who have seen the business world as it exists rather than as academics would perceive it; and our friends and colleagues Bert Balk and Erwin Diewert for teaching us much. Although our book is inspired by the work of these and other innovators, it also contains much original material that extends their work in hopefully productive ways.

We thank Bert Balk for his thoughtful comments on part of the book; Ephraim Sudit for sharing his insights into productivity measurement at the company level; audiences at seminars and conferences around the world for their questions, comments, suggestions, and references; and graduate students in Barcelona, Chapel Hill, and Athens, whose reactions to half-baked ideas and preliminary drafts have contributed productively to the development of this book.

Thanks to our original editor Scott Parris, for his enthusiasm for and support of this project, but whose patience understandably finally ran out, to his successor Kristin Purdy, and to our current editors Karen Maloney and Kate Gavino, whose patience we have not yet tested.

We started this project with the financial support of Fundación Banco Bilbao Vizcaya Argentaria (BBVA) and continued with the financial support of Generalitat de Catalunya, project 2009SGR 1001, and Ministerio de Ciencia y Technología projects SEJ2007–67737-C03–01 and ECO2010–21242-C03–01.

Chapter 7 is a revised and greatly expanded version of "Advances in Cost Frontier Analysis of the Firm," chapter 4 in C. R. Thomas and W. F. Shughart II, eds., *The Oxford Handbook of Managerial Economics*. New York: Oxford University Press (2013). Chapter 8 is a revised, refocused, and expanded version of "Productivity, Price Recovery, Capacity Constraints and Their Financial Consequences," *Journal of Productivity Analysis* 41:1 (February 2014), 3–17.

1 Introduction

1.1 MANAGEMENT, ACCOUNTING, ECONOMICS, AND THE BUSINESS PRESS

Managers make business decisions; they do so at the company level and, in different guises, at the industry or sector level, and the national economy level. Koopmans (1951) referred to these decision makers as "helmsmen," for the way they steer their businesses. Management decisions determine the economic performance of the business, and have financial implications for its owners, its lenders, its customers, and its resource suppliers.

Accountants construct accounts from the outcomes of management decisions; they do so at the same three levels. These accounts describe financial performance and can be compared through time and across production units at each level. Although accounts record the financial consequences of management decisions, they also inform management decision making. Kline and Hessler (1952), Chandler (1962), Johnson (1972, 1975, 1978), and the historical papers collected in Temin (1991) describe in great detail the procedures by which accounts were used to guide management decision making at major businesses a century or more ago. Accounts thus guide management decisions and record their consequences. They contain an enormous amount of useful financial information, but they generally contain no entry labelled "productivity."

Economists have analytical skills and interests that are complementary to those of managers and accountants. Although accounts contain no direct productivity information, economists are able to extract productivity information from them. This information enables them to quantify the

1

contribution of productivity change to change in the financial health of a business. They also are able to quantify the financial contributions of the main drivers of productivity change, generally but not exclusively identified with improvements in operating efficiency and the adoption of new technologies, and this information can be used to inform business and public policy. Finally they are able to identify the beneficiaries of the financial fruits of productivity change, and to quantify their gains or losses. The ability to extract so much relevant economic information from the accounts was emphasized many years ago by Mason (1941), who asserted in a preface to Dean (1941) that Dean's study of the relationship between cost and output in a leather belt shop "is a model of the way in which significant economic relationships may be derived from the accounting and operating data of a business firm." This ability also forms the cornerstone of the seminal contributions of Davis (1955) and Kendrick and Creamer (1961) that we discuss in Section 1.5 and exploit throughout the book.

With this complementary financial and productivity information at hand it becomes possible to associate alternative management practices with higher or lower productivity, and hence with better or worse financial performance. It is also possible to associate various features of the operating environment with productivity and hence financial performance. This information does not appear in company accounts, but it plays an important role in the relationship between productivity and financial performance. Accounting for variation in the operating environment, either through time or across businesses, levels the playing field when conducting a comparative performance evaluation. We discuss internal and external drivers of productivity and financial performance in Section 1.3. The relationship between productivity and financial performance is also influenced by movements in prices paid for resources and received for goods and services. The role of productivity and prices in influencing financial performance is an old theme that permeates the book.

Much of what we know about the relationship between productivity and business financial performance comes from business accounts. It is difficult to overstate the significance of the synergies between accountants and economists, or the significance of the resulting information. Most importantly, it is difficult to overstate the significance of productivity itself. At the company level, improvements in productivity go straight to the bottom line, to the benefit of various beneficiaries. Profitable companies expand, and their hiring and investment activities contribute to growth in the economy. At the economy level, these productivity gains raise income per capita and contribute to a higher standard of living. Productivity patterns go a long way to explaining the Schumpeterian creative destruction responsible for the survival and disappearance of companies, and at the aggregate level to answering Landes's (1990) rhetorical question "Why are we so rich and they so poor?"

We gain additional insight into the relationship between productivity and financial performance from the business press, which reports on a regular basis on a number of issues bearing on events and trends in business productivity and financial performance. Although the press rarely provides precise definitions of critical terms such as "productivity," "profit," and "margin," much of its reporting is informative regardless of the definitions of these and related terms. At the aggregate economy level it reports and analyzes trends in various performance indicators released by government agencies. At the sector or industry level it chronicles trends in employment, productivity, sales revenue, and profit, frequently against a backdrop of regulation or overseas competition and occasionally based on information contained in consultancy studies. At the company level it regularly reports and analyzes corporate earnings results. We offer a brief analysis of aggregate economy and industry productivity and financial performance in Section 1.2, and we provide illustrative examples throughout the book.

Particularly at the aggregate economy level the business press is interested in three key issues:

(i) What is the nature of the relationship between trends in productivity and financial performance? The business press acknowledges the link between productivity change and some notion of profit change, and attributes any divergence to the presence of variation in pricing power in output and input markets, which has varied, both in magnitude and source. A popular topic in the press is the attribution of price variation to variation in market power. An important objective of this book is to provide an analytical framework within which change in financial performance can be attributed to price change and productivity change.

(ii) What factors drive productivity change? The business press cites internal factors under management influence, such as waste reduction, adoption of new technologies and business practices, and changes in business size and diversification. It also cites external factors such as the diffusion of technologies, and the overall business environment as characterized by the strength of competition, the regulatory structure, the availability and quality of public infrastructure, and other factors contained in the popular phrase "the institutional arrangement." A second objective of this book is to provide an analytical framework within which the drivers of productivity change can be identified and their contributions quantified.

(iii) How are the financial benefits of productivity growth distributed? The business press acknowledges that productivity change creates winners and losers in the distribution game, and it mentions several groups, including, in order of popularity, consumers, employees, suppliers of intermediate goods, and business itself. To cite one example, the press writes that consumers typically benefit from productivity growth, most recently the ICT revolution. The means by which consumers benefit include falling prices, improving quality, or more generally falling quality-adjusted prices, and the introduction of new goods and services. David (1990), Crafts (2004), and many other writers remind us that this is not a new phenomenon; the benefits of previous general purpose technological revolutions, ranging from textiles production and steam power to railroads and electricity, *initially* accrued to business, but *eventually* went to consumers. A third objective of this book is to provide an analytical framework within which the distribution of the fruits of productivity change can be quantified.

Our investigations in Sections 1.2 to 1.4 address each of these issues, although not in great detail. The detail awaits the development of formal models in the remainder of the book. Indeed the primary objective of this book is to provide an analytical framework within which each of these key issues can be addressed.

1.2 PRODUCTIVITY AND FINANCIAL PERFORMANCE

Scholars have long known that the long-term relationship between productivity and financial performance is positive and relatively stable, but that the short-term relationship can be volatile. Scott (1950; 4) notes that "profit in itself cannot always be taken as a measure of industrial efficiency, for it is vitally affected by factors of supply and demand ... A long history of satisfactory net profits is, however, substantial evidence of past efficiency..." Smith (1973; 53–55) emphasizes the importance of the relationship in the design of collective bargaining agreements intended to allocate the gains arising from productivity improvements. He observes that "the existence of a relationship between the productivity of the firm and profits cannot be denied but there can be no certainty that they will move in the same direction at all times and under all circumstances." He continues by noting that "there needs to be more research and analysis on the relationship between productivity and profitability [by which he means profit]." Kendrick (1984; 52) notes that "over the long run, probably the most important factor influencing profit margins is the relative rate of productivity advance ... In the short run, the effects of productivity trends may be obscured."

Many writers share this long-term view of productivity-driven profit growth, particularly at aggregate levels. However, the ability to discern a short-term relationship between productivity and profit *at the company level* hinges on whether conventional accounting data incorporate, or can be modified to incorporate, information required to measure productivity change. Diebold (1952; 62–63) observes that "[p]roductivity (or man-hour) accounting need in no way clash with good cost accounting; rather, it can effectively be made a working part of a company's accounting system and used by management in a variety of ways." He continues: "The data are generated by day-to-day operations and can be collected in a manner similar to cost data." Davis (1955; 1) notes that an editorial in the February 1947 *Journal of Accountancy* suggests that company income statements be developed that "will indicate increases or decreases in productivity of the company and also the distribution of the 'fruits of production' among all parties of interest." Davis's interest in distribution is a recurring theme in this book. Wait (1980; 29) describes productivity measurement as "a management accounting challenge," and notes that "it should be helpful to management to know both what gross improvements in productivity have been obtained and how those improvements have been shared." Thus, even though productivity does not appear in the accounts, accountants clearly care about productivity.

Widespread interest in the relationship between productivity and profit provides us with an opportunity to forge a linkage between the business and economics literatures, in an effort to encourage interaction.[1] We call this relationship productivity accounting. Davis (1955) defines the term, which he attributes to Diebold, as the use of financial statements to construct the ratio of, or the difference between, revenue and cost, expressed in real rather

---

[1] The distinction between business and economics literatures is admittedly arbitrary, but we find it useful.

than nominal terms by adjusting for changing prices. The significance of productivity accounting is its ability to separate the impacts of productivity change and price change on business financial performance. Simply comparing nominal revenue and cost through time conceals the possibility that a relatively productive company is financially unsuccessful because it lacks pricing power, or that a relatively unproductive company is financially successful because it enjoys pricing power. Accounting for price change converts the comparison to one between real revenue and real cost, thereby accounting for the impact of productivity change on change in financial performance.

Productivity accounting provides answers to two of the three business press questions above.

(i) What is the nature of the relationship between trends in productivity and financial performance?

Formal models characterizing the relationship have been developed by Davis (1955), Kendrick and Creamer (1961), and Vincent (1968 and elsewhere). We examine these models and extensions to them developed by others in Chapters 2 to 6. The ratio models in Chapters 2 and 3 are based on index numbers, and the difference models in Chapters 4 to 6 are based on indicators. The models in Chapters 7 and 8 exploit both index numbers and indicators.

(ii) What factors drive productivity change?

Productivity accounting cannot answer this question, but it does provide the data and an analytical framework within which economic analysis can identify, and quantify the contributions of, the primary drivers of productivity change. The analysis is based on primal (production) or dual (cost, revenue, or profit) best-practice frontiers. We introduce these frontiers in Section 1.6, and we use them within a productivity-accounting framework, throughout the book.

(iii) How are the financial benefits of productivity growth distributed?

Davis's procedure for productivity accounting not only quantifies productivity change, it also quantifies the sharing of the fruits of productivity change. Both productivity accounting and accounting for the distribution

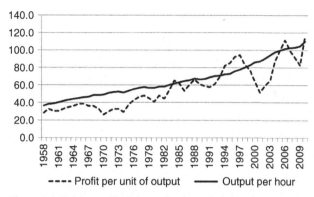

Figure 1.1 Labor productivity and unit profit in the US economy

of the fruits of productivity change have been implemented by Kendrick and Creamer and, extensively, by writers associated with the French public institution CERC (Centre d'Étude des Revenues et des Coûts) (1969a and elsewhere). We illustrate the distribution issue throughout the book.

1.2.1 Some empirical evidence

We provide scattered evidence on productivity, financial performance, and distribution from three sources: US Bureau of Labor Statistics (BLS)[2] data on US non-financial corporations, Organization for Economic Cooperation and Development (OECD)[3] data on Germany and Italy, and US Bureau of Transportation Statistics data on US airlines (www.bts.gov).

The US economy

Figure 1.1 depicts trends in labor productivity (output per hour) and unit profit (profit per unit of output) for the nonfinancial corporate sector since 1958, both indexed to 100 in 2005. The BLS does not measure total factor productivity in this sector, but labor productivity in this sector behaves similarly to total factor productivity in the private business and private nonfarm business sectors, increasing more rapidly due to the positive

---

[2] The BLS productivity page has five areas: labor productivity and costs; multifactor productivity; international productivity; productivity research; and productivity overview. We use the first three throughout the book, but rather than refer to each area separately we simply refer to the BLS and provide a link to its productivity page www.bls.gov/bls/productivity.htm.

[3] As we do with the BLS, we refer to all OECD references with a single link to its economy page www.oecd.org/economy.

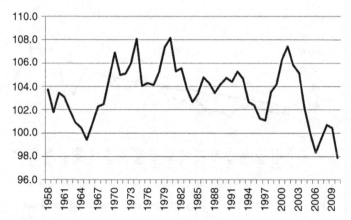

Figure 1.2 Labor's cost share in the US economy

impact of capital deepening. Figure 1.1 illustrates a point raised by Kendrick (1984) and many other writers; over a long period of time productivity and financial performance increase apace, but over short periods (say, from 1993 to 2010) the relationship can be much more volatile, with sub-periods of rising productivity and falling, as well as rising, unit profits. Because the volatility comes from the behavior of profits, it is clear that prices play a role in financial performance, a fact we revisit throughout the book.

Figure 1.2 shows the trend in labor's cost share (labor compensation as a share of value added) in the nonfinancial corporate sector, also indexed to 100 in 2005. The trend is upward and volatile until its 1980 peak, and downward and volatile thereafter, with the 2010 value being the lowest on record at the time. The volatility has relatively narrow amplitude about an actual 2005 value of about 67%. Since value added consists of payments to labor and capital, capital's cost share was the highest on record in 2010. The peaks and troughs in labor's share correspond to troughs and peaks in unit profits in Figure 1.1. It is clear that the benefits of recent productivity growth have not increased labor's share of value added. We examine the distributional impacts of productivity change in Section 1.4 and throughout the book.

Germany and Italy

In this exercise we compare labor productivity (output per unit labor input), wages (labor compensation per unit labor input), and unit labor cost (labor compensation per unit of output), each indexed to 100 in 2005,

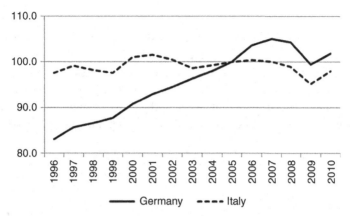

Figure 1.3 Labor productivity in Germany and Italy

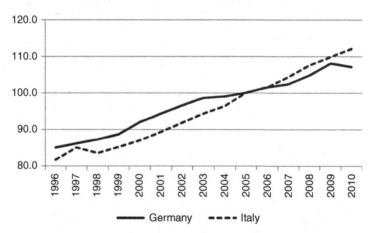

Figure 1.4 Wage rates in Germany and Italy

since 1996 in two countries seemingly headed in opposite directions. Figures 1.3, 1.4, and 1.5 tell the story, with one qualification. Each country's data are indexed separately, allowing a comparison of trends between countries but precluding a comparison of levels between countries. Nonetheless it is clear that labor productivity has grown much faster in Germany and wages have grown faster in Italy, with the inevitable consequence that unit labor cost has grown far faster in Italy, by over 37% compared to just 2.5% in Germany. Italy's international competitiveness has suffered as a result. We study labor productivity and its cost consequences in Chapter 7.

US airlines

The US Bureau of Transportation Statistics groups US airlines into three groups, low-cost, regional, and network. Figure 1.6 tracks operating expenses per available seat mile, the industry measure of unit cost, for each group quarterly from 2007/1 through 2011/2. Low-cost carriers do indeed have the lowest unit costs, although the regional carriers have managed to reduce unit costs since 2008/2 to a point where the two groups

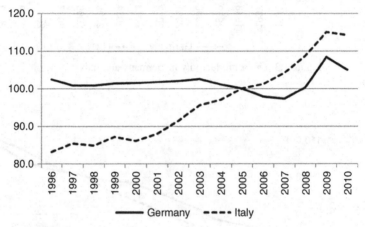

Figure 1.5 Unit labor cost in Germany and Italy

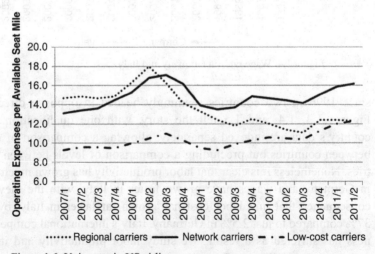

Figure 1.6 Unit costs in US airlines

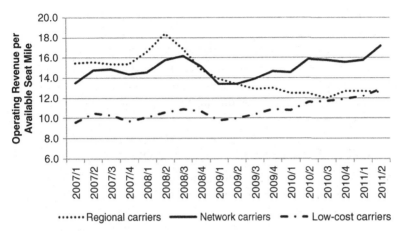

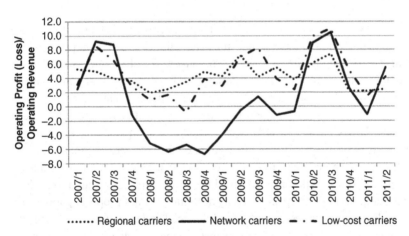

Figure 1.7 Unit revenues in US airlines

Figure 1.8 Profit margins in US airlines

have the same unit costs, and the large network carriers have had the highest unit costs since 2008/3.

Figure 1.7 tracks operating revenue per available seat mile. The network carriers earn the highest unit revenue while, as is the case with unit costs, the other two groups are converging toward a common unit revenue level.

Figure 1.8 tracks the profit margin, defined as operating profit/loss as a percentage of operating revenue, for the three groups. Profit margins have been extremely volatile at the network airlines, and remained negative for much of the period. Margins in the other two groups have been less volatile, positive throughout the period with one quarterly exception, and have averaged over 4%.

It is natural to wonder how much of the intergroup variation in each of these three financial performance indicators is attributable to productivity variation, and how much to variation in pricing power (or, in the case of jet fuel, pricing impotence). Throughout the book we develop models capable of addressing this issue.

1.2.2 Differing perspectives on the relationship

We find differing perspectives, both within and between the business and economics literatures, on productivity, financial performance, and the relationship between the two.

1. The impacts of quantity changes and price changes on financial performance

A trend has developed in the business literature seeking to integrate measures of productivity into business accounts, and thereby to decompose value changes into quantity changes and price changes. The challenge is to structure accounting information in a managerially useful way, and many alternative structures have been developed. Most recognize the fact that accounting data are nominal values that include the effects of quantity changes and price changes. Davis (1955; 1, 113) notes that "[t]he sharply rising price level following World War II has focused attention on the shortcomings of money profits as a measure of the economic performance of a business enterprise." He provides an extensive history and analysis of common price accounting, noting that "[p]roductivity accounting is not proposed, however, as a replacement for present methods of financial and cost accounting; rather, as a supplement." Supposing that a business keeps both standard and common price accounts, Davis notes that this would enable the business "to distinguish the effect of price changes from other changes on output and costs and to measure continuously both profit and productivity performance." In a brief summary of the history of corporate productivity accounting, Kendrick (1984; 51–52) concurs, noting that "[t]he idea of separating the influence of relative changes of prices of outputs and of inputs on profit margins, as distinguished from changes in productivity, was slow to spread until after World War II." He claims that "[a] major motivation for managements to develop productivity measurement is the realization of the importance of levels and changes in productivity to profit rates and the need to track productivity explicitly as an aspect of cost control."

It is not necessary to separate prices from quantities if the sole objective is to measure profit(ability). All that is required are measures of revenue and cost, which are readily available in company financial statements and which do not require separation of values into quantities and prices. At the economy-wide level, however, accounting convention equates income and expenditure, and so attention shifts from a focus on profit at the business level to a focus on productivity. The measurement of productivity does require separation of individual values into quantities and prices. These individual quantities and prices must then be aggregated into indexes (or indicators) of output and input quantities and prices, after which productivity is measured as the ratio of an output quantity index to an input quantity index (or the difference between an output quantity indicator and an input quantity indicator). Under some circumstances productivity can also be measured as the ratio of an input price index to an output price index, as we discuss in Chapter 2 (Section 2.9), or as the difference between an input price indicator and an output price indicator, as we discuss in Chapter 5 (Section 5.5). We utilize quantity and price indexes (and quantity and price indicators) throughout the book.

2. The impacts of productivity change on the company bottom line and on aggregate prosperity

Business literature tends to concentrate on the short-term linkage between productivity and financial performance at individual companies whose financial statements provide the raw data, while economics literature is interested primarily in the long-term linkage between productivity and living standards at aggregate sectors of the economy, for which data are provided by government statistical and regulatory agencies. However, the rapid growth and availability of large longitudinal data sets and the continuing increase in computing power have enabled the economics literature to place increasing significance on a short-term micro perspective.

The opening sentence in van Loggerenberg and Cucchiaro (1981–2; 87) expresses a common view in business literature. "The overall purpose of productivity analysis is to improve business operations and competitive position in order to serve the longer-term goals of improving profitability and, ultimately, shareholders' value in the firm." Wait (1980; 27) expresses a similar opinion. "Profits represent the 'bottom line' *financial* measure in a business enterprise while productivity measures represent the 'bottom line' *physical* measurement independent of costs and prices in the market place. A closer tie-in of productivity and profitability measures, accordingly, should provide management with greater insight into past and potential effects on profitability of productivity changes" (emphasis in the original). Additional short-term perspectives on the linkage between productivity and the company bottom line appear in CERC (1969b and elsewhere), Siegel (1980, 1986), Eldor and Sudit (1981), and Sudit (1984).

A particularly valuable source of information on the linkage is *Productivity Measurement Review*, a journal published from 1955 through 1965 by the European Productivity Agency (EPA) of the Organization for European Economic Cooperation. The *Review*, which published just 43 issues, focused on interfirm comparisons, based on productivity, cost, and financial ratios, as well as what would now be known as "pin factory" studies. European Productivity Agency (1956) provides a detailed introduction to methods, data, and findings. We refer to EPA studies published in the journal throughout the book, beginning with Section 1.3.4.[4]

From the prosperity perspective, Fabricant (1961; xxxv), in an introduction to Kendrick (1961), expresses a common view in economics literature. "Higher productivity is a means to better levels of economic well-being and greater national strength. Higher productivity is a major source of the increment in income over which men bargain and sometimes quarrel. And higher – or lower – productivity affects costs, prices, profits, output, employment, and investment, and thus plays a part in business fluctuations, in inflation, and in the rise and decline of industries." Kendrick (1961; 3) concurs, noting that "[t]he story of productivity, the ratio of output to input, is at heart the record of man's efforts to raise himself from poverty.... Of the fourfold increase in real net national product per capita between 1889 and 1957, productivity advance accounted for about three-fourths. This meant not only a large gain in the plane of living, but an increase in the quality and variety of goods and an expansion of leisure time, while increasing provision was made for future growth and for national security."

---

[4] European Productivity Agency documents are archived at the European University Institute's Historical Archives of the European Communities in Florence, Italy. Boel (2003) provides an in-depth political and economic history of the Agency.

3. Alternative definitions of productivity

We consider three related measures of productivity. One is total factor productivity (in a value-added framework), another is total productivity (in a gross-output framework). The OECD, the BLS, and many writers use the term "multi-factor productivity" in both frameworks. The third is partial productivity, typically labor productivity (although carbon productivity is currently in vogue). The first two incorporate all relevant inputs, while the third incorporates just one. The first two are preferred, but the third is widely used. Economists steeped in neoclassical theory associate either of the first two with technical change; our concept is broader.

We use the term "productivity change" in two distinct contexts. It can refer to variation through time; a notable example is provided by the "productivity paradox" introduced by Solow (1987), which refers to the widely chronicled productivity stagnation in the United States and elsewhere in the 1970s and 1980s. Solow summarized his productivity paradox with the apt phrase "[y]ou can see the computer age everywhere but in the productivity statistics." It also can refer to variation across producing units; macro examples are provided by the much discussed productivity gap between the United States and EU countries and by the large literature on convergence, and micro examples include the interfirm comparison literature we discuss in Section 1.3.4.

4. Alternative objectives of a firm's management

A firm's management has either a single objective or multiple objectives. Objectives may vary from one firm to another.

Friedman (1970) distinguishes a company from its management, and assigns a single objective to management. In his view a company has no responsibility, social or otherwise. Management has a responsibility, not to society but to the owners of the company, and society is not part of this principal–agent relationship. Quoting from his *Capitalism and Freedom*, Friedman concludes that "there is one and only one social responsibility of business – to use its resources and engage in activities designed to increase its profits so long as it stays within the rules of the game." Other writers assign similar single objectives to management. Gilchrist (1971) and Davis and Kay (1990) suggest the maximization of "added value," which Lawrence, Diewert, and Fox (2006) call gross operating surplus, and Jensen (2010) suggests "value" maximization. At the opposite extreme, Drucker (1954, 1955), noting the structural complexity of a business, proposes no fewer than nine often conflicting financial and nonfinancial objectives of its management. In Drucker's (1954; 63) opinion management cannot manage by a single objective, and *"[o]bjectives are needed in every area where performance and results directly and vitally affect the survival and prosperity of the business"* (emphasis in the original). This seems to be the philosophy behind the French *Tableau de bord*, which dates back to the 1930s, and the more recent balanced scorecard of Kaplan and Norton (1992). Advocates of corporate social responsibility (CSR) broaden the maximand still further, to include indirect stakeholders representing diverse segments of society, and CSR scoreboards and league tables proliferate, making CSR a performance indicator as well as an objective. The central issues are whether or not the pursuit of CSR enhances productivity, and whether or not it is profitable. The literature surrounding CSR is huge and growing, and inconclusive on both issues. Friedman describes the social responsibility philosophy underlying CSR as "pure and unadulterated socialism." Kitzmuller and Shimshack (2012) provide a balanced overview of the literature.

The discussion of managerial objectives prompts three observations:

(i) Managements pursue one or more objectives, but not necessarily successfully. Failure to optimize is a key feature of our economic analyses of the relationship between productivity and financial performance because sub-optimization exists, and has deleterious financial consequences.

(ii) It is important to distinguish clearly between managerial objectives and indicators of a firm's financial performance. Thus, Arthur D. Little (2008) distinguishes a single objective from multiple key performance indicators directed toward that objective. Davis (2005), who at the time was Worldwide Managing Director of McKinsey & Company, refers to a "contract between business and society," and claims that profit is a critical indicator of, and reward for, business success in pursuing its ultimate objective of the efficient provision of goods and services that society wants. We consider several financial performance indicators throughout the book without assigning objectives.

(iii) It is worth asking whether managerial objectives are even relevant to an investigation of the relationship between productivity and financial performance. Amey (1969) and Gilchrist (1971), among many others, suggest that, regardless of managerial objectives, return on assets (ROA) is the key indicator of business financial performance. Our economic analyses of the relationship are independent of managerial objectives.

5. *Alternative indicators of a firm's financial performance*

As a very broad generalization, economics literature tends to use a single financial performance indicator (profit), while business literature employs a suite of financial performance indicators (profit, profitability, ROA, return on equity (ROE), etc.). However, both literatures use several financial performance indicators as dependent variables in explorations of the impacts of alternative management practices and of variation in the operating environment on business financial performance. The balanced scorecard and the *Tableau de bord* incorporate nonfinancial success indicators along with ROE.

Regardless of managerial objectives, we accept, and use, multiple indicators of business financial performance, but one at a time. We use four related indicators of financial performance. In Chapters 2 and 3 we use profitability, the ratio of revenue to cost. In Chapters 4 to 6 we use profit, the difference between revenue and cost. In Chapter 7 we use cost, more likely than revenue to be under management control. In Chapter 8 we use ROA, the ratio of profit to assets. Each of these definitions has variants, there being latitude in deciding the items to be included in cost, revenue, and assets, for example. Consequently, for the most part we remain as generic as possible in our definitions.

6. *Expensing profit*

The US Bureau of Economic Analysis (www.bea.gov) reported 2012 corporate profits from domestic industries, after inventory valuation and capital consumption adjustments and taxes, in excess of 1.1 trillion dollars. At roughly the same time global mining giant BHP Billiton reported 2012 profit from operations of nearly 24 billion US dollars, and an ROA of 23%, both down significantly from 2011. The business press regularly reports corporate profits and losses, as well as government statistical agency data on aggregate profit. Neither is zero by construction, but rather a nonzero residual, the difference between revenue and a measure of cost. The central issue is how to incorporate profit into an analysis of the relationship between productivity and financial performance. The treatment of profit varies more within the two literatures than between them.

In the aggregate accounts the fundamental accounting identity requires nominal income to equal nominal expenditure, the latter including what is usually called gross operating surplus or the gross return to capital, which provides remuneration for the suppliers of capital inputs. Whatever it is called, it closes the gap between nominal revenue and nominal noncapital expense by treating remuneration for capital inputs as an expense. Unlike other expenses, it is expressed as a value that cannot easily be split into quantity and price components.

Many writers adapt the fundamental accounting identity framework at the level of the firm. Davis (1955) and Kendrick and Creamer (1961) call the gross return to capital "investor input," and treat it as the opportunity cost of the capital assets required to operate a business. This opportunity cost is distinct from the explicit depreciation cost associated with the use of capital equipment.[5] As in the aggregate accounts, investor input is a value without quantity and price dimensions, although it can be split into debt and equity components.

If investor input is not treated as an expense, revenue and cost can differ, and investor input becomes a new name for profit. The majority of studies in both literatures do not expense investor input, and profit becomes a financial performance indicator to be examined.

The distinction between the two treatments of investor input has implications that go beyond the different values of nominal profit in each accounting period. However, neither procedure forces *real* profit to be zero in any accounting period, and neither signals the absence of productivity change, which can be nonzero from one accounting period to the next.

In Chapters 2 and 3 we do not expense investor input, because it would make nominal profitability unity by definition. We do show, however, an interesting consequence of expensing investor input in Section 2.9. In Chapters 4 to 6 we conduct separate analyses in which investor input is, and is not, expensed. We pay particular attention to Davis (1955), who expenses investor input, because he also considers whether the decision to expense profit or not has an impact on productivity measurement. The issue is irrelevant in the cost-oriented Chapter 7, and we do not expense investor input when we analyze ROA in Chapter 8 because it would make nominal ROA zero by definition.

7. Exogeneity of prices

The nature of price determination plays a key role in productivity accounting. The business literature tends to see prices as being determined

---

[5] Kraus (1978) and Eldor and Sudit (1981) are among the writers who treat depreciation as a separate expense, in which case the gross return to capital is the difference between revenue and noncapital expense.

endogenously, with pricing strategies as complements to productivity strategies as a way of enhancing the bottom line. Miller (1984) exemplifies the endogeneity of prices in the business literature by emphasizing "pricing strategies" and "renegotiations with vendors and customers." Banker, Chang, and Majumdar (1996b; 695) provide more detail, noting that "[f]irms pursuing a differentiation strategy, including firms with strong marketing and product development skills, command higher output prices, and tend to exhibit a high price recovery ratio. In addition, firms with strong purchasing abilities, either through scale economies or through alliances with suppliers, can significantly lower their input prices. Such a competitive advantage is also reflected in a high price recovery ratio." In the economics literature prices are generally taken to be determined exogenously, the result of the forces of competition. An important situation in which output prices are exogenous occurs in regulated industries. Saal and Parker (2001) and many others emphasize the importance of the relationship between productivity and profit in a regulatory setting, in which the regulator controls monopoly product prices with the objective of forcing utilities to raise productivity, and to share the benefits of productivity improvements with consumers. However, there is also a large literature on market power and margins, or markups of prices over marginal costs, which allows for empirical testing of the exogeneity hypothesis. Applebaum (1979) developed a procedure for testing price-taking behavior, and Kutlu and Sickles (2012) extend the procedure to include the inefficiencies that market power allows, as Hicks's (1935) quiet life hypothesis posits.

Throughout most of the book we make no assumption about how prices are determined, although when our analysis is based on cost frontiers we require exogeneity of input (but not output) prices.

8. Capacity and its rate of utilization

Productivity is alleged to be pro-cyclical. During a downturn output growth slows more rapidly than input growth slows, as businesses build excess capacity, and productivity change is beneath trend. During a recovery the opposite happens; with spare capacity already in place, input growth lags behind output growth and productivity change is above trend. The macroeconomic evidence is abundant, and Basu and Fernald (2001) provide a survey and their own empirical analysis. However, Ohanian (2001) and Field (2003) disagree about productivity patterns in the United States during the Great Depression.

Three difficulties arise. First, we do not have a single preferred definition of capacity utilization. An output-oriented approach associated with Gold (1955) and Johansen (1968) defines capacity output as the maximum output that can be produced with some input quantities fixed and with no limit on the availability of other inputs. The rate of capacity utilization is the ratio of actual to full capacity output. A pair of output-oriented *economic* approaches defines full capacity output as the output that maximizes either revenue or variable profit, conditional on fixity of some inputs and with no limit on the availability of other inputs. The rate of capacity utilization is the ratio of actual output to the output that maximizes either revenue or variable profit. An input-oriented *economic* approach, associated with Klein (1960), de Leeuw (1962), Schultze (1963), and Hickman (1964), is based on a comparison of short-term (with some input quantities fixed) and long-term average cost functions. The comparison has generated alternative definitions of full capacity output, but the rate of capacity utilization remains the ratio of actual to full capacity output. In contrast to the output-oriented approaches, input-oriented capacity utilization rates can exceed unity.

Second, partly because we lack a single preferred definition of capacity utilization, we also lack a single preferred analytical framework that links financial performance, productivity, and capacity utilization. Empirical evidence and the business press suggest that productivity and financial performance are both pro-cyclical, although it is easy to imagine a scenario in which a demand-driven increase in output prices, and consequently in capacity utilization, reduces productivity and increases profit. In this scenario productivity is counter-cyclical. We develop alternative models linking the three phenomena in Chapter 8.

Third, it is not clear that the rate of capacity utilization is under management control. Is it exogenous, driven purely by trends in demand, or is it controllable independently of demand, driven my managerial hoarding of skilled labor and other inputs for use when demand recovers? At the company level neither Davis (1955) nor Kendrick and Creamer (1961) incorporates capacity and its rate of utilization among the list of drivers of productivity change. However, Davis does suggest that productivity exhibits a ∩–shaped relationship with the rate of capacity utilization, which he defines as the ratio of output to plant and equipment assets. He defends the second-tier status accorded to capacity and its utilization rate by suggesting, with an apparent short-term perspective, that management has little control over the rate of capacity utilization.

For these reasons, and others as well, we ignore capacity utilization in Chapters 2 to 7. We do, however, explore the issue in some detail in Chapter 8, where we incorporate change in the rate of capacity utilization among the drivers of change in ROA.

1.3 PRODUCTIVITY DRIVERS, DISPERSION, AND PERSISTENCE

Productivity change and variation do not just happen; both are driven by a wide range of factors. Some are under the control of management, some are not, and the controllability of others depends on the circumstances.

We begin at the aggregate level, where presumably all productivity drivers are under the control of a nation's helmsmen. The OECD attributes productivity change to technical change, economies of scale, efficiency change, and the rate of capacity utilization. The BLS attribution is nearly the same, replacing capacity utilization with reallocation of resources and adding other factors. We refer to these drivers as "primary" drivers, and we discuss them throughout the book, although since economies of (or returns to) scale has a precise meaning not applicable in some contexts in which it is used, we use the imprecise term "size change," a term we borrow from Davis (1947) and use throughout the book. The economics literature has largely adopted these definitions, although agreement on the role of size (and diversification) change *as a productivity driver* under management control is far from unanimous, and the "other factors" vary in importance from one situation to another. Kendrick (1961; 11) observed that productive efficiency (an expression he occasionally used for productivity) "may change as a result of technological innovation, changes in scale of output, and changes in the rate of utilization of capacity." He also warned that "[m]ere *descrip-tion* of the components of changing productive efficiency does not, of course, *explain* the causes of the changes." Denison (1962, 1974) compiled a much longer list of productivity drivers, including improved resource allocation, advances in knowledge, and relaxation of restrictions against optimum use of resources.

The list of drivers is far more extensive at the micro level, where the distinction between controllable and uncontrollable drivers is important. Davis (1955; 3) cites "changes in the production process, changes in methods of using existing processes, changes in input proportions or output mix, and changes in the rate or scale at which existing processes are utilized." He later adds changes in operating policies and practices, changes in product design and changes in process technology. Kendrick and Creamer (1961) distinguish short-term drivers (the rate of capacity utilization) from long-term drivers (improvements in productive efficiency arising from technical change). The drivers identified by Davis and Kendrick and Creamer are arguably controllable and, although the terminology and the levels of aggregation differ, Davis and Kendrick identify essentially the same sources of productivity change as the BLS and the OECD. Schmitz (2005) provides an interesting illustration of the variety of productivity drivers. In the 1980s a number of factors conspired to allow Brazilian iron ore producers to deliver iron ore to Chicago at prices beneath domestic prices. The dramatic increase in competition forced US and Canadian producers to increase productivity. Schmitz rejected the following popular productivity drivers before settling on improved work practices as the primary driver of US and Canadian productivity: closing low-productivity mines, adjusting scale at continuing mines, adoption of new technology, increases in skill, increases in the price of labor relative to other inputs, and changes in restrictions on purchasing inputs.

In Section 1.3.1 we discuss internal productivity drivers that are presumably under management control. In Section 1.3.2 we discuss external drivers that are not controllable by firm management, but presumably are controllable by the economy's helmsmen. In Section 1.3.3 we pose a challenge of allocating these many internal and external productivity drivers to the few primary drivers identified by the BLS and the OECD. If internal productivity drivers are under the control of business management, and if external productivity drivers are under the control of an economy's helmsmen, one might expect productivity convergence, as laggards adopt the policies and practices of leaders. However, empirical evidence built up over half a century or more demonstrates the opposite; productivity variation across plants, firms, and nations is large and remarkably persistent. In Section 1.3.4 we present evidence of, and potential explanations for, persistent productivity dispersion.

1.3.1 Internal productivity drivers

The internal productivity drivers discussed in the following sub-sections are garnered from a host of academic studies, and some recent citations are provided for each driver. Each of these drivers, and no doubt more, also can be found in consultancy reports. Lewis (2004) surveys a dozen years of experience exploring productivity drivers and deterrents at the McKinsey Global Institute.

1. *Quality of management: general*

The American Engineering Council (1921), headed at the time by Herbert Hoover, later to become the thirty-first President of the United States (1929–33) and preside over the Great Depression, published a volume titled *Waste In Industry*. This volume was reviewed by Gadsby (1921), who reports the Council's definition of waste as "that part of the material, time, and human effort expended in production represented by the difference between the average attainments on the one hand and performance actually attained," or in our parlance the difference between average and best practice. Across six industries this gap ranged from 1.7:1 to nearly 5:1. The study identified a number of sources of waste, most of which are catalogued below. The study also assigned responsibility for waste; across the six industries the study found management responsible for anywhere from 50% to over 80%.

Management has been the omitted variable in econometric studies of production, cost, and productivity for the better part of a century. Years ago Drucker (1954; 71) claimed that "the only thing that differentiates one business from another in any given field is the quality of its management on all levels. And the only way to measure this crucial factor is through a measurement of productivity that shows how well resources are utilized and how much they yield." Hoch (1955) and Mundlak (1961; 44) agreed, with Mundlak noting in a somewhat more technical vein that "estimates of the parameters of production functions are subject to bias as a result of excluding the variable which represents management," which Hoch called entrepreneurial capacity. Mundlak developed what is essentially a fixed effects panel data estimation model intended to eliminate the bias, assuming that "whatever management is, it does not change considerably over time." However, management can vary through time, and it comingles with other unobserved sources of heterogeneity. In fisheries the management effect is called the skipper effect or the good captain effect. Alvarez and Schmidt (2006) test the good captain hypothesis by estimating and distinguishing skill (captaincy) from luck (random shocks), applying econometric techniques described in Section 1.6.2 to panel data on hake fishery in northern Spain. Even better, Wolff, Squires, and Guillotreau (2013) are able to track skippers across vessels and through time, enabling them to identify a skipper effect and to distinguish the skipper effect from other sources of heterogeneity, also applying econometric techniques to a panel of French purse-seine vessels harvesting in the Indian Ocean.

The concept of management is hard to define, but since management is the (collective) decision maker it is clear that what matters is the decisions managers make, not the managers themselves. Recently, Bloom and Van Reenen (2007, 2010) and Bloom et al. (2013) explored variation in management practices among firms and across countries. They identify eighteen key management practices spread over four areas: shop floor operations, monitoring, targets, and incentives. Scoring each firm from 1 to 5 in each practice and averaging generates an overall management score for each firm. They find management practices to vary "tremendously," and identify product-market competition, labor-market regulation, and ownership structure as key drivers of variation in management practices. They call the corresponding productivity variation "astounding," and they find the management score to be a significant driver of sales, sales growth, sales per employee, return on capital employed, Tobin's q, and the probability of firm exit. In these and additional related studies Bloom and his colleagues have created an interesting proxy for the omitted variable identified by Hoch and Mundlak.

2. Quality of management: human resource management practices

The huge literature on human resource management (HRM) practices covers pay practices (e.g., salary, hourly rate, piece rate, seniority, profit sharing), promotion and retention practices, training procedures, and the role of teamwork. The primary empirical finding, reflected in the studies of Ichniowski, Shaw, and Prennushi (1997) and Black and Lynch (2004), is that innovative workplace and employment practices raise productivity. A secondary finding is that synergies cause groups of complementary HRM practices to raise productivity by more than individual practices do. Another finding, reported by Freeman and Kleiner (2005), is that changing pay practices can reduce productivity but raise profit, illustrating the potential divergence between the two first raised in Section 1.2. Bloom and Van Reenen (2011) survey the literature on the impacts of alternative human resource management practices.

3. Quality of management: misallocation and reallocation

Management engages in resource allocation across divisions, product lines, plants, and outlets, in a usually unstated effort to equalize marginal productivities, and hence to raise overall productivity and, ultimately, to improve financial performance. Conversely, heterogeneity in plant- or firm-level productivity (misallocation), exerts a drag on aggregate productivity. The extent and productivity impact of misallocation is the subject of a rapidly growing literature directed at the structure, extent, and productivity impacts of misallocation and reallocation.

A static allocation analysis typically compares productivity and market share, the hypothesis being that competition leads high-productivity producers to have larger market share than low-productivity producers. An intertemporal allocation analysis compares productivity and future growth in market share or output, the hypothesis being that competition expands the market share gap through time. An alternative intertemporal allocation analysis compares productivity and the probability of exit within the next few time periods, the hypothesis being similar. Summarizing, an allocation analysis attributes aggregate productivity change to productivity change within incumbent producers, to changing market share among incumbent producers, and to the entry of new producers and exit of incumbent producers. Foster, Haltiwanger, and Syverson (2008) provide an empirical illustration based on a pooled sample of over 17,000 establishment-year observations over five US census years. Findings are somewhat sensitive to alternative definitions of productivity, but a general finding is that incumbent firms contribute positively to aggregate productivity growth, share changes among incumbent firms also contribute positively, new entrants enhance aggregate productivity, as do exiting firms by removing their relatively low productivities from the sample. Collard-Wexler and De Loecker (in press) find qualitatively similar results in the US steel industry, with additional insight into aggregate productivity change provided by the changing fortunes of the incumbent vertically integrated mills and the new minimills.

Bartelsman, Haltiwanger, and Scarpetta (2013) provide international evidence in support of the misallocation hypothesis, and the hypothesis is the subject of a Special Issue: Misallocation and Productivity of the *Review of Economic Dynamics* (2013). This recent reallocation literature is an extension of the old "poor but efficient" literature initiated by Tax (1953), Schultz (1964), and Hopper (1965), who argued that poor farmers had no alternative but to allocate resources efficiently.

4. Quality of management: adoption of new technology

This literature studies the impacts of the adoption of information and communications technology (ICT), just-in-time practices, supply chain management, electronic commerce, including B2B, and other new technologies. Two key findings emerge: the impact of any new technology depends on the presence of complementary inputs, including skilled labor and organizational capital, and while the adoption of any new technology may increase productivity, it may also increase competition, thereby threatening financial performance. Draca, Sadun, and Van Reenen (2007) provide a guided tour of theory and evidence, and provide new evidence suggesting that Solow's paradox no longer exists, if it ever did. Bloom, Sadun, and Van Reenen (2012) find US multinationals operating in Europe achieved a higher productivity boost from IT adoption than did non-US multinationals, and they attribute the gap to superior human resource management in US multinationals.

5. Quality of management: product range and diversification

The research issue is whether or not changes in the range and mix of a firm's outputs affect productivity. A large theoretical literature on endogenous product selection suggests that product range and mix are under management control, and that product selection influences financial performance. Bernard, Redding, and Schott (2010) and Schoar (2002) provide empirical evidence suggesting that diversification and product switching both raise productivity, but with an uncertain impact on financial performance.

6. Quality of management: cost cutting and waste elimination

The business press regularly reports company announcements of intentions to cut or manage costs, or to down-size or right-size operations. Borenstein and Farrell (2000) characterize these practices as "fat trimming" and "re-optimization," the latter analogous to reallocation discussed earlier. It is likely that implementation of these practices does raise productivity and improve financial performance, but there is little systematic empirical evidence. Outsourcing, including offshoring, represents an attempt at cost cutting. Thouin, Hoffman, and Ford (2009) examined the impacts of outsourcing of IT services of nearly 1,500 Integrated Healthcare Delivery Systems, which resulted in large cost savings and a roughly 25% increase in profit. Castellani and Pieri (2013) address the concern that R&D offshoring may reduce knowledge and competitiveness in advanced economies. They find quite the opposite in Europe, where offshoring R&D is positively associated with home region productivity growth, in part through reverse technology transfer, and that the strength of the association depends on the location of the recipient region, being strongest in Southeast Asia.

Further evidence from academic studies and the *McKinsey Quarterly* is similarly positive.[6]

7. *Quality of labor*

Unmeasured variation in labor quality constitutes a widely acknowledged source of measured productivity dispersion. The BLS attempts to account for variation in labor quality by scaling labor hours by a labor composition index that incorporates age, education, and gender. In their study of Danish manufacturing industries Fox and Smeets (2011) adjust the labor input for a host of human capital variables, and find the adjustment decreases a measure of productivity dispersion across firms, but only by 18%.

8. *Quality of capital (and intermediate inputs in a gross output context)*

Unmeasured variation in the quality of capital is another potential source of measured productivity dispersion. The BLS also attempts to account for capital quality variation by decomposing the capital input into an "information processing equipment and software" component and a residual component. Another potential source of variation in capital quality is variation in maintenance activity. Alsyouf (2007) conducted a case study at a Swedish paper mill and found that elimination of all unplanned production stoppages and bad quality production due to maintenance-related causes would raise productivity and increase profit by over 12% of the mill's maintenance budget.

9. *Quality of outputs or services*

Improvements in output quality can generate improved financial performance, either by way of productivity gains or through increases in output prices commanded by higher quality output. Corredor and Goñi (2011) examined 800 Spanish firms over a 13 year period, and found that firms that received EFQM awards out-performed other firms on both productivity and profitability criteria. Sharma (2005) examined seventy companies listed on the Singapore stock exchange over a 6-year period, and found that firms

---

[6] Throughout the book we make frequent reference to the *McKinsey Quarterly* and the McKinsey Global Institute, because we find their productivity studies insightful, informative, and methodologically complementary to academic studies. Studies from both sources can be accessed at www. mckinsey.com.

with ISO 9000 certification had higher profit margins, sales growth, and earnings per share than firms without certification.[7]

1.3.2 External productivity drivers

External productivity drivers are beyond the control of business management. The external drivers discussed in the following sub-sections are collected from a host of academic studies, with some recent citations provided for each driver. These drivers also feature prominently in consultancy reports; the *McKinsey Quarterly* and the McKinsey Global Institute publish extensively in the area of productivity, competitiveness, and growth, at industry and aggregate economy levels.

1. Institutions

North (1990) describes institutions as the rules of the game that shape human interaction. Institutions influence the performance of an economy, and the businesses in it, by affecting the costs of production, communication, and exchange. Institutions are numerous, and the surrounding literature voluminous. Klein and Luu (2003) document the impacts of variation in legal, regulatory, and political institutions on productivity over a panel of countries. They conclude that economic freedom (a composite of several indicators) and policy stability are mutually reinforcing and together exert a strong positive influence on productivity. Many McKinsey Global Institute studies identify inadequate institutions as the primary barrier to improved productivity and prosperity.

2. Ownership

Economists have been debating the impacts of alternative ownership structures on business performance for generations. Hansmann (1988) provides a largely theoretical comparison of investor-owned firms, customer-owned firms, worker-owned firms, and firms without owners. More recently Bloom and Van Reenen (2010) and Bloom et al. (2012) have gathered management data on over 10,000 organizations, including more than just traditional firms, across twenty countries. They find substantial variation across

---

[7] EFQM is a global not-for-profit foundation based in Brussels that confers organizational excellence awards similar to the Malcolm Baldridge National Quality awards. ISO 9000 and its successors comprise a collection of quality standards. Participation in both is voluntary, and receiving an EFQM award or ISO 9000 certification may act as a signal of high quality to customers and other stakeholders.

ownership forms in the quality of management practices of the sort we discussed in Section 1.3.1. Management practices in the public sector trail those in the private sector by a large margin, largely due to inferior incentive structures. Management practices at family-owned and -managed firms trail those at family-owned and externally managed firms, a gap they attribute to primogeniture. Firms with private equity ownership and multinational firms are both relatively well managed.

3. The competitive environment

Competition allows entry, creates exit, and generates pressure to improve productivity, but its effect on financial performance is uncertain. Conversely, market power can enhance financial performance by improving margins, but its impact on productivity is debatable. Aw, Chung, and Roberts (2003) compared industry structure in manufacturing industries in Taiwan and South Korea. They found Taiwanese industries to be less concentrated, to have more producer turnover, smaller productivity dispersion, and a smaller percentage of plants operating at low productivity levels than comparable industries in South Korea, and they attribute these structural differences to greater competition in Taiwan and barriers to exit and entry in South Korea. Van Reenen (2011), quoting Adam Smith, surveyed several recent studies showing that increased competition leads to improved management practices, and, as we noted earlier, Bloom and Van Reenen (2007) found that improved management practices raise *both* productivity *and* financial performance. Darwinian reallocation across firms through entry and exit is the subject of the productivity dynamics literature.

4. Regulation, deregulation, and regulatory structure

Types of regulation are numerous (a short list includes regulation of price and quality in product and labor markets, entry to and exit from product and labor markets, health and safety, and environmental quality), and variation in the tautness of regulatory constraints is large. Empirical findings vary, but a common theme is that, by imposing constraints on economic activity, regulations reduce measured productivity.[8] Greenstone, List, and Syverson (2012) found that air quality regulations are associated with a nearly 5%

---

[8] Another, offsetting, common theme is that, while regulations tend to reduce *measured* productivity, they also generate *unmeasured*, or at least external, benefits such as a cleaner environment. It should also be noted that incentive regulation is designed to improve measured productivity, and there is considerable evidence suggesting that it does.

decline in productivity in US manufacturing over a two-decade period, at a cost of over US$450 billion. Casu, Ferrari, and Zhao (2013) found that reforms in Indian banking regulation fostered productivity growth, although the impacts have been stronger for foreign-owned banks than for private and state-owned banks. Poschke (2010) attributes a substantial part of the productivity lag of the EU behind the United States to its higher entry barriers in product and labor markets, and exit barriers in labor markets, which reduce the incentive to invest in productivity-enhancing new technologies. The OECD has analyzed the sources of Germany's dual economy, which combines a dynamic industrial sector with a stagnant service sector. Over-regulation is the key constraint on the service sector, including employment protection legislation, zoning laws that favor incumbents, licensing rules and advertising restrictions that protect professions, and restrictions on domestic transportation.

5. Structural reform and liberalization

This driver covers a lot of ground, including privatization, microeconomic reform, and trade liberalization. In a pair of studies, Eslava et al. (2004, 2010) study the impact of a suite of domestic structural reforms on productivity in a panel of Colombian manufacturing plants. They find a positive impact that works primarily through a reallocation of inputs away from low-productivity businesses to higher-productivity businesses. The Colombian data have also been used to estimate the impact of various measures of trade liberalization on productivity. As with domestic reforms, trade reforms, including the reduction of both tariff and nontariff barriers, have positive impacts on productivity. Additional studies of the productivity impacts of regulatory change and trade liberalization focus on Chile, Germany, India, Indonesia, Mexico, and the United States.

6. Demographics

Demographic factors influence productivity. The fabled productivity slow-down began in the 1970s and ended in the 1990s. The baby boomers entered the labor market in the 1960s and 1970s and reached their prime working years in the 1990s. Feyrer (2011) shows that the timing is not coincidental, and that the linkage between the two is provided by the impact of the baby boomers on management quality. He finds the management effects of the baby boom to have accounted for as much as 20% of the measured US productivity slowdown.

The impact of immigration on domestic employment and wages has been widely studied, and immigration also influences domestic productivity. West (2011) relates numerous potential domestic benefits of immigration, and proposes several policy changes that would create a "brain gain" for domestic producers. The Executive Office of the President (2013) asserts that immigration reform will have numerous desirable domestic impacts, and in particular will "increase overall U.S. productivity, resulting in higher GDP and higher wages." Peri (2012) focuses narrowly on the impact of immigration on domestic productivity. He studies immigration into US states, and finds that immigration has a positive impact on total factor productivity. Once again the impact works through a reallocation channel, with domestic and immigrant workers sorting into different skill groups.

7. Geography

A country's distance from the equator has long been a popular, and powerful, explanatory variable in international productivity comparisons. Hall and Jones (1997) find distance to the equator to be the single strongest predictor of a country's economic performance. Another geographic issue concerns agglomeration versus dispersion. When producers are clustered, consumers can substitute more easily than when producers are dispersed. Substitutability prevents less productive producers from operating profitably, and so increases average productivity and reduces its dispersion. The rise of the Internet has created something akin to an agglomeration effect that increases substitutability. Syverson (2004a, 2004b) and Andersson and Lööf (2011) provide theory and plant-and firm-level evidence in support of the hypothesis that agglomeration raises average productivity and reduces its dispersion. The agglomeration versus dispersion concept has morphed naturally into the notion of proximity versus fragmentation, and the geographical dimension has expanded to include cultural and relational proximity fragmentation, as evidenced by the study of trade patterns within and beyond regions by Johnson and Noguera (2012) and the study of outsourcing in the European automotive industry by Schmitt and Van Biesebroeck (2013). The *Journal of Economic Geography* regularly publishes empirical studies on the topic.

8. Public infrastructure and research & development (R&D)

Variation in the quantity and quality of public infrastructure, such as public transport services, contributes to variation in private productivity across firms and nations. Cohen (2010) surveys methods and findings, and incorporates a spatial multiplier to account for geographic spillovers from transportation infrastructure in the United States. Public R&D expenditure provides much the same private services as public infrastructure provision. Wang et al. (2013) examine the impacts on private productivity of both public and private R&D, which may have either competitive or complementary impacts on private productivity. In their study of US agriculture over the 1970–2009 period they find evidence of complementarity, although R&D affects productivity with a lag.

1.3.3 A challenge

The lists of internal and external productivity drivers are suggestive rather than comprehensive, and are intended to emphasize that productivity is controllable, either by firm management or by the aggregate economy's helmsmen. None of these drivers, internal or external, appears in company or economy accounts. They and their impacts must be inferred using various analytical techniques.

At the beginning of Section 1.3 we note that the BLS and the OECD identify essentially the same set of primary productivity drivers – efficiency change, technical change, and size change. Primary drivers are most frequently identified by applying quantitative techniques, econometrics, and mathematical programming, to data contained in company financial statements or economy accounts. Internal secondary drivers are typically identified by site visits, interviews, and the like. The challenge is to assign the internal productivity drivers listed in Section 1.3.1 to the primary drivers. Internal drivers (2), (3), and (6), HRM, reallocation, and waste elimination, are assigned to efficiency change, internal driver (4), adoption of new technology, is assigned to technical change, and so on. Assignment is important because it is useful to know what is driving efficiency change, for example, if we find efficiency change to be a source of productivity change. We do not assign external drivers to primary drivers; we use them as control variables in empirical analysis.

1.3.4 Productivity dispersion and persistence

Productivity gaps among nations are large, long-lasting, and widely analyzed. Here we focus on interfirm, or even interplant, gaps that Syverson (2011) finds to be ubiquitous, large, and persistent. This finding is not new.

The US BLS began publishing *Monthly Labor Review* in 1915. Almost from the beginning the *Review* published labor productivity studies. Many collected data on output, hours worked, and wages per hour, enabling them to report labor productivity, unit labor requirements, and unit labor cost. Some were aggregate within industry through time, and others were aggregate across industries for one year or through time. A few were detailed interplant comparisons that addressed productivity gaps and their persistence. Many reported productivity gaps together with a what-if scenario: if labor productivity at all observations were raised to the level achieved at the most productive observation, an enormous amount of labor could be saved. (The irony of this scenario will become apparent in Section 1.4.)

In one remarkable early interplant comparison in the lumber industry Squires (1917) compared labor productivity and unit labor cost, for up to twenty-one occupational categories or production processes "from tree to lumber pile," across twenty-six sawmills. One of several comparisons was based on eleven representative sawmills and five production processes. Squires found dispersion in labor productivity within a process ranging from 3:1 to 50:1, and dispersion in unit labor cost within a production process ranging from 4:1 to 12:1. Unit labor cost, aggregated across processes, ranged from US$1.45 to US$4.85 per thousand board feet. Squires attributed an unknown part of this large dispersion to heterogeneity in the characteristics of trees being logged. Stewart (1922), at the time Commissioner of Labor Statistics, reported on a survey of labor productivity in copper mining commissioned by the Department of Labor, "with a view to closing down, if necessary, the mines that were the least productive." In a sample of 1,006 mines, labor productivity ranged from 38 to 416 pounds per worker per day in 1916; a year later the gap was 30 to 372. In a later interplant comparison in the boot and shoe industry Stern (1939) compared labor productivity levels and growth rates across forty-three plants from 1923 to 1936. In the twenty-three plants making men's shoes Stern found dispersion in labor productivity on the order of 4:1 in the early years, increasing to 5:1 in later years, and he found dispersion in the rate of growth of labor productivity of nearly 2:1. The twenty plants making women's and growing girls' shoes exhibited lower levels of labor productivity, slightly less dispersion in labor productivity, a growing productivity gap, and slightly more dispersion in the rate of growth of labor productivity. Stern attributed some of the findings to variation in the rates of adoption of new labor-saving machinery, to a growing range of styles (to which Stern attributed much of the productivity gap between men's shoes and women's and growing girls' shoes), and to the effects of the depression (since many workers would be on the job part time but would be carried on the books full time).

From its inception in 1955 to its demise in 1966, *Productivity Measurement Review* was filled with European interfirm and interplant productivity comparisons. The samples were usually small, but the activities being compared were detailed, for example, inserting spokes in the wheel construction department in the Dutch bicycle industry. Productivity measures were usually confined to output per unit of labor, or its reciprocal unit labor requirements. Findings were usually expressed in "highest, lowest, and the ratio of the two" format, with reported ratios of two or more the norm and five or more not unusual. Productivity dispersion leads naturally to unit labor cost and unit cost dispersion, and several studies compare unit labor cost or unit cost at the activity level in the same format. Unit cost variation has further repercussions, and a few studies examined dispersion in operating ratios such as ROA and profit margin, with broadly similar findings. Since virtually all studies were cross-sectional, lacking a temporal dimension, the persistence of dispersion in productivity, unit cost, and operating ratios was not addressed.

During the 1950s, the International Labor Office Productivity Demonstration Missions documented organizational inefficiencies within firms, and the consequent large potential productivity gains available, in underdeveloped economies. Kilby (1962) summarized some of the studies, many of which were interfirm comparisons similar to those conducted under the auspices of the BLS and the European Productivity Agency, and traced costly inefficiency to internal organizational deficiencies and external impediments including inadequate infrastructure. At about the same time Ingham and Harrington (1958) were conducting similar studies of British firms and plants for the British Institute of Management. A decade later Rowan and Dunning (1968) reported findings of an extensive comparison of US and UK firms located in the United Kingdom. The comparison involved both physical productivity measures and financial indicators, and the study documented both dispersion and the superior performance of the US firms.

Salter (1966) compared best practice and average practice labor productivity, and its reciprocal, across plants in a number of industries in the United States and the United Kingdom, and found ratios in the neighborhood of 2:1. His study is of interest primarily for the sources of productivity dispersion he considers. He mentions variation in the quality of management, but his favored source of productivity dispersion is captured by the title of his book. He attributes a large share of measured productivity dispersion to variation in the age of plant and variation in the timing of investment in new plant and equipment.

Kendrick (1984; ch. 8) provides a brief overview of interfirm comparison efforts around the globe, and summarizes work then underway by the American Productivity Center (about which more later) and the US Census Bureau. His summary includes averages across all plants of labor productivity at each quartile and overall in a large number of narrowly defined industries. Citing another study, he also reports high/median/low values of productivity ratios and various financial performance ratios for all firms in a single Canadian sector.

More recent evidence documents wide dispersion across plants in total factor productivity in the production of relatively homogeneous products, for example, cement. Given sufficient geographic dispersion or other barriers to competition, high-cost plants and firms coexist with low-cost plants and firms. Some studies, being blessed with panel data, document the persistence of productivity and unit-cost dispersion. Evidence on the sources of productivity and cost dispersion and its persistence is growing, with the most likely sources being variation in both the internal management and external institutions drivers that we chronicled in Sections 1.3.1 and 1.3.2.

The various methodologies employed in these studies raise an important measurement issue. Early studies lack information on the capital input, and so they are forced to study labor productivity and its dispersion. On the other hand, the bulk of these studies are conducted at the firm or plant level, where information on physical outputs is typically available, and so they can study physical productivity and its dispersion. The tables have turned since then. Most productivity studies have, or can create, an index of capital services, and so are able to study total, or total factor, productivity. On the other hand, most productivity studies have moved away from the plant level to a higher level of aggregation, where information on physical outputs is of necessity replaced by real value added (usually based on an industry-level price deflator) or some similar indicator of revenue productivity. However, this revenue-based productivity measure has a serious shortcoming. If prices vary across production units, and if prices are correlated with physical productivities, an industry-level price deflator is inappropriate and revenue productivity differs from the preferred physical productivity. Onerous data requirements have conspired to make empirical investigation into the revenue versus physical productivity relationship rare. A pair of enlightening studies by Foster, Haltiwanger, and Syverson (2008) and García Marín and Voigtländer (2013) illustrate the differences in trend and dispersion of the two productivity measures.

Productivity varies. It progresses unevenly through time. It varies considerably across producing units, and we have some evidence that this variation can persist. In both cases variation has causes and consequences. We have identified numerous internal and external causes documented in the literature. The consequences are primarily financial; other things equal, productivity gains add value to the bottom line and to the aggregate economy. Throughout the book we examine the relationship between productivity variation and variation in financial performance. In the next section we conduct a preliminary investigation into how the financial fruits of productivity gains are distributed.

1.4 DISTRIBUTION OF THE FRUITS OF PRODUCTIVITY GROWTH

By "distribution" we mean the functional allocation of the financial benefits of productivity growth among employees and other factors of production, consumers, suppliers of capital, and the business itself. Consumers typically benefit from productivity growth through falling prices, improved quality broadly defined, or more generally falling quality-adjusted prices, and through the availability of new goods and services such as mobile telephones. Labor and other input suppliers typically benefit also, although their fortunes are also influenced by market power. The returns to labor and capital providers also tend to be volatile.

An early example of the focus on distribution in the business literature is provided by Bell (1940; 4), who examined the distribution of the benefits of productivity gains within several sectors of the US economy during the interwar period 1919 to 1938. He sought to trace "the immediate effects of technological changes upon the several participants in the productive process and also upon the consuming public." He identified the participants as employees, who receive wage and salary incomes; holders of capital, who receive rent, interest and dividends; and the business itself, which retains earnings to be used to fund future expansion or to meet current expenses or dividends in times of slack demand.

Davis (1947; chs 1–3) places particular emphasis on the aggregate distributional consequences of productivity growth. Historically, productivity growth has contributed to growth in output, and to growth in output per capita. Davis says "[b]ut more output for a given input is not enough. In fact, increasing efficiency could be self-defeating if the labor and other resources saved by improved technology were not sufficiently re-employed to bring about further expansion in national output." Davis considers a concept broader and vaguer than growth in output per capita; he calls it "economic progress" and he wonders, rhetorically, if productivity growth is sufficient for economic progress. He refers to a school of thought that associates productivity growth with economic progress, "on the assumption that distribution will take care of itself." He rejects this narrow concept of economic progress in favor of a broader one that distributes the productivity gains broadly throughout the community "without any idleness of men or machines, or wasteful or unsocial practices." Like Jerome (1932, 1934) before him, Davis writes extensively about conditions of re-employment (of those men and machines displaced by productivity growth), alternative views on sharing the benefits of increasing efficiency (i.e., productivity growth), and various social costs of industrial development.[9]

Davis identifies six potential participants in the financial distribution of the benefits of productivity growth (which he calls increasing efficiency): customers (who may pay lower prices or receive higher quality products), wage and salary workers (who may receive higher compensation), materials suppliers (who may receive higher prices), investors (who may receive higher dividends), the business itself (which may increase its retained earnings), and the government (which may receive higher tax payments). He also analyzes alternative techniques for examining distribution developed by Mills (1937) and Bell (1940), and he bravely surveys a literature concerned with how the financial benefits "should" be distributed. Later Davis (1955) provides an empirical application to a single business in which, following Bell's methodology, he attaches a monetary value to productivity growth and distributes this value among consumers, labor and management, materials suppliers, providers of supplies and business services, depreciation, and investors.

Kendrick explores the distribution of the financial benefits of productivity change, both at the aggregate level and within a single business. In his 1961 study of the US private domestic economy over the period 1919 to 1957 he finds productivity growth of 2.1% per year leading to product prices increasing at a slower pace (1.2%) than factor prices (3.4%). He also finds

---

[9] There was a great deal of concern in the 1920s and 1930s that labor displacement would result in longer-term technological unemployment. J. J. Davis (1927), at the time Secretary of Labor, wrote "[w]ith invention of every labor-saving machine should come invention of ways of using the man whose labor is saved. There is no other way; otherwise our new machinery does not 'save' labor, but wastes it."

that labor's price grew at a faster pace (4.0%) than capital's price (1.5%) over the same period. As a result, labor's share of national income increased from 72% to 81%. In Kendrick (1984; appendix A, case 2), he examines the distribution of the financial benefits of productivity change at a durable goods manufacturing company. Beneficiaries include customers, suppliers, employees, stockholders, and the federal government.

Salter (1966; ch. 12) argues that the distribution of the benefits of productivity change should depend on the sources of the productivity change. After finding that productivity growth in British industry came primarily from two sources, neutral technical change and the exploitation of scale economies, he finds that the gains have largely been passed on to consumers. He finds this distributional outcome plausible, even desirable, because "[e]conomies of scale and improving technology are not the product of any particular group ... No particular group has any economic or ethical right to appropriate the fruits of productivity increases of this nature."

A prominent group of French scholars also emphasize the importance of the distribution of the benefits of productivity change. Because this literature appears to be little known in English-speaking circles, we pay close attention to its treatment of the beneficiaries of productivity change. Led by Vincent, who in turn was greatly influenced by Kendrick, the methodology was developed at CERC in the 1960s, with the objective of applying the methodology to public and private firms across France. The public firms included Electricité de France (EDF), Gaz de France, les Charbonnages de France, and Société Nationale des Chemin de Fer Français, with the contract between EDF and the state obliging EDF to meet productivity gain targets in exchange for greater business autonomy. However, CERC encountered stiff resistance in the private sector, which Houéry (1977) attributes partly to management opposition to political intrusion into the *generation* of a productivity surplus, but primarily to labor union hostility to political intrusion into the *distribution* of the surplus. We return to the CERC methodology in Chapter 4 and at various other points in the book.

1.5 THE INTELLECTUAL INFLUENCE OF HIRAM S. DAVIS AND JOHN W. KENDRICK

Our initial influence is Hiram Simmons Davis (1903–99), who in a remarkable pair of books addressed many of the issues raised in the first four sections of this chapter. Davis was a member of the staff of the

Industrial Research Department of the Wharton School of Finance and Commerce at the University of Pennsylvania for over two decades, and Director of the Department for part of that period. In his 1947 book he addressed the relationship between productivity change and economic progress at the industry level. In his 1955 book he addressed the relationship between productivity change and financial performance at the individual business level, using for illustrative purposes an anonymous cotton textile manufacturer. In both books he is concerned primarily with the drivers of productivity change and the distribution of its benefits. Among his many contributions, Davis

(i) was an early contributor to the measurement of productivity, particularly multifactor productivity;

(ii) emphasized the link between productivity and business financial performance, noting that the latter was not necessarily a good indicator of the former;

(iii) identified the primary economic drivers of productivity change as technical change, technical efficiency change, changes in input proportions and the output mix, and changes in the scale of operations, and assigned a secondary role to the rate of capacity utilization;

(iv) emphasized the distribution of the financial benefits of productivity change, identifying the beneficiaries as consumers, employees, suppliers, investor/owners, the business itself, and government;

(v) emphasized that productivity growth was necessary, but not sufficient, for "economic progress," a broader concept that also includes relatively rapid re-employment following labor displacement brought on by productivity growth;

(vi) expressed concern for the external social costs arising from production activities, offering as examples insecurity of jobs and incomes, industrial impairment of health, wasteful use of natural resources, and more general social costs;

(vii) saw the need to aggregate heterogeneous inputs and heterogeneous outputs into meaningful aggregates, and stated that the only unit of measure "is the unit of the accountant – the national unit of value, the dollar in the case of the United States" (1955; 4);

(viii) considered replacing product price weights with product unit cost weights in the presence of market imperfection, and addressed the challenges confronting the allocation of cost to multiple products;

(ix) proposed real unit cost as a useful way to aggregate multiple inputs in a productivity index, and proposed the ratio of real revenue to real cost as a productivity index in the presence of multiple outputs and multiple inputs;

(x) saw the need to adjust current dollar aggregates to account for fluctuations in the value of the unit of value, a critical component of what he called productivity accounting;

(xi) described five internal uses for productivity accounting: to provide an overall measure of the efficiency of a firm; to provide an analytical audit of past performance; to provide budget control of current performance; to provide common price financial statements; and to measure the initial distribution of the benefits flowing from gain or loss in productivity in the firm;

(xii) related productivity accounting to the longstanding business practice of using variance analysis for budget control purposes;

(xiii) introduced the concept of "investor input" as an expense that absorbs nominal profit in the base and comparison accounting periods; and

(xiv) recognized and thought creatively about various technical issues such as the "new and disappearing goods" problem (1955; 39–44) and the choice between fixed base and chaining of empirical price and quantity index numbers (1955; 44–53).

Siegel (1986; 35) claims that Davis (1955) "occupies an important place in the history of American productivity measurement at the enterprise level ... It brought the accounting viewpoint into a field of quantitative activity that had been virtually monopolized by economic statisticians and industrial engineers."

Our second influence is John Whitefield Kendrick (1917–2009), who was deeply influenced by Davis, and who extended many of his contributions. Kendrick worked for the US Department of Commerce and served on the staff of the National Bureau of Economic Research, where he worked for Solomon Fabricant, after which he spent his academic career with the George Washington University until his death in 2009, although his work continued to extend beyond academe. He was associated with the American Productivity Center from its inception in 1977 and with the Conference Board (which sponsored his 1961 study with Creamer and his 1980 study with Grossman). Among his many achievements, Kendrick

(i) extended and applied many of the contributions of Davis just enumerated;

(ii) placed particular emphasis on the concept of investor input;

(iii) stressed that strong financial performance is not necessarily a sign of strong productivity performance, and vice-versa;

(iv) distinguished productivity in a gross output context (total productivity) from productivity in a value added context (total factor productivity);

(v) emphasized the advantage of a total (or total factor) productivity index over a suite of partial productivity indexes;

(vi) gave equal importance to the economic drivers of productivity change and the distribution of its financial benefits;

(vii) emphasized the differences between the value, quantity, and price of labor and those of capital, and explored the complexities of the latter;

(viii) distinguished clearly between the widespread use of "general purpose" quantity and price deflators and the use of more appropriate firm-specific quantity and price deflators, an issue we discussed in Section 1.3.4;

(ix) produced the seminal work on productivity trends in the aggregate US economy (Kendrick 1961); and

(x) conducted case studies quantifying the sources and benefits of productivity change at individual companies (Kendrick and Creamer 1961, Kendrick 1984).

Vincent (1968; 12, 71) asserts that "[d]e très nombreuses publications ont été consacrées, depuis vingt-cinq ans, à la productivité et à ses divers aspects; mais seuls quelques ouvrages ont fait une place importante à la mesure de la productivité.[1]" Vincent's footnote 1 lists six works, three in French, European Productivity Agency (1955, 1956), and Kendrick (1961). He continues with "[l]a mise en œuvre de la productivité totale des facteurs est due essentiellement à un auteur américain, John W. Kendrick, dont les recherches ont fait l'objet d'un important ouvrage."

We are not alone in being influenced by Davis and Kendrick. The influence of Davis on Kendrick is clear, and is explicitly acknowledged in Kendrick and Creamer and in Kendrick's introduction to a 1978 reprint of Davis (1955). The subsequent line of influence from Kendrick to the early French writers, including Vincent (1965, 1968), Courbis and Templé (1975), and Houéry (1977), is widely acknowledged. Many other contributors to the accounting and management literatures, including Gold (1955, 1971), Kaplan (1983), Sudit (1984), and Banker, Datar, and Kaplan (1989) among many others, have been influenced directly by Kendrick, and so indirectly if not directly by Davis. Their influence permeates this book.

1.6 SOME USEFUL TECHNICAL MATERIAL

Throughout the book we make use of the theory of producer behavior and related concepts of production efficiency. We summarize this theoretical material in Section 1.6.1. Additional theoretical background can be found in chapter 2 of Kumbhakar and Lovell (2000), from which Section 1.6.1 is extracted, and in more detail in Färe and Primont (1995). The production, cost, and other frontiers that emerge from Section 1.6.1 must be estimated using observed data that may or may not reflect optimizing behavior. We summarize alternative empirical techniques suitable for situations in which optimizing behavior is a testable hypothesis rather than an underlying assumption in Section 1.6.2. Estimation can be implemented with a linear programming technique known as Data Envelopment Analysis (DEA) (Charnes, Cooper, and Rhodes 1978) or with an econometric technique known as Stochastic Frontier Analysis (SFA) (Aigner, Lovell, and Schmidt 1977). Fried, Lovell, and Schmidt (2008) offer an accessible introduction to both techniques, and Cooper, Seiford, and Tone (2000) and Kumbhakar and Lovell (2000) provide the details. Commercial software and freeware are widely available for both techniques.

1.6.1 Production theory

We begin by introducing notation and terminology. Output vectors are denoted $y = (y_1, \ldots, y_M) \in R_+^M$ and input vectors are denoted $x = (x_1, \ldots, x_N) \in R_+^N$. The set of technologically feasible combinations of output vectors and input vectors is given by the production set $T = \{(y,x): x \text{ can produce } y\}$ depicted in Figure 1.9. T is closed and bounded, and monotonic in the sense that $(y,x) \in T \Rightarrow (y, \lambda x) \in T$ for $\lambda \geq 1$ and $(y,x) \in T \Rightarrow (\lambda y, x) \in T$ for $0 \leq \lambda \leq 1$. If $M = 1$, which requires either a single output or a real output aggregate of multiple outputs, then we can define a *production frontier* $f(x) = max\{y: (y,x) \in T\}$ as the outer boundary of the production set T, which is also depicted in Figure 1.9. $f(x)$ is the locus of maximum outputs that can be produced with any input vector and existing technology, or, equivalently, the locus of minimum inputs required to produce any output vector with existing technology.

The set of input vectors that are feasible for any given output vector y is the input set $L(y) = \{x: (x,y) \in T\}$, which is bounded below by the input isoquant $IL(y)$. The set of output vectors that are feasible for any given input vector x is the output set $Q(x) = \{y: (y,x) \in T\}$, which is bounded above by the output isoquant $IQ(x)$. The sets $L(y)$ and $Q(x)$ are assumed to be closed

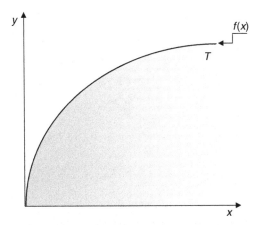

Figure 1.9 A production set and its frontier

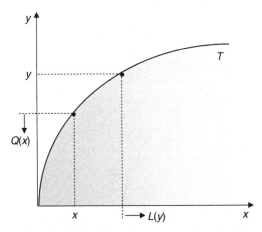

Figure 1.10 Input sets and output sets of production technology ($M = 1, N = 1$)

and convex. Input sets and output sets are depicted in Figure 1.10 for output y and input x. An input set and its isoquant are depicted in Figure 1.11 for output vector y, and an output set and its isoquant are depicted in Figure 1.12 for input vector x.

It is not necessary that producers operate on the surface of the production set T, or on the input isoquant $IL(y)$, or on the output isoquant $IQ(x)$, and we need a concept of distance to these technological boundaries. The concept is that of a radial distance function. An *input distance function* $D_i(y,x) = max\{\lambda: x/\lambda \in L(y)\}$ gives the maximum amount by which a

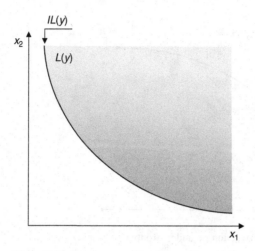

Figure 1.11 Input sets and isoquants of production technology ($N=2$)

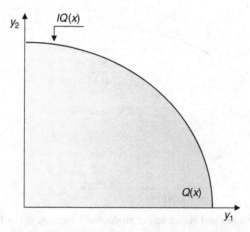

Figure 1.12 Output sets and isoquants of production technology ($M=2$)

producer's input vector x can be contracted radially and still remain feasible for output vector y. In Figures 1.13 and 1.14 optimal $\lambda > 1$ because input usage is wasteful, being located on the interior of T and $L(y)$. Input usage is not wasteful if (x, y) is located on the boundary of T, or if $x \in IL(y)$, in which case $\lambda = 1$. An input distance function is non-increasing in y and non-decreasing, concave, and homogeneous of degree $+1$ in x. An *output distance function* $D_o(x, y) = min\{\mu: y/\mu \in Q(x)\}$ gives the minimum amount by which an output vector can be deflated and still remain feasible for input

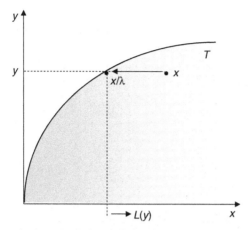

Figure 1.13 An input distance function ($M=1$, $N=1$)

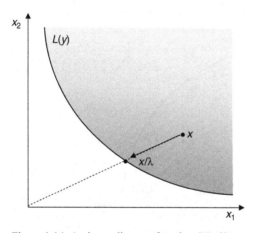

Figure 1.14 An input distance function ($N=2$)

vector x. In Figures 1.15 and 1.16 optimal $\mu < 1$ because output vector y can be expanded radially without requiring additional input, and so is located on the interior of T and $Q(x)$. Output usage is maximal in a radial sense if (y, x) is on the boundary of T, or if $y \in IQ(x)$, in which case $\mu = 1$. An output distance function is non-increasing in x, and non-decreasing, convex, and homogeneous of degree +1 in y.

We are now prepared to introduce measures of the technical efficiency of production. If $M=1$, the appropriate best practice standard is the production frontier $f(x)$ in Figure 1.9. An output-oriented measure of technical

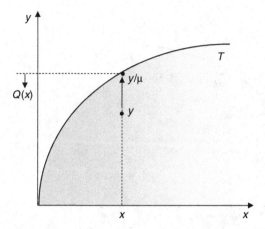

Figure 1.15 An output distance function ($M = 1$, $N = 1$)

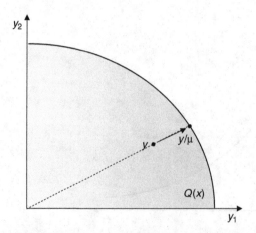

Figure 1.16 An output distance function ($M = 2$)

efficiency is $TE_o(x, y) = [max\{\phi : \phi y \leq f(x)\}]^{-1} \leq 1$. An input-oriented measure of technical efficiency is $TE_i(y, x) = min\{\theta : y \leq f(\theta x)\} \leq 1$.

If $M > 1$, the appropriate best practice standards are provided by the production set T and, equivalently, by the input sets $L(y)$ and the output sets $Q(x)$. An output-oriented measure of technical efficiency is $TE_o(x, y) = [max\{\phi : \phi y \in Q(x)\}]^{-1} = D_o(x, y) \leq 1$. An input-oriented measure of technical efficiency is $TE_i(y, x) = min\{\theta : \theta x \in L(y)\} = [D_i(y, x)]^{-1} \leq 1$. The two measures are depicted in Figure 1.17 for $M = N = 1$, and in Figures 1.18 and 1.19 for input vector x and output vector y.

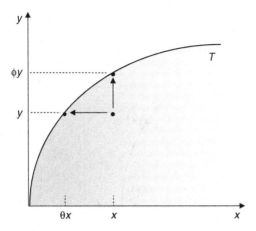

Figure 1.17 Input-oriented and output-oriented measures of technical efficiency ($M=1$, $N=1$)

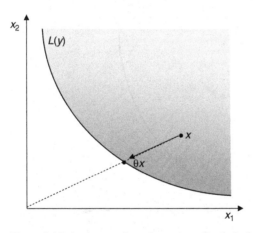

Figure 1.18 An input-oriented measure of technical efficiency ($N=2$)

Thus far the analysis has been technical, appropriate when price information is unavailable or ignored. The benefit of having access to, and using, price information is that we can augment measures of technical efficiency with measures of economic efficiency. This requires additional notation and terminology.

Input price vectors are denoted $w = (w_1, ..., w_N) \in R_{++}^N$ and output price vectors are denoted $p = (p_1, ..., p_M) \in R_{++}^M$. Total cost $C = w^T x = \sum w_n x_n$ is bounded below by the cost frontier $c(y, w) = min_x \{w^T x : x \in L(y)\}$. A cost

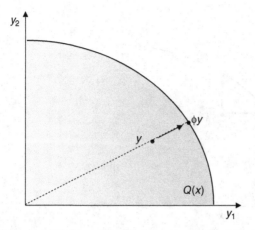

Figure 1.19 An output-oriented measure of technical efficiency ($M=2$)

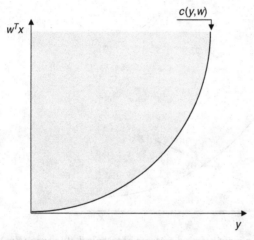

Figure 1.20 A cost frontier ($M=1$)

frontier $c(y,w)$ is non-decreasing in y and non-decreasing, concave, and homogeneous of degree $+1$ in w. A cost frontier is illustrated in Figure 1.20. Total revenue $R=p^Ty=\sum p_m y_m$ is bounded above by the revenue frontier $r(x,p)=max_y\{p^Ty: y \in Q(x)\}$. A revenue frontier $r(x,p)$ is non-decreasing in x and non-decreasing, convex, and homogeneous of degree $+1$ in p. A revenue frontier is illustrated in Figure 1.21. Finally, profit $\pi=R-C$, and profitability $\Pi=R/C$. We analyze variation in profit and

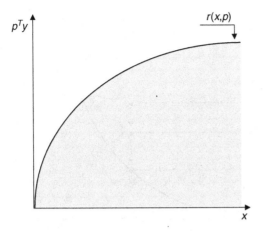

Figure 1.21 A revenue frontier ($N=1$)

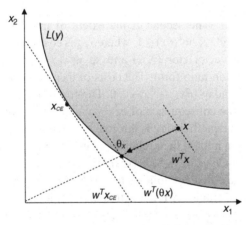

Figure 1.22 The measurement and decomposition of cost efficiency ($N=2$)

profitability throughout the book, but we do not make use of profit or profitability frontiers, although both exist.

Producers are not required to operate on their cost or revenue frontiers, which suggests the need for measures of departure from (above and below, respectively) these frontiers.

A measure of cost efficiency is a function $CE(y, w, x) = c(y, w)/w^T x \leq 1$. In Figures 1.22 and 1.23, the cost efficiency of input vector x, given output quantity vector y and input price vector w, is broken down into two components. The first is the extent of input-oriented technical inefficiency

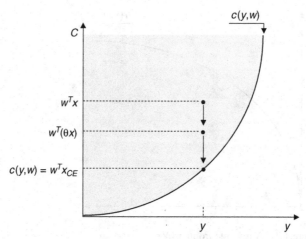

Figure 1.23 The measurement and decomposition of cost efficiency ($M=1$)

$TE_i(y,x) = w^T(\theta x)/w^T x \leq 1$. The second is the extent of input allocative inefficiency $AE_i(y,w,x) = w^T x_{CE}/w^T(\theta x) \leq 1$, where x_{CE} is cost-efficient (i.e., a cost minimizing input vector) for (y,w) and so $w^T x_{CE} = c(y,w)$. Both components are expressed in ratio form. The costs of these two inefficiencies are $w^T x - w^T(\theta x) \geq 0$ and $w^T(\theta x) - w^T x_{CE} \geq 0$. The cost of input-oriented technical inefficiency is the consequence of excessive input use, or waste. The cost of input allocative inefficiency is the consequence of using inputs in the wrong proportions in light of their relative prices. The measure of cost efficiency decomposes as $CE(y,w,x) = TE_i(y,x) \times AE_i(y,w,x) \leq 1$.

The analysis of revenue efficiency follows that of cost efficiency step for step. A measure of revenue efficiency is a function $RE(x,p,y) = p^T y/r(x,p) \leq 1$. In Figures 1.24 and 1.25, the revenue efficiency of output vector y, given input quantity vector x and output price vector p, is broken down into two components. The first is the extent of output-oriented technical inefficiency $TE_o(x,y) = p^T y/p^T(\phi y) \leq 1$. The second is the extent of output allocative inefficiency $AE_o(x,p,y) = p^T(\phi y)/p^T y_{RE} \leq 1$, where y_{RE} is a revenue maximizing output vector for (p,y) and so $p^T y_{RE} = r(x,p)$. These ratios can be converted to expressions for the revenue lost to output-oriented technical inefficiency $p^T(\phi y) - p^T y \geq 0$ and the revenue lost to output allocative inefficiency $p^T y_{RE} - p^T(\phi y) \geq 0$. The revenue lost to output-oriented technical inefficiency is due to a failure to produce maximum feasible output, given the available resources. The revenue lost to output allocative inefficiency is due to producing the wrong mix of outputs, given their relative prices.

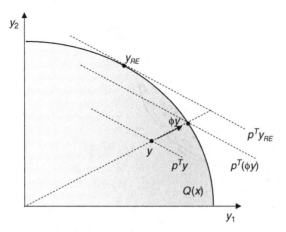

Figure 1.24 The measurement and decomposition of revenue efficiency ($M=2$)

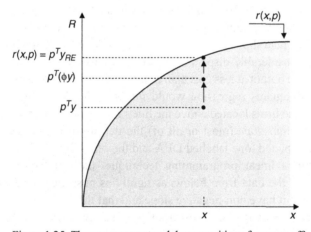

Figure 1.25 The measurement and decomposition of revenue efficiency ($N=1$)

The measure of revenue efficiency decomposes as $RE(x,p,y) = TE_o(x,y) \times AE_o(x,p,y) \leq 1$.

1.6.2 Empirical techniques

Much of the analysis in subsequent chapters is based on a production frontier $f(x)$ or a cost frontier $c(y,w)$, or occasionally a unit cost frontier $ac(y,w)$ or a revenue frontier $r(x,p)$. Estimation of these frontiers can be

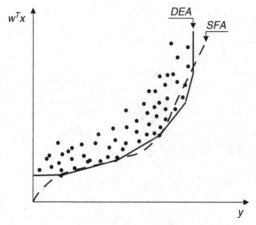

Figure 1.26 SFA and DEA cost frontiers

implemented with either DEA or SFA. Here we sketch the essentials of both empirical techniques, with the assistance of Figure 1.26.

Figure 1.26 shows a sample of firms incurring cost $w^T x$ in the production of output y. The data show a positive cost–output relationship, although they also exhibit considerable dispersion in the relationship, with some firms producing more output at less cost than other firms. A cost *function* fitted by ordinary least squares regression would *intersect* the data, with positive slope, with some firms located above the fitted function and others below it. A cost *frontier envelops* (most or all of) the data from below. Two such frontiers are depicted, one labelled DEA and the other SFA.

DEA being a linear programming technique, the DEA cost frontier envelops *all* of the data from below, as tightly as possible, subject to the restrictions that it have non-negative slope and that the feasible cost-output set bounded below by the DEA cost frontier be a convex set. The DEA cost minimization linear program is calculated for each of I firms in the sample. The program for a firm having data (y^o, x^o) is

$$\min_{x, \lambda} w^T x^o$$
$$\text{s.t. } y^o \leq \sum_{i=1}^{I} \lambda_i y_i$$
$$x^o \geq \sum_{i=1}^{I} \lambda_i x_i$$
$$\sum_{i=1}^{I} \lambda_i = 1$$
$$\lambda_i \geq 0,$$

where λ is an $I \times 1$ weighting vector. The objective is to select an input vector that minimizes expenditure, given input prices w. The first two sets of linear constraints require that the firm under evaluation (i) produce no more of each output than a convex combination (with non-negative weights summing to one) of other firms does ($y^\circ \leq \sum_{i=1}^{I} \lambda_i y_i$), while (ii) using no less of each input than the same convex combination of other firms does ($x^\circ \geq \sum_{i=1}^{I} \lambda_i x_i$). The final constraints require the combinations to have non-negative weights summing to unity. In Figure 1.26, firms defining the DEA cost frontier are cost-efficient, and the cost efficiency of the remaining firms located above the DEA cost frontier is measured by the ratio of their cost to the minimum cost of producing the same output vector, and so $w^T x_{CE}/w^T x \leq 1$, with $w^T x_{CE}$ located on the DEA cost frontier. Since this is a linear program, it has a dual linear program that provides information on the structure of the DEA cost frontier.

Construction of an SFA cost frontier begins with the understanding that actual cost is at least as great as minimum cost, and so $w_i^T x_i \geq c(y_i, w_i; \beta)$, where i indexes firms and β is a parameter vector characterizing the structure of the SFA cost frontier. In the belief that the relationship is stochastic, we allow for random shocks by writing $w_i^T x_i \geq c(y_i, w_i; \beta) + v_i$, in which v_i is a normally distributed random error term with zero mean and constant variance. The SFA stochastic cost frontier in Figure 1.26 is $c(y_i, w_i; \beta) + v_i$, but all that is visible is the deterministic component $c(y_i, w_i; \beta)$. Firms having $v_i > 0$ lie above $c(y_i, w_i; \beta)$, and firms having $v_i < 0$ can (not must) lie beneath $c(y_i, w_i; \beta)$. Finally, converting the inequality into an equality is achieved by adding an additional error term, and so the SFA cost frontier regression is

$$w_i^T x_i = c(y_i, w_i; \beta) + v_i + u_i,$$

in which $u_i \geq 0$ captures the cost inefficiency of firm i relative to the stochastic cost frontier $c(y_i, w_i; \beta) + v_i$. The cost inefficiency error component thus has a one-sided distribution, usually but not necessarily the non-negative half of a normal distribution. Most firms lie above $c(y_i, w_i; \beta)$, but some firms can lie beneath it if $v_i + u_i < 0$.

DEA and SFA cost frontiers are likely to tell similar stories about cost efficiency in a sample of firms. The only essential difference between the two techniques is that DEA is deterministic, while SFA is stochastic, and allows random events to influence cost-efficiency estimation via the random error component v_i.

1.7 THE ORGANIZATION OF THE BOOK

Our objective is to merge the economics literature on productivity and its drivers with the business literature on the sources and beneficiaries of variation in business financial performance, in an effort to uncover and exploit synergies between the two literatures and their respective toolkits. Since financial performance can be defined in alternative ways, we develop more than one analytical framework.

Our analysis contributes to the business literature by incorporating the economic drivers of productivity change into productivity accounting, by incorporating multiple outputs as well as multiple inputs into the analysis, by using modern index number and indicator techniques to aggregate multiple inputs and multiple outputs, and by exploiting duality theory when we find it useful. Our analysis contributes to the economics literature by reorienting the analysis away from an aggregate context toward a business context, and by relating productivity change to change in business financial performance.

The remainder of the book is divided into three parts. In Part I, comprising Chapters 2 and 3, we define financial performance in terms of profitability, the *ratio* of revenue to cost, and we express change in financial performance in ratio form, as a pure number. In Part II, comprising Chapters 4 to 6, we define financial performance in terms of profit, the *difference* between revenue and cost, and we express change in financial performance in difference form, in monetary units. In Part III, comprising Chapters 7 and 8, we define financial performance in terms of cost and ROA, and we evaluate change in financial performance in both ratio and difference forms. We express change in both ratio and difference forms because various authors (e.g., Miller 1984, Balk 2003) assert that the business community is more comfortable with performance analysis expressed in difference form, and economists are more comfortable with performance analysis expressed in ratio form (making it somewhat ironic that the concept of profitability, a ratio, is not as popular in economics as profit, a difference). A complementary analytic reason for expressing change in both ratio and difference forms is that the two forms have offsetting advantages and disadvantages. Perhaps in an effort to reach both communities, several authors conduct performance analysis in one form, and then convert their analysis to the other form.

Davis (1955) and Kendrick and Creamer (1961) were perhaps the first to report both ratio and difference forms of change in financial performance. This enabled them to report productivity change in both percent and value terms, a practice adopted later by Puiseux and Bernard (1965), Houéry

(1977), and Sink, Tuttle, and DeVries (1984), among others. Kendrick (1984; 59) explains the logic behind reporting both forms. "Both are necessary, because an organization is typically interested in knowing which factors show the largest percentage changes, but it is also interested in identifying those factors that provide the largest net impact in dollars."

In Part I we decompose change in financial performance using ratios. The basic ratio is profitability, the ratio of revenue to cost. We begin by motivating the use of profitability as a financial performance indicator. We continue by introducing theoretical and empirical quantity and price index numbers. Our initial objective is to use these index numbers to decompose profitability change into a quantity change component and a price change component. The quantity change component is the ratio of an output quantity index to an input quantity index, and provides an index of productivity change. The price change component is the ratio of an output price index to an input price index, and provides an index of price recovery change. We pursue our initial objective in Chapter 2, in which we take both theoretical and empirical approaches. We also transform the profitability change decomposition in a way that enables us to analyze the distribution of the fruits of productivity change.

Our decomposition of change in financial performance using ratios is not new. It is frequently described as "the APC performance measurement system," with reference to the American Productivity Center, a strong proponent and user of the ratio system. However, the APC system is in fact a modification of a system developed previously and described in van Loggerenberg and Cucchiaro (1981–82). Thus, even though the idea did not originate with the APC, we refer to the APC system because the APC has been very influential in promoting the linkage between productivity and profitability.[10]

We refer above to quantity and price indexes. The ultimate objective of the APC performance measurement system is to go inside these indexes to

---

[10] The American Productivity Center (APC) was founded in 1977 as a privately funded nonprofit organization developing and marketing practical programs to improve business productivity. In the belief that productivity and quality go hand in hand, in 1988 it expanded its name to the American Productivity and Quality Center. Kendrick was associated with the APC from its inception. At the invitation of Dr Jackson Grayson, founder and chairman of the APC, Kendrick collaborated with APC staff to produce Kendrick (1984), an updated revision of Kendrick and Creamer (1961). Chapter 7 of Kendrick (1984), written by Carl Thore, then APC vice-president for measurement, describes "The APC Performance Measurement System," which Thore states was developed at the National Productivity Institute of the Republic of South Africa. Basil van Loggerenberg, described as "[t]he key developer," outlined the method to the APC in 1978, and subsequently the APC transformed the method into the APC performance measurement system. Belcher (1987) provides an insider's guide to implementing the APC performance measurement system.

attribute change in profitability to its sources, changes in the quantities and prices of individual outputs and inputs. This is possible using an empirical approach, but not using a theoretical approach. However, the theoretical approach has the virtue of supporting an alternative decomposition, of the productivity index into its economic drivers.

Our second objective is to extend the APC system in a different direction, by decomposing the index of productivity change into the product of its primary drivers. We pursue this objective in Chapter 3. We begin by using empirical index numbers to implement the decomposition. We do not make much progress with this strategy unless we augment empirical index numbers with economic theory. We continue by using theoretical productivity and price recovery indexes to implement the decomposition. This strategy enables us to decompose productivity change, not by variable, as is achieved using empirical index numbers, but by economic driver. We conclude by combining a theoretical productivity index with an empirical price recovery index.

In Part II we decompose change in financial performance using differences. Various writers refer to a strategy based on differences as "the AT&T approach" or "the NIPA (Net Income and Productivity Analysis) approach used by AT&T," presumably to distinguish this strategy from the APC approach based on ratios. Some writers convert differences to ratios and others do not. Alternative variants differ in their details, but not in their focus on monetary differences.[11]

In Chapter 4 we provide an introduction to the concept of profit as a business financial performance indicator, and we systematically survey the business literature on the topic. We introduce an initial decomposition of profit change into a quantity effect and a price effect. We carry out the decomposition under two scenarios. In the first profit is included among the

[11] In the late 1960s the Economic Analysis Section at AT&T was charged with developing total factor productivity studies. Among other things the section developed and introduced a difference model for analyzing the distribution of the impressive productivity gains in the Bell System. Specifically, they estimated the dollar values of the productivity gains that were passed on to customers (rate reductions), employees (compensation), shareholders (profits), suppliers (prices), creditors (interest), and governments (taxes). This analysis was a recurring procedure at AT&T and an inseparable part of its productivity analysis framework. It was later used in a regulatory context to assess whether an adequate portion of productivity gains was passed on as benefits to customers (in the form of rate cuts or smaller rate increases) relative to higher profits for shareholders. Kendrick (1984) relates part of the story, and the AT&T website www.att.com/history/ has additional information. Chaudry (1982) provides an accessible entry into the AT&T/NIPA model and its uses, and he discusses the use of NIPA for corporate planning and budgetary control purposes at the "major corporation" of Eldor and Sudit (1981). Grossman (1984a, 1984b) provides short and long comparisons of the APC and NIPA approaches to productivity accounting.

expenses, a procedure advocated by Davis and Kendrick. In the second profit is not expensed. We also introduce the distribution of the quantity effect to its beneficiaries, under both scenarios. The French writers, beginning with Vincent (1965, 1968), decompose profit change and analyze the distribution of the quantity effect under both scenarios.

The analysis in Chapter 5 is a bit more formal. We begin by introducing quantity and price indicators, the difference equivalents of quantity and price index numbers. Armed with indicators, we decompose profit change into a quantity change component and a price change component. The quantity change component is the difference between an output quantity indicator and an input quantity indicator. The price change component is the difference between an output price indicator and an input price indicator. We next decompose the quantity change component. When profit is not expensed the quantity change component decomposes into a productivity effect and what we call a margin effect. When profit is expensed the quantity change component decomposes into a productivity effect and what we call an earnings on capital expansion effect. Under both scenarios the quantity change component decomposes, and provides information about the sources of profit change that is unavailable in the ratio approach in Part I, in which the quantity change component coincides with the productivity effect.

In Chapter 6 we decompose the productivity effect, when profit is expensed and when it is not. When profit is not expensed we develop two decomposition strategies. One is based on the margin effect framework introduced in Chapter 5, and the other replaces the margin effect with what we call an activity effect. The difference between the two strategies depends on whether the size of the business is considered to be under the control of management, and this difference influences our definition of productivity change. The margin effect framework generates three productivity change drivers – technical efficiency change, technical change, and size change – and the activity effect framework omits size change as a productivity change driver on the assumption that size change is not under management control.

In Part III we study the linkage between productivity and different financial performance indicators. In Chapter 7 we ignore the revenue half of profitability and profit, and study the linkage between productivity and cost. One motive for doing so is that it is closely related to the business practice of variance analysis. A second motive is the large number of scenarios in which cost is under management control but revenue is not. In the frameworks we develop cost change decomposes into an input price change effect and an output quantity change effect, and the latter decomposes further. These decompositions hold for both ratio form and difference form, and we develop theoretical and empirical approaches in both forms. Due to their popularity we also consider the linkages between productivity and unit cost, and between productivity and unit labor cost.

In Chapter 8 we analyze the linkage between productivity and ROA, a popular financial performance indicator. Our motives are twofold. First, ROA is a widely reported performance indicator. Second, and more importantly, relating productivity to ROA provides an introduction to the duPont Triangle performance evaluation system, which combines the ratio and difference features of financial performance analysis. This material in turn provides an introduction to the literature on productivity networks, managerial control ratios, and financial ratios associated with Eilon, Gold, and their associates. We conduct the analysis both without and with incorporating variation in the rate of capacity utilization into the analysis of the duPont Triangle system. We have noted the importance of productive capacity and its rate of utilization for both productivity and price recovery, and so for business financial performance. Throughout much of the book we ignore the issue, but here we discuss its incorporation into the analysis because it plays such a prominent role in the literature on productivity networks and managerial control ratios.

Figure 1.27, adapted from van Loggerenberg and Cucchiaro (1981–82), illustrates the basic ideas, and applies equally well to the ratio approach in Part I and the difference approach in Part II. Reading across the top row identifies the two sources of revenue change, and reading across the bottom row identifies the two sources of cost change. The resulting middle column identifies revenue change and cost change as one pair of sources of profit(ability) change. An alternative approach reads down columns. Reading down the left column identifies the two sources of productivity change, and reading down the right column identifies the two sources of price recovery change. The resulting middle row identifies productivity change and price recovery change as an alternative pair of sources of profit(ability) change.

Figure 1.28, borrowed from the New South Wales Treasury (1999), extends Figure 1.27. It repeats the notion that both high productivity and favorable price recovery enhance financial performance, and adds that the preferred outcome is in the "Lean & Mean" quadrant characterized by high productivity and low price recovery. The high productivity and high price recovery quadrant is "Too good to last." van Loggerenberg and Cucchiaro (1981–82) explain why: a high price recovery strategy is "unsafe" because a favorable price structure will quickly be eroded by competition. Throughout the book we compare the contributions of productivity and price recovery to business financial performance.

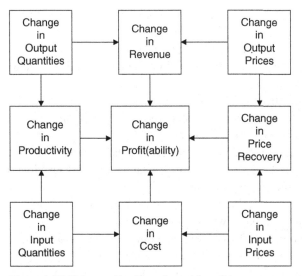

Figure 1.27 Drivers of business financial performance

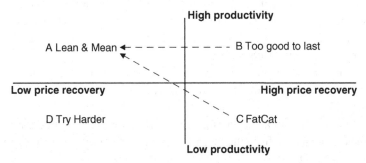

Figure 1.28 Productivity, price recovery, and financial performance

1.8 SOME USEFUL SOURCES OF DATA AND OTHER RELEVANT INFORMATION

Data relevant to the study of productivity, and occasionally financial performance, are widely available from numerous sources. We offer a very selective list of sources.

The OECD provides a rich source of economic data for its member countries at http://stats.oecd.org/Index.aspx

The OECD Composite Indicators contain a wide variety of economically relevant data at http://composite-indicators.jrc.ec.europa.eu/

The EU KLEMS database includes non-EU countries as well, and is available at http://www.euklems.net/

The US BEA (Bureau of Economic Analysis) publishes the US economic accounts from four perspectives, national, regional, industry, and international at www.bea.gov

The US BLS (Bureau of Labor Statistics) reports similar data for the US economy at http://www.bls.gov/bls/productivity.htm and most national statistical agencies report similar data.

The National Bureau of Economic Research publishes books and working papers, hosts a wealth of relevant data, and provides links to other relevant sites. www.nber.org

The World Bank publishes an annual ranking of the most business-friendly countries at http://www.doingbusiness.org/

The US Conference Board Total Economy Database is available at http://www.conference-board.org/data/economydatabase/

Agricultural and fishery productivity and related data are reported at the national and sub-national levels. In Australia the source is ABARES (Australian Bureau of Agricultural and Resource Economics and Sciences) http://www.daff.gov.au/abares and in the United States the agricultural data source is the Department of Agriculture Economic Research Service http://www.ers.usda.gov/

Industry-level data are frequently reported by national and supra-national regulatory agencies and trade associations. One example is provided by the airline industry.

Productivity, financial performance, and other data for international airlines are available from the International Air Transport Association at http://www.iata.org

Productivity, financial performance, and other data for US airlines and other transport carriers are available from the US Bureau of Transportation Statistics at http://www.bts.gov

The Association of American Railroads reports profitability both as ROE and as the "operating ratio," the ratio of operating expense to operating revenue, productivity as "freight revenue per ton mile" and also as "revenue ton-miles per constant dollar operating expense," essentially the reciprocal of unit cost, and additional economic information, for each US Class I railroad, at http://www.aar.org

Productivity and related data for individual firms are available from three sources. One is the proliferation of longitudinal databases currently used for economic research. Another is the agencies that regulate public and private utilities. A third is company annual reports.

One company whose performance we examine later in the book is international retailing giant Walmart, whose annual reports are available at http://investors.walmartstores.com/

Two more are international mining giants BHP Billiton and Rio Tinto, whose Annual Reports are available at http://www.bhpbilliton.com and http://www.riotinto.com

A fertile source of productivity studies at national, industry and firm level that we have found extremely informative is the consultancy McKinsey & Company. The McKinsey Global Institute publishes large-scale studies, and *McKinsey Quarterly*, the online business journal of McKinsey & Company, publishes article-length studies of productivity and related topics. Both are available at http://www.mckinsey.com

The Management and Accounting Web maintains extensive bibliographies on 136 topics of particular relevance at http://maaw.info/

PART I

Productivity and Profitability

2 Profitability Change:
Its Generation and Distribution

2.1 INTRODUCTION

This chapter is the first of two dealing with the generation of profitability and the distribution of its financial impacts. Inspired by Davis (1947, 1955), we define profitability as the ratio of revenue to cost, and for the time being we avoid the task of defining cost and revenue precisely. Profitability is not as popular a measure of business financial performance as is profit, the difference between revenue and cost. Regardless of its popularity, however, profitability is surely a useful financial performance measure.

Our primary objective in Chapters 2 and 3 is to identify the factors that generate change in profitability. One set of factors, which we refer to as *sources*, consists of changes in quantities and prices of outputs and inputs. Individual quantity changes aggregate to the overall impact of quantity change on profitability change, which we call *productivity change*. Individual price changes aggregate to the overall impact of price change on profitability change, which we call *price recovery* change. In this framework profitability change consists exclusively of productivity change and price recovery change. A second set of factors, which we refer to as *drivers*, consists of phenomena such as technical change, change in the efficiency of resource allocation, and size change. The ability of management to harness these factors drives productivity change, which is one component of profitability change. Thus, the term *sources* refers to quantities and prices of individual outputs and inputs, whose changes influence productivity change

65

or price recovery change, either of which influences profitability change. The term *drivers* refers to phenomena related to technology and management practices that influence productivity change (but not price recovery change), and hence profitability change.[1]

Our second objective in Chapters 2 and 3 is to identify the *recipients* of the financial impacts of productivity change. Among the potential claimants to these impacts are consumers, resource suppliers including labor, and lenders to and owners of the enterprise. Thus, the sources of productivity change are changes in quantities of outputs and inputs, and the recipients of the fruits of productivity change are those agents paying or receiving changes in prices of individual outputs and inputs. Throughout Chapters 2 and 3 the changes mentioned above and illustrated in Figure 1.27 in Chapter 1 are expressed, at least initially, in ratio form.

We stress that, in devoting two chapters to the analysis of profitability and its change, we are by no means suggesting that firms seek to maximize profitability. We do not assign an objective to firms because our analysis does not require that we do so. We treat profitability not as a business objective, but as an indicator of the financial health of the business, an indicator, we might add, that is widely used.

We lay the analytical groundwork in this chapter, where we attribute change in profitability to change in productivity and change in price recovery. We analyze both sources and drivers of productivity change, and we identify the recipients of the financial benefits of productivity change. We begin by using theoretical index numbers, and we quickly turn to empirical index numbers to achieve our objectives. In Section 2.2 we review some early studies that exploit the concept of profitability. In Section 2.3 we provide background material on theoretical index numbers, which decompose value change (in this case revenue change and cost change) into quantity change and price change. In Section 2.4 we develop empirical index numbers as approximations to their theoretical counterparts. In Section 2.5 we discuss empirical estimation of theoretical index numbers as an alternative to the use of empirical index numbers.

---

[1] A loose analogue to profitability exists at the aggregate economy level, where improvements in well-being, or living standards, or real incomes, are attributed to productivity growth and to improvements in the "terms of trade," the ratio of export prices to import prices. This is of particular importance to Australia, where improved terms of trade have replaced productivity growth as the primary driver of real income growth since 2000, and there is concern that terms of trade cannot continue to improve; see Gruen (2012).

There is good reason to discuss two alternative approaches to the use of index numbers in Sections 2.4 and 2.5: the two approaches are complementary. Theoretical index numbers are appropriate for analyzing the economic drivers of the productivity change component of profitability change, but they are not appropriate for analyzing the individual variables responsible for either component of profitability change. Conversely, empirical index numbers are appropriate for analyzing the generation and distribution of profitability by *individual and aggregate quantity and price variables*, but they are not well suited to the decomposition of productivity change by *economic driver*. The economic drivers of productivity change (technical change, efficiency change, and size change) are not directly observed in the data, and efforts limited to empirical index numbers to identify the economic drivers of productivity change have not proved very successful. We defer much of our discussion of the economic drivers of productivity change to Chapter 3, where we replace empirical index numbers with empirical estimates of theoretical productivity indexes, and also with the economic theory of production, to identify the economic drivers of productivity change, and hence of profitability change.

In Section 2.6 we combine approximation with estimation in an effort to avoid the use of prices distorted by cross-subsidy in the measurement of productivity change. In Section 2.7 we reinterpret the price recovery term as describing the distribution of the fruits of productivity change to individual agents paying or receiving the price changes. This reinterpretation enables us to analyze the distribution of the financial impacts of productivity change. In Section 2.8 we reorganize the basic "profitability change equals productivity change times price recovery change" expression. This reorganization generates a series of alternative expressions for productivity change. In Section 2.9 we examine a special case of the relationship linking profitability change to productivity change and price recovery change. In this special case profitability is constant, so there is no change in profitability to be explained. However, this also implies that productivity change and price recovery change are reciprocally related. This offers an alternative way of measuring productivity change – as the reciprocal of price recovery change. Because it uses price changes instead of quantity changes, we refer to it as a dual productivity index. In Section 2.10 we acknowledge that many firms (Boeing and Airbus, for example) operate in more than one country, and that some commodities (minerals and commercial aircraft, for example) are traded in US dollars (USD). In both situations exchange rate movements constitute additional price changes, and we show how they expand the price recovery component of profitability change.

2.2 EARLY RECOGNITION OF PROFITABILITY AS A PERFORMANCE INDICATOR

The concept of profitability has a long history in the business literature. Our presentation is largely chronological, but it is apparent that the influential contributors are Davis (1955); Kendrick and Creamer (1961); Kendrick (1961); and Vincent (1968).

In an early and influential treatise on financial ratio analysis, Bliss (1923; 104) compares two fundamental business relationships. One is unit cost, the ratio of cost to the quantity of output produced, which is appropriate for "businesses having satisfactory measures of physical volume," and which we analyze in Sections 7.5 and 7.6 of Chapter 7. The other is the reciprocal of what we call profitability, the ratio of cost to revenue, which we analyze here and in Chapter 3. Bliss recommends the use of unit cost for short-term performance evaluation and comparison, but for longer-term assessment he recommends the use of profitability because unit cost is more sensitive than profitability to fluctuations in prices. He also cautions against interindustry comparisons, noting that both indicators are apt to be highly characteristic of industries.[2]

Davis (1947; 22) describes profitability as "the measure of efficiency which is used by business, . . . the relation of money income to money expenditure, or revenue received per dollar expended." He reveals an awareness of the productivity and price recovery components of profitability, by emphasizing the distinction between two measures of managerial prowess that he calls productive efficiency and efficiency in bargaining for inputs.[3]

---

[2] The concept of profitability, with a variety of definitions of cost and revenue, has assumed a variety of names since, including "operating ratio" (Davis 1955, Waters and Street 1998), "efficiency index" (Downie 1958), the "Downie ratio" (O'Donnell and Swales 1982), "business efficiency" (Amey 1969), "rentability" (Kurosawa 1975), "profitability margin" (Banker, Chang, and Majumdar 1993), "cost recovery" (PC 2001, 2008), and even "profitability" (Abb 1961, Sink, Tuttle, and De Vries 1984, and Brayton 1985).

[3] Anonymous (1955) wrote a review of an article Alessandro Costanza published in *Produttivita* (1955). Costanza wrote, in our notation, $\Pi = (Y/X) \times (P/W)$, in which Y is production, measured in physical units, X is manhours, Y/X is physical productivity, P is a weighted mean of output prices, W is a weighted mean of wages, and P/W "something like the 'terms of trade' of the particular industry or sector studied." Costanza attributed this formula, which we recognize as a decomposition of profitability, to Benedetto Barberi (1901–76), an Italian mathematician who was at one

Davis (1955; 80, 8, 84) associates profitability with the operating ratio then (and still) in use in the railroad industry, and he claims that the trouble with financial indicators such as operating ratios "is that they reflect too much." By this he means that operating ratios combine rather than separate the impacts of quantities and prices on financial performance. He then describes productivity accounting as a measure of productivity change given by "change in output value per dollar of input . . . after price changes have been eliminated." Productivity accounting thus expresses profitability change in real rather than nominal terms, as the ratio of deflated revenue change (an implicit output quantity index) to deflated cost change (an implicit input quantity index), with deflation being accomplished by output and input price indexes. This procedure separates the impacts of quantities and prices on financial performance, and creates Davis's measure of overall company efficiency. He provides a numerical example that offers an explicit comparison of the operating ratio and productivity accounting, and he states that "the operating ratio can be derived from the productivity ratio simply by multiplying the latter by the ratio of the 'implicit' output and input price indexes." He expresses productivity change first as a ratio, as just described, and then as a monetary difference, both in real terms. This procedure of reporting the impact of productivity change in both formats has influenced many subsequent writers.[4]

Lest the preceding discussion leave the impression that productivity accounting is nothing more than an analysis of profitability change in real rather than nominal terms, Davis devotes the bulk of chapter 4 to additional uses of productivity accounting. In addition to its use in the measurement of business efficiency, he proposes productivity accounting for use in analytical audits, in budget control, and in common price accounting. In chapter 5 he also uses productivity accounting to analyze the distribution of the financial benefits of productivity change. However, unlike his practice of reporting the impact of productivity change in ratio and difference forms, his interest in the distributional impacts of productivity change has not been followed by many subsequent writers, Kendrick being a prominent exception.

---

time Director of ISTAT, Statistics Italy, and 1953–55 Chairperson of the International Association for Research in Income and Wealth.

[4] Davis (1955) credits Jones (1933) with being the first to use price weights to construct real output and input aggregates in the measurement of industrial productivity. Griliches (2000) traces productivity measurement based on output and input quantity indexes back to Copeland (1937) and Copeland and Martin (1938).

Downie (1958) apparently was unaware of the works of Davis. He was interested in two features of postwar British industry: the existence of wide differences in the efficiencies of firms in the same industry, and the rate at which industrial efficiency increases. His ultimate concern was with determining whether the "rules of the game" (essentially antitrust laws influencing industrial structure) have influenced the dispersion and growth of efficiency. These interests require a definition of efficiency, and Downie proposes the "efficiency index" $\varepsilon = (v + \check{r}K)/s = (v/s) + \check{r}\beta$, where s is the revenue (turnover), v is the cost of current inputs and depreciation (operating expense), $\check{r}K$ is the cost of employing capital (defined as the product of the average rate of profit in the industry $\check{r}$ and the value of capital employed in the company K), and $\beta = K/s$ is the ratio of the value of capital employed to the value of turnover, a monetary expression for the familiar capital–output ratio. All terms are firm specific except for $\check{r}$. This efficiency index is essentially the ratio of the sum of variable cost and capital cost to revenue, or the reciprocal of profitability. Downie defines the firm's internal rate of profit as $r = (s - v)/K$, which enables him to convert his measure of efficiency from ratio form to difference form $\varepsilon = 1 - \beta(r - \check{r})$. Assuming that interfirm differences in β are small enough to be neglected, it follows that $\varepsilon \lesseqgtr 1$ as $(r - \check{r}) \gtreqless 0$, or as the firm's internal rate of profit exceeds, equals, or falls short of the industry average rate of profit. Relatively profitable firms are relatively efficient on Downie's definition. We will see in Chapters 4 to 6 that, apart from his use of $\check{r}$, Downie's treatment of the cost of employing capital is very similar to the investor input concept introduced by Davis (1955) and Kendrick and Creamer (1961).

Downie notes that the efficiency index includes both technical efficiency and a sort of marketing efficiency (skill in producing what is most in demand), and that variation in pricing power also may influence it. He clearly recognizes that his efficiency index has productivity and price recovery components, although he does not explicitly decompose the efficiency index. However, he does devote much of the book to an exploration of the magnitudes of and trends in dispersion in ε across firms, seeking to determine whether the rules of the game favor a "transfer mechanism" that facilitates entry and exit or an "innovation mechanism" that facilitates catching up and falling behind. In these mechanisms he anticipates the subsequent literature on industry dynamics. He provides extensive empirical results for UK industry. He finds "very substantial" dispersion in efficiency that persists through time, sufficient entry and exit to provide modest support for the transfer mechanism, and sufficient churning to provide strong support for the innovation mechanism.

Kendrick and Creamer (1961) follow Davis (1955) by defining the "value" attributed to the capital input in such a way as to force nominal profitability to unity in each period. They deflate comparison period values to obtain comparison period real profitability. This deflation exercise, in conjunction with the unit nominal profitability convention, effectively decomposes nominal profitability change into productivity change and price recovery change components. They also follow Davis by expressing productivity change both as a ratio and as a monetary value, reflecting their belief that the two concepts provide complementary information about business performance. A series of case studies of individual companies illustrates the procedure.[5]

Vincent was directly influenced by Kendrick, as we note in Chapter 1, and in turn he influenced a generation of French writers. We discuss Vincent's work in detail in Chapters 4 to 6 because most of his work is in difference form rather than ratio form. However, we introduce Vincent here because he begins in ratio form by analyzing profitability and its productivity and price recovery components, and because many of his ideas are relevant to the material we discuss here and in Chapter 3.

Vincent distinguishes between two situations. In the first situation, nominal profit is allowed to be nonzero in the base period and the comparison period, which allows profitability to be non-unitary in both periods. In the second situation, nominal profit is defined in such a way as to force it to be zero in the base period and the comparison period, which forces profitability to be unitary in both periods. The second situation features prominently in the works of Davis and Kendrick, and Vincent considers alternative explanations for nominal profit being zero in both periods. In the more general first situation, nonzero profit in both periods allows $PY \neq WX$, Y and X being output and

---

[5] The Kendrick and Creamer terminology is admirably precise. The productivity concept in a model containing gross output and labor, capital, and intermediate inputs is termed "total" productivity, while productivity in a model with value added and labor and capital inputs is termed "total factor" productivity. Vincent and other French writers use the terms "productivité globale" in a gross output model and "productivité total" in a value added model. Kendrick and Creamer do not express a preference for total productivity or total factor productivity, and in two case studies they calculate both. They recognize that a total factor productivity index must exceed a total productivity index in absolute value, although they point out that the two monetary values coincide. The relationship between the two *productivity indexes* depends on the ratio of nominal gross output to nominal value added, a relationship first explored by Domar (1961). The relationship between the two *monetary values* has been explored by Balk (2009, 2010).

input quantity indexes and P and W being output and input price indexes. Vincent rearranges terms and parameterizes the inequality to obtain a general expression for productivity change, $Y/X = m(W/P)$, where the scalar $m = \Pi^1/\Pi^0$, Π being profitability, the ratio of revenue R to cost C, and superscripts 1 and 0 indicating comparison period and base period. One interpretation of m is that it represents a markup of product prices over their marginal costs resulting from product market power (or a markdown of input prices beneath the value of their marginal products due to input market power), and we revisit this possibility immediately below. Vincent writes that in this situation the relationship between the "surplus de productivité" and its distribution is lost, a debatable claim we return to in Section 2.9. In the less general second situation, $PY = WX$, $m = 1$, and consequently $Y/X = W/P$. In this situation W/P becomes a dual price-based measure of productivity change, and we revisit this possibility in Section 2.9.

Bahiri and Martin (1970) also analyze profitability, although they do not provide a decomposition of it. Their "primary, total earnings productivity index" is profitability, the ratio of revenue to cost, and they show that $R/C = (\pi/C) + 1$, where $\pi = R - C$ is profit and π/C is "the rate of profit generation," a "secondary, profit productivity index." They note that maximization of the primary total earnings productivity index implies maximization of the secondary profit productivity index. They define the two indexes for each output separately, which requires allocating cost to outputs. The procedure, which they call productivity costing, "takes into account any variable expenses ... and adds a minimal overhead apportionment based on optimal facilities usage. Products with the highest total earnings productivity characteristics ... are the most useful in achieving an industrial-commercial system's primary objective" (p. 67). Norman and Bahiri (1972) apply the primary and secondary productivity indexes to an interfirm comparison for management, and to an intertemporal analysis of British industry. In Chapter 8 we relate the primary total earnings productivity index R/C and the secondary profit productivity index π/C to the apex of the duPont Triangle, return on assets π/A, A representing assets. We also relate the secondary profit productivity index to the literature on markups (or margins), in which the markup $\mu = \pi/C \Rightarrow 1 + \mu = R/C = \Pi$, our measure of profitability.

Wait (1980) offers an initial definition of productivity as the ratio of revenue to cost, but he notes that this is valid only if there are no price changes, and he suggests deflating revenue and cost in the comparison period to base period price levels. Thus, his decomposition of profitability into productivity and price recovery is implicit rather than explicit. He notes that productivity and profitability analyses can reinforce one another, and he develops an "analysis of variance in net income" that converts ratios to differences, with monetary price and quantity effects. He decomposes the price effect by variable, so as to identify the individual contributors to profitability change. His productivity change index has three components: product mix, volume, and "performance," the latter being a residual that may capture "pure" productivity change. He also notes that the productivity index can be linked to indexes of percent of capacity used. However, as we demonstrate in Chapter 3, any attempt to use empirical index numbers to decompose productivity change by economic driver is doomed to failure. While the idea that productivity change can be attributed to drivers such as changes in product mix, volume, and capacity utilization is a good one, the techniques are ill-suited to the task.

van Loggerenberg and Cucchiaro (1981–82; 87–91) construct an analytical model of profitability change, which they then convert to an empirical model of profit change, with an application to a division of a large manufacturing firm. They claim that their profitability decomposition model enables companies to "measure how much, in dollars or percent return on investment, profits were affected by productivity growth or decline." This dual focus on monetary and percent impacts follows Davis (1955) and has remained influential. They note that "with the same basic accounting information used to calculate revenues and costs, it is possible to gain more insight into precisely what is driving profits." They explicitly mention productivity change and price recovery change as the two drivers.

van Loggerenberg and Cucchiaro also consider a select list of economic drivers of productivity change, attributing it to "two distinct and measurable components": change in capacity utilization and change in efficiency. They define change in capacity utilization as an increase in output, which they view as being uncontrollable in the short term, holding certain resources fixed. They define change in efficiency as a reduction in either the quantity of fixed resources or the quantity of variable resources per unit of output, which they view as being potentially controllable. "The total factor productivity measurement approach ... measures the profit contribution of each resource in terms of capacity utilization, efficiency, and price recovery." However, when they attempt to decompose productivity change by economic driver, their analysis becomes opaque.

Kendrick (1984; 62–63) refers to the decomposition of profitability change as the APC Performance Measurement System, and attributes its original development to van Loggerenberg. He expresses changes in ratio form and then in difference form, noting that "[t]he APC system goes beyond these ratios and also translates them into their dollar effects on profitability." He reports changes in aggregate quantities and prices of output and input, and also for the individual components of each, using firm-specific empirical quantity indexes and price indexes: "The total dollar effects of both productivity and price recovery are combined for all inputs and collectively become the total explanation of the change in profit" Although he considers the primary impact of price changes to be that on financial performance, he is one of the few to follow Davis by exploring the secondary impact of price changes as signaling the distributional impacts of productivity change.

Sink, Tuttle, and DeVries (1984; 265) begin with the astute observation that "[p]roductivity is a component of performance, not a synonym for it." They decompose change in financial performance, as measured by profitability change, into productivity change and price recovery change. They also convert ratios to differences to decompose profit change by individual output and individual input. As is common in the literature, they interpret price recovery and its components exclusively as sources of profitability change. Unlike some previous studies, they do not make a futile attempt to decompose productivity change by economic driver. They provide a case study, using base period price weights to aggregate outputs and inputs, and comparison period quantity weights to aggregate output prices and input prices.

Brayton (1985; 58) recounts the Touche Ross & Co. version of the APC approach to develop a "Total Productivity Measurement System." He examines the decomposition of profitability change, expresses results in ratio form and in difference form, and decomposes profitability change and profit change by variable. He also emphasizes the role of price recovery and its components as contributors to financial performance, and he claims that this decomposition analysis enables companies to "identify the causes of deterioration or improvement in profitability, determine where attention should be focused to apply available resources with the maximum beneficial effect, project the impact of possible changes in productivity and pricing, . . . and take corrective actions when necessary." These contributions of the decomposition analysis echo the additional uses of productivity accounting identified by Davis (1955).[6]

---

[6] Hayzen and Reeve (2000) and Rao (2000, 2002) also analyze the generation of profitability, although not its distribution.

The concept of profitability has a much shorter history in the economics literature. Georgescu-Roegen (1951; 103) apparently introduced the concept of profitability into the economics literature, calling it "an *economic criterion*" on which to evaluate business performance. He called his economic criterion "*return to the dollar*," and he notes an important advantage of profitability: a performance criterion "*must be independent of the scale of production*," and he notes that revenue, cost, and profit are not (emphasis in the original). He also notes that von Neumann (1945–46) refers to the ratio of revenue to cost as having no economic meaning, and suggests that "a direct interpretation of the function would be highly desirable." Davis and subsequent writers provide economic meaning and interpretation to the profitability function.

Despite this distinguished introduction, the concept of profitability has suffered from relative neglect in the economics literature, where the bottom line is represented by profit, and where there exists a well-established duality theory based on a profit frontier first proposed by Hotelling (1932). The theoretical underpinnings of profitability have their origins outside the field of economics, in fractional programming, and have been surveyed by Schaible (1981).

There are many ways to express business financial performance. The use of profitability to represent the bottom line has some potential advantages, not all of which have been widely appreciated, much less fully exploited. Among these advantages are:

(i) Profitability is appropriate for the comparison of the financial performance of firms of varying size; whereas small firms may be disadvantaged by performance criteria expressed in difference form (such as profit), they are not necessarily disadvantaged by the ratio criterion of profitability;

(ii) Profitability does not take on zero or negative values frequently encountered with profit, which simplifies analysis;

(iii) Profitability change decomposes into the product of a productivity change component and a price recovery change component;

(iv) The two components of profitability change decompose by individual variable, which is useful if the goal is to "separate the ps and qs" that contribute to change in the bottom line; indeed deflation of nominal values to obtain real values is one procedure for decomposing profitability change into productivity change and price recovery change;

  (v) Decompositions by individual variable can be implemented using empirical index numbers;

 (vi) If empirical index numbers are replaced with empirical estimation of theoretical index numbers, or augmented with the economic theory of production, the productivity change component of profitability change also decomposes into the economic drivers of productivity change, as we demonstrate in Chapter 3; and

(vii) Profitability is, or can be made, the centerpiece of much business financial ratio analysis since, for example, $ROA = \pi/A = (\pi/R)$ $(R/A) = [1 - (C/R)](R/A) = [1 - \Pi^{-1}](R/A)$, where R is revenue, C is cost, A is assets, $\pi = R - C$ is profit, and $\Pi = R/C$ is profitability. This makes profitability a core component of ROA.[7]

2.3 THEORETICAL DECOMPOSITION OF PROFITABILITY CHANGE

We are interested in comparing quantities and prices in two situations, a base situation 0 and a comparison situation 1. The pair of situations $(0,1)$ can represent a pair of time periods, a pair of producers, or an actual outcome and a target outcome (as in benchmarking and variance analysis). For the most part we refer to a pair of situations as an adjacent pair of time periods. In any event, the terminology "base" and "comparison," while popular, is by no means unique. Davis (1955) refers to "base" and "given" periods, and Kendrick and Creamer (1961) refer to "base" and "measured" periods, to cite just two of many departures from our terminology, which we borrow from Balk (1998).

---

[7] The concept of profitability (or its reciprocal cost recovery) has found widespread use beyond academe. In a study for McKinsey & Company, Dohrmann and Pinshaw (2009) use the reciprocal of profitability, the expense per dollar of tax revenue collected, as a measure of the efficiency of national tax collection administrations. Arthur D. Little (www.adlittle.com) uses cost recovery to analyze the cost efficiency of European banks, KPMG (www.kpmg.com.au) does the same for Australian banks, and the US Federal Deposit Insurance Corporation (www2.fdic.gov/qbp) reports quarterly efficiency ratios for US commercial banks. The Australian Productivity Commission (www.pc.gov.au/research/commission/gte0607) reports cost recovery as one indicator of the financial performance of government-owned or government-controlled entities that provide services such as electricity, water, transport, and the like. In its annual reports, Tyson Foods reports revenue, cost, profit, and the reciprocal of profitability. It also reports annual changes in revenue and cost, and it decomposes revenue change into "change in average sales price" and "change in sales volume." (http://ir.tyson.com/phoenix.zhtml?c=65476&p=irol-reportsAnnual)

Comparing scalars such as R^1 and R^0, C^1 and C^0, π^1 and π^0, and Π^1 and Π^0 between two situations is easy; comparing vectors such as y^1 and y^0, x^1 and x^0, p^1 and p^0, and w^1 and w^0 between two situations is not. This is because one vector may be larger in some elements and smaller in others than another vector, and so neither is larger than the other in a mathematical sense. It is nonetheless possible to rank them economically. Economic indexes enable us to make an economic comparison of a pair of vectors, by converting them to a single scalar. A price index is such a scalar, one that enables the comparison of a pair of price vectors, while a quantity index is another such scalar that enables the comparison of a pair of quantity vectors.

We now outline the procedure for constructing theoretical quantity and price indexes. These indexes are called "theoretical" because they are defined on the underlying production technology, when necessary under the assumption of optimizing behavior on the part of producers. In Section 2.3.1 we discuss theoretical quantity and productivity indexes, and in Section 2.3.3 we discuss theoretical price and price recovery indexes. In Section 2.3.4 we put the two together to analyze a theoretical decomposition of profitability change.

Because they are defined on the underlying technology, if the technology is well behaved the quantity and productivity indexes in Section 2.3.1 satisfy a number of desirable properties, including monotonicity in both y^1 and y^0, homogeneity of degree $+1$ in y^1 and degree -1 in y^0, identity, proportionality, and independence of units of measurement. The price and price recovery indexes in Section 2.3.3 satisfy the same properties in prices, for the same reason. Balk (1998, 2008) enumerates desirable properties of theoretical index numbers.

2.3.1 Theoretical quantity and productivity indexes

A theoretical output quantity index is a scalar-valued function $Y(x, y^1, y^0)$ that compares output quantity vectors y^1 and y^0, given some input quantity vector x. A Malmquist output quantity index is defined as

$$Y_M(x, y^1, y^0) = D_o(x, y^1) / D_o(x, y^0), \qquad (2.1)$$

in which the functions $D_o(x, y^1)$ and $D_o(x, y^0)$ are output distance functions defined in Section 1.6.1 of Chapter 1. The output quantity index $Y_M(x, y^1, y^0)$ converts a comparison of two output quantity vectors y^1 and y^0 to a ratio of two scalars, and this ratio satisfies $Y_M(x, y^1, y^0) \gtreqless 1$ as $D_o(x, y^1) \gtreqless D_o(x, y^0)$.

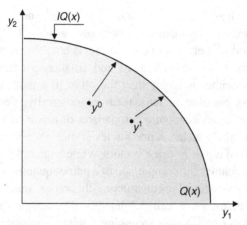

Figure 2.1 Malmquist output quantity index

A Malmquist output quantity index is illustrated in Figure 2.1, in which output quantity vectors y^1 and y^0 cannot be ranked mathematically because $y^1 \not> y^0$ and $y^0 \not> y^1$. They can be ranked economically, however, and $Y_M(x, y^1, y^0) > 1$ because y^1 is closer than y^0 to the output isoquant $IQ(x)$.

The output quantity index $Y_M(x, y^1, y^0)$ in expression (2.1) and in Figure 2.1 compares output vectors from two periods, but it is a generic index that does not specify the period from which the input vector and the technology are drawn. It is common practice to select both from the same period, leading to three choices for an output quantity index, a base period output quantity index $Y_M^0(x^0, y^1, y^0)$ and a comparison period output quantity index $Y_M^1(x^1, y^1, y^0)$ and, because the two are not generally equal, the geometric mean of the two $Y_M(x^1, x^0, y^1, y^0) = [Y_M^1(x^1, y^1, y^0) \times Y_M^0(x^0, y^1, y^0)]^{1/2}$ is often used, at the cost of losing the separate information contained in each.

A theoretical input quantity index is a scalar-valued function $X(y, x^1, x^0)$ that compares input quantity vectors x^1 and x^0, given some output quantity vector y. A Malmquist input quantity index is defined as

$$X_M(y, x^1, x^0) = D_i(y, x^1) / D_i(y, x^0), \tag{2.2}$$

in which the functions $D_i(y, x^1)$ and $D_i(y, x^0)$ are input distance functions also defined in Chapter 1. The input quantity index $X_M(y, x^1, x^0)$ converts a comparison of two input quantity vectors x^1 and x^0 to a ratio of two scalars, and this ratio satisfies $X_M(y, x^1, x^0) \gtreqless 1$ as $D_i(y, x^1) \gtreqless D_i(y, x^0)$.

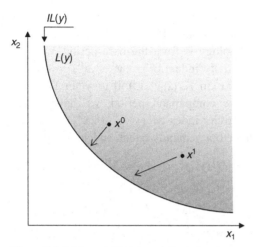

Figure 2.2 Malmquist input quantity index

A Malmquist input quantity index is illustrated in Figure 2.2, in which input quantity vectors x^1 and x^0 cannot be ranked mathematically. They can be ranked economically, however, and $X_M(y, x^1, x^0) > 1$ because x^1 is farther than x^0 from the input isoquant $IL(y)$.

The input quantity index $X_M(y, x^1, x^0)$ in expression (2.2) and Figure 2.2 is also a generic index that compares input vectors from two periods without specifying the period from which the output vector y and the technology $L(y)$ are drawn. It is common practice to select both from the same period, leading to three choices for an input quantity index, a base period input quantity index $X_M^0(y^0, x^1, x^0)$, a comparison period input quantity index $X_M^1(y^1, x^1, x^0)$, and their geometric mean $X_M(y^1, y^0, x^1, x^0) = [X_M^1(y^1, x^1, x^0) \times X_M^0(y^0, x^1, x^0)]^{1/2}$.

A theoretical productivity index is the ratio of a theoretical output quantity index to a theoretical input quantity index. A Malmquist productivity index is defined as

$$M(x, y^1, y^0, y, x^1, x^0) = Y_M(x, y^1, y^0) / X_M(y, x^1, x^0), \qquad (2.3)$$

in which $Y_M(x, y^1, y^0)$ and $X_M(y, x^1, x^0)$ are defined in expressions (2.1) and (2.2). $M(x, y^1, y^0, y, x^1, x^0) \gtreqless 1 \iff Y_M(x, y^1, y^0) \gtreqless X_M(y, x^1, x^0)$ signals productivity growth, stagnation, or decline because output growth as measured by the output quantity index exceeds, equals, or trails input growth as measured by the input quantity index.

The Malmquist productivity index in expression (2.3) is a generic index that leaves information unspecified. If $x=x^0$ in $Y_M(x,y^1,y^0)$, if $y=y^0$ in $X_M(y,x^1,x^0)$, and if technology is from the base period, we have a base period Malmquist productivity index $M^0(y^1,y^0,x^1,x^0) = Y_M^0(x^0,y^1,y^0)/X_M^0(y^0,x^1,x^0)$, while if $x=x^1$ in $Y_M(x,y^1,y^0)$, if $y=y^1$ in $X_M(y,x^1,x^0)$, and if technology is from the comparison period, we have a comparison period Malmquist productivity index $M^1(y^1,y^0,x^1,x^0) = Y_M^1(x^1,y^1,y^0)/X_M^1(y^1,x^1,x^0)$. The two are not generally equal, and so the geometric mean

$$
\begin{aligned}
M(y^1,y^0,x^1,x^0) &= [M^1(y^1,y^0,x^1,x^0) \times M^0(y^1,y^0,x^1,x^0)]^{1/2} \\
&= \{[Y_M^0(x^0,y^1,y^0)/X_M^0(y^0,x^1,x^0)] \\
&\quad \times [Y_M^1(x^1,y^1,y^0)/X_M^1(y^1,x^1,x^0)]\}^{1/2} \\
&= Y_M(x^1,x^0,y^1,y^0)/X_M(y^1,y^0,x^1,x^0)
\end{aligned}
\tag{2.4}
$$

is often used. $M(y^1,y^0,x^1,x^0) \gtreqless 1$ as productivity change is growth, stagnation, or decline.

Summarizing, the geometric mean Malmquist productivity index in expression (2.4) has (at least) four virtues: (i) each quantity index is expressed in terms of distance functions and so has desirable theoretical properties; (ii) it is based on both output distance functions and input distance functions, and so is not oriented; (iii) it is expressed as the ratio of an output quantity index to an input quantity index, which makes it structurally similar to empirical productivity indexes such as the Fisher productivity index; and (iv) it decomposes into separate indexes of technical change, technical efficiency change, and size change, the latter encompassing economies of scale and changes in the output mix and the input mix. This tripartite decomposition makes it appropriate for use with profit change decompositions that include a margin effect, which we discuss in Chapter 6.

It is worth noting that Malmquist did not propose the productivity index (2.4) that bears his name. Malmquist (1953) developed a quantity index of different consumption bundles but at the same level of utility. His consumption quantity index has been adapted to the construction of input quantity indexes, output quantity indexes and productivity indexes in the context of production economics. The adaptation was anticipated by Moorsteen (1961), and formally proposed as a productivity index, and named, by Bjurek (1996). Diewert (2008; 20) refers to Malmquist output and input quantity indexes as "our best theoretical quantity index[es]" because they satisfy the proportionality property, and the ratio of the two is the Malmquist productivity index named by Bjurek that is now recommended by Diewert and Nakamura (2007).

However, the Malmquist productivity index in expression (2.4) is not the only Malmquist productivity index. A second Malmquist productivity index, also not proposed by Malmquist himself, is far more popular. Its popularity requires that we introduce it, which we do in Section 2.3.2.[8]

2.3.2 An alternative Malmquist productivity index

Another Malmquist productivity index was introduced by Caves, Christensen, and Diewert (1982) (CCD). This index cannot be expressed as the ratio of an output quantity index to an input quantity index, which breaks the structural similarity with empirical productivity indexes. Like the Malmquist index we introduced in Section 2.3.1, the CCD Malmquist productivity index is expressed in terms of distance functions, and can be expressed as a base period index or comparison period index or the geometric mean of the two. Unlike the other Malmquist productivity index, the CCD index can have an output orientation based exclusively on output distance functions, or an input orientation based exclusively on input distance functions. The variant we use here decomposes into separate indexes of technical change and technical efficiency change, which makes it appropriate for use with profit change decompositions that include an activity effect, which we also discuss in Chapter 6, and for use in decomposing change in ROA, which we discuss in Chapter 8.

A generic output-oriented CCD Malmquist productivity index is

$$M_{o\,\text{CCD}}(x^1, x^0, y^1, y^0) = D_o(x^1, y^1) / D_o(x^0, y^0), \qquad (2.5)$$

which defines productivity change as the ratio of two output distance functions, and so compares the productivity of comparison period quantities (x^1, y^1) to that of base period quantities (x^0, y^0) against a generic technology. A base period output-oriented CCD Malmquist productivity index is $M_o^0{}_{\text{CCD}}(x^1, x^0, y^1, y^0) = D_o^0(x^1, y^1)/D_o^0(x^0, y^0)$, a comparison period output-oriented CCD Malmquist productivity index is $M_o^1{}_{\text{CCD}}(x^1, x^0, y^1, y^0) = D_o^1(x^1, y^1)/D_o^1(x^0, y^0)$, and a geometric mean output-oriented CCD Malmquist productivity index is

---

[8] Stigler's (1966; 77) observation that "If we should ever encounter a case where a theory is named for the correct man, it will be noted" seems particularly relevant here.

$$M_{o \text{ CCD}}(x^1, x^0, y^1, y^0) = [D_o^0(x^1, y^1)/D_o^0(x^0, y^0) \times D_o^1(x^1, y^1)/D_o^1(x^0, y^0)]^{1/2}.$$

$$(2.6)$$

$M_{o \text{ CCD}}(x^1, x^0, y^1, y^0) \gtreqless 1$ as productivity change is growth, stagnation, or decline.

The two Malmquist productivity indexes given in expressions (2.4) and (2.6) do not coincide except under very restrictive conditions on either the underlying production technology or the quantity vectors y and x; Färe, Grosskopf, and Roos (1996) and Balk (1998) provide the details. However, limited empirical evidence suggests that estimates of the two tend to be numerically close. Additional limited empirical evidence also suggests that calculated empirical productivity indexes such as Fisher (1922) and Törnqvist (1936) provide close approximations to estimates of both Malmquist productivity indexes. Our preference for the Malmquist productivity index in expression (2.4) is based partly on its structural similarity to empirical index numbers, as the ratio of an output quantity index to an input quantity index, and partly on the fact that it includes size change as a driver of productivity change. The CCD Malmquist productivity index in expression (2.6), on the other hand, cannot be expressed as the ratio of an output quantity index to an input quantity index, and it does not include size change as a driver of productivity change, a point first raised by Grifell-Tatjé and Lovell (1995). Consequently, since then it has become popular to impose constant returns to scale on the underlying technology, which allows the alternative Malmquist productivity index to include size change as a driver of productivity change. However, when we use the alternative Malmquist productivity index in Chapters 6 and 8, we use the original CCD specification that does not impose constant returns to scale on the underlying technology.

As a concluding observation, the Malmquist productivity index in expression (2.4) is not oriented, being defined on both output distance functions and input distance functions. The CCD Malmquist productivity index introduced in this section is output-oriented, being defined on output distance functions. An input-oriented CCD Malmquist productivity index $M_{i \text{ CCD}}(y^1, y^0, x^1, x^0)$ defined on input distance functions also exists, and is appropriate when the economic problem under investigation is oriented toward resource conservation.

2.3.3 Theoretical price and price recovery indexes

A theoretical output price index is a scalar-valued function $P(x,p^1,p^0)$ that compares output price vectors p^1 and p^0, given some input quantity vector x. A Konüs (1939) output price index is defined as

$$P_K(x,p^1,p^0) = r(x,p^1) / r(x,p^0), \qquad (2.7)$$

in which the revenue frontiers $r(x,p^1)$ and $r(x,p^0)$ are defined in Chapter 1. The output price index $P_K(x,p^1,p^0)$ converts a comparison of two output price vectors p^1 and p^0 to a ratio of two scalars, and this ratio satisfies $P_K(x,p^1,p^0) \gtreqless 1$ as $r(x,p^1) \gtreqless r(x,p^0)$ in the sense of generating greater, the same, or less potential revenue from a given technology and input quantity vector.

The output price index $P_K(x,p^1,p^0)$ in expression (2.7) is yet another generic index that compares output price vectors from two periods without specifying the period from which the input quantity vector and the technology are drawn. Three options are a base period output price index $P_K^0(x^0,p^1,p^0)$, a comparison period output price index $P_K^1(x^1,p^1,p^0)$, and the geometric mean of the two, $P_K(x^1,x^0,p^1,p^0) = [P_K^1(x^1,p^1,p^0) \times P_K^0(x^0,p^1,p^0)]^{1/2}$; since the first two options are not generally equal except under restrictive conditions, the third option is often used.

A Konüs output price index is illustrated in Figure 2.3, in which $p^1 > p^0$ is not required. $P_K(x,p^1,p^0) > 1$ because p^1 allows larger maximum revenue than p^0 does, for any $x \geq 0$ and regardless of the mathematical relationship between the two price vectors.

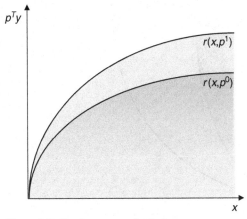

Figure 2.3 Konüs output price index

A theoretical input price index is a scalar-valued function $W(y, w^1, w^0)$ that compares input price vectors w^1 and w^0, given some output quantity vector y. A Konüs input price index is defined as

$$W_K(y, w^1, w^0) = c(y, w^1) / c(y, w^0), \tag{2.8}$$

in which the cost frontiers $c(y, w^1)$ and $c(y, w^0)$ are also defined in Chapter 1. The input price index $W_K(y, w^1, w^0)$ converts a comparison of two input price vectors w^1 and w^0 to a ratio of two scalars, and this ratio satisfies $W_K(y, w^1, w^0) \gtreqless 1$ as $c(y, w^1) \gtreqless c(y, w^0)$ in the sense of requiring greater, the same, or smaller minimum cost to produce output quantity vector y.

The input price index $W_K(y, w^1, w^0)$ in expression (2.8) compares input price vectors from two periods without specifying the period from which the output quantity vector y and the technology $L(y)$ are drawn. As usual, the three options are a base period input price index, $W_K^0(y^0, w^1, w^0)$, a comparison period input price index, $W_K^1(y^1, w^1, w^0)$, and the geometric mean of the two, $W_K(y^1, y^0, w^1, w^0) = [W_K^1(y^1, w^1, w^0) \times W_K^0(y^0, w^1, w^0)]^{1/2}$.

A Konüs input price index is illustrated in Figure 2.4, where there is no presumption that $w^1 > w^0$. However, $W_K(y, w^1, w^0) > 1$ because w^1 generates higher minimum cost than w^0 does, for any $y \geq 0$ and regardless of the mathematical relationship between the two price vectors.

A theoretical price recovery index is the ratio of a theoretical output price index and a theoretical input price index. A Konüs price recovery index is defined as

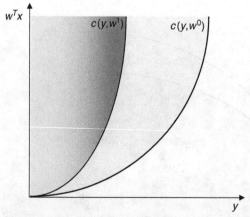

Figure 2.4 Konüs input price index

$$K(x,p^1,p^0,y,w^1,w^0) = P_K(x,p^1,p^0) / W_K(y,w^1,w^0), \qquad (2.9)$$

in which $P_K(x,p^1,p^0)$ and $W_K(y,w^1,w^0)$ are defined in expressions (2.7) and (2.8). $K(x,p^1,p^0,y,w^1,w^0) \gtreqless 1 \Leftrightarrow P_K(x,p^1,p^0) \gtreqless W_K(y,w^1,w^0)$ signals positive, zero, or negative price recovery because output price growth as measured by the output price index exceeds, equals, or falls short of input price growth as measured by the input price index.

The Konüs price recovery index in expression (2.9) is a generic index leaving information unspecified. If $x=x^0$ in $P_K(x,p^1,p^0)$, if $y=y^0$ in $W_K(y,w^1,w^0)$, and if base period technology is specified, we have a base period Konüs price recovery index, $K^0(x^0,p^1,p^0,y^0,w^1,w^0)=P_K^0(x^0,p^1,p^0)/W_K^0(y^0,w^1,w^0)$, while if $x=x^1$ in $P_K(x,p^1,p^0)$, if $y=y^1$ in $W_K(y,w^1,w^0)$, and if comparison period technology is specified, we have a comparison period Konüs price recovery index $K^1(x^1,p^1,p^0,y^1,w^1,w^0)=P_K^1(x^1,p^1,p^0)/W_K^1(y^1,w^1,w^0)$. It is also possible to specify the geometric mean of the two, $K(x^1,x^0,p^1,p^0,y^1,y^0,w^1,w^0)=[K^1(x^1,p^1,p^0,y^1,w^1,w^0) \times K^0(x^0,p^1,p^0,y^0,w^1,w^0)]^{1/2} = P_K(x^1,x^0,p^1,p^0) / W_K(y^1,y^0,w^1,w^0).$[9]

2.3.4 Theoretical decomposition of profitability change

We are now prepared to provide a theoretical decomposition of profitability change. Recalling that profitability $\Pi=R/C$, change in profitability from base period to comparison period is expressed as

$$\begin{aligned} \Pi^1/\Pi^0 &= (R^1/C^1) / (R^0/C^0) \\ &= (R^1/R^0) / (C^1/C^0), \end{aligned} \qquad (2.10)$$

where R^1/R^0 is nominal revenue change and C^1/C^0 is nominal cost change. We wish to associate nominal revenue change with change in the output quantity index (2.1) and the output price index (2.7), and we wish to associate nominal cost change with the input quantity index (2.2) and the input price index (2.8). We use generic expressions rather than geometric mean expressions to lighten the notational burden.

---

[9] Konüs developed a consumer's "true" cost of living index as the ratio of a pair of expenditure functions evaluated at different commodity price vectors and the same utility (or standard of living) level. His consumer cost of living index has been adapted to the construction of input price indexes and output price indexes in the context of production economics, and we extend Konüs price indexes to a Konüs price recovery index.

The pair of indexes in expressions (2.1) and (2.7), and the pair of indexes in expressions (2.2) and (2.8), do not satisfy the product test, in the sense that

$$R^1/R^0 \approx Y_M(x,y^1,y^0) \times P_K(x,p^1,p^0)$$
$$C^1/C^0 \approx X_M(y,x^1,x^0) \times W_K(y,w^1,w^0), \tag{2.11}$$

so that the product of quantity and price indexes only approximates the nominal value change. Consequently, substituting the generic versions of the theoretical index numbers given in expressions (2.1), (2.2), (2.7), and (2.8) into expression (2.10) for profitability change yields

$$
\begin{aligned}
\Pi^1/\Pi^0 &= (R^1/R^0)/(C^1/C^0) \\
&\approx [Y_M(x,y^1,y^0) \times P_K(x,p^1,p^0)]/[X_M(y,x^1,x^0) \times W_K(y,w^1,w^0)] \\
&= [Y_M(x,y^1,y^0) \times X_M(y,x^1,x^0)]/[P_K(x,p^1,p^0) \times W_K(y,w^1,w^0)] \\
&= M(x,y^1,y^0,y,x^1,x^0) \times K(x,p^1,p^0,y,w^1,w^0).
\end{aligned}
\tag{2.12}
$$

The first line of expression (2.12) repeats the second equality in expression (2.10). The second line states that the ratio of revenue change to cost change is only approximated by the ratio of the product of theoretical output price and quantity indexes to the product of theoretical input price and quantity indexes; the ratio of two approximations in expression (2.11) remains an approximation. The third and fourth lines rearrange and combine indexes to show that profitability change is approximated by the product of a theoretical productivity index and a theoretical price recovery index.[10]

Despite the approximate nature of expression (2.12), it remains a valuable expression. The first virtue of decomposition (2.12) of Π^1/Π^0 is that it provides an initial attribution of change in (one indicator of) business financial performance to four theoretical indexes, two quantity indexes [$Y_M(x,y^1,y^0)$ and $X_M(y,x^1,x^0)$] and two price indexes [$P_K(x,p^1,p^0)$ and $W_K(y,w^1,w^0)$]. These four indexes define two economic aggregates, a productivity index [$M(x,y^1,y^0,y,x^1,x^0) = Y_M(x,y^1,y^0)/X_M(y,x^1,x^0)$] and a price recovery index [$K(x,p^1,p^0,y,w^1,w^0) = P_K(x,p^1,p^0)/W_K(y,w^1,w^0)$]. Both productivity

[10] Balk (1998; sections 3.5 and 4.4) makes repeated use of Mahler's inequality to show that the product of base period price and quantity indexes over- (under-)states value change, and the product of comparison period price and quantity indexes under- (over-)states value change, and so the products of geometric mean price and quantity indexes "satisfy the product test approximately." In this context "approximately" is a mathematical, not a statistical, concept.

change and price recovery change contribute to profitability change, and the product of their two indexes approximates profitability change.

The second virtue of the decomposition is that it formalizes the warnings of Davis, Kendrick and others cited in Chapter 1 that productivity growth is neither necessary nor sufficient for an increase in profitability, which also depends on change in price recovery. The beneficial impact of productivity growth on profitability can be negated by poor price recovery, and strong price recovery can generate growth in profitability in the absence of productivity growth.

However, the decomposition is only approximate; it is not exact because the theoretical quantity and price indexes satisfy the product test approximately, not exactly. Nonetheless, Malmquist and Konüs pairs do satisfy the product test in two circumstances. They satisfy the product test when $M = N = 1$, because then all theoretical index numbers collapse to ratios of scalars such as $Y_M(x, y^1, y^0) = y^1/y^0$, $P_K(x, p^1, p^0) = p^1/p^0$, and so on, but this case is uninteresting. A more interesting case allows $M > 1$, $N > 1$, but imposes restrictions on the data and on producer behavior. Diewert (1981) shows that, for the cost change part of expression (2.11), although the product test is not satisfied at $y = y^0$, and is not satisfied at $y = y^1$, there exists an intermediate output quantity vector $y^* = \lambda y^0 + (1-\lambda)y^1$, $0 \leq \lambda \leq 1$, for which $X_M(y^*, x^1, x^0) \times W_K(y^*, w^1, w^0) = C^1/C^0$, where $X_M(y^*, x^1, x^0)$ is a generic Malmquist input quantity index, $W_K(y^*, w^1, w^0)$ is a generic Konüs input price index, and cost minimizing behavior (which can be relaxed to input allocative efficiency) is assumed in both periods. The same argument applies to the output side. Although the product test is not satisfied at $x = x^0$ and is not satisfied at $x = x^1$, there exists an intermediate input quantity vector $x^* = \mu x^0 + (1-\mu)x^1$, $0 \leq \mu \leq 1$, for which $Y_M(x^*, y^1, y^0) \times P_K(x^*, p^1, p^0) = R^1/R^0$, where $Y_M(x^*, y^1, y^0)$ is a generic Malmquist output quantity index, $P_K(x^*, p^1, p^0)$ is a generic Konüs output price index, and output allocative efficiency is assumed. The implication of Diewert's analysis is that the approximations in expressions (2.11) and (2.12) may be quite good if producers are allocatively efficient and quantities do not vary much from base period to comparison period. This is likely to be the case in most time series situations, and less likely in most cross-sectional situations.

It is possible to force satisfaction of the product test by defining implicit Malmquist price indexes $PI_M(x, p^1, p^0, y^1, y^0) = (R^1/R^0)/Y_M(x, y^1, y^0)$ and $WI_M(y, w^1, w^0, x^1, x^0) = (C^1/C^0)/X_M(y, x^1, x^0)$, but neither implicit price index satisfies the identity property unless $M = 1$ or $y^1 = \lambda y^0$, $\lambda > 0$. The implicit Konüs quantity indexes $YI_K(x, p^1, p^0, y^1, y^0) = (R^1/R^0)/P_K(x, p^1, p^0)$ and

$XI_K(y, w^1, w^0, x^1, x^0) = (C^1/C^0)/W_K(y, w^1, w^0)$ also fail to satisfy an analogous identity property. There is thus a trade-off between the identity property satisfied by Konüs price indexes and Malmquist quantity indexes that do not satisfy the product test, and the product test satisfied by Malmquist quantity indexes and implicit price indexes, or Konüs price indexes and implicit quantity indexes, that do not satisfy the identity property. We explore this trade-off in Chapter 3, where we derive some new and interesting properties of implicit Malmquist price indexes and implicit Konüs quantity indexes in Section 3.3.2, and in Section 3.4 we examine the magnitude and statistical significance of the failure of Malmquist quantity and productivity indexes to satisfy the product test with Fisher price and price recovery indexes.

The fact that the theoretical quantity and price indexes only approximately satisfy the product test is unfortunate but by no means fatal. This is because in practice we do not use them. In Section 2.4 we approximate them with empirical index numbers, and in Section 2.5 we estimate them using econometric methods or mathematical programming techniques. We revisit this issue in Chapter 3.

Summarizing Section 2.3, we have developed theoretical quantity and price indexes that aggregate many dimensions to one, and that satisfy desirable properties. We have used these indexes to construct theoretical productivity and price recovery indexes that also satisfy desirable properties. However, no pair of theoretical quantity and price indexes satisfies the relevant product test, and consequently the productivity and price recovery indexes also fail the relevant product test. Consequently, expressions (2.11) and (2.12) provide just approximate decompositions of revenue change, cost change and profitability change into their respective quantity change and price change components. In addition, no pair decomposes by individual variable. We shall show, however, that each pair decomposes by economic driver. We pursue the pairing of explicit and implicit quantity and price indexes to ensure satisfaction of the product test in Chapter 3, where we also explore the seriousness of failure of the product test.

2.4 EMPIRICAL DECOMPOSITION OF PROFITABILITY CHANGE

Index numbers are aggregator functions. They aggregate possibly disparate changes in individual quantities (or prices) into a scalar-valued index of aggregate quantity (or price) change. Theoretical index numbers are defined directly on the underlying production technology, and they inherit desirable properties from those of the technology. But because technology is unobserved, they are unobserved as well, and must be estimated. In this section we analyze empirical index numbers, which are constructed from observable market transactions and provide approximations to their theoretical counterparts. Some empirical index numbers provide better approximations than others. The great virtue of all popular empirical index numbers, however, is that they decompose by individual variable. Such decompositions offer valuable insight to managers seeking to enhance financial performance, by directing their attention to those variables contributing the most and the least.

Like their theoretical counterparts, empirical index numbers satisfy desirable properties, although some satisfy more properties than others. Eichhorn and Voeller (1976) list five basic properties, including monotonicity, homogeneity, identity, dimensionality, and invariance to units of measurement, that an empirical function must satisfy to qualify as a price (or quantity) index, and they prove that no function satisfies all five. Despite this impossibility result, the functions we study in this section are generally well behaved.

Empirical quantity and price indexes are widely used to approximate theoretical quantity and price indexes. Laspeyres (1871) output quantity and price indexes are given by $Y_L(y^1, y^0, p^1, p^0)$ and $P_L(p^1, p^0, y^1, y^0)$, respectively, and we conserve on notation by writing

$$
\begin{aligned}
Y_L &= p^{0T}y^1/p^{0T}y^0 = \sum U_m^0(y_m^1/y_m^0) \\
P_L &= p^{1T}y^0/p^{0T}y^0 = \sum U_m^0(p_m^1/p_m^0),
\end{aligned}
\tag{2.13}
$$

where $U_m = p_m y_m/p^T y$ is the revenue share of output y_m. The second equality in both expressions shows that Y_L and P_L decompose by variable. The intuition behind Y_L and P_L is that each is a weighted sum of individual changes, with individual quantity changes (y_m^1/y_m^0) and individual price changes (p_m^1/p_m^0) being weighted by their relative importance, as measured by their base period revenue shares.

Paasche (1874) output quantity and price indexes $Y_P(y^1, y^0, p^1, p^0)$ and $P_P(p^1, p^0, y^1, y^0)$ also decompose by variable, and are given in simplified notation by

$$
\begin{aligned}
Y_P &= p^{1T}y^1/p^{1T}y^0 = [\sum U_m^1(y_m^1/y_m^0)^{-1}]^{-1}, \\
P_P &= p^{1T}y^1/p^{0T}y^1 = [\sum U_m^1(p_m^1/p_m^0)^{-1}]^{-1}.
\end{aligned}
\tag{2.14}
$$

The intuition behind Y_P and P_P is the same as that behind Y_L and P_L, with base period revenue share weights replaced with comparison period revenue share weights.

It is conventional practice to pair a Laspeyres quantity index with a Paasche price index, and less frequently to pair a Paasche quantity index with a Laspeyres price index. This is because, although $Y_L P_L \neq R^1/R^0$ and $Y_P P_P \neq R^1/R^0$,

$$Y_L P_P = (p^{0T}y^1/p^{0T}y^0) \times (p^{1T}y^1/p^{0T}y^1) = p^{1T}y^1/p^{0T}y^0 = R^1/R^0, \quad (2.15)$$

and also $Y_P P_L = R^1/R^0$. Thus, the product of a Laspeyres quantity index and a Paasche price index (and the reverse) equals the revenue change ratio. Both Laspeyres–Paasche pairings satisfy the product test exactly, not as an approximation, because P_P is an implicit Laspeyres price index and P_L is an implicit Paasche price index. Neither $Y_L P_L$ nor $Y_P P_P$ equals the revenue change ratio.[11]

Laspeyres–Paasche index number pairs are widely used, but because they use different weights, they generate different results. This has led to the construction of index numbers that combine base period and comparison period information, although in various ways.

Edgeworth (1925)–Marshall (1887) (EM) index numbers combine base period and comparison period information, and they are highly regarded by Fisher, who writes: "The best practical all-around formula, taking all four points into account – accuracy, speed, minimum legitimate circular discrepancy, simplicity – is the Edgeworth-Marshall formula" (p. 365). Fabricant (1940) and Kendrick (1961) use EM index numbers in their monumental studies of productivity growth in the US, and Kendrick indicates that the EM weighting convention was used in most other National Bureau studies at the

---

[11] Davis (1955), Kendrick (1961), Kendrick and Creamer (1961), and Vincent (1961) all pair Laspeyres quantity indexes with Paasche price indexes. Failure of the pairs (Y_L, P_L) and (Y_P, P_P) to satisfy the product test has not prevented the use of these two incompatible index number pairs. In the accounting literature, in the context of variance analysis, the residual arising from failure to satisfy the product test is called a joint, or residual, variance. Weber (1963) traces the treatment of the joint variance back to a pair of studies in 1927 and 1932. Bashan et al. (1973) provide a careful analysis of the joint variance based on Laspeyres quantity and price indexes. An implication of their analysis (that they derive but do not discuss) is that the joint variance is zero if $Y_L + P_L = 2$. In the productivity dynamics literature, the pairing of Laspeyres (or Paasche) quantity and price indexes creates a similar problem: failure of the product test and the consequent appearance of a residual covariance term that is difficult to interpret; Balk (2003) provides a clear exposition with references to the productivity dynamics literature.

time.[12] EM output quantity and price indexes are given in simplified notation by

$$Y_{EM} = \sum {}^1\!/_2 (p_m^0 + p_m^1) y_m^1 \Big/ \sum {}^1\!/_2 (p_m^0 + p_m^1) y_m^0 = \sum (\bar{p}_m y_m^0 / \bar{p}^T y^0)(y_m^1 / y_m^0),$$
$$P_{EM} = \sum {}^1\!/_2 (y_m^0 + y_m^1) p_m^1 \Big/ \sum {}^1\!/_2 (y_m^0 + y_m^1) p_m^0 = \sum (\bar{y}_m p_m^0 / \bar{y}^T p^0)(p_m^1 / p_m^0),$$

$$(2.16)$$

which use the arithmetic mean of base period and comparison period prices to weight individual quantity changes, and the arithmetic mean of base period and comparison period quantities to weight individual price changes. The intuition behind EM indexes is to replace an arbitrary reliance on either base period or comparison period weights with arithmetic mean weights. Fabricant (1940) shows that EM output quantity and price indexes are bounded by their Laspeyres and Paasche counterparts. The second equalities demonstrate that Y_{EM} and P_{EM} decompose by variable, with $\bar{p}_m$ and $\bar{y}_m$ being arithmetic mean prices and quantities, so that $\bar{p}_m y_m^0 / \bar{p}^T y^0$ are revenue shares using base period quantities and arithmetic mean prices, and $\bar{y}_m p_m^0 / \bar{y}^T p^0$ are revenue shares using base period prices and arithmetic mean quantities. However, $Y_{EM} P_{EM} \neq R^1 / R^0$, and so EM quantity and price indexes do not satisfy the product test. It is possible to pair Y_{EM} with an implicit EM output price index $PI_{EM} = (R^1/R^0)/Y_{EM}$, or to pair P_{EM} with an implicit EM output quantity index $YI_{EM} = (R^1/R^0)/P_{EM}$. Both pairings satisfy the product test by construction, but the implicit indexes PI_{EM} and YI_{EM} fail to satisfy the linear homogeneity test for quantity and price indexes.[13]

Although each of these empirical index numbers decomposes by variable, and some pairs of them satisfy the product test exactly, they do not necessarily approximate theoretical indexes closely; they provide what we call "good" approximations to their theoretical counterparts, depending on the circumstances. For this reason we are interested in more sophisticated empirical index numbers that provide "better" approximations to their theoretical counterparts. Such index numbers are referred to as "superlative" index numbers.[14]

---

[12] Gold and Kraus (1964), Eilon and Teague (1973), Eilon, Gold, and Soesan (1975, 1976), Harper (1984) and New South Wales Treasury (1999) all use EM quantity indexes. Eilon et al. (1976) compare EM arithmetic mean price weights with Walsh (1924) geometric mean price weights; with their data both indexes provide a close approximation to the Fisher index.

[13] $Y_{EM} P_{EM} \neq R^1 / R^0$ unless the M × M matrix $[\bar{p} \bar{y}^T]$ is a scalar matrix.

[14] Loosely speaking, "good" indexes are consistent with ("exact for" in the literature) functional forms that provide first-order approximations to their theoretical counterparts. Laspeyres and Paasche indexes are good indexes because both are exact for linear and fixed-proportions

Fisher (1922) suggested taking the geometric means of Laspeyres and Paasche quantity and price indexes. The intuition is similar to that of EM indexes; rather than constructing importance weights exclusively from base period data, or exclusively from comparison period data, it is preferable to use both. Fisher output quantity and price indexes are given in simplified notation by

$$
\begin{aligned}
Y_F &= (Y_L \times Y_P)^{1/2} = [(p^{0T}y^1/p^{0T}y^0) \times (p^{1T}y^1/p^{1T}y^0)]^{1/2}, \\
P_F &= (P_L \times P_P)^{1/2} = [(p^{1T}y^0/p^{0T}y^0) \times (p^{1T}y^1/p^{0T}y^1)]^{1/2}.
\end{aligned}
\tag{2.17}
$$

It is not difficult to show that $Y_F P_F = R^1/R^0$, so that this pairing also satisfies the product test exactly. Y_F and P_F also decompose by variable, as Balk (2004, 2008) demonstrates.

Törnqvist (1936) proposed a third combination of base period and comparison period importance weights. His approach is similar to the EM approach, although arithmetic mean price and quantity weights are replaced by arithmetic mean share weights. Törnqvist output quantity and price indexes are expressed in geometric mean form and simplified notation as

$$
\begin{aligned}
Y_T &= \Pi(y_m^1/y_m^0)^{1/2(U_m^1+U_m^0)}, \\
P_T &= \Pi(p_m^1/p_m^0)^{1/2(U_m^1+U_m^0)},
\end{aligned}
\tag{2.18}
$$

in which individual output quantity changes are weighted by their arithmetic mean revenue shares and individual output price changes also are weighted by their arithmetic mean revenue shares. Törnqvist output quantity and price indexes decompose by variable, but $Y_T P_T \neq R^1/R^0$, and so they do not satisfy the product test. Consequently, it is conventional to force satisfaction of the product test by pairing Y_T with an implicit Törnqvist output price index $PI_T = (R^1/R^0)/Y_T$, or by pairing P_T with an implicit Törnqvist output quantity index $YI_T = (R^1/R^0)/P_T$.

---

functional forms. "Better" indexes are called "superlative" because they are exact for functional forms that provide second-order approximations to their theoretical counterparts. Fisher and Törnqvist indexes are superlative indexes because they are exact for quadratic and log-quadratic ("translog") functional forms, respectively. Diewert (2008) provides details and references to the literature. However, the accuracy of even superlative index numbers depends on assumptions concerning optimizing behavior, and we are not aware of empirical evidence concerning the sensitivity of accuracy to violations of the optimization assumptions. Hill (2006) provides two sets of empirical evidence showing that even superlative indexes can diverge from one another by substantial margins. In Section 2.6 we discuss a strategy for dealing with violations of the optimization assumptions.

The preceding material extends naturally to the input side, where the input quantity and price indexes are X_L and W_L, X_P and W_P, X_{EM} and W_{EM}, X_F and W_F, and X_T and W_T, respectively. The pairings $X_L W_P = X_P W_L = X_{EM} WI_{EM} = XI_{EM} W_{EM} = X_F W_F = X_T WI_T = XI_T W_T = C^1/C^0$, and so satisfy the product test exactly, where WI_{EM} and XI_{EM} are implicit EM input price and quantity indexes and WI_T and XI_T are implicit Törnqvist input price and quantity indexes.

We are now prepared to provide an empirical decomposition of profitability change. Recalling that profitability $\Pi = R/C$, change in profitability from base period to comparison period is expressed in ratio form, using expression (2.10), as

$$
\begin{aligned}
\Pi^1/\Pi^0 &= (R^1/R^0)/(C^1/C^0) \\
&= (Y/X) \times (P/W),
\end{aligned}
\tag{2.19}
$$

where R^1/R^0 is revenue change and C^1/C^0 is cost change, and the empirical index number pairs Y, P and X, W are required to satisfy the product test. Pairs that satisfy the product test and provide "good" approximations to their theoretical counterparts include Laspeyres quantity (or price) and Paasche price (or quantity) indexes. Pairs that satisfy the product test and provide "better" approximations to their theoretical counterparts include EM quantity (or price) and implicit EM price (or quantity) indexes, Fisher quantity and price indexes, and Törnqvist quantity (or price) and implicit Törnqvist price (or quantity) indexes.

We provide an illustration, using Laspeyres quantity indexes and Paasche price indexes because these pairs satisfy the product test and decompose by variable, and because their use is widespread. We have

$$
\begin{aligned}
\Pi^1/\Pi^0 &= (Y_L/X_L) \times (P_P/W_P) \\
&= \sum U_m^0 (y_m^1/y_m^0)/ \sum V_n^0 (x_n^1/x_n^0) \\
&\quad \times [(\sum U_m^1 (p_m^1/p_m^0)^{-1})^{-1}/\sum V_n^1 (w_n^1/w_n^0)^{-1})^{-1}],
\end{aligned}
\tag{2.20}
$$

in which $V_n = w_n x_n / w^T x$ is the cost share of the nth input. Expression (2.20) attributes quantity change to $M + N$ individual quantity changes, and attributes price change to $M + N$ individual price changes.

Summarizing the results of Section 2.4:

(i) The two ratios Y/X and P/W of empirical index numbers provide information on two aggregate sources of profitability change;

(ii) This information is slightly but informatively disaggregated to the two empirical quantity indexes Y and X and the two empirical price indexes P and W to provide information on four sources of profitability change;

(iii) Any of the three empirical index number pairs ($Y_L P_P$, $Y_P P_L$, and $Y_F P_F$) that decomposes and satisfies the product test can be used to provide a complete decomposition of the productivity change component into $M + N$ quantity changes and the price recovery change component into $M + N$ price changes;

(iv) The business literature stresses index number pairs that satisfy the product test, and so provide exact decompositions of profitability change, but it is not much concerned with the choice between "good" and "better" index numbers; and conversely

(v) The economics literature is concerned with the use of "better" index number pairs that satisfy the product test, but it freely uses implicit index numbers because it is not much concerned with the decomposition of profitability change.

2.5 EMPIRICAL ESTIMATION OF THEORETICAL INDEXES

In Section 2.4 we used empirical index numbers to approximate their theoretical counterparts, and so to approximate and decompose productivity change and price recovery change by individual variable. An alternative approach is to use econometric or mathematical programming techniques to estimate the structure of the production technology underlying the theoretical indexes. Once the technology is estimated, productivity change can be quantified and decomposed, with the decomposition by economic driver rather than by individual variable. Because production technology has both primal and dual representations, it can be estimated using either a primal (production frontier or distance function) approach or a dual (cost or revenue frontier) approach. Indeed, estimation of a primal representation of technology dates at least from Cobb and Douglas (1928), and estimation of a dual representation of technology dates at least from the time series study of Dean (1941) and the cross section study of Nerlove (1963). In this section we offer a brief introduction to primal and dual approaches to the estimation of the productivity change component of profitability change, leaving the details to Chapter 3.[15]

The primal approach to estimation proceeds as follows. A Malmquist productivity index is given in expression (2.4). The output quantity indexes are ratios of pairs of output distance functions, as indicated in expression (2.1), and the input quantity indexes are ratios of pairs of input distance functions, as indicated in expression (2.2). Given appropriate quantity data, it is possible to estimate the distance functions, which generate estimated output and input quantity indexes which, when substituted into expression (2.4), generate an estimated Malmquist productivity index. The estimated index can then be decomposed into the economic drivers of productivity change following procedures outlined in Chapter 3. The primal approach also applies to M_o CCD(x^1, x^0, y^1, y^0) and M_i CCD(y^1, y^0, x^1, x^0) introduced in Section 2.3.2.

The dual approach to estimation proceeds as follows. Under certain conditions, output distance functions in expression (2.1) are dual to revenue frontiers in the sense that they provide equivalent characterizations of the underlying production technology. Under similar conditions, input distance functions in expression (2.2) are dual to cost frontiers in the same sense. Given appropriate quantity and price data, this suggests the strategy of estimating a revenue frontier or a cost frontier and, after estimation, evaluating the estimated frontier at base period and comparison period values of (x, p) or (y, w) as required. After estimation and evaluation, a revenue or cost frontier can be decomposed into the economic drivers of productivity change; we provide details in Chapters 3 and 7. We provide a brief introduction to estimation in both primal and dual approaches in Section 1.6 of Chapter 1.

2.6 COMBINING APPROXIMATION TO AND ESTIMATION OF THEORETICAL INDEXES

Caves, Christensen, and Swanson (1980) modify a conventional index number framework within which to estimate productivity change, and they apply their modified framework to the US railroad industry. At the

---

[15] Griliches (2000) dates the first empirical estimation of production functions, using time series data and for the explicit purpose of estimating productivity growth (usually under another name, such as efficiency change or technical change), to the early 1940s.

core of their framework is the Törnqvist productivity index defined as the ratio of Y_T in expression (2.18) to the analogous input quantity index $X_T = \Pi(x_n^1/x_n^0)^{1/2(V_n^1+V_n^0)}$, expressed in logarithmic form as

$$lnY_T - lnX_T = \sum \tfrac{1}{2}(U_m^1 + U_m^0)(lny_m^1 - lny_m^0)$$
$$-\sum \tfrac{1}{2}(V_n^1 + V_n^0)(lnx_n^1 - lnx_n^0), \qquad (2.21)$$

where all variables are defined in Section 2.4. Normally expression (2.21) would be calculated using observed quantity and price data. However, during their study period rate regulation resulted in the cross-subsidization of passenger service by freight service. This led Caves et al. (1980) to conclude that output prices provide poor approximations to marginal costs of service provision, being higher than marginal cost for freight service and lower than marginal cost for passenger service. It follows that revenue shares provide inappropriate weights for aggregating changes in the two outputs, with the freight revenue share overstating its cost elasticity. No such concern affects input weights, and so expression (2.21) is replaced by

$$lnY_T - lnX_T = \sum \tfrac{1}{2}\{[\partial lnc(y,w)/\partial lny_m]^1 + [\partial lnc(y,w)/\partial lny_m]^0\}(lny_m^1 - lny_m^0)$$
$$-\sum \tfrac{1}{2}(V_n^1 + V_n^0)(lnx_n^1 - lnx_n^0), \qquad (2.22)$$

in which the $\partial lnc(y,w)/\partial lny_m$ are elasticities of cost with respect to outputs. Although revenue shares in expression (2.21) are observed, output cost elasticities in expression (2.22) are not, and must be estimated. Caves et al. (1980) do so, and find substantial divergences between estimated output cost elasticities and observed revenue shares, and a corresponding substantial divergence between estimated rates of productivity change based on expressions (2.21) and (2.22). Expression (2.21) attaches too small a weight to passenger service, which was shrinking, and too large a weight to freight service, which was expanding. Expression (2.22) increases the weight attached to passenger service, reduces the weight attached to freight service, and consequently reduces the estimated rate of productivity growth in the industry.

Expression (2.22) is a hybrid productivity change expression. The input change component is an empirical Törnqvist input quantity index obtained from observed quantity and price data. The output change component has the same functional form, but observed revenue shares are replaced by estimated cost elasticities to weight individual output changes. A complementary interpretation of the output change component of expression (2.22) is that it combines two strategies: the theoretical output quantity index $Y(x, y^1, y^0)$ is approximated by an empirical output quantity index Y_T, but with observed revenue shares replaced with empirical estimates of theoretical output cost elasticities.

It is possible to extend the exercise. Expression (2.22) decomposes by variable, making it possible to identify the quantity variables that have most promoted or retarded productivity growth. It is also possible to calculate price recovery change, using a Törnqvist functional form and the input price data embedded in the input cost shares and the output price data embedded in the output revenue shares. The price recovery expression also decomposes by variable, making it possible to identify the price variables that have most promoted or retarded price recovery. However, the product of Törnqvist productivity change and Törnqvist price recovery change only approximates profitability change. Equality can be forced by replacing the Törnqvist price recovery change component with an implicit Törnqvist price recovery change component, but at the sacrifice of the ability to quantify the contributions of individual price changes.

An appealing alternative to the use of implicit indexes is available. From either expression (2.21) or (2.22) calculate Y_T. From the data underlying expression (2.21) calculate P_T. Form the product $Y_T \times P_T$, using either Y_T series, and compare the product with R^1/R^0 to obtain an estimate of the magnitude of the product test gap.

2.7 DISTRIBUTION OF THE FINANCIAL IMPACTS OF PRODUCTIVITY CHANGE

Davis (1947, 1955), Evans (1947; 221), and Kendrick and Creamer are much concerned with the way the financial impacts of productivity change are distributed among a company's customers, input suppliers, and owners. Evans describes a scenario that generates the "Too good to last" quadrant in Figure 1.28 in Chapter 1: a firm increases its productivity and realizes higher profit, but "this favored position may not be long maintained. Other companies will adopt the improved methods, and there may be price reductions. At the same time, there may also be pressure for wage increases." Vincent and other French writers associated with CERC express similar concerns in the context of public service provision. Davis uses company accounting records to calculate a rate of productivity growth, expressed in percentage terms, and he converts this growth rate to a monetary value. He then distributes this productivity bonus to all participants, in both percentage and monetary terms. In a macroeconomic context Kendrick (1961; 14) does likewise, and makes the linkage between productivity and distribution succinctly: "Rising productivity has meant that the prices of final goods and services have risen less than the prices (average unit compensations) of the factors of production. It is in this way that the fruits of productivity advance have been distributed to those who provided the factor services." Of course disaggregation may produce losers as well as winners.

In Sections 2.3 and 2.4 we interpreted price recovery change P/W as one of two *sources of profitability change*. Here we associate price recovery change with the *financial consequences of productivity change*, with the elements of P/W identifying the recipients of the financial impacts of productivity change.

There are many reasons to be concerned with how the financial impacts of productivity change are distributed among the various participants. We mention just a few.

  (i) As competition intensifies, profitability of nonexiting firms is forced toward unity, with the bulk of the financial impacts of productivity change accruing to consumers and input suppliers;

 (ii) As market power increases, profitability is likely to expand, to the detriment of consumers under monopoly and to the detriment of input suppliers under monopsony;

(iii) Utilities are regulated to deter abuse of market power. Incentive regulation is designed to encourage utilities to become more productive, and to force them to share the fruits of their productivity growth with consumers. Regulators monitor productivity change and the allocation of its financial benefits;

(iv) Service providers in the public sector have objectives and face constraints unlike those in the private sector, and these differences may have very different distributional consequences. Responsible public agencies track productivity change and its distributional consequences; and

 (v) Labor unions have an incentive to exploit their bargaining power to expand their share of the fruits of productivity change. Agents on both sides of the bargaining table track changes in productivity and compensation.

To study the distribution of the financial impacts of productivity change, we rearrange terms in expression (2.19), and assume that we are using pairs of empirical index numbers that satisfy the product test to maintain the equality, and that decompose by variable to identify individual beneficiaries. We obtain Vincent's (1968) expression

$$Y/X = (\Pi^1/\Pi^0)/(P/W) \\ = (\Pi^1/\Pi^0) \times (W/P), \tag{2.23}$$

which states that the fruits of productivity growth Y/X accrue to three groups: the business itself Π^1/Π^0, consumers who pay the output price index P, and resource suppliers who receive the input price index W. However, since the empirical price indexes P and W decompose by variable, expression (2.23) also identifies consumers of M individual products as winners or losers, and suppliers of N individual inputs as winners or losers. Because Π is a scalar, Π^1/Π^0 needs no decomposition, and we are deliberately vague about the ultimate destination of Π^1/Π^0. Expression (2.23) encapsulates Davis's distributional concerns in a single line.

Davis (1955) provides an empirical illustration, based on data from a single company over an eight-year period. On the assumption that $\Pi^1 = \Pi^0 = 1$ (an assumption we explore in detail in Section 2.9), expression (2.23) simplifies to $Y/X = W/P$, and all fruits of productivity change go to consumers and input suppliers. Davis calculates $Y_L/X_L = 1.18 = W_P/P_P$, so that productivity growth enables input prices to grow 18% faster than output prices. He also calculates individual components of both W_P and P_P so as to identify individual resources whose suppliers have benefitted or suffered and individual commodities whose consumers have suffered or benefitted.

Kendrick (1961; 111) applies this framework to the US private domestic economy over the first half of the twentieth century. Although he does not write down anything like expression (2.23), he has exactly this relationship in mind when he states "[i]f productivity advances, wage rates and capital return necessarily rise in relation to the general product price level, since this is the means whereby the fruits of productivity gains are distributed to workers and investors by the market mechanism." Necessity follows from the equality between revenues and expenses in the national accounts, which implies that nominal profitability is unitary in each year and expression (2.23) collapses to $Y/X = W/P$, as with Davis. Over the period 1919–57, Kendrick finds productivity growth of 2.1% per annum. Focusing on distribution, Kendrick finds input price growth of 3.4% per annum and output price growth of 1.2% per annum. However, the labor price component of W increased by 4.0% per annum, while the capital price component increased by just 1.5% per annum. Consequently, labor received nearly all of the benefits of productivity growth, and as a result labor's share in national income increased from 72% to 81%.

Kendrick (1984; appendix A, case 2) implements expression (2.23) for a single company. A productivity index increases by 4.5%. Kendrick then converts ratios to monetary units to facilitate his focus on the financial consequences of productivity growth. The productivity increase of 4.5% creates a \$4.7 million productivity bonus available for distribution. He reports the distribution of the bonus, both in percentage form and in monetary values, to customers as a 0.5% price cut, to suppliers of inter- mediate materials and services as a 1% increase in purchase prices, to employees as a 3% increase in wages and fringe benefits, to stockholders as a higher rate of return on average investment, and to the federal govern- ment as taxes on the higher rate of return. In this case study the impacts of productivity growth are positive for all participants.

Waters and Street (1998) ask, with reference to a decade of microeco- nomic reform in Australia, "[h]ave these reforms delivered?" To answer the question they require measures of productivity performance and financial performance, which they link by means of the profitability change expres- sion (2.19). They do not convert this expression to the distribution expres- sion (2.23), although it is possible to draw limited distributional inferences from their delivery findings. Unlike Davis and Kendrick, they allow nonzero profit. They provide an application to Australian National Railways (AN) in the 1980s, using Fisher quantity and price indexes. They report trends in Π, Y/X (but neither Y nor X), P/W, P, and W. They do not decompose quantity and price indexes by variable, and so their interest in the distributional consequences of productivity change extends only as far as the three indexes Π^1/Π^0, P, and W. Their answer to "[h]ave these reforms delivered?" is that the financial performance of AN worsened significantly over the period even as productivity increased, because output price increases failed to keep pace with input price increases. Because $W > P > 0$ and Π declined more or less continuously, the sole beneficiaries from productivity growth are input suppliers, and W is not disaggregated. Waters and Tretheway (1999) conduct a similar analysis of two Canadian railways (Canadian National and Canadian Pacific) during 1956–95, using Törnqvist quantity indexes and implicit Törnqvist price indexes. They report trends in Y/X, PI/WI, PI, and WI for both railways. They report declining profitability despite productivity growth at both railways, and they attribute declining PI/WI to competitive pressures, noting that "on average, both railways are more than passing on all productivity gains to their customers" (p. 216).[16]

Salerian (2003) is also concerned with the performance consequences of microeconomic reform in Australia: his performance indicators are profitability, productivity, and price recovery, and he also provides an application to AN during the 1980s. His study differs from that of Waters and Street in two significant respects: he is interested in the distribution of the financial impacts of productivity growth, even though he does not explicitly derive expression (2.23) from the profitability expression (2.19), and he disaggregates P and W. He uses Fisher quantity and price indexes, which satisfy the product test and decompose by variable. It is the decomposability property that permits attribution of profitability change to individual quantities and prices. Over the study period, an 18% growth in productivity failed to keep pace with a 21% decline in price recovery, and financial performance deteriorated. He reports indexes of Π, R, C, Y/X, P/W, Y, X, P, and W, and he also reports trends in the contributions to profitability change of individual quantities and prices of three outputs and six inputs.

Saal and Parker (2001) are concerned with the performance consequences of the 1989 privatization and price cap regulation of water and sewerage companies in England and Wales. Performance is characterized by profitability, and they are interested in the relative contributions of productivity change and price recovery change to profitability change. If price recovery is the main driver of (positive) profitability change, this may reflect a lax regulatory regime. However, they also pay particular attention to the distributional impacts of productivity change, "because criticism has been directed at the high profits earned in the industry since privatization" (p. 62). Thus, they are concerned with expression (2.23), especially with the Π^1/Π^0 component but also with the P component because it is P that reflects the performance of the regulator. They note that $\Pi^1/\Pi^0 = 1$ is unlikely in this regulated monopoly environment, and so they contrast trends in Y/X with trends in W/P. They construct Törnqvist quantity indexes and implicit Törnqvist price indexes, both for the industry and for individual utilities. They report trends in Π, Y/X, PI/WI, PI, and WI for the industry and for individual utilities, over the period 1985–99. For the industry as a whole

---

[16] Additional studies that disaggregate the distributional impacts of productivity change include Fluet and Lefebvre (1987) (Canadian manufacturing), Fuglie, MacDonald, and Ball (2007) (US agriculture), and Eakin et al. (2010) (US railroads).

they find that the observed increase in profitability (2.9% per annum) can be attributed almost equally to productivity gains (1.6% per annum) and to increases in price recovery (1.3% per annum). The implication they draw from this is that "the regulatory régime has been lax ... in the sense of allowing a substantial increase in economic profitability that cannot be attributed to productivity gains" (p. 87).

2.8 ADDITIONAL PRODUCTIVITY INDEXES

In Section 2.7 we centered our discussion of the distribution of the financial impacts of productivity change on expression (2.23). Here we use this expression to derive alternative productivity indexes. We begin by rewriting expression (2.23), which satisfies the product test, as

$$
\begin{aligned}
Y/X &= (\Pi^1/\Pi^0)/(P/W) \\
&= [(R^1/R^0)/P]/[(C^1/C^0)/W] \\
&= [(R^1/P)/(C^1/W)]/[R^0/C^0] \\
&= \Pi_0^1/\Pi^0,
\end{aligned}
\tag{2.24}
$$

in which Π_0^1 is deflated comparison period profitability, defined as nominal comparison period revenue R^1 deflated by an output price index P, divided by nominal comparison period cost C^1 divided by an input price index W. The terms $(R^1/R^0)/P$ and $(C^1/C^0)/W$ in the second equality are an implicit output quantity index and an implicit input quantity index. We make extensive use of implicit quantity (and price) indexes in Section 3.3.2 of Chapter 3. Implicit price indexes are generated by rearranging terms in expression (2.24) to obtain $P/W=(\Pi^1/\Pi^0)/(Y/X)$ and following the same procedures. The terms R^1/P and C^1/W in the third equality are deflated comparison period revenue and deflated comparison period cost. The final equality in expression (2.24) states that an alternative measure of productivity change is provided by the ratio of deflated comparison period profitability and nominal base period profitability.

In the first line of expression (2.24) suppose, following Norman and Bahiri (1972), that $\Pi^t=R^t/C^t=(1 + \mu^t)$, $t=0,1$, where μ^t is the period t margin of profit over cost. In this case the first line of expression (2.24) becomes $Y/X=[(1 + \mu^1)/(1 + \mu^0)]/(P/W)$, which expresses productivity change as real margin change, nominal margin change adjusted for price change. If the margin (or markup) does not change between base period and comparison period, which does not require the margin to be zero in both periods, then $Y/X = W/P$.

The final equality in expression (2.24) is exactly the procedure employed by Davis (1955) and Kendrick and Creamer to measure productivity change. If, for whatever reason, accounting or economic, cost equals revenue in the base period, then $\Pi^0 = 1$ and productivity change simplifies to $Y/X = \Pi_0^1$. If cost equals revenue in the comparison period as well, the first three equalities in expression (2.24) collapse to $Y/X = W/P$, a dual measure of productivity change we examine in some detail in Section 2.9.

It is possible to compromise between expression (2.24) and a conventional primal productivity index Y/X, by deflating either nominal comparison period revenue or nominal comparison period cost, but not both. This leads to two more alternative measures of productivity change given by

$$
\begin{aligned}
Y/X &= Y/[(C^1/C^0)/W] \\
&= [(R^1/R^0)/P)]/X.
\end{aligned}
\tag{2.25}
$$

The first equality in expression (2.25) states that productivity change can be measured by the ratio of an output quantity index to an implicit input quantity index that can be interpreted as cost change not accounted for by changes in input prices. The second equality states that productivity change can also be measured by the ratio of an implicit output quantity index that can be interpreted as revenue change not accounted for by changes in output prices to an input quantity index.

2.9 A DUAL PRODUCTIVITY INDEX

Suppose, for whatever reason, that $\Pi^1 = \Pi^0$, so that nominal profitability remains unchanged from base period to comparison period. In this situation there is no change in profitability to be explained, and this is the primary objective of the exercise. However, the challenge of distinguishing productivity change from price recovery change remains. If $\Pi^1 = \Pi^0$, expression (2.23) collapses to

$$
Y/X = W/P,
\tag{2.26}
$$

which states that productivity change can be measured in two equivalent ways. The first is the conventional primal measure, the ratio of an output quantity index to an input quantity index. The second is the neglected dual measure, the ratio of an input price index to an output price index. The challenge of distinguishing productivity change from price recovery change has been met: one is the reciprocal of the other, and so an increase in Y/X generates an equivalent reduction in P/W, as Kendrick noted in Section 2.7.

The dual measure of productivity change was apparently introduced by Siegel (1952). Siegel (1955; 53) paraphrases expression (2.26) as "a productivity index may be written as a ratio of appropriate 'price' indexes." He relates the dual productivity measure nicely to our discussion of income distribution with the brief phrase "productivity indexes tell us that the impact of technology, etc., is to make output cheap compared to input". Kendrick (1961; chapter 5) calculates a dual measure of productivity change in the US private domestic economy.[17]

Fourastié (1957;12) is more emphatic than either Siegel or Kendrick, asserting that the objective and the consequence of productivity growth "*is to bring down selling prices and consequently speed up social progress and more particularly raise living standards and the purchasing power of wages and salaries*" (emphasis in the original). Fourastié prefers the dual measure, arguing that prices are easier to measure than quantities, particularly at the aggregate level and over long periods of time. Fourastié expresses all inputs in terms of the number of labor hours required in their production, which enables him to aggregate all inputs into a single input he calls "integrated labor." He provides a wide range of empirical applications of what he calls indirect productivity measurement. To cite two of many examples: "The price [of cognac] to the producer between 1780 and 1785 was 380–550 h.w. per litre, and between 1945 and 1953 it was 145 to 600 h.w." In contrast, "[t] he real price of transport for one person from Paris to Toulouse has fallen from 2,500 h.w. in 1725–50 to 32 h.w. in 1950" (pp. 57, 63, with h.w. being the real hourly wage). Fourastié attributes the divergent price trends to negligible productivity growth in the production of cognac and rapid productivity growth in passenger transport. Primal productivity measures

---

[17] The term "dual" seems to have been introduced by Jorgenson and Griliches (1967), and has a different meaning in the context of index numbers than it does in the economic theory of production. In the latter context duality refers to a relationship between a primal, technology-based, frontier and a dual, price-based, frontier, this relationship relying on assumptions concerning the structure of technology and optimizing behavior. In the index number context a different assumption generates duality between a primal ratio of quantity indexes and a dual ratio of price indexes. In both contexts duality allows one to reach the same conclusion from two different starting points. Siegel does not use the word. Fourastié uses the terms "direct" and "indirect" productivity measurement.

would be exceedingly difficult to calculate for these examples, and for most other examples Fourastié considers.

Many years later, following the lead of Fourastié, Hsieh (2002) re-examines the East Asian productivity growth miracle from a dual perspective, arguing that factor prices are measured more accurately than factor quantities, particularly in the case of capital. He finds primal and dual estimates of productivity growth "remarkably similar" for Korea, and finds dual estimates substantially higher than primal estimates for Singapore. Fernald and Neiman (2011) extend the investigation, arguing that market distortions arising from heterogeneous capital subsidies and market power cause primal and dual productivity measures to diverge. They find virtually no gap in Hong Kong and Korea, and gaps of around 2% for Singapore and Taiwan. Most usefully, they obtain a closed form expression for the gap between primal and dual productivity measures that depends on primal and dual measures of real wage growth and real capital payment growth.

We stress that expression (2.26) has been obtained from the assumption that $\Pi^1 = \Pi^0 \gtrless 1$, which does not imply the stronger assumption that $\Pi^1 = \Pi^0 = 1$. The latter assumption is equivalent to $\pi^1 = \pi^0 = 0$, while the former implies only that $\pi^1 = \lambda \pi^0 \gtrless 0$, $\lambda > 0$. Siegel (1961; 27) makes the stronger assumption that $\pi^1 = \pi^0 = 0$, and obtains "a productivity index as a ratio of appropriately constructed *price* measures for input and output" as follows (in our notation): if $PY = R^1/R^0 = C^1/C^0 = WX$, then $Y/X = [(R^1/R^0)/P]$ / $[(C^1/C^0)/W] = W/P$ because $R^1 = C^1$ and $R^0 = C^0$, although he does not explain what phenomena would cause $R = C$ in both periods. Still later Siegel (1986; 9) provides a bit more insight into the zero profit assumption: "Our 'quantity' definition of productivity has an equivalent 'price' version that may be intuitively more appealing to finance-oriented managers and executives. In this version, as in conventional accounting, the value of any period's output is regarded as equal to the value of input, and profit (actual or imputed) is reflected in both values rather than left separate. Accordingly . . . 'profitability' collapses to unity so that . . . 'price recovery' becomes simply the reciprocal of the 'quantity' definition of productivity." This explanation cites a business accounting convention that treats profit in such a way that revenue equals cost.

The business accounting convention to which Siegel (1961) refers is consistent with the approaches of Davis (1955) and Kendrick and Creamer, but it is not as precise about how the value of input is equated to the value of output. Davis and Kendrick and Creamer identify profit with a return to providers of capital, and they treat the return to capital as an additional expense, which equates cost with revenue. This business accounting convention of treating capital as having both cost and return elements is commonplace, and has been adopted by Eldor and Sudit (1981) and Lawrence, Diewert, and Fox (2006) among many others. We discuss this convention in detail in Chapter 4.

Vincent (1961) provides an English language introduction to a special issue of *Etudes et Conjoncture* devoted exclusively to productivity measurement. His "price method" approach to productivity measurement offers yet another way of making nominal profit zero. In this approach all outputs and all inputs are valued at their current prices, and profit is included among the inputs, resulting in a "book-keeping equality" between revenue and cost, so that $\Pi = R/C = 1$. In our notation Vincent obtains $Y/X = W/P$. He does not, however, explain how profit, treated as an input, is separated into its quantity and price components. Perhaps because he was unaware of the work of Davis (1955) and Kendrick and Creamer, he notes that "[a]s this is never done, the method can only yield rough, and in the short run sometimes mediocre results" (p. 13).

Puiseux and Bernard (1965, 1966) and Roger-Machart (1969) apply Vincent's methodology to analyze the productivity and distribution behavior of Electricité de France (EDF). They make the (relatively) weak assumption that $\Pi^1 = \Pi^0$ rather than the strong assumption that $\Pi^1 = \Pi^0 = 1$, and they deduce that $Y/X = W/P$. They interpret the primal productivity change index Y/X as indicating the *sources* of productivity change, and they interpret the dual index W/P not as a dual measure of productivity change, but as indicating the "utilisation" of the financial impacts of productivity change. Puiseux and Bernard (1965; 91) explain that "[l]'intérêt de cette nouvelle façon de mesurer la productivité est de mettre en évidence la répartition des emplois de productivité entre les divers facteurs de production d'une part, la clientéle d'autre part." They do not explain what accounting or other convention makes profitability constant through time. However, given this convention, they make a useful distinction between agents whose prices are favorably ("emploi") or unfavorably ("héritage") impacted by productivity change, with the latter group augmenting the productivity bonus to be distributed to the former group. They accomplish this by converting productivity growth rates to a productivity bonus expressed in monetary units. We revisit this procedure of augmenting the productivity bonus in Chapters 4 to 6.

Davis (1955) and Kendrick and Creamer apply these techniques to private businesses, for which profit is a plausible objective and consequently profit plays a role in the distribution of the productivity bonus. Puiseux and Bernard and Roger-Machart were perhaps the first to apply these techniques to a prominent public sector entity, EDF, for which the role of profit is diminished and the significance of the distribution of the productivity bonus among the remaining agents is magnified. Over the 1952–62 decade, Puiseux and Bernard (1965) find annual values of profit tending toward zero, suggesting that the productivity bonus is almost fully distributed. They find a 2.8% annual productivity bonus, and they find the main beneficiaries to be consumers and employees, who more than exhaust the productivity bonus, receiving annual price reductions on the order of 1.9% and annual compensation increases of over 1.1%. The only losers in the distribution exercise are providers of intermediate inputs and capital.

Jorgenson and Griliches (1967) make the strong assumption that $\pi^1 = \pi^0 = 0$ in order to obtain the dual productivity change expression (2.26), but their justification is quite different. Their context is aggregate, the US private domestic economy, and their time period is long, 1945–65. They write that "the fundamental identity for each accounting period is that the value of output is equal to the value of input" (p. 251). In these circumstances they show that Y/X and W/P provide equivalent measures of productivity change. This explanation cites a macroeconomic accounting convention, a fundamental identity in the aggregate accounts, that the value of output equals the value of input.

Jorgenson and Griliches also offer an alternative explanation, based on economic theory rather than business or macroeconomic accounting conventions. If production is characterized by locally constant returns to scale, and if marginal rates of substitution equal input price ratios and marginal rates of transformation equal output price ratios, competition forces profit to zero, and consequently $Y/X = W/P$. This explanation cites optimizing producers operating under competitive conditions that drive equality of revenue and cost.

Vincent (1968) cites yet another explanation, one based on the construction of empirical index numbers. If output price weights are replaced with unit cost weights in the output quantity index Y, then profit so defined is zero. The procedure we discussed in Section 2.6 provides motivation for this strategy, although it does not require the difficult allocation of cost to individual outputs.

The conventions adopted by Siegel, Jorgenson and Griliches, and Vincent have somewhat different motivations, but they share an important implication: nominal profit being zero in both base period and comparison period, the entire productivity bonus is passed forward to consumers and backward to input suppliers. Some output prices may rise and some input prices may decline, but W/P increases by the rate of productivity growth. The second Jorgenson and Griliches explanation is particularly appealing: competitive pressure forces producers to fully distribute the financial benefits of productivity growth. Indeed Diewert (1992; 168) asserts that the dual measure of productivity change "does not make much sense" unless profit is zero in each period.

This assertion is popular, but inaccurate. The requirement that nominal profit be zero in each period is equivalent to $\Pi^1 = \Pi^0 = 1$, which is stronger than the equality condition $\Pi^1 = \Pi^0$ with which we began. It is therefore sufficient, but not necessary, for the dual productivity change expression (2.26) to hold. Balk (2003; 20) is very clear on this point. In our notation he writes $Y/X = \Pi^1/\Pi^0 \times W/P$, and continues "if the profitability of the firm were not changing over time, then TFP change could be measured by the ratio of an input price index number over an output price index number." He also warns that "constant profitability is not the same thing as constant profit."

Expression (2.26) is a distribution expression as much as a productivity expression, but the distributional story needs to be told carefully. Suppose that $\Pi^1 = \Pi^0 > 1$. If productivity increases by $\delta\%$, this is reflected in a $\delta\%$ increase in Y/X and an equivalent $\delta\%$ increase in W/P. It may appear that the financial benefits of the productivity gain are fully distributed to consumers and resource suppliers, but this appearance is deceiving. The financial consequences for the producer of these two equivalent increases are offsetting *in a ratio sense*, because profitability remains unchanged at $\Pi^1 = \Pi^0 > 1$. But they may or may not be offsetting *in a monetary sense* because constant profitability is consistent with variable profit, and the impact on profit depends on how the four indexes Y, X, P, and W change. Under the original supposition that $\Pi^1 = \Pi^0 > 1$, several outcomes are possible. (i) If $y^1 = (1+\delta)y^0$, $\delta > 0$ and $p^1 = p^0/(1+\delta)$, revenue, cost, and profit are all unchanged, and the productivity bonus is fully distributed to consumers. (ii) If $x^1 = x^0/(1+\delta)$ and $w^1 = (1+\delta)w^0$, revenue, cost, and profit are all unchanged, and the productivity bonus is fully distributed to input suppliers. In both cases (i) and (ii) residual claimants receive none of the productivity bonus. (iii) However, if $y^1 = (1+\delta)y^0$ and $w^1 = (1+\delta)w^0$, revenue, cost, and profit all increase by $(1+\delta)$, and input suppliers share the productivity bonus (since $w^1 > w^0$) with residual claimants (since $\pi^1 > \pi^0$). (iv) Alternatively, if $x^1 = x^0/(1+\delta)$ and $p^1 = p^0/(1+\delta)$, revenue, cost, and profit all decline by $(1+\delta)$, and so consumers win (since $p^1 < p^0$) and residual claimants lose (since $\pi^1 < \pi^0$). (v) If $p^1 = (1+\delta)p^0$ and $w^1 = (1+\delta)w^0$, revenue, cost, and profit all increase by $(1+\delta)$, and inflation brings a transfer from consumers to input suppliers and residual claimants. (vi) Finally, if $y^1 = (1+\delta)y^0$ and $x^1 = (1+\delta)$ x^0, there is no productivity bonus to share, but residual claimants nonetheless benefit from expansion with positive profit. In each of these and many more cases, the consistency of constant profitability with variability of profit allows residual claimants to benefit from productivity growth (and lose from productivity decline), despite their apparent absence from expression (2.26). Only under the stronger assumption that $\Pi^1 = \Pi^0 = 1$, so that $\pi^1 = \pi^0 = 0$, are the financial benefits of productivity growth fully distributed to consumers and resource suppliers.

We conclude this section with a summary of the issues surrounding dual productivity indexes. What are the implications of unchanging profitability?

(i) $\Pi^1 = \Pi^0$ is a necessary condition for the existence of a dual productivity index $W/P = Y/X$;

(ii) The more popular condition $\pi^1 = \pi^0 = 0$ is sufficient, but not necessary, for $W/P = Y/X$;

(iii) $\Pi^1 = \Pi^0$ means that there is no change in profitability to be explained, which was the original objective of the exercise;

(iv) All that remains to be explained is the change in Y/X and the equivalent change in W/P;

(v) Considerations of data availability and accuracy determine whether Y/X or W/P is used to measure productivity change. Fourastié emphasizes this possibility, and it is finding growing applications;

(vi) Under conditions stated above, W/P provides a dual productivity index. However, the main thrust of the preceding discussion shifts the focus from productivity to income distribution. Davis, Kendrick, and Siegel appear to attach equal weight to the two roles of W/P, and the French writers emphasize its contribution to the analysis of income distribution; and

(vii) Equality of Y/X and W/P does not mean that all benefits of productivity change are distributed to consumers and input suppliers, because unchanging profitability, assuming $\Pi^1 = \Pi^0 > 1$, in a growing business generates an increase in profit to be distributed to the residual claimants of the business.

2.10 EXCHANGE RATE MOVEMENTS

Commercial aircraft are priced in USD. An appreciation of the USD against the euro benefits Airbus, whose costs are largely in €, and hurts Boeing, whose aircraft become dearer, at least in the eurozone. Conversely, a weakening of the USD against the € benefits Boeing and hurts Airbus. EADS, the parent company of Airbus, reports "Currency translation adjustments for foreign operations" in its Annual Consolidated Statements of Comprehensive Income. Indeed, exchange rates matter for the financial performance of all exporters (and importers), whether or not their products are priced in USD. Exchange rates are additional prices (of foreign currencies) that must be incorporated into the price recovery effect.

We follow Hilmola (2006), who appears to be the first to incorporate exchange rate movements into a decomposition of profitability change. For simplicity we assume that a producer incurs all costs in € and generates all revenues in USD, an assumption that easily can be relaxed to accommodate Airbus and Daimler and other multinationals. Then for this producer

$$
\begin{aligned}
\Pi^1/\Pi^0 &= (Y/X) \times (P^{USD}/W^€) \\
&= (Y/X) \times [(P^€/W^€) \times (P^{USD}/P^€)].
\end{aligned} \tag{2.27}
$$

Change in financial performance, expressed in €, is driven by productivity change and price recovery change ($P^{USD}/W^€$). Price recovery change is expressed in two different currencies, and so can be decomposed. One component is price recovery change expressed in € ($P^€/W^€$). The other is movement in the exchange rate at which USD revenue is converted to € ($P^{USD}/P^€$). An appreciation of the USD increases the domestic value of the price recovery effect.

Figure 2.5, borrowed from Lovell and Lovell (2013), illustrates decomposition (2.27) for Australian coal exporters, who incur costs in AUD and generate revenues in USD. All three variables are normalized to unity in 2000–01. From 1991/92 through 2000–01, international price recovery ($P^{USD}/W^€$) declined by 70%, largely due to declining international coal prices. The decline was partly offset by a weakening AUD that led to a 45% increase in the USD/AUD, which reduced the decline in domestic price recovery (P^{AUD}/W^{AUD}) to 56%. After 2000–01 all three trends reversed. International price recovery increased by 167%, primarily due to booming global minerals demand. However, a strengthening AUD caused the USD/AUD to decline by 33%, shrinking the increase in domestic price recovery to

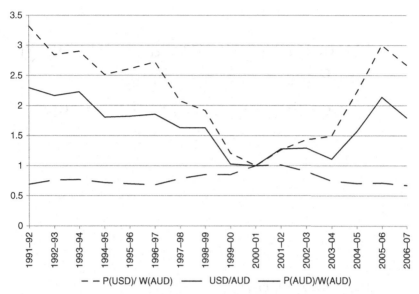

Figure 2.5 Decomposing price recovery, Australian coal mining

80%. It is not surprising that Australian coal exporters such as BHP Billiton and Rio Tinto include the cost or benefit of exchange rate movements that occurred during the financial year in their annual financial reports. Some also include a sensitivity analysis of the expected impacts on financial performance of a hypothetical 10% change in the value of all foreign currencies to which they are exposed.

3 Decomposing the Productivity Change and Price Recovery Change Components of Profitability Change

3.1 INTRODUCTION

In Chapter 2 we decomposed change in business financial performance, as measured by profitability, into two components, the contributions of productivity change and price recovery change. In this chapter we extend the decomposition process by decomposing each component, but in different ways in order to satisfy different objectives. We want to attribute the productivity change component to economic drivers, so as to quantify the individual influences of management practices and technology on productivity change. We want to attribute the price recovery change component to individual variables, both to quantify the contributions of individual price changes to price recovery change and to explore the distribution of the financial impacts of productivity change.

We have three options for meeting these objectives. First, we can pair an empirical index of productivity change with an empirical index of price recovery change; we explore this option in Section 3.2. Second, we can pair a theoretical index of productivity change with a theoretical index of price recovery change; we explore this option in Section 3.3. Finally, we can pair a theoretical index of productivity change with an empirical index of price recovery change; we explore this option, with an empirical application, in Section 3.4. In Section 3.5 we summarize the analyses of Chapters 2 and 3 of profitability change, its drivers, and its distribution.

Each option has advantages and disadvantages.

The first option is very popular, in part because empirical productivity and price recovery indexes can be paired in such a way as to ensure satisfaction of the product test. It also provides valuable information by quantifying the contribution of individual quantities to productivity change, and of individual prices to price recovery change. We discuss several such studies in Section 2.7 of Chapter 2. However, this popular option has two drawbacks. Empirical index numbers, even superlative index numbers, are not guaranteed to provide accurate approximations to the unobserved true rates of productivity change and price recovery change. In addition, we show in Section 3.2.1 that empirical index numbers by themselves are incapable of modeling the contributions of the economic drivers of productivity change. Thus, if one is interested in determining the extent to which the exploitation of scale economies, for example, has contributed to productivity growth and improved financial performance, an empirical productivity index by itself is uninformative. However, as we show in Section 3.2.2, augmenting an empirical productivity index with economic theory generates an analytical framework that enables the decomposition of productivity change by economic driver.

The second option, to pair a theoretical index of productivity change with a theoretical index of price recovery change, has not to our knowledge been pursued. This option has the distinct advantage of allowing the modeling of the economic drivers of productivity change; indeed modeling and decomposition of a Malmquist productivity index has become a cottage industry in recent years. However, this option has at least three drawbacks. First, if theoretical indexes are not approximated with empirical index numbers, as in the first option, they must be estimated, and reliable estimation of a theoretical index requires a reasonably large sample. Second, as we noted in Section 2.3.4 of Chapter 2, even our preferred theoretical indexes, a Malmquist productivity index and a Konüs price recovery index, fail the product test except under extremely restrictive conditions on the true but unknown technology. Finally, a theoretical price recovery index does not decompose by variable, which precludes both the quantification of the contributions of individual prices to price recovery change and an analysis of the distributive implications of productivity change.

The third option, to pair a theoretical index of productivity change with an empirical index of price recovery change, apparently has not been pursued either, for two of the reasons the second option has not been pursued. We know of no theoretical productivity index that, when paired with any empirical price recovery index, satisfies the product test with more than two variables. In addition, reliable estimation of a theoretical productivity index requires a reasonably large sample. However, despite these drawbacks the third option is appealing, for two reasons. The primary argument in favor of the third option is that it is the only option that offers the possibility of meeting the twin objectives outlined in the opening paragraph; estimating a theoretical productivity index permits the identification of the economic drivers of productivity change, and calculation of an empirical price recovery index permits the identification of the individual prices contributing to price recovery change and characterizing the impact of productivity change on income distribution. A secondary argument rests on the fact that economic theory provides no guidance concerning the seriousness of the failure to satisfy the product test. Combining an estimate of a productivity index with an approximation to a price recovery index may yield a numerically small or large failure. The magnitude of the gap between the product of a quantity index and a price index and the corresponding nominal value change is partly data dependent, and partly a matter of choosing the best estimation techniques and the best functional forms available.[1]

Because the product test looms so large in this chapter, in Section 3.4 we provide one piece of empirical evidence bearing on the seriousness of the product test gap. The evidence is encouraging. In Section 3.5 we provide an overall evaluation of the ratio approach to profitability change and its decomposition, based on the material in Chapters 2 and 3.

The strategy underlying our preferred third option is illustrated in Figure 3.1. The productivity change component of profitability change is *estimated* using a theoretical productivity index such as the Malmquist index. Decomposition by economic driver follows procedures outlined in Section 3.3.1. The price recovery change component of profitability change is *approximated* using an empirical price recovery index such as the Fisher index. Decomposition by individual prices to identify the primary sources of price recovery change and the primary recipients of the financial benefits of productivity change is discussed in Chapter 2.

After exploring the various options for decomposing the productivity change and price recovery change components of profitability change in

---

[1] In analogous situations the literature contains ample precedent for introducing a "residual" to make up the gap. A particularly relevant example is provided by the Denny, Fuss, and Waverman (1981) study estimating the rate of productivity change in Canadian telecommunications, and decomposing the estimated rate into the contributions of economic drivers. Over their sample period the economic drivers account for 101.3% of measured productivity change, although the residual is larger than 1.3% in absolute value in each sub-period.

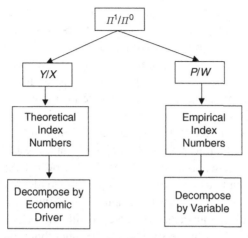

Figure 3.1　Decomposing profitability change

Sections 3.2 to 3.4, in Section 3.5 we summarize the analyses of Chapters 2 and 3 of ratio models of profitability change.

3.2 PAIRING EMPIRICAL PRODUCTIVITY AND PRICE RECOVERY INDEXES

We established in Chapter 2 that profitability change decomposes into the product of an empirical productivity index and an empirical price recovery index. We also demonstrated that these empirical productivity and price recovery indexes decompose by variable. This enables us to identify the output and input quantities having the greatest influence on productivity change, and also to identify the output and input prices having the greatest influence on price recovery change.

We also establish that some pairs of empirical productivity and price recovery indexes satisfy the product test. Two Laspeyres and Paasche pairs, a Fisher pair, an EM/implicit EM pair, and a Törnqvist/implicit Törnqvist pair all satisfy the product test. We defer consideration of implicit index numbers to Section 3.3.2, although an implicit Konüs index does make an appearance in Section 3.2.2. In this section we restrict our analysis to the first three pairs of empirical index numbers.

We also establish a preference for superlative Fisher indexes over Laspeyres and Paasche indexes, which are not superlative. However, even superlative indexes can provide inaccurate approximations to the unknown truth if the requisite allocative efficiency conditions are not satisfied, and so we do not discard Laspeyres and Paasche indexes out of hand.

In Section 3.2.1 we briefly discuss a pair of studies that successfully pair Laspeyres and Paasche indexes in pursuit of the modest but entirely appropriate objective of decomposing profitability change into the product of productivity and price recovery indexes. We also discuss two additional studies that pair Laspeyres and Paasche indexes in the more ambitious pursuit of a further objective, the subsequent decomposition of productivity change into its economic drivers. These efforts fail, not because they use indexes that are not superlative, but because they do not exploit economic theory. Despite numerous efforts, it is not possible to identify the economic drivers of productivity change using empirical index numbers without some assistance from economic theory, because identification of economic drivers requires a specification of the structure of the underlying production technology and how it shifts through time. But this information is not provided by data, and must be extracted from the data using economic theory. In Section 3.2.2 we discuss three studies that pair Fisher indexes in an effort to decompose the productivity change component of profitability change by economic driver. These studies succeed, to varying degrees, not because they use superlative indexes, but because they exploit economic theory.

3.2.1 Empirical indexes without the assistance of economic theory

An empirical index of productivity change decomposes by variable, but without the assistance of economic theory it does not decompose credibly by economic driver. This fact does not discredit the use of empirical indexes of productivity change without theory. They are ideally suited to the decomposition of profitability change into its productivity change and price recovery change components, and also to the further decomposition of each component by individual variable, although this praise is subject to the qualification that empirical index numbers are quite capable of providing unsatisfactory approximations to productivity change and price recovery change. We illustrate the appropriate use of an empirical productivity index with two examples.

Houéry (1977)

Houéry is one of several French contributors to the "comptes de surplus" methodology; we mentioned other writers in Section 2.9 of Chapter 2.

Inspired directly by Vincent (1968), and indirectly by Kendrick and Creamer (1961), Houéry believes the appropriate orientation for measuring productivity is an input conserving orientation focused on cost, and he asserts that variation in cost has three components: (i) variation in the quantities of inputs, (ii) variation in the prices of inputs, and (iii) "adaptation of the cost structure," which we interpret as the adjustment of the input mix to changes in relative input prices. A similar term appears in many subsequent productivity index decompositions.

Houéry's input quantity index and input price index are both of Laspeyres form, and so

$$X_L = w^{0T}x^1 \, / \, w^{0T}x^0,$$
$$W_L = w^{1T}x^0 / w^{0T}x^0. \tag{3.1}$$

He then introduces a third index that measures "l'adaptation de la structure des coûts aux variations relatives de prix des facteurs. (Choix des facteurs de production les moins chers.)" (p. 60) as

$$I_x = X_P \, / X_L, \tag{3.2}$$

in which X_P is a Paasche input quantity index. Adaptation of the cost structure is weighted by comparison period prices in the numerator and base period prices in the denominator, and consequently one would expect $I_X < 1$. Multiplying X_L, W_L, and I_X generates

$$X_L \times W_L \times I_x = w^{1T}x^1 \, / w^{0T}x^0 = C^1/C^0, \tag{3.3}$$

so that the change in cost between base period and comparison period is fully "explained" by changes in input quantities X_L, changes in input prices W_L, and adaptation of the cost structure to the new input price structure I_X. An alternative interpretation of expression (3.3) is that X_L and W_L fail the product test, and I_X measures the product test gap between $X_L \times W_L$ and C^1/C^0. This gap is easily quantified, and can be characterized using expression (3.2) as the Paasche–Laspeyres spread expressed in ratio form.

Houéry defines a productivity index as

$$Y/X = Y_L \, /(X_L \times I_X), \tag{3.4}$$

in which Y_L is a Laspeyres output quantity index and X_L and I_X are defined above. Substituting expression (3.2) into expression (3.4) yields

$$Y/X = Y_L \, /X_P, \tag{3.5}$$

an unusual combination of quantity indexes that Houéry justifies by claim-
ing that it corrects the denominator for changes in the cost structure. If we
apply the same adaptation strategy to the output side, by introducing an
adaptation of the revenue structure to changing output prices, expression
(3.5) becomes $Y/X = (Y_L \times I_Y)/(X_L \times I_X) = Y_P/X_P$, and both quantity indexes
are of Paasche form, a structure that has been advocated by Frankel (1963).[2]

Houéry does not attempt a further decomposition of the productivity
index by economic driver. After expressing productivity change as in
expression (3.5), Houéry converts his analysis to difference form, and we
continue with his difference form analysis in Chapters 4 to 6.

Banker, Chang, and Majumdar (1996a)

The authors apply Houéry's framework by defining and decomposing
profitability change as

$$\Pi^1/\Pi^0 = (Y_L/X_P) \times (P_P/W_L). \tag{3.6}$$

Like Houéry before them, their productivity change index pairs a Laspeyres
output quantity index with a Paasche input quantity index. Consequently,
satisfaction of the product test requires their price recovery index to pair a
Paasche output price index with a Laspeyres input price index. Unlike
Houéry, they offer no intuition behind these unusual pairings.

Neither Houéry nor Banker et al. (1996a) go beyond a simple empirical
decomposition of profitability change. The next pair of studies attempt to go
further, by decomposing their empirical productivity indexes. Their
attempts are unsuccessful.

Kurosawa (1975, 1991)

Kurosawa is perhaps the first to use the empirical index number approach in
an effort to obtain an analytical decomposition of the productivity change
component of profitability change. He begins by introducing a "relative
value system," in which "rentability" is defined as we define profitability,
$\Pi = R/C = p^T y/w^T x$. Rentability change is expressed in ratio form and decomposed as

---

[2] In a review of Kendrick and Creamer, Frankel (1963) recommends the use of Paasche quantity
indexes because, being based on comparison period price weights, they are better suited to a
company's current needs than are the more popular Laspeyres quantity indexes. Hansen, Mowen,
and Hammer (1992) echo Frankel's recommendation, which nonetheless remains a minority
opinion.

$$\Pi^1/\Pi^0 = (Y/X) \times (P/W)$$
$$= [(p^{0T}y^1/p^{0T}y^0)/(w^{0T}x^1/w^{0T}x^0)] \times [(p^{1T}y^1/p^{0T}y^1)/(w^{1T}x^1/w^{0T}x^1)]$$
$$= (Y_L/X_L) \times (P_P/W_P).$$
$$(3.7)$$

Change in rentability decomposes into a Laspeyres "index of total productivity" and a Paasche "index of relative price, effect of the terms of trade (market effect)." The structure of expression (3.7) coincides with that of expression (2.20), having explicit functional forms for the quantity and price indexes that decompose by variable and satisfy the product test.

Kurosawa decomposes the productivity index in an attempt to identify the economic drivers of productivity change. Because the output quantity index "reflects not only changes in the quantity but changes in product mix as well" it is rewritten as

$$Y_L = [(p^{0T}S_y^1)/(p^{0T}S_y^0)] \times \sum y_m^1 / \sum y_m^0$$
$$= I_{Sy} \times I_{Qy},$$
$$(3.8)$$

in which $Sy = (y_1/\sum y_m, \ldots, y_M/\sum y_m)$ is a normalized output quantity vector, I_{Sy} is a Laspeyres normalized output quantity index defined as "effect of product mix measured by constant prices," and I_{Qy} is defined as "effect of output change measured by physical terms." A similar result holds for the input quantity index, and so

$$X_L = [(w^{0T}S_x^1)/(w^{0T}S_x^0)] \times \sum x_n^1 / \sum x_n^0$$
$$= I_{Sx} \times I_{Qx},$$
$$(3.9)$$

in which $Sx = (x_1/\sum x_n, \ldots, x_N/\sum x_n)$ is a normalized input quantity vector, I_{Sx} is a Laspeyres normalized input quantity index defined as "effect of distribution change of input factors," and I_{Qx} is defined as "effect of input factors." The terms I_{Sy} and I_{Sx} are similar in intent, if not content, to Houéry's adaptation indexes.

It follows from expressions (3.8) and (3.9) that productivity change can be written as

$$Y_L/X_L = (I_{Sy}/I_{Sx}) \times (I_{Qy}/I_{Qx}),$$
$$(3.10)$$

with the four components on the right side defined above. Expression (3.10) decomposes productivity change into the product of two terms; the first term is an aggregate mix effect expressed as a ratio of Laspeyres index numbers, and the second term is an aggregate scale effect expressed as a ratio of ratios.

However, Kurosawa's (1975; 161) interpretation is different: "Variations in the productivity index are caused in the main by the following factors: the effects of the use of new technology and methods or better use of existing techniques." It is difficult to see either factor, which we would translate as technical change and efficiency change, in either component of Y_L/X_L.

Expressions (3.8) and (3.9) are not units invariant, and so expression (3.10) has an apples and oranges problem. The aggregate mix and scale effects in (3.10) both involve unweighted sums of outputs and unweighted sums of inputs. Davis (1955) saw the apples and oranges problem clearly, noting that the sum operator is "proper" under product homogeneity or for a constant product mix. Kurosawa (1991; 301) acknowledges that expression (3.10) "is not always possible because of the heterogeneity of the products and input resources." The unweighted sum operator is a serious limitation when applied to outputs because its validity requires homogeneity of outputs (e.g., a single commodity sold in M markets). Absent homogeneity, aggregation must be weighted. Given homogeneity, if outputs are sold at a common price the problem collapses to a single product firm and product mix is not an issue, while if they are sold at different prices an explanation is required. The unweighted sum operator is a far more serious limitation when applied to inputs, where not even labor is likely to be homogeneous, much less labor, capital, and disparate intermediate inputs. Some sort of weighted aggregation is essential; indeed, this is why we have quantity index numbers, with price or other weights.

As Kurosawa (1991) recognizes, it is possible to avoid the apples and oranges problem by exploiting the decomposability property of Laspeyres index numbers (appearing in expression (2.13) of Chapter 2) to rewrite Y_L as

$$Y_L = p^{0T}y^1/p^{0T}y^0 = \sum U_m^0(y_m^1/y_m^0), \qquad (3.11)$$

in which the $U_m = p_m y_m/p^T y$ are output revenue shares that provide the weights missing from expression (3.8). Defining X_L in the same way and taking the ratio leads to the revised productivity index

$$Y_L/X_L = \sum U_m^0(y_m^1/y_m^0) / \sum V_n^0(x_n^1/x_n^0), \qquad (3.12)$$

in which the $V_n = w_n x_n/w^T x$ are input cost shares that provide the weights missing from expression (3.9). A similar transformation can be applied to P_P and W_P to obtain

$$P_P/W_P = \left[\sum U_m^1(p_m^1/p_m^0)^{-1}\right]^{-1} / \left[\sum V_n^1(w_n^1/w_n^0)^{-1}\right]^{-1}. \qquad (3.13)$$

The apples and oranges problem has disappeared, and expressions (3.12) and (3.13), which replicate expression (2.20) in Chapter 2, have the virtue of being far more transparent than expression (3.7) in identifying the quantities and prices of individual outputs and inputs most responsible for promoting or retarding productivity change and price recovery change.

Summarizing, expressions (3.8) to (3.10), which attempt to decompose productivity change by economic driver, have two serious drawbacks. First, although mix and scale (or technical change and technical efficiency change) are valid drivers of productivity change, neither pair of drivers is likely to tell the whole story. Second, the lack of units invariance creates the apples and oranges problem that is serious on the output side and fatal on the input side. However, expressions (3.12) and (3.13) are useful because they provide a transparent identification of the sources of profitability change by individual variable.

Banker, Chang, and Majumdar (1993, 1995, 1996b)

These three studies go well beyond Banker et al. (1996a), by decomposing what they call the "profitability margin," defined as we define profitability, into productivity change and price recovery change components. However, they view this two-way decomposition as inadequate because it omits components such as changes in the product mix and changes in the rate of capacity utilization, both of which they consider to be distinct from the productivity effect rather than components of it. They modify both the productivity change component and price recovery change component, motivated by a desire to introduce the two new drivers of profitability change without running afoul of the product test. They also augment empirical index numbers with input use targets, or standards, which serve as benchmarks and also facilitate decomposition. The introduction of targets gives these three studies more promise than that of Banker et al. (1996a), but none of these studies succeeds in identifying anything like a full set of economic drivers of productivity change. The analytical framework being identical in the three studies, we focus on the first, borrowing an occasional clarifying remark from the others.[3]

---

[3] Banker et al. distinguish variable inputs from fixed inputs and exploit the distinction in an effort to incorporate variation in the rate of capacity utilization as a driver of profitability change. We simplify their model by allowing all inputs to be variable. Our version of their model therefore omits their capacity utilization change ratio. We return to the role of capacity utilization in Chapter 8. Fraquelli and Vannoni (2000) apply the approach of Banker et al., with capacity

Banker et al. begin by writing profitability change in conventional form as in our expression (2.19) in Chapter 2. They express the productivity change component as

$$Y_L/X_P = (p^{0T}y^1/p^{0T}y^0) / (w^{1T}x^1/w^{1T}x^0), \qquad (3.14)$$

as in Houéry and Banker et al. (1996a). They express the price recovery change component as

$$P_P/W_L = (p^{1T}y^1/p^{0T}y^1) / (w^{1T}x^0/w^{0T}x^0), \qquad (3.15)$$

as in Banker et al. (1996a). The pairing of Laspeyres and Paasche indexes is unusual, but it is easily verified that $\Pi^1/\Pi^0 = Y_L/X_P \times P_P/W_L$, so that the product test is satisfied.

However, satisfaction of the product test presents a challenge for the incorporation of any additional sources of profitability change that are assumed not to be components of productivity change. It requires that the conventional definitions of productivity change and/or price recovery change be modified to accommodate the introduction of any new sources of profitability change. Banker et al. therefore decompose Π^1/Π^0 into three components: a modified productivity change ratio, a modified price recovery change ratio, and a remainder term that they refer to as a product mix change ratio. These three ratios, when multiplied together, yield the original profitability change ratio.

They implement this three-way decomposition through the introduction of benchmarks, or standard input requirements. These standards could be any of several benchmarks, including previous usage, a current target usage, usage of another firm, or an industry average usage. They choose as their benchmarks industry average usage, across firms and through time. Their use of standards sets them apart from Kurosawa and Houéry, and brings them close to cost variance analysis, which we discuss in Chapter 7.

The modified productivity change ratio compares actual input use to standard input requirements, given actual outputs. It is exclusively input-oriented, focuses only on input use for actual outputs, and differs markedly from the original productivity change ratio in expression (3.14). The modified productivity change ratio is given by

---

utilization included, to an investigation into the sources of variation in the financial performance of five major European telecommunications operators under various forms of incentive regulation. They find regulation to have had little impact on profitability, due to offsetting productivity increases and declining price recovery.

$$Y/X = (w^{1T}\chi^1/w^{1T}x^1)/(w^{0T}\chi^0/w^{0T}x^0), \tag{3.16}$$

in which $\chi^t = \Sigma a_{nm}^t y_m^t$, $t=0,1$, is a vector of standard input quantities, and the standard input requirements a_{nm}^t are time-varying industry average input–output ratios. Banker et al. assume that the standard input requirements are time invariant, but we allow them to be time varying. The standard input quantities χ^t are predicted input quantities obtained by applying standard input requirements to actual output quantities y^t.

Because the base period is defined such that $\chi^0 = x^0$, $w^{0T}\chi^0/w^{0T}x^0 = 1$, the denominator of expression (3.16) is unity. The modified productivity change ratio becomes the ratio of comparison period standard input use to comparison period actual input use, both evaluated at comparison period prices, and so the final expression for the modified productivity change ratio becomes

$$Y/X = (w^{1T}\chi^1/w^{1T}x^1), \tag{3.17}$$

which is a Paasche quantity index comparing χ^1 and x^1, leading us to interpret it as a comparison period measure of cost efficiency relative to an industry average benchmark. To see that the modified productivity change ratio can be interpreted as a cost efficiency measure, insert the definition of χ^1 into the numerator of expression (3.17) to obtain

$$\begin{aligned} Y/X &= w^{1T}\sum a_{nm}^1 y_m^1/w^{1T}x^1 \\ &= w^{1T}[a^1]y^1/w^{1T}x^1, \end{aligned} \tag{3.18}$$

in which $[a^1]$ is an $N \times M$ matrix of comparison period standard input requirements. Thus, Y/X is the ratio of predicted standard cost to actual cost in the comparison period. If actual cost is less than predicted standard cost, productivity growth has occurred (because the normalization requires equality between standard cost and actual cost in the base period).

Profitability change as defined in expression (3.6) is clearly intertemporal. But the first component of profitability change, modified productivity change as defined in expressions (3.17) and (3.18), is just as clearly atemporal, with only comparison period data involved. In these two expressions "change" refers to a comparison of actual cost with target cost, both in the comparison period.

The modified price recovery change ratio compares comparison period and base period prices, using comparison period quantity weights, and is expressed as

$$P/W = (p^{1T}y^1/p^{0T}y^1) / (w^{1T}\chi^1/w^{0T}\chi^1)$$
$$= P_P / (w^{1T}\chi^1/w^{0T}\chi^1). \tag{3.19}$$

This expression differs from the original price recovery change ratio in expression (3.15) in two ways: it is entirely Paasche (rather than a mixture of Paasche and Laspeyres), and it replaces actual input quantities, which the firm does use, with standard input quantities χ, which the firm does not use, in the denominator.

The third component of profitability change, the new product mix change ratio, is intended to capture the impact on profitability change of change in the actual output mix, and is expressed as

$$PM = (p^{0T}y^1/p^{0T}y^0)/(w^{0T}\chi^1/w^{0T}\chi^0)$$
$$= Y_L /(w^{0T}\chi^1/w^{0T}\chi^0) \tag{3.20}$$
$$= Y_L /(w^{0T}[a^1]y^1/w^{0T}[a^0]y^0).$$

The second equality defines PM as the ratio of a Laspeyres output quantity index to a Laspeyres standard input quantity index. The third equality uses the definition of standard input quantities to redefine PM as the ratio of a pair of Laspeyres output quantity indexes, with base period output prices in the numerator and what might be called standard industry unit cost prices in the denominator. However, the denominator fails the identity property in outputs unless $a^1 = a^0$, an assumption Banker et al. make and we find unrealistic. Even with this assumption it is difficult to see a product mix change in expression (3.20).

Collecting expressions (3.17), (3.19), and (3.20) generates the profitability change decomposition

$$\Pi^1/\Pi^0 = [w^{1T}\chi^1/w^{1T}x^1] \times [P_P/(w^{1T}\chi^1/w^{0T}\chi^1)] \times [Y_L/(w^{0T}\chi^1/w^{0T}\chi^0)]. \tag{3.21}$$

The three components multiply to Π^1/Π^0. Profitability change is the product of modified productivity change $[w^{1T}\chi^1/w^{1T}x^1]$, modified price recovery change $[P_P/(w^{1T}\chi^1/w^{0T}\chi^1)]$, and change in the product mix $[Y_L/(w^{0T}\chi^1/w^{0T}\chi^0)]$. The definitions of each component are idiosyncratic. The impact of scale economies is missing or buried inside one of the components, as are the impacts of other conventional drivers of productivity change such as change in technology and change in productive efficiency.

Conclusions

The first conclusion of this section is that empirical index numbers can be used to meet the worthy objective of decomposing profitability change by variable, as Houéry and Banker et al. (1996a) demonstrate. The second conclusion is that, although empirical index numbers are appropriate for attributing profitability change to changes in individual quantities and prices, they are ill-suited for attributing profitability change to changes in its economic drivers. An exclusive reliance on empirical index numbers, with no assistance from the economic theory of production, is an unsatisfactory option if the objective is to identify the economic drivers of productivity change. This is illustrated most forcefully by Banker et al. (1993, 1995, 1996b), whose decomposition in expression (3.21) is unconvincing. The third conclusion is that the introduction of targets, or standards, into the analysis promises much but delivers little in attributing productivity change to its economic drivers, because the targets are typically established in terms of *industry averages*. However, technical change, efficiency change, and scale economies are features of *best practice* technology. Even if targets provide managerially useful information, and their longevity suggests that they surely do, within an empirical index number framework and with industry average standards they are of limited value in identifying, much less quantifying, the economic drivers of productivity change.

3.2.2 Empirical indexes with the assistance of economic theory

In this section we show, through an analysis of three studies based on very similar models, that empirical index numbers, properly augmented by the economic theory of production, can provide a credible decomposition of productivity change by economic driver. In each study superlative Fisher indexes replace Laspeyres and Paasche indexes, but this is not essential to the analysis. The first two studies do not decompose a profitability index into the product of productivity and price recovery indexes, but this is not the objective of either study. We show how easy it is to embed the productivity change decomposition in the first study in a larger decomposition of profitability change, and we are able to convert the productivity change decomposition in the second study into a complete decomposition of profitability change. The third study does decompose a profitability index into the product of productivity and price recovery indexes, and also decomposes the productivity index into the product of its drivers.

Expressing profitability change in Fisher form yields

$$\Pi^1/\Pi^0 = (Y_F/X_F) \times (P_F/W_F), \tag{3.22}$$

in which Y_F and P_F are defined in expression (2.17) in Chapter 2 and X_F and W_F are defined similarly. Both the Fisher productivity index Y_F/X_F and the Fisher price recovery index P_F/W_F decompose by variable. The objective now becomes one of decomposing the Fisher productivity index by economic driver.

Ray and Mukherjee (1996)

Ray and Mukherjee exploit the economic theory of production to decompose a Fisher productivity index. Their decomposition identifies four economic drivers of productivity change: change in technical efficiency, change in the efficiency with which inputs are allocated, change in production technology, and change in the scale of production. These are the four economic drivers identified by the BLS and the OECD.

Their model has multiple inputs, but just a single output. With a single output the concept of size collapses to scale, since there is no product mix component, and the Fisher output quantity index is $Y_F = (Y_L \times Y_P)^{1/2} = y^1/y^0$, and the Fisher productivity index to be decomposed is

$$\begin{aligned}
Y_F/X_F &= (y^1/y^0)/[(w^{0T}x^1/w^{0T}x^0) \times (w^{1T}x^1/w^{1T}x^0)]^{1/2} \\
&= \{[(w^{0T}x^0/y^0)/(w^{0T}x^1/y^1)] \times [(w^{1T}x^0/y^0)/(w^{1T}x^1/y^1)]\}^{1/2}, \\
&= (Z_L^{-1} \times Z_P^{-1})^{1/2}. \tag{3.23}
\end{aligned}$$

The second equality in expression (3.23) verifies that Y_F/X_F is the geometric mean of Y_L/X_L and Y_P/X_P, and since $M = 1$ the terms in the second equality are mixed-period expressions for change in average cost. The third equality expresses Y_F/X_F in terms of input/output quantity indexes. We make extensive use of input/output quantity indexes in Chapter 7.

Expression (3.23) relies exclusively on observed data. The Ray and Mukherjee decomposition augments data with theory, which is provided in detail in Section 1.6 of Chapter 1. Their decomposition can be expressed as

$$\begin{aligned}
Y_F/X_F &= \Delta TE_i(y^1, y^0, x^1, x^0) \times \Delta AE_i(y^1, y^0, w^1, w^0, x^1, x^0) \\
&\quad \times \Delta SE_i(y^1, y^0, w^1, w^0) \times \Delta T_i(y^1, y^0, w^1, w^0), \tag{3.24}
\end{aligned}$$

which attributes productivity change to four economic drivers, each with an input orientation: change in technical efficiency, change in input allocative efficiency, change in scale efficiency, and technical change. The product of the first two drivers is change in cost efficiency.

The first component on the right side of decomposition (3.24) is change in technical efficiency, defined as

$$\Delta TE_i(y^1, y^0, x^1, x^0) = TE_i^1(y^1, x^1)/TE_i^0(y^0, x^0), \tag{3.25}$$

with $\Delta TE_i(y^1, y^0, x^1, x^0) \gtreqless 1$ as technical efficiency improves, stagnates or declines from base period to comparison period.

The second component is change in input allocative efficiency, defined as

$$\Delta AE_i(y^1, y^0, w^1, w^0, x^1, x^0)$$
$$= [\{[c^1(y^1, w^0)/w^{0T}(x^1/D_i^1(y^1, x^1))]/[c^0(y^0, w^0)/w^{0T}(x^0/D_i^0(y^0, x^0))]\}$$
$$\times \{[c^1(y^1, w^1)/w^{1T}(x^1/D_i^1(y^1, x^1))]/[c^0(y^0, w^1)/w^{1T}(x^0/D_i^0(y^0, x^0))]\}]^{1/2}$$
$$= \{[AE_i^1(y^1, w^0, x^1)/AE_i^0(y^0, w^0, x^0)]$$
$$\times [AE_i^1(y^1, w^1, x^1)/AE_i^0(y^0, w^1, x^0)]\}^{1/2}, \tag{3.26}$$

which is the geometric mean of two mixed-period indexes of input allocative efficiency change. The first is the ratio of the allocative efficiency of (y^1, x^1) relative to comparison period technology with that of (y^0, x^0) relative to base period technology, using base period input prices; the second is the same ratio, but using comparison period input prices. $\Delta AE_i(y^1, y^0, w^1, w^0, x^1, x^0) \gtreqless 1$ as input allocative efficiency so defined improves, stagnates, or declines from base period to comparison period.

The third component is change in scale efficiency, defined as

$$\Delta SE_i(y^1, y^0, w^1, w^0) = [\{[c^1(y^0, w^0)/y^0]/[c^1(y^1, w^0)/y^1]\}$$
$$\times \{[c^0(y^0, w^1)/y^0]/[c^0(y^1, w^1)/y^1]\}]^{1/2}, \tag{3.27}$$

which is the geometric mean of two mixed-period indexes of frontier average cost change. The first measures the change in frontier average cost from y^0 to y^1 along comparison period technology using base period input prices; the second measures the same change along base period technology using comparison period input prices. $\Delta SE_i(y^1, y^0, w^1, w^0) \gtreqless 1$ as frontier average cost is lower, the same, or higher at comparison period output than at base period output.

The final component is technical change, defined as

$$\Delta T_i(y^1, y^0, w^1, w^0) = \{[c^0(y^0, w^0)/c^1(y^0, w^0)] \times [c^0(y^1, w^1)/c^1(y^1, w^1)]\}^{1/2},$$

(3.28)

which is the geometric mean of two indexes of technical change. The first measures the shift in the cost frontier between base and comparison periods at base period data (y^0, w^0); the second measures the same shift at comparison period data (y^1, w^1). $\Delta T_i(y^1, y^0, w^1, w^0) \gtreqless 1$ as technical change is progress that shifts the cost frontier downward, absent, or regress that shifts the cost frontier upward from base period to comparison period.

Substituting expressions (3.25) to (3.28) into expression (3.24) yields a decomposition of the Fisher index of single output productivity change. Substituting expression (3.24) into expression (3.22) generates a decomposition of profitability change into the economic drivers of productivity change and the individual price components of price recovery change

$$\Pi^1/\Pi^0 = [\Delta TE_i(y^1, y^0, x^1, x^0) \times \Delta AE_i(y^1, y^0, w^1, w^0, x^1, x^0)$$
$$\times \Delta SE_i(y^1, y^0, w^1, w^0) \times \Delta T_i(y^1, y^0, w^1, w^0)] \times (P_F/W_F).$$

(3.29)

Expression (3.29) has a very attractive feature. By construction, $[\Delta TE_i(y^1, y^0, x^1, x^0) \times \Delta AE_i(y^1, y^0, w^1, w^0, x^1, x^0) \times \Delta SE_i(y^1, y^0, w^1, w^0) \times \Delta T_i(y^1, y^0, w^1, w^0)]$ is mathematically equivalent to Y_F/X_F, and so it satisfies the product test with P_F/W_F. However, the model has two shortcomings. The use of mixed-period data in $\Delta AE_i(y^1, y^0, w^1, w^0, x^1, x^0)$ and $\Delta SE_i(y^1, y^0, w^1, w^0)$ makes both expressions difficult to interpret and, perhaps consequently, it is easy to show that $AE_i^1(y^1, w^1, x^1) = AE_i^0(y^0, w^0, x^0)$ does not imply $\Delta AE_i(y^1, y^0, w^1, w^0, x^1, x^0) = 1$ because of the presence of the mixed-period terms $AE_i^1(y^1, w^1, x^0)$ and $AE_i^0(y^0, w^0, x^1)$. In addition, the contribution of scale economies to productivity change is based on the concept of frontier average cost, which is well defined only in a single output setting. Since most firms produce more than one output, it is desirable to modify the model to incorporate $M > 1$. The next study provides a step in this direction.

Kuosmanen and Sipiläinen (2009)

Kuosmanen and Sipiläinen also exploit the economic theory of production to generate an alternative decomposition of a Fisher productivity index. Their decomposition identifies five economic drivers of productivity change. Four of the drivers have the same economic interpretation, but different analytical structure, as those identified by Ray and Mukherjee. The fifth driver is change in what they call a price effect. The virtue of their decomposition is not the introduction of the fifth driver, which we find strange, but rather the ability to incorporate multiple outputs.

The Kuosmanen and Sipiläinen decomposition is

$$
\begin{aligned}
Y_F/X_F &= \Delta TE(y^1,y^0,x^1,x^0) \times \Delta AE(y^1,y^0,w^1,w^0,x^1,x^0,p^1,p^0) \\
&\quad \times \Delta SE(y^1,y^0,w^1,w^0,x^1,x^0,p^1,p^0) \times \Delta T(p^1,p^0,w^1,w^0) \quad (3.30) \\
&\quad \times \Delta PE(p^1,p^0,w^1,w^0),
\end{aligned}
$$

which, apart from the final component $\Delta PE(p^1,p^0,w^1,w^0)$, is structurally identical to the Ray and Mukherjee decomposition, although the details of the first four components differ. The Ray and Mukherjee components are input-oriented, while the Kuosmanen and Sipiläinen components are simultaneously input- and output-oriented.

The first component is change in technical efficiency, defined as

$$
\begin{aligned}
&\Delta TE(y^1,y^0,x^1,x^0) \\
&= \{[TE_i^1(y^1,x^1)/TE_i^0(y^0,x^0)] \times [TE_o^1(x^1,y^1)/TE_o^0(x^0,y^0)]\}^{1/2} \\
&= \{[D_i^0(y^0,x^0)/D_i^1(y^1,x^1)] \times [D_o^0(x^0,y^0)/D_o^1(x^1,y^1)]\}^{1/2}, \quad (3.31)
\end{aligned}
$$

which is the geometric mean of input-oriented and output-oriented measures of technical efficiency change. $\Delta TE(y^1,y^0,x^1,x^0) \gtreqless 1$ as technical efficiency so defined improves, stagnates or declines from base period to comparison period.

The second component is change in allocative efficiency, defined as

$$
\begin{aligned}
&\Delta AE(y^1,y^0,w^1,w^0,x^1,x^0,p^1,p^0) \\
&= [\{[c^1(y^1,w^1)/w^{1T}(x^1/D_i^1(y^1,x^1))]/[c^0(y^0,w^0)/w^{0T}(x^0/D_i^0(y^0,x^0))]\} \\
&\quad \times \{[p^{1T}(y^1/D_o^1(x^1,y^1))/r^1(x^1,p^1)]/[p^{0T}(y^0/D_o^0(x^0,y^0))/r^0(x^0,p^0)]\}]^{1/2} \\
&= \{[AE_i^1(y^1,w^1,x^1)/AE_i^0(y^0,w^0,x^0)] \times [AE_o^1(x^1,p^1,y^1)/AE_o^0(x^0,p^0,y^0)]\}^{1/2}, \\
&\hspace{11cm} (3.32)
\end{aligned}
$$

which is the geometric mean of two ratios. The first is the ratio of input allocative efficiency in the comparison period to input allocative efficiency in the base period. The second is the ratio of output allocative efficiency in the comparison period to output allocative efficiency in the base period. $\Delta AE(y^1,y^0,w^1,w^0,x^1,x^0,p^1,p^0) \gtreqless 1$ as overall allocative efficiency so defined improves, remains unchanged, or declines from base period to comparison period. $\Delta AE(y^1, y^0, w^1, w^0, x^1, x^0, p^1, p^0)$ decomposes into its input-oriented and output-oriented components, so that the two can be analyzed separately.

The third component is change in scale efficiency, defined as

$$\Delta SE(y^1, y^0, w^1, w^0, x^1, x^0, p^1, p^0)$$
$$= \{[(p^{1T}y^1/c^1(y^1, w^1))/\rho^1(p^1, w^1)] \times [r^1(x^1, p^1)/(w^{1T}x^1))/\rho^1(p^1, w^1)]\}^{1/2}$$
$$/\{[(p^{0T}y^0/c^0(y^0, w^0))/\rho^0(p^0, w^0)] \times [(r^0(x^0, p^0)/(w^{0T}x^0))/\rho^0(p^0, w^0)]\}^{1/2},$$
$$(3.33)$$

in which $\rho(p, w) = max_{y,x}\{p^T y/w^T x \mid (y, x) \in T\} = max_{y,x}\{\Pi \mid (y, x) \in T\}$ is a profitability frontier indicating the maximum profitability achievable with prices (p, w) and production technology T. The profitability frontier is analogous to the more familiar profit frontier $\pi(p, w) = max_{y,x}\{p^T y - w^T x \mid (y, x) \in T\}$, but expressed in ratio form rather than in difference form.[4] $\Delta SE(y^1, y^0, w^1, w^0, x^1, x^0, p^1, p^0)$ is the ratio of a pair of scale efficiency measures. The numerator is the geometric mean of an input-oriented scale efficiency measure and an output-oriented scale efficiency measure, both based on comparison period prices and technology. Each component of the numerator is bounded above by unity, and achieves its upper bound if $p^{1T}y^1 = r^1(x^1, p^1)$ and $w^{1T}x^1 = c^1(y^1, w^1)$. The denominator is the geometric mean of an input-oriented scale efficiency measure and an output-oriented scale efficiency measure, both based on base period prices and technology, and is interpreted the same way as the numerator is. $\Delta SE(y^1, y^0, w^1, w^0, x^1, x^0, p^1, p^0) \gtreqqless 1$ as scale efficiency so defined improves, remains unchanged, or declines from base period to comparison period.

The fourth component is technical change, defined as

$$\Delta T(p^1, p^0, w^1, w^0) = \{[\rho^1(p^0, w^0)/\rho^0(p^0, w^0)] \times [\rho^1(p^1, w^1)/\rho^0(p^1, w^1)]\}^{1/2},$$
$$(3.34)$$

which is the geometric mean of a pair of shifts of the profitability frontier, one evaluated at base period prices and the other at comparison period prices. $\Delta T(p^1, p^0, w^1, w^0) \gtreqqless 1$ as maximum profitability increases, stagnates,

---

[4] If technology satisfies free disposability, convexity, and constant returns to scale, then $\rho(p, w)$ is dual to T in the sense that T can be recovered from $\rho(p, w)$ by means of $T = (y, x) \mid p^T y/w^T x \leq \rho(p, w) = (y, x) \mid \Pi \leq \rho(p, w) \forall (p, w) \in R_{++}^{M+N}\}$, and if technology does not satisfy constant returns to scale, then $\rho(p,w)$ is dual to the convex conical hull of T. Kuosmanen and Sipiläinen provide the technical details.

or declines from base period to comparison period. The intuition is that, with given prices, the only way *maximum* profitability in the comparison period can exceed *maximum* profitability in the base period is through an improvement in technology.

The final component is change in the price effect, defined as

$$\Delta PE(p^1, p^0, w^1, w^0)$$
$$= \{[\rho^0(p^1, w^1)/\rho^0(p^0, w^0)] \times [\rho^1(p^1, w^1)/\rho^1(p^0, w^0)]\}^{1/2}/(P_F/W_F),$$
$$(3.35)$$

in which the numerator is the geometric mean of a pair of ratios. The first measures the change in maximum profitability attributable to changes in prices of inputs and outputs, with base period technology. The second is the same ratio, but with comparison period technology. To convert the numerator from nominal to real terms, it is deflated by a Fisher index of price recovery change. $\Delta PE(p^1, p^0, w^1, w^0) \gtreqless 1$ as the price effect so defined improves, remains unchanged, or deteriorates from base period to comparison period.[5]

The Kuosmanen and Sipiläinen decomposition has two virtues. It is free of the average cost concept, and so easily accommodates multiple outputs. The $\Delta AE(y^1, y^0, w^1, w^0, x^1, x^0, p^1, p^0)$ and $\Delta SE(y^1, y^0, w^1, w^0, x^1, x^0, p^1, p^0)$ drivers are free of mixed-period functions, and so each driver equals unity if base period and comparison period values are equal, as they are defined.

However, their decomposition introduces a new problem, with the inclusion of $\Delta PE(p^1, p^0, w^1, w^0)$. We do not think of price change, however defined, as a driver of productivity change. We think of it as a complement to productivity change in explaining profitability change. Multiplying both sides of expression (3.30) by P_F/W_F yields

$$\Pi^1/\Pi^0 = (Y_F/X_F) \times (P_F/W_F)$$
$$= [\Delta TE(y^1, y^0, x^1, x^0) \times \Delta AE(y^1, y^0, w^1, w^0, x^1, x^0, p^1, p^0)$$
$$\times \Delta SE(y^1, y^0, w^1, w^0, x^1, x^0, p^1, p^0) \times \Delta T(p^1, p^0, w^1, w^0)] \qquad (3.36)$$
$$\times \{[\rho^0(p^1, w^1)/\rho^0(p^0, w^0)] \times [\rho^1(p^1, w^1)/\rho^1(p^0, w^0)]\}^{1/2}.$$

---

[5] Kuosmanen and Sipiläinen illustrate their decomposition using a sample of 459 Finnish farms over 1992–2000. The story is one of productivity decline despite technical progress, improvements in scale efficiency resulting from increased farm size, and improvements in overall allocative efficiency. The main driver of productivity decline as they define it in expression (3.30), and profitability decline as we define it in expression (3.36), is diminished price strength, or market power, brought on by the increased competitive pressures subsequent to Finland's 1995 entry into the EU.

The first equality in expression (3.36) is an empirical decomposition of profitability change that satisfies the product test. The second equality is a theoretical decomposition that also satisfies the product test. Although it is tempting to associate $[\Delta TE(y^1,y^0,x^1,x^0) \times \Delta AE(y^1,y^0,w^1,w^0,x^1,x^0,p^1,p^0) \times \Delta SE(y^1,y^0,w^1,w^0,x^1,x^0,p^1,p^0) \times \Delta T(p^1,p^0,w^1,w^0)]$ with Y_F/X_F, and equally tempting to associate $\{[\rho^0(p^1,w^1)/\rho^0(p^0,w^0)] \times [\rho^1(p^1,w^1)/\rho^1(p^0,w^0)]\}^{1/2}$ with P_F/W_F, the nature of the two associations is one of approximation rather than equality. Because $[\Delta TE(y^1,y^0,x^1,x^0) \times \Delta AE(y^1,y^0,w^1,w^0,x^1,x^0,p^1,p^0) \times \Delta SE(y^1,y^0,w^1,w^0,x^1,x^0,p^1,p^0) \times \Delta T(p^1,p^0,w^1,w^0)]$ is not mathematically equivalent to Y_F/X_F, it does not satisfy the product test with P_F/W_F. The conditions under which the two approximations become equalities appear to be unlikely to hold.[6]

Thus, expression (3.36) has some shortcomings: (i) the first equality satisfies the product test but does not identify the economic drivers of productivity change; (ii) the second equality satisfies the product test but its price recovery change component does not decompose by variable; and (iii) neither component of the second equality equals the corresponding component of the first equality except under unlikely conditions. As a consequence, pairing $[\Delta TE(y^1,y^0,x^1,x^0) \times \Delta AE(y^1,y^0,w^1,w^0,x^1,x^0,p^1,p^0) \times \Delta SE(y^1,y^0,w^1,w^0,x^1,x^0,p^1,p^0) \times \Delta T(p^1,p^0,w^1,w^0)]$ from the second equality with P_F/W_F from the first equality, which meets our twin objectives of identifying the economic drivers of productivity change and the individual price changes driving the price recovery change term, fails the product test.

Diewert (2014)

Diewert continues the efforts of Ray and Mukherjee and Kuosmanen and Sipiläinen, with a novel approach. He decomposes profitability change using a combination of Fisher and Konüs indexes, an unusual pairing that follows in the tradition, if not the specifics, of Houéry. His decomposition is

$$\Pi^1/\Pi^0 = [\Delta CE_i(y^1,y^0,w^1,w^0,x^1,x^0) \times \Delta S(y^1,y^0,p^1,p^0,w^1,w^0) \times \Delta T_i(y^1,y^0,w^1,w^0)] \times [P_F/W_k(y^1,y^0,w^1,w^0)], \quad (3.37)$$

---

[6] $[\Delta TE(y^1,y^0,x^1,x^0) \times \Delta AE(y^1,y^0,w^1,w^0,x^1,x^0,p^1,p^0) \times \Delta SE(y^1,y^0,w^1,w^0,x^1,x^0,p^1,p^0) \times \Delta T(p^1,p^0,w^1,w^0)] = Y_F/X_F$ if, and only if, $P_F/W_F = \{[\rho^0(p^1,w^1)/\rho^0(p^0,w^0)] \times [\rho^1(p^1,w^1)/\rho^1(p^0,w^0)]\}^{1/2}$. A sufficient condition for the latter is $[(p^{1T}y^1/w^{1T}x^1)/\rho^1(p^1,w^1)] = [(p^{0T}y^0/w^{0T}x^0)/\rho^0(p^0,w^0)] = [(p^{0T}y^1/w^{0T}x^1)/\rho^0(p^0,w^0)] = [(p^{1T}y^0/w^{1T}x^0)/\rho^0(p^1,w^1)]$. Equality of these four ratios of actual to maximum profitability seems unlikely. Unlike the Ray and Mukherjee decomposition, the Kuosmanen and Sipiläinen decomposition only approximates a Fisher index of productivity change.

which attributes profitability change to productivity change (the first three components) and price recovery change, the latter being the ratio of a Fisher output price index to a Konüs input price index.

The first component

$$\Delta CE_i(y^1, y^0, w^1, w^0, x^1, x^0) = [c^1(y^1, w^1)/w^{1T}x^1]/[c^0(y^0, w^0)/w^{0T}x^0], \quad (3.38)$$

measures the contribution of change in cost efficiency to productivity change. $\Delta CE_i(y^1, y^0, w^1, w^0, x^1, x^0) \gtrless 1$ as cost efficiency improves, remains unchanged or deteriorates from base period to comparison period.

The second component

$$
\begin{aligned}
\Delta S(y^1, &y^0, p^1, p^0, w^1, w^0) \\
&= [\{[p^{0T}y^1/c^0(y^1, w^0)]/[p^{0T}y^0/c^0(y^0, w^0)]\} \\
&\quad \times \{[p^{1T}y^1/c^1(y^1, w^1)]/[p^{1T}y^0/c^1(y^0, w^1)]\}]^{1/2} \\
&= Y_F/\{[c^0(y^1, w^0)/c^0(y^0, w^0)] \times [c^1(y^1, w^1)/c^1(y^0, w^1)]\}^{1/2},
\end{aligned}
\quad (3.39)
$$

is a "not quite conventional" measure of the contribution of change in scale economies along the two cost frontiers; not quite conventional in part because the movement from y^0 to y^1 may include the impact of change in the output mix as well as a pure scale effect (which we refer to as size change). The numerator is a Fisher output quantity index. Diewert interprets the denominator as an input quantity index, the geometric mean of two cost frontier ratios. The first uses base period input prices and technology, and the second uses comparison period input prices and technology. The idea is that movements along a cost frontier reflect changes in cost-efficient input usage. Based on this idea, expression (3.39) is the ratio of an output quantity index to a cost-efficient input quantity index, and this ratio provides a measure of multiproduct returns to scale, with $\Delta S(y^1, y^0, p^1, p^0, w^1, w^0) \gtrless 1$ as returns to scale are increasing, constant, or decreasing on $[y^0, y^1]$.[7]

The third component

$$\Delta T_i(y^1, y^0, w^1, w^0) = \{[c^0(y^0, w^1)/c^1(y^0, w^1)] \times [c^0(y^1, w^0)/c^1(y^1, w^0)]\}^{1/2} \quad (3.40)$$

---

[7] An alternative interpretation of the denominator of expression (3.39) is that it is a Konüs output quantity index defined as $Y_K(y^1, y^0, w^1, w^0) = \{[c^0(y^1, w^0)/c^0(y^0, w^0)] \times [c^1(y^1, w^1)/c^1(y^0, w^1)]\}^{1/2}$. On this interpretation Diewert's scale effect becomes $\Delta S(y^1, y^0, p^1, p^0, w^1, w^0) = Y_F/Y_K(y^1, y^0, w^1, w^0)$, the ratio of a pair of output quantity indexes.

is a Konüs sort of measure of the contribution of technical change to productivity change. This measure is also somewhat unconventional because each component cost frontier is a function of mixed-period data. $\Delta T_i(y^1, y^0, w^1, w^0) \gtreqless 1$ as technical change so defined is progress that shifts the cost frontier down, leaves it unchanged, or is regress that shifts it up.

The product of the first three components constitutes Diewert's productivity index, which is driven by change in input-oriented cost efficiency, by size change, and by input-oriented technical change. The final component

$$P_F/W_K(y^1, y^0, w^1, w^0)$$
$$= P_F / \{[c^0(y^0, w^1)/c^0(y^0, w^0)] \times [c^1(y^1, w^1)/c^1(y^1, w^0)]\}^{1/2}, \quad (3.41)$$

is a hybrid price recovery index having a Fisher output price index in the numerator and a Konüs input price index in the denominator. The price recovery index has the same basic structure as the scale effect in expression (3.39), replacing quantity indexes with price indexes.

The three drivers of productivity change satisfy the product test with the hybrid price recovery index $P_F/W_K(y^1, y^0, w^1, w^0)$. Consequently, Diewert's productivity index collapses to the hybrid form $Y_F/XI_K(y^1, y^0, w^1, w^0, x^1, x^0)$, where $XI_K(y^1, y^0, w^1, w^0, x^1, x^0) = (C^1/C^0)/W_K(y^1, y^0, w^1, w^0)$ is an implicit Konüs input quantity index. The profitability change expression (3.37) becomes

$$\Pi^1/\Pi^0 = [Y_F/XI_K(y^1, y^0, w^1, w^0, x^1, x^0)] \times [P_F/W_K(y^1, y^0, w^1, w^0)], \quad (3.42)$$

in which both the productivity effect and the price recovery effect combine empirical and theoretical indexes, one of which is implicit.

Conclusions

The very large advantage of the approach developed in Section 3.2.2 over that proposed in Section 3.2.1 is that it is capable of providing an economically plausible decomposition of the productivity change component of profitability change, while at the same time providing a decomposition of the price recovery change component by individual variable. The principal finding is that augmenting empirical index numbers with economic theory bears fruit. Structurally similar decompositions of productivity change that differ in their details are provided by the studies we examine.

It is encouraging that all three studies attribute productivity change to the same three drivers: change in cost efficiency, size change, and technical change, once one aggregates technical efficiency change and allocative efficiency change into cost efficiency change in the first two studies and allows for the double orientation and removes the price recovery term in the second study. All three studies struggle with the concept of the contribution of size change to productivity change, and the allocative efficiency change term in the first study does not collapse to unity in the absence of allocative efficiency change. A virtue of the second study is its double orientation, which is reminiscent of the structure of the Malmquist productivity index. The third study has two notable features. Its pairing of empirical and theoretical price indexes in the price recovery index is novel, although its input price index does not decompose by individual prices. Its reliance on an implicit Konüs input quantity index to ensure satisfaction of the product test with $W_K(y^1, y^0, w^1, w^0)$, which is standard practice in the empirical index number literature, is creative in the theoretical index number literature. Implicit quantity and price indexes, including $XI_K(y^1, y^0, w^1, w^0, x^1, x^0)$, play an important role in Section 3.3.2.

3.3 PAIRING THEORETICAL PRODUCTIVITY AND PRICE RECOVERY INDEXES

Malmquist quantity and productivity indexes, and Konüs price and price recovery indexes, are our best theoretical indexes because they satisfy a host of desirable properties, so their use in a decomposition exercise is appealing. Unfortunately, it turns out that their theoretical appeal does not translate to comparable practical value. Nonetheless, it is worth exploring what can, and cannot, be accomplished when the analysis is limited to theoretical indexes.

In Section 3.3.1 we pair a Malmquist productivity index with a Konüs price recovery index. This pairing runs afoul of the product test, and its Konüs component does not decompose by individual variables. In Section 3.3.2 we consider various pairings of explicit, implicit, and hybrid Malmquist productivity indexes and Konüs price recovery indexes. The use of implicit indexes ensures satisfaction of the product test, although implicit indexes run afoul of the identity test. Nonetheless, these pairings generate interesting new results.

3.3.1 Explicit theoretical indexes

Consider pairing a Malmquist productivity index $M(x, y^1, y^0, y, x^1, x^0) = Y_M(x, y^1, y^0)/X_M(y, x^1, x^0)$ set out in expressions (2.1) to (2.4) in Chapter 2 with a Konüs price recovery index $K(x, p^1, p^0, y, w^1, w^0) = P_K(x, p^1, p^0)/W_K(y, w^1, w^0)$

set out in expressions (2.7) to (2.9) in Chapter 2. This pairing is appealing because it involves our two best theoretical indexes, and because $M(x, y^1, y^0, y, x^1, x^0)$ decomposes into the product of the economic drivers of productivity change identified by the BLS and the OECD. We follow Lovell (2003) to illustrate the decomposition of $M(x, y^1, y^0, y, x^1, x^0)$.

$M(x, y^1, y^0, y, x^1, x^0)$ is expressed in generic form, but decomposition requires a base period and a comparison period. The base period output quantity index

$$Y_M^0(x^0, y^1, y^0) = D_o^0(x^0, y^1)/D_o^0(x^0, y^0) \tag{3.43}$$

decomposes as

$$Y_M^0(x^0, y^1, y^0)$$
$$= [D_o^1(x^1, y^1)/D_o^0(x^0, y^0)] \times [D_o^0(x^1, y^1)/D_o^1(x^1, y^1)] \times [D_o^0(x^0, y^1)/D_o^0(x^1, y^1)]$$
$$= \Delta TE_o(x^1, x^0, y^1, y^0) \times \Delta T_o(x^1, y^1) \times [D_o^0(x^0, y^1)/D_o^0(x^1, y^1)], \tag{3.44}$$

in which $\Delta TE_o(x^1, x^0, y^1, y^0)$ is a measure of output-oriented technical efficiency change and $\Delta T_o(x^1, y^1)$ is a measure of output-oriented technical change. We ignore the third term for the moment.

The base period input quantity index $X_M^0(y^0, x^1, x^0) = D_i^0(y^0, x^1)/D_i^0(y^0, x^0)$ decomposes as

$$X_M^0(y^0, x^1, x^0)$$
$$= [D_i^1(y^1, x^1)/D_i^0(y^0, x^0)] \times [D_i^0(y^1, x^1)/D_i^1(y^1, x^1)] \times [D_i^0(y^0, x^1)/D_i^0(y^1, x^1)]$$
$$= \Delta TE_i(y^1, y^0, x^1, x^0) \times \Delta T_i(y^1, x^1) \times [D_i^0(y^0, x^1)/D_i^0(y^1, x^1)], \tag{3.45}$$

in which $\Delta TE_i(y^1, y^0, x^1, x^0)$ is a measure of input-oriented technical efficiency change and $\Delta T_i(y^1, x^1)$ is a measure of input-oriented technical change. We continue to ignore the third term.

Since the base period Malmquist productivity index $M^0(y^1, y^0, x^1, x^0) = Y_M^0(x^0, y^1, y^0)/X_M^0(y^0, x^1, x^0)$, it follows directly from expressions (3.44) and (3.45) that $M^0(y^1, y^0, x^1, x^0)$ decomposes as

$$M^0(y^1, y^0, x^1, x^0)$$
$$= [\Delta TE_o(x^1, x^0, y^1, y^0)/\Delta TE_i(y^1, y^0, x^1, x^0)] \times [\Delta T_o(x^1, y^1)/\Delta T_i(y^1, x^1)]$$
$$\times \{[D_o^0(x^0, y^1)/D_o^0(x^1, y^1)]/[D_i^0(y^0, x^1)/D_i^0(y^1, x^1)]\}. \tag{3.46}$$

This decomposition double counts both technical efficiency change and technical change. One strategy is to replace the first two terms with their square roots and multiply the third term by the product of their square roots. This would generate a decomposition that is similar in both spirit and structure to that proposed by Kuosmanen and Sipiläinen. Another strategy is to merge either the denominators or the numerators of the first two terms with the third term. Merging the denominators generates the decomposition

$$
\begin{aligned}
M^0(y^1,y^0,x^1,x^0) &= \Delta TE_o(x^1,x^0,y^1,y^0) \times \Delta T_o(x^1,y^1) \\
&\quad \times \{[D_o^0(x^0,y^1)/D_o^0(x^1,y^1)]/[D_i^0(y^0,x^1)/D_i^0(y^0,x^0)]\} \\
&= \Delta TE_o(x^1,x^0,y^1,y^0) \times \Delta T_o(x^1,y^1) \times \Delta S^0(y^1,y^0,x^1,x^0),
\end{aligned}
\tag{3.47}
$$

in which $\Delta TE_o(x^1,x^0,y^1,y^0)$ and $\Delta T_o(x^1,y^1)$ are measures of output-oriented technical efficiency change and technical change, respectively, and $\Delta S^0(y^1,y^0,x^1,x^0)$ is a nonoriented measure of the contribution of size change, defined on the base period technology and measured on the interval $[(y^1-y^0),(x^1-x^0)]$.[8]

Expression (3.47) provides a decomposition of the base period Malmquist productivity index. The comparison period Malmquist productivity index $M^1(y^1,y^0,x^1,x^0)$ decomposes in exactly the same way, as does the geometric mean of the two $M(y^1,y^0,x^1,x^0)=[M^0(y^1,y^0,x^1,x^0)\times M^1(y^1,y^0,x^1,x^0)]^{1/2}$ $= Y_M(x^1,x^0,y^1,y^0)/X_M(y^1,y^0,x^1,x^0)$.

The geometric mean Konüs price recovery index was defined at the end of Section 2.3.3 as $K(x^1,x^0,p^1,p^0,y^1,y^0,w^1,w^0)=P_K(x^1,x^0,p^1,p^0)/W_K(y^1,y^0,w^1,w^0)$. We know from Section 2.3.4 of Chapter 2 that pairing a Malmquist productivity index with a Konüs price recovery fails the product test with profitability change, which we express using geometric mean versions of each as

$$
\begin{aligned}
\Pi^1/\Pi^0 &\approx M(y^1,y^0,x^1,x^0) \times K(x^1,x^0,p^1,p^0,y^1,y^0,w^1,w^0) \\
&= [Y_M(x^1,x^0,y^1,y^0)/X_M(y^1,y^0,x^1,x^0)] \\
&\quad \times [P_K(x^1,x^0,p^1,p^0)/W_K(y^1,y^0,w^1,w^0)] \\
&= [\Delta TE_o(x^1,x^0,y^1,y^0) \times \Delta T_o(x^1,x^0,y^1,y^0) \times \Delta S(y^1,y^0,x^1,x^0)] \\
&\quad \times K(x^1,x^0,p^1,p^0,y^1,y^0,w^1,w^0).
\end{aligned}
\tag{3.48}
$$

---

[8] The association of $\Delta S^0(y^1,y^0,x^1,x^0)$ with a size effect is an assertion, not a theorem. However, Lovell proves, for the $M=N=1$ case, that $\Delta S^0(y^1,y^0,x^1,x^0)$ does provide a measure of scale economies on the base period technology. Also, $\Delta TE_o(x^1,x^0,y^1,y^0) \times \Delta T_o(x^1,y^1) = D_o^0(x^1,y^1)/D_o^0(x^0,y^0)$, which is the Caves, Christensen, and Diewert (1982) version of the base period Malmquist productivity index, and which Grifell-Tatjé and Lovell (1995) show ignores the contribution of size change to productivity change. It follows directly that $M^0(y^1,y^0,x^1,x^0)/M_{o\,CCD}(x^1,x^0,y^1,y^0) = [D_o^0(x^0,y^1)/D_o^0(x^1,y^1)]/[D_i^0(y^0,x^1)/D_i^0(y^0,x^0)]$ is a base period (multidimensional) size effect.

Expression (3.48) states that profitability change is approximated by the product of a Malmquist index of productivity change (which itself is the ratio of Malmquist indexes of output quantity change and input quantity change) and a Konüs price recovery index (which itself is the ratio of Konüs indexes of output price change and input price change). The Malmquist productivity index is the product of indexes of technical efficiency change, technical change, and size change. We decompose a Konüs implicit input quantity index in Chapter 7.

Despite the theoretical appeal of Malmquist and Konüs indexes, this pairing has two empirical drawbacks. As we noted in Chapter 2, neither $[P_K(x^1,x^0,p^1,p^0) \times Y_M(x^1,x^0,y^1,y^0)]$ nor $[W_K(y^1,y^0,w^1,w^0) \times X_M(y^1,y^0,x^1,x^0)]$ satisfies the product test, except under very severe restrictions on the structure of production technology. These failures are responsible for the "$\approx$" in expression (3.48). Nonetheless, the magnitude of the two failures is an empirical issue, in two senses. First, $P_K(x^1,x^0,p^1,p^0)$ and $Y_M(x^1,x^0,y^1,y^0)$ must be estimated, and the product of their *estimates* may provide an acceptable approximation to observed revenue change, and $W_K(y^1,y^0,w^1,w^0)$ and $X_M(y^1,y^0,x^1,x^0)$ must also be estimated, and the product of their *estimates* may provide an acceptable approximation to observed cost change. Moreover, our interest centers on profitability change, which is approximated by the ratio of $P_K(x^1,x^0,p^1,p^0) \times Y_M(x^1,x^0,y^1,y^0)$ to $W_K(y^1,y^0,w^1,w^0) \times X_M(y^1,y^0,x^1,x^0)$, and an empirical estimate of this ratio may come closer to satisfying the product test than do empirical estimates of either of its components. The second drawback of this pairing is that neither $M(y^1,y^0,x^1,x^0)$ nor $K(x^1,x^0,p^1,p^0,y^1,y^0,w^1,w^0)$ decomposes by variable. This is of no concern with the productivity index, which decomposes by economic driver, but it is a serious concern with the price recovery index, which we want to decompose by individual price change.

We conclude that pairing two theoretical indexes is an unsatisfactory option. No matter how small the approximation error caused by failure to satisfy the product test, the inability to decompose the price recovery index by individual price change is fatal, in light of our objectives of decomposing the productivity change component by economic driver and decomposing the price recovery component by individual price change.

3.3.2 Explicit and implicit theoretical indexes

Our two best theoretical quantity and price indexes fail the product test. This motivates the generation of implicit theoretical price and quantity indexes, whose sole purpose is to satisfy the product test. However, this achievement comes at a cost.

Consider pairing a generic Malmquist output quantity index $Y_M(x, y^1, y^0)$ with a generic implicit Malmquist output price index $PI_M(x, p^1, p^0, y^1, y^0) = (R^1/R^0)/Y_M(x, y^1, y^0)$. Similarly, on the input side we can pair a generic Malmquist input quantity index $X_M(y, x^1, x^0)$ with a generic implicit Malmquist input price index $WI_M(y, w^1, w^0, x^1, x^0) = (C^1/C^0)/X_M(y, x^1, x^0)$. Both pairs satisfy the product test by construction, for base period, comparison period, and geometric mean specifications.

We can reverse the procedure. Consider pairing a generic Konüs output price index $P_K(x, p^1, p^0)$ with a generic implicit Konüs output quantity index $YI_K(x, p^1, p^0, y^1, y^0) = (R^1/R^0)/P_K(x, p^1, p^0)$. On the input side we can pair a generic Konüs input price index $W_K(y, w^1, w^0)$ with a generic implicit Konüs input quantity index $XI_K(y, w^1, w^0, x^1, x^0) = (C^1/C^0)/W_K(y, w^1, w^0)$. These two pairs also satisfy the product test by construction, for base period, comparison period, and geometric mean specifications.

The introduction of implicit theoretical price and quantity indexes generates the following options:

(i) Pair a generic Malmquist productivity index $Y_M(x, y^1, y^0)/X_M(y, x^1, x^0)$ with a generic implicit Malmquist price recovery index $PI_M(x, p^1, p^0, y^1, y^0)/WI_M(y, w^1, w^0, x^1, x^0)$;

(ii) Pair a generic Konüs price recovery index $P_K(x, p^1, p^0)/W_K(y, w^1, w^0)$ with a generic implicit Konüs productivity index $YI_K(x, p^1, p^0, y^1, y^0)/XI_K(y, w^1, w^0, x^1, x^0)$;

(iii) Pair a generic hybrid productivity index $Y_M(x, y^1, y^0)/XI_K(y, w^1, w^0, x^1, x^0)$ with a generic hybrid price recovery index $PI_M(x, p^1, p^0, y^1, y^0)/W_K(y, w^1, w^0)$; and

(iv) Pair another generic hybrid productivity index $YI_K(x, p^1, p^0, y^1, y^0)/X_M(y, x^1, x^0)$ with another generic hybrid price recovery index $P_K(x, p^1, p^0)/WI_M(y, w^1, w^0, x^1, x^0)$.

It is easy to see that the product test is satisfied by construction for numerator and denominator of all four combinations of explicit and implicit theoretical indexes. Thus, in contrast to the approximate decomposition of profitability change provided by expression (3.48), all four pairings above generate exact decompositions of profitability change. However, forcing satisfaction of the product test by means of introducing implicit theoretical indexes comes at a cost. The implicit price indexes $PI_M(x, p^1, p^0, y^1, y^0)$ and $WI_M(y, w^1, w^0, x^1, x^0)$ in options (i), (iii), and (iv) fail the identity test in prices, and the implicit quantity indexes $YI_K(x, p^1, p^0, y^1, y^0)$ and $XI_K(y, w^1, w^0, x^1, x^0)$ in options (ii), (iii), and (iv) fail the identity test in quantities. Nonetheless, each of these pairings can be given an interesting economic interpretation.

3.3.2.1 Implicit Malmquist price and price recovery indexes

A base period implicit Malmquist output price index is

$$
\begin{aligned}
PI_M^0(x^0, p^1, p^0, y^1, y^0) &= (R^1/R^0)/Y_M^0(x^0, y^1, y^0) \\
&= [p^{1T}y^1/D_o^0(x^0, y^1)]/[p^{0T}y^0/D_o^0(x^0, y^0)],
\end{aligned}
\tag{3.49}
$$

in which $Y_M^0(x^0, y^1, y^0) = D_o^0(x^0, y^1)/D_o^0(x^0, y^0)$ is a base period Malmquist output quantity index. Multiplying and dividing by $p^{0T}y^1/D_o^0(x^0, y^1)$ yields

$$
\begin{aligned}
PI_M^0(x^0, p^1, p^0, y^1, y^0) &= \{[p^{1T}y^1/D_o^0(x^0, y^1)]/[p^{0T}y^1/D_o^0(x^0, y^1)]\} \\
&\quad \times \{[p^{0T}y^1/D_o^0(x^0, y^1)]/[p^{0T}y^0/D_o^0(x^0, y^0)]\} \\
&= P_P \times \{[p^{0T}y^1/D_o^0(x^0, y^1)]/[p^{0T}y^0/D_o^0(x^0, y^0)]\},
\end{aligned}
\tag{3.50}
$$

which is the product of a Paasche output price index and a base period output mix effect that is the ratio of the revenue generated by two technically efficient output vectors $y^1/D_o^0(x^0, y^1)$ and $y^0/D_o^0(x^0, y^0)$.

Revenue change is

$$
\begin{aligned}
R^1/R^0 &= Y_M^0(x^0, y^1, y^0) \times PI_M^0(x^0, p^1, p^0, y^1, y^0) \\
&= Y_M^0(x^0, y^1, y^0) \times P_P \times \{[p^{0T}y^1/D_o^0(x^0, y^1)]/[p^{0T}y^0/D_o^0(x^0, y^0)]\},
\end{aligned}
\tag{3.51}
$$

which states that the product of a base period Malmquist output quantity index, a Paasche output price index, and the base period output mix effect identified in expression (3.50) satisfies the product test with revenue change. Expression (3.51) combines a theoretical quantity index with an empirical price index, with the base period output mix effect filling the product test gap.

If $M = 1$ or if $M > 1$ and $y^1 = \lambda y^0$, $\lambda > 0$, the output mix effect equals unity and consequently $PI_M^0(x^0, p^1, p^0, y^1, y^0) = P_P$ and $R^1/R^0 = Y_M^0(x^0, y^1, y^0) \times P_P$, which states that, under either of the stipulated conditions, (i) a base period implicit Malmquist output price index is equal to a Paasche output price index, and (ii) the product of a base period Malmquist output quantity index and a Paasche output price index satisfies the product test with revenue change. The single output condition is satisfied in many empirical applications, and the proportionality condition is plausible when output price ratios do not vary much. If neither of these conditions holds, base period output allocative efficiency (but not technical efficiency) of y^0 relative to p^0 is sufficient for the output mix effect to be bounded above by unity, and thus for $PI_M^0(x^0,p^1,p^0,y^1,y^0) \leq P_P$ and $R^1/R^0 \leq Y_M^0(x^0,y^1,y^0) \times P_P$. A less restrictive sufficient condition for both inequalities requires only that y^0 be more allocatively efficient than y^1 relative to p^0 on base period technology.

A comparison period implicit Malmquist output price index is

$$PI_M^1(x^1,p^1,p^0,y^1,y^0) = (R^1/R^0)/Y_M^1(x^1,y^1,y^0)$$
$$= P_L \times \{[p^{1T}y^1/D_o^1(x^1,y^1)]/[p^{1T}y^0/D_o^1(x^1,y^0)]\},$$
(3.52)

after multiplying and dividing by $p^{1T}y^0/D_o^1(x^1,y^0)$, where $Y_M^1(x^1,y^1,y^0) = D_o^1(x^1,y^1)/D_o^1(x^1,y^0)$ is a comparison period Malmquist output quantity index.

Revenue change is

$$R^1/R^0 = Y_M^1(x^1,y^1,y^0) \times P_L \times \{[p^{1T}y^1/D_o^1(x^1,y^1)]/[p^{1T}y^0/D_o^1(x^1,y^0)]\},$$
(3.53)

which states that the product of a comparison period Malmquist output quantity index, a Laspeyres output price index, and a comparison period output mix effect satisfies the product test with revenue change.

The same conditions as above make the comparison period output mix effect unity, which in turn makes $PI_M^1(x^1,p^1,p^0,y^1,y^0) = P_L$ and $R^1/R^0 = Y_M^1(x^1,y^1,y^0) \times P_L$, and so under either of these conditions a comparison period implicit Malmquist output price index is equal to a Laspeyres output price index, and the product of a comparison period Malmquist output quantity index and a Laspeyres output price index satisfies the product test with revenue change. The weaker condition that y^1 be more allocatively efficient than y^0 relative to p^1 on comparison period technology is sufficient for the comparison period output mix effect to be bounded below by unity, and thus for $PI_M^1(x^1,p^1,p^0,y^1,y^0) \geq P_L$ and $R^1/R^0 \geq Y_M^1(x^1,y^1,y^0) \times P_L$.

An implicit Malmquist output price index is the geometric mean of expressions (3.50) and (3.52), and so

$$PI_M(x^1,x^0,p^1,p^0,y^1,y^0) = P_F \times [\{[p^{0T}y^1/D_o^0(x^0,y^1)]/[p^{0T}y^0/D_o^0(x^0,y^0)]\}$$
$$\times \{[p^{1T}y^1/D_o^1(x^1,y^1)]/[p^{1T}y^0/D_o^1(x^1,y^0)]\}]^{1/2},$$

$$(3.54)$$

in which the Fisher output price index $P_F=[P_P \times P_L]^{1/2}$. Revenue change is given by the geometric mean of expressions (3.51) and (3.53), and so

$$R^1/R^0 = Y_M(x^1,x^0,y^1,y^0) \times P_F \times [\{[p^{0T}y^1/D_o^0(x^0,y^1)]/[p^{0T}y^0/D_o^0(x^0,y^0)]\}$$
$$\times \{[p^{1T}y^1/D_o^1(x^1,y^1)]/[p^{1T}y^0/D_o^1(x^1,y^0)]\}]^{1/2}.$$

$$(3.55)$$

The same conditions as above make the geometric mean output mix effect equal to unity, which in turn makes $PI_M(x^1,x^0,p^1,p^0,y^1,y^0)=P_F$ and $R^1/R^0 = Y_M(x^1,x^0,y^1,y^0) \times P_F$, and so under either of these conditions an implicit Malmquist output price index is equal to a Fisher output price index, and the product of a Malmquist output quantity index and a Fisher output price index satisfies the product test with revenue change. If neither of these conditions holds, the output allocative efficiency conditions above imply that the base period component of the geometric mean output mix effect is bounded above by unity and the comparison period component is bounded below by unity, making it likely that their geometric mean is approximately unity, and thus $PI_M(x^1,x^0,p^1,p^0,y^1,y^0) \approx P_F$ and $R^1/R^0 \approx Y_M(x^1,x^0,y^1,y^0) \times P_F$. To conserve on notation we write expressions (3.54) and (3.55) as

$$PI_M(x^1,x^0,p^1,p^0,y^1,y^0) = P_F \times \gamma_y^M$$

$$(3.56)$$

and

$$R^1/R^0 = Y_M(x^1,x^0,y^1,y^0) \times P_F \times \gamma_y^M,$$

$$(3.57)$$

with γ_y^M measuring the gap between $PI_M(x^1,x^0,p^1,p^0,y^1,y^0)$ and P_F associated with the geometric mean output mix effect in expressions (3.54) and (3.55).

The revenue change expression (3.57) generates an explicit relationship between an empirical Fisher output quantity index and a theoretical Malmquist output quantity index. Since $Y_F \times P_F=R^1/R^0$, it follows directly that

$$Y_F = Y_M(x^1,x^0,y^1,y^0) \times \gamma_y^M.$$

$$(3.58)$$

Since γ_y^M is defined in closed form in expressions (3.54) and (3.55), it is possible to calculate the gap between the two indexes.

This completes the analysis of the implicit Malmquist output price index in options (i) and (iii) in the introduction to this section. The implicit Malmquist input price index is developed in a similar manner, using the same strategies and the same allocative efficiency logic. The base period implicit Malmquist input price index is $WI_M^0(y^0, w^1, w^0, x^1, x^0) = (C^1/C^0)/X_M^0(y^0, x^1, x^0)$ and the comparison period implicit Malmquist input price index is $WI_M^1(y^1, w^1, w^0, x^1, x^0) = (C^1/C^0)/X_M^1(y^1, x^1, x^0)$. We omit all intermediate steps and arrive at the geometric mean of the two, the implicit Malmquist input price index

$$WI_M(y^1, y^0, w^1, w^0, x^1, x^0) = W_F \times \{[(w^{0T}x^1/D_i^0(y^0, x^1))/(w^{0T}x^0/D_i^0(y^0, x^0))]$$
$$\times [(w^{1T}x^1/D_i^1(y^1, x^1))/(w^{1T}x^0/D_i^1(y^1, x^0))]\}^{1/2}$$
$$= W_F \times \gamma_x^M, \tag{3.59}$$

and the corresponding expression for cost change

$$C^1/C^0 = X_M(y^1, y^0, x^1, x^0) \times W_F \times \{[(w^{0T}x^1/D_i^0(y^0, x^1))/(w^{0T}x^0/D_i^0(y^0, x^0))]$$
$$\times [(w^{1T}x^1/D_i^1(y^1, x^1))/(w^{1T}x^0/D_i^1(y^1, x^0))]\}^{1/2}$$
$$= X_M(y^1, y^0, x^1, x^0) \times W_F \times \gamma_x^M, \tag{3.60}$$

in which γ_x^M is the gap between $WI_M(y^1, y^0, w^1, w^0, x^1, x^0)$ and W_F associated with the input mix effect in expressions (3.59) and (3.60). If either $N=1$ or $x^1 = \mu x^0$, $\mu > 0$, then $\gamma_x^M = 1$, the gap vanishes, and so $WI_M(y^1, y^0, w^1, w^0, x^1, x^0) = W_F$ and $C^1/C^0 = X_M(y^1, y^0, x^1, x^0) \times W_F$. If neither of these conditions holds, we exploit the fact that γ_x^M is the geometric mean of a base period input mix effect bounded above by unity and a comparison period input mix effect bounded below by unity, and so we expect $\gamma_x^M \approx 1$. If the input mix is relatively stable in the two periods, we also expect $\gamma_x^M \approx 1$.

The cost change expression (3.60) can be used to relate an empirical Fisher input quantity index and a theoretical Malmquist input quantity index. Since $X_F \times W_F = C^1/C^0$, it follows that

$$X_F = X_M(y^1, y^0, x^1, x^0) \times \gamma_x^M, \tag{3.61}$$

and it is possible to calculate the gap between the two indexes using the definition of γ_x^M in expressions (3.59) and (3.60).

We now construct a price recovery index. We ignore base period and comparison period indexes and proceed directly to an implicit Malmquist price recovery index. The ratio of expressions (3.56) and (3.59) is

$$PI_M(x^1,x^0,p^1,p^0,y^1,y^0)/WI_M(y^1,y^0,w^1,w^0,x^1,x^0) = (P_F/W_F) \times \gamma_{yx}^M,$$
(3.62)

in which $\gamma_{yx}^M = \gamma_y^M/\gamma_x^M$ measures the gap between $PI_M(x^1,x^0,p^1,p^0,y^1,y^0)/$ $WI_M(y^1,y^0,w^1,w^0,x^1,x^0)$ and (P_F/W_F), and for reasons explained above we expect $\gamma_{yx}^M \approx 1$, in which case the implicit Malmquist price recovery index is approximately equal to a Fisher price recovery index. $\gamma_{yx}^M = 1$ would require equality between the output mix effect and the input mix effect, a sufficient but not necessary condition for which is $y^1 = \lambda y^0$, $\lambda > 0$, and $x^1 = \mu x^0$, $\mu > 0$.

An expression for profitability change is given by the ratio of expressions (3.57) and (3.60), and is

$$\begin{aligned}\Pi^1/\Pi^0 &= (R^1/R^0)/(C^1/C^0) \\ &= [Y_M(x^1,x^0,y^1,y^0)/X_M(y^1,y^0,x^1,x^0)] \times (P_F/W_F) \times \gamma_{yx}^M,\end{aligned}$$
(3.63)

and if $\gamma_{yx}^M \approx 1$ a Malmquist productivity index and a Fisher price recovery index approximately satisfy the product test with profitability change. We provide an empirical application in Section 3.4 in which we test the hypothesis that $\gamma_{yx}^M = 1$.

Since $(P_F/W_F) \times (Y_F/X_F) = (R^1/R^0)/(C^1/C^0)$, it follows that

$$Y_F/X_F = [Y_M(x^1,x^0,y^1,y^0)/X_M(y^1,y^0,x^1,x^0)] \times \gamma_{yx}^M,$$
(3.64)

which relates an empirical Fisher productivity index to a theoretical Malmquist productivity index, with gap γ_{yx}^M defined beneath expression (3.62).

3.3.2.2 Implicit Konüs quantity and productivity indexes

We have discussed implicit Malmquist output price, input price, and price recovery indexes. We now consider implicit Konüs output quantity, input quantity, and productivity indexes. We begin with a base period implicit Konüs output quantity index. We have

$$\begin{aligned}YI_K^0(x^0,p^1,p^0,y^1,y^0) &= (R^1/R^0)/P_K^0(x^0,p^1,p^0) \\ &= [p^{1T}y^1/r^0(x^0,p^1)]/[p^{0T}y^0/r^0(x^0,p^0)],\end{aligned}$$
(3.65)

in which $P_K^0(x^0,p^1,p^0) = r^0(x^0,p^1)/r^0(x^0,p^0)$ is a base period Konüs output price index. Multiplying and dividing by $p^{1T}y^0/r^0(x^0,p^1)$ yields

$$YI_K^0(x^0,p^1,p^0,y^1,y^0) = \{[p^{1T}y^1/r^0(x^0,p^1)]/[p^{1T}y^0/r^0(x^0,p^1)]\}$$
$$\times \{[p^{1T}y^0/r^0(x^0,p^1)]/[p^{0T}y^0/r^0(x^0,p^0)]\} \quad (3.66)$$
$$= Y_P \times \{[p^{1T}y^0/r^0(x^0,p^1)]/[p^{0T}y^0/r^0(x^0,p^0)]\},$$

which expresses a base period implicit Konüs output quantity index as the product of a Paasche output quantity index and a base period output allocative efficiency effect, so named because it can be written as $[p^{1T}y^0/r^0(x^0,p^1)]/$ $[p^{0T}y^0/r^0(x^0,p^0)] = [p^{1T}(y^0/D_o^0(x^0,y^0))/r^0(x^0,p^1)]/[p^{0T}(y^0/D_o^0(x^0,y^0))/r^0(x^0,p^0)]$ $= [D_o^0(x^0,y^0) \times AE_o^0(x^0,p^1,y^0)]/[D_o^0(x^0,y^0) \times AE_o^0(x^0,p^0,y^0)] = AE_o^0(x^0,p^1,y^0)/$ $AE_o^0(x^0,p^0,y^0)$, the ratio of two output allocative efficiency effects, each the ratio of actual revenue to maximum revenue. This ratio is bounded above by unity if y^0 is allocatively efficient relative to p^0, or if y^0 is more allocatively efficient relative to p^0 than to p^1. In this case a base period implicit Konüs output quantity index is bounded above by a Paasche output quantity index, and so $YI_K^0(x^0,p^1,p^0,y^1,y^0) \leq Y_P$, with $YI_K^0(x^0,p^1,p^0,y^1,y^0) = Y_P$ if either $M=1$ or $p^1=\lambda p^0$, $\lambda > 0$.

Revenue change is

$$R^1/R^0 = P_K^0(x^0,p^1,p^0) \times YI_K^0(x^0,p^1,p^0,y^1,y^0)$$
$$= P_K^0(x^0,p^1,p^0) \times Y_P \times [AE_o^0(x^0,p^1,y^0)/AE_o^0(x^0,p^0,y^0)], \quad (3.67)$$

which states that the product of a base period Konüs output price index, a Paasche output quantity index, and a base period output allocative efficiency effect satisfies the product test with R^1/R^0. As above, we expect $R^1/R^0 \leq P_K^0(x^0,p^1,p^0) \times Y_P$. However, if either $M=1$ or $p^1=\lambda p^0$, $\lambda > 0$, expressions (3.66) and (3.67) collapse to $YI_K^0(x^0,p^1,p^0,y^1,y^0) = Y_P$ and $R^1/R^0 = P_K^0(x^0,p^1,p^0) \times Y_P$, in which case a base period implicit Konüs output quantity index is equal to a Paasche output quantity index, and consequently a Konüs output price index and a Paasche output quantity index satisfy the product test with R^1/R^0.

We now sketch the results of a comparison period implicit Konüs output quantity index. Following the same procedures as above, after multiplying and dividing by $p^{0T}y^1/r^1(x^1,p^0)$ we have

$$YI_K^1(x^1,p^1,p^0,y^1,y^0) = (R^1/R^0)/P_K^0(x^1,p^1,p^0)$$
$$= Y_L \times [p^{1T}y^1/r^1(x^1,p^1)]/[p^{0T}y^1/r^1(x^1,p^0)], \quad (3.68)$$

in which $P_K^1(x^1,p^1,p^0) = r^1(x^1,p^1)/r^1(x^1,p^0)$ is a comparison period Konüs output price index. A comparison period implicit Konüs output quantity index is the product of a Laspeyres output quantity index and a comparison period output allocative efficiency effect. Because the allocative efficiency effect collapses to $AE_o^1(x^1,p^1,y^1)/AE_o^1(x^1,p^0,y^1)$, if y^1 is more allocatively efficient relative to p^1 than to p^0, then $YI_K^1(x^1,y^1,y^0) \geq Y_L$.

Revenue change is

$$
\begin{aligned}
R^1/R^0 &= P_K^1(x^1,p^1,p^0) \times YI_K^1(x^1,p^1,p^0,y^1,y^0) \\
&= P_K^1(x^1,p^1,p^0) \times Y_L \times [AE_o^1(x^1,p^1,y^1)/AE_o^1(x^1,p^0,y^1)],
\end{aligned}
\tag{3.69}
$$

which states that the product of a comparison period Konüs output price index, a Laspeyres output quantity index, and a comparison period output allocative efficiency effect satisfies the product test with R^1/R^0. Under the conditions above, $R^1/R^0 \geq P_K^1(x^1,p^1,p^0) \times Y_L$. If either $M=1$ or $p^1=\lambda p^0$, $\lambda > 0$, $YI_K^1(x^1,p^1,p^0,y^1,y^0) = Y_L$ and $R^1/R^0 = P_K^1(x^1,p^1,p^0) \times Y_L$.

The geometric mean of expressions (3.66) and (3.68) is an implicit Konüs output quantity index

$$
\begin{aligned}
YI_K(x^1,x^0,p^1,p^0,y^1,y^0) &= Y_F \times \{[AE_o^0(x^0,p^1,y^0)/AE_o^0(x^0,p^0,y^0)] \\
&\quad \times [AE_o^1(x^1,p^1,y^1)/AE_o^1(x^1,p^0,y^1)]\}^{1/2}
\end{aligned}
\tag{3.70}
$$

and the geometric mean of expressions (3.67) and (3.69) yields the expression for revenue change

$$
\begin{aligned}
R^1/R^0 &= P_K(x^1,x^0,p^1,p^0) \times Y_F \times \{[AE_o^0(x^0,p^1,y^0)/AE_o^0(x^0,p^0,y^0)] \\
&\quad \times [AE_o^1(x^1,p^1,y^1)/AE_o^1(x^1,p^0,y^1)]\}^{1/2}.
\end{aligned}
\tag{3.71}
$$

Expression (3.70) states that an implicit Konüs output quantity index is the product of a Fisher output quantity index and an output allocative efficiency effect. Because one component of the output allocative efficiency effect is bounded above by unity and the other bounded below by unity, we expect $YI_K(x^1,x^0,p^1,p^0,y^1,y^0) \approx Y_F$. Expression (3.71) states that a Konüs output price index and a Fisher output quantity index approximately satisfy the product test with R^1/R^0.

To conserve on notation, we write expressions (3.70) and (3.71) as

$$
YI_K(x^1,x^0,p^1,p^0,y^1,y^0) = Y_F \times \gamma_y^K
\tag{3.72}
$$

and

$$R^1/R^0 = P_K(x^1,x^0,p^1,p^0) \times Y_F \times \gamma_y^K, \qquad (3.73)$$

in which γ_y^K is the gap between $YI_K(x^1,x^0,p^1,p^0,y^1,y^0)$ and Y_F associated with the output allocative efficiency effect in expressions (3.70) and (3.71).

Expression (3.73) can be used to relate empirical Fisher and theoretical Konüs output price indexes, exactly as we used expression (3.58) to relate Fisher and Malmquist output quantity indexes. $P_F \times Y_F = R^1/R^0$, and so

$$P_F = P_K(x^1,x^0,p^1,p^0) \times \gamma_y^K, \qquad (3.74)$$

and the definition of γ_y^K in expressions (3.70) and (3.71) enables us to calculate the gap between the theoretical and empirical output price indexes.

This completes the analysis of the implicit Konüs output quantity index in options (ii) and (iv) in the introduction to this section. We consider next the implicit Konüs input quantity index. The base period implicit Konüs input quantity index is $XI_K^0(y^0,w^1,w^0,x^1,x^0) = (C^1/C^0)/W_K^0(y^0,w^1,w^0)$ and the comparison period implicit Konüs input quantity index is $XI_K^1(y^1,w^1,w^0,x^1,x^0) = (C^1/C^0)/W_K^1(y^1,w^1,w^0)$. The geometric mean of the two, the implicit Konüs input quantity index, is

$$XI_K(y^1,y^0,w^1,w^0,x^1,x^0) = X_F \times \{[AE_i^0(y^0,w^1,x^0)/AE_i^0(y^0,w^0,x^0)]$$
$$\times [AE_i^1(y^1,w^1,x^1)/AE_i^1(y^1,w^0,x^1)]\}^{1/2}$$
$$= X_F \times \gamma_x^K, \qquad (3.75)$$

in which γ_x^K is the gap between $XI_K(y^1,y^0,w^1,w^0,x^1,x^0)$ and X_F associated with the input allocative efficiency effect, which is defined analogously to the output allocative efficiency effect beneath expression (3.66). In the base period, for example, $AE_i^0(x^0,y^0,w^1)/AE_i^0(x^0,y^0,w^0) = [w^{1T}(x^0/D_i^0(y^0,x^0))/c^0(y^0,w^1)]/[w^{0T}(x^0/D_i^0(y^0,x^0))/c^0(y^0,w^0)]$, which is the ratio of a pair of ratios of technically efficient cost to minimum cost.

The implicit Konüs input quantity index $XI_K(y^1,y^0,w^1,w^0,x^1,x^0)$ appears in Diewert's profitability change decomposition in expression (3.42).

Cost change is

$$C^1/C^0 = W_K(y^1,y^0,w^1,w^0) \times X_F \times \{[AE_i^0(y^0,w^1,x^0)/AE_i^0(y^0,w^0,x^0)]$$
$$\times [AE_i^1(y^1,w^1,x^1)/AE_i^1(y^1,w^0,x^1)]\}^{1/2}$$
$$= W_K(y^1,y^0,w^1,w^0) \times X_F \times \gamma_x^K. \qquad (3.76)$$

Since $W_F \times X_F = C^1/C^0$, expression (3.76) generates the following relationship between Fisher and Konüs input price indexes:

$$W_F = W_K(y^1, y^0, w^1, w^0) \times \gamma_x^K, \qquad (3.77)$$

with γ_x^K defined in expressions (3.75) and (3.76).

We now construct an implicit Konüs productivity index. We ignore base period and comparison indexes and proceed directly to an implicit Konüs productivity index. The ratio of expressions (3.72) and (3.75) is

$$YI_K(x^1, x^0, p^1, p^0, y^1, y^0)/XI_K(y^1, y^0, w^1, w^0, x^1, x^0) = (Y_F/X_F) \times \gamma_{yx}^K, \quad (3.78)$$

in which $\gamma_{yx}^K = \gamma_y^K / \gamma_x^K$ is the gap between $YI_K(x^1, x^0, p^1, p^0, y^1, y^0)/$ $XI_K(y^1, y^0, w^1, w^0, x^1, x^0)$ and Y_F/X_F. We expect $\gamma_{yx}^K \approx 1$, in which case the implicit Konüs productivity index is approximately equal to a Fisher productivity index. $\gamma_{yx}^K = 1$ would require equality between the output and input allocative efficiency effects γ_y^K and γ_x^K, a sufficient but not necessary condition for which is $p^1 = \lambda p^0$, $\lambda > 0$ and $w^1 = \mu w^0$, $\mu > 0$.

The ratio of expressions (3.73) and (3.76) provides an implicit Konüs measure of profitability change

$$\begin{aligned} \Pi^1/\Pi^0 &= (R^1/R^0)/(C^1/C^0) \\ &= [P_K(x^1, x^0, p^1, p^0)/W_K(y^1, y^0, w^1, w^0)] \times (Y_F/X_F) \times \gamma_{yx}^K, \end{aligned} \qquad (3.79)$$

and if $\gamma_{yx}^K \approx 1$, a Konüs price recovery index and a Fisher productivity index approximately satisfy the product test with profitability change.

Since $P_F/W_F \times Y_F/X_F = (R^1/R^0)/(C^1/C^0)$, it follows that

$$P_F/W_F = [P_K(x^1, x^0, p^1, p^0)/W_K(y^1, y^0, w^1, w^0)] \times \gamma_{yx}^K, \qquad (3.80)$$

which relates an empirical Fisher price recovery index to a theoretical Konüs price recovery index, with gap γ_{yx}^K defined beneath expression (3.78).

The results of this section are summarized in Table 3.1, which contains six pairings of theoretical (either Malmquist or Konüs) and empirical (Fisher) indexes. Revenue change, cost change, and profitability change each have two decompositions. None of these pairs is equal unless $\gamma_y^M = \gamma_y^K$ or $\gamma_x^M = \gamma_x^K$ or $\gamma_{yx}^M = \gamma_{yx}^K$, which is unlikely since γ_y^M, γ_x^M, and γ_{yx}^M are mix terms that hold prices constant while comparing values generated by different quantities, while γ_y^K, γ_x^K, and γ_{yx}^K are allocative efficiency terms that hold quantities constant while comparing values generated by different prices. Price recovery change and productivity change have just a single decomposition.

Table 3.1 Explicit and implicit theoretical price and quantity indexes

	Implicit Malmquist Approach		Implicit Konüs Approach
3.56	$PI_M(x^1,x^0,p^1,p^0,y^1,y^0) = P_F \times \gamma_y^M$	3.72	$YI_K(x^1,x^0,p^1,p^0,y^1,y^0) = Y_F \times \gamma_y^K$
3.57	$R^1/R^0 = Y_M(x^1,x^0,y^1,y^0) \times P_F \times \gamma_y^M$	3.73	$R^1/R^0 = P_K(x^1,x^0,p^1,p^0) \times Y_F \times \gamma_y^K$
3.58	$Y_F = Y_M(x^1,x^0,y^1,y^0) \times \gamma_y^M$	3.74	$P_F = P_K(x^1,x^0,p^1,p^0) \times \gamma_y^K$
3.59	$WI_M(y^1,y^0,w^1,w^0,x^1,x^0) = W_F \times \gamma_x^M$	3.75	$XI_K(y^1,y^0,w^1,w^0,x^1,x^0) = X_F \times \gamma_x^K$
3.60	$C^1/C^0 = X_M(y^1,y^0,x^1,x^0) \times W_F \times \gamma_x^M$	3.76	$C^1/C^0 = W_K(y^1,y^0,w^1,w^0) \times X_F \times \gamma_x^K$
3.61	$X_F = X_M(y^1,y^0,x^1,x^0) \times \gamma_x^M$	3.77	$W_F = W_K(y^1,y^0,w^1,w^0) \times \gamma_x^K$
3.62	$\dfrac{PI_M(x^1,x^0,p^1,p^0,y^1,y^0)}{WI_M(y^1,y^0,w^1,w^0,x^1,x^0)} = \dfrac{P_F}{W_F} \times \gamma_{yx}^M$	3.78	$\dfrac{YI_K(x^1,x^0,p^1,p^0,y^1,y^0)}{XI_K(y^1,y^0,w^1,w^0,x^1,x^0)} = \dfrac{Y_F}{X_F} \times \gamma_{yx}^K$
3.63	$\dfrac{\Pi^1}{\Pi^0} = \dfrac{Y_M(x^1,x^0,y^1,y^0)}{X_M(y^1,y^0,x^1,x^0)} \times \dfrac{P_F}{W_F} \times \gamma_{yx}^M$	3.79	$\dfrac{\Pi^1}{\Pi^0} = \dfrac{P_K(x^1,x^0,p^1,p^0)}{W_K(y^1,y^0,w^1,w^0)} \times \dfrac{Y_F}{X_F} \times \gamma_{yx}^K$
3.64	$\dfrac{Y_F}{X_F} = \dfrac{Y_M(x^1,x^0,y^1,y^0)}{X_M(y^1,y^0,x^1,x^0)} \times \gamma_{yx}^M$	3.80	$\dfrac{P_F}{W_F} = \dfrac{P_K(x^1,x^0,p^1,p^0)}{W_K(y^1,y^0,w^1,w^0)} \times \gamma_{yx}^K$

Beneath the revenue change, cost change, and profitability change rows we exploit the ability of Fisher quantity and price indexes to satisfy the product test with the relevant value change to generate six separate relationships between Fisher indexes and their theoretical Malmquist and Konüs counterparts. Each of these relationships contains a gap variable that we argue is likely to be close to unity, making it likely that a Fisher index has magnitude close to that of its theoretical quantity or price counterpart. Moreover, each gap variable has a closed form expression, and can be calculated to quantify the gap.

We prefer the Malmquist measures of revenue change in expression (3.57), cost change in expression (3.60), and profitability change in expression (3.63) to the corresponding Konüs measures in expressions (3.73), (3.76), and (3.79). The Malmquist measures decompose quantity change Y_M and X_M and productivity change Y_M/X_M by economic driver, and they decompose price change P_F and W_F and price recovery change P_F/W_F by individual price, while the Konüs measures do just the opposite. The Konüs measures do, however, generate valuable relationships between Fisher and Konüs output price, input price, and price recovery indexes. Our preferred Malmquist choice corresponds to option (i) among the four options with which we began this section, while the Konüs choice corresponds to option (ii). The two hybrid options (iii) and (iv) generate less useful pairings of Y_M, X_F with P_F, W_K or Y_F, X_M with P_K, W_F.

3.4 PAIRING A THEORETICAL INDEX WITH AN EMPIRICAL INDEX

We are down to the third and final option for meeting the dual objective set forth in the introduction to this chapter, namely, the pairing of a theoretical index with an empirical index. The analysis of explicit and implicit theoretical indexes in Section 3.3.2 generated six such pairings, and we stated a preference for the three pairings that emerged from an analysis of implicit Malmquist price and price recovery indexes. These three pairings appeared in expressions (3.57), (3.60), and (3.63), and in the left side of Table 3.1. Each pairing includes a product test gap variable associated with a mix effect. Each gap variable is expressed in closed form as the geometric mean of a variable bounded above by unity and a variable bounded below by unity, and so we expect each gap variable to be approximately unity. The empirical question is whether the gap variables are close enough to unity to justify the pairings of our best theoretical and empirical indexes.

The hypotheses of interest are that the three product test gap variables do not differ significantly from unity, which we test by way of

$$H_{oy} : \gamma_y^M = (R^1/R^0)/[Y_M(x^1,x^0,y^1,y^0) \times P_F] = 1$$
$$H_{ox} : \gamma_x^M = (C^1/C^0)/[X_M(y^1,y^0,x^1,x^0) \times W_F] = 1$$
$$H_{oyx} : \gamma_{yx}^M = (\Pi^1/\Pi^0)/\{[Y_M(x^1,x^0,y^1,y^0)/X_M(y^1,y^0,x^1,x^0)] \times (P_F/W_F)\} = 1.$$

R^1/R^0 and C^1/C^0 are contained in the data, P_F and W_F are calculated from the data, and $Y_M(x^1,x^0,y^1,y^0)$ and $X_M(y^1,y^0,x^1,x^0)$ are estimated from the data. Since Fisher price and quantity indexes satisfy the product test with the relevant value change, these three hypotheses are equivalent to the hypotheses that $Y_F = Y_M(x^1,x^0,y^1,y^0)$, $X_F = X_M(y^1,y^0,x^1,x^0)$ and $Y_F/X_F = Y_M(x^1,x^0,y^1,y^0)/X_M(y^1,y^0,x^1,x^0) = M(x^1,x^0,y^1,y^0)$, or that $\gamma_y^M = 1$, $\gamma_x^M = 1$ and $\gamma_{yx}^M = 1$.

We provide empirical evidence (and a quotation) borrowed from Brea, Grifell-Tatjé, and Lovell (2011) bearing on the size of the three gaps. The evidence is drawn from a panel of US agriculture production covering 48 contiguous states and running from 1960 through 2004. The data include price and quantity indexes for three outputs (crops, livestock, and other products) and four inputs (land, labor, materials, and capital). We construct R^1/R^0, C^1/C^0 and Π^1/Π^0 directly from the data, we calculate P_F and W_F from the data, and we use linear programming techniques to estimate $Y_M(x^1,x^0,y^1,y^0)$, $X_M(y^1,y^0,x^1,x^0)$ and their ratio.[9]

The evidence summarized in Table 3.2 is based on 2,112 observations (48 states and 44 ratios of comparison period to base period variables). Column (2) examines the product test gap on the output side, using the ratio of observed revenue change to the product of an estimated Malmquist output quantity index and a calculated Fisher output price index. If this ratio does not differ from unity in a statistically significant way, we fail to reject the hypothesis that $Y_M(x^1,x^0,y^1,y^0)$ and P_F satisfy the product test, or equivalently that $Y_M(x^1, x^0, y^1, y^0) = Y_F$. Column (3) conducts the same exercise on the input side, and column (4) examines the overall product test gap, using the ratio of observed profitability change to the product of an estimated Malmquist productivity index and a calculated Fisher price recovery index. Hypothesis tests based on these two ratios are interpreted in the same way.

It is not possible to reject, at a 95% confidence level, either the hypothesis that $Y_M(x^1,x^0,y^1,y^0) = Y_F$ or the hypothesis that $X_M(y^1,y^0,x^1,x^0) = X_F$.

---

[9] The data are available at www.ers.usda.gov/data-products/agricultural-productivity-in-the-us.aspx.

Table 3.2 Statistical tests of the product test gap

	$\gamma_y^M = (R^1/R^0)/[Y_M(x^1,x^0,y^1,y^0) \times P_F]$	$\gamma_x^M = (C^1/C^0)/[X_M(y^1,y^0,x^1,x^0) \times W_F]$	$\gamma_{yx}^M = (\Pi^1/\Pi^0)/[M(x^1,x^0,y^1,y^0) \times (P_F/W_F)]$
Mean	1.0014	0.9987	1.0041
Standard Dev.	0.0501	0.0391	0.0616
Maximum	1.3175	1.2484	1.3461
Minimum	0.6072	0.8425	0.6160
Observations	2,112	2,112	2,112
95% Conf. Int.	[1.0035,0.9992]	[1.0004,0.9970]	[1.0058,1.0015]

However, it is possible to reject the hypothesis that $M(x^1, x^0, y^1, y^0) = Y_F/X_F$ at the same confidence level. From a statistical perspective, therefore, our evidence on the product test is mixed: we find that Malmquist quantity indexes satisfy the product test with Fisher price indexes, but a Malmquist productivity index does not satisfy the product test with a Fisher price recovery index. However, the mean product test gap is extremely small, barely 0.4%, probably far smaller than the calculation error (Fisher calls it "formula error") associated with the Fisher price recovery index and the estimation error associated with the Malmquist productivity index. In light of the importance we attach to our dual objective of decomposing a Malmquist productivity index by economic driver and decomposing a Fisher price recovery index by individual price change, we are willing to live with a 0.4% product test gap. Applying Fisher's unwillingness to require exact fulfillment of the circular test to the satisfaction of the product test in our context, we believe that "a necessary irreducible minimum of divergence from such fulfilment is entirely right and proper" (p. 271).

Figure 3.2 tracks annual means (across states) of profitability change constructed directly from the data and the product of an estimated Malmquist productivity index and a calculated Fisher price recovery index. The product of an estimated Malmquist productivity index and a calculated Fisher price recovery index tracks observed profitability change very closely, with slightly smaller amplitude.

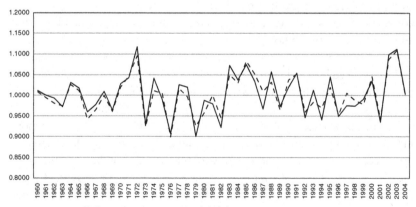

Solid line expresses Π^1/Π^0; Dashed line expresses $M(x^1, x^0, y^1, y^0) \times (P_F/W_F)$

Figure 3.2 Profitability change and the product of a Malmquist productivity change index and a Fisher price recovery index

3.5 CONCLUSIONS ON RATIO MODELS OF PROFITABILITY CHANGE

In Chapters 2 and 3 we have measured business financial performance with profitability, the ratio of revenue to cost. One virtue of profitability as a performance indicator is that it levels the playing field when comparing the financial performance of firms of varying size. In evaluating business financial performance it is important to distinguish the contribution of productivity change from that of changes in the prices the business pays and receives. This is the central message of Davis (1955) and Kendrick and Creamer.

Accordingly, the primary objective of Chapter 2 was to decompose profitability change into its productivity change and price recovery change components. We began by developing theoretical quantity and price indexes, and empirical quantity and price indexes, and we discussed the virtues of each. We used these indexes to develop theoretical productivity and price recovery indexes, and empirical productivity and price recovery indexes, and we discussed their virtues as well. We also discussed three special cases of profitability change that have appeared in the literature. In one case profitability is unchanged, in which case price recovery change provides a reciprocal measure of productivity change. In another, more restrictive, case profitability is not just unchanged, but unchanged at a value of unity, making profit unchanged at zero. In a third, intermediate, case profitability is unity in the base period and unrestricted in the comparison period, making profit zero in the base period and unrestricted in the comparison period; this case is considered in detail by Davis and Kendrick and Creamer, among others.

We also emphasized the distributional impacts of productivity change, and we showed how to identify winners and losers and how to quantify their gains and losses. The French writers associated with CERC place special emphasis on the distributional impacts of productivity change.

The primary objective of Chapter 3 is to extend Chapter 2 by decomposing productivity change into its economic drivers, and by decomposing price recovery change by individual variable. It turns out that decomposing price recovery change by individual variable requires an empirical price recovery index, such as the ratio of a Fisher output price index to a Fisher input price index. We obtain two productivity indexes that decompose by economic driver. Both theoretical Malmquist productivity indexes decompose by economic driver, although in different ways, and so does an empirical Fisher productivity index. The combination of empirical Fisher productivity and price recovery indexes is appealing because (i) the Fisher productivity index decomposes by economic driver, although we uncovered some problems with two such decompositions in Section 3.2.2, and (ii) the Fisher price recovery index decomposes by individual variable. An alternative combination of a theoretical Malmquist productivity index and an empirical Fisher price recovery index is also appealing, for the same two reasons, and despite the fact that this pair does not satisfy the product test. However, we have theoretical arguments, backed by explicit closed form expressions for the product test gap that can be calculated numerically, and supported by (one piece of) empirical evidence, that lead us to believe that the product test gap is likely to be small, and possibly no larger than the approximation error associated with (even superlative) empirical indexes and the estimation error resulting from having to estimate theoretical indexes. We conclude, pending additional empirical investigation, that change in business financial performance, as measured by profitability change, is best decomposed using either (i) the product of an estimated theoretical Malmquist productivity index and a calculated empirical Fisher price recovery index, or (ii) the product of Fisher productivity and price recovery indexes.

PART II

Productivity and Profit

4 Profit Change: Its Generation and Distribution

4.1 INTRODUCTION

Our objective in this chapter is to initiate a decomposition of profit change analogous to the decomposition of profitability change we initiated in Chapter 2. This chapter shares a core objective with Chapter 2, a desire to analyze the generation of change in business financial performance and an equally strong desire to analyze the distribution of the financial impacts of business growth or contraction. However, there are two major differences between the ratio analysis of profitability change in Chapters 2 and 3 and the difference analysis of profit change initiated in this chapter and continuing through Chapters 5 and 6. First, and obviously, business financial performance is assessed with different measuring rods. In Chapters 2 and 3, profitability change and its components were expressed as ratios, as pure numbers, while in Chapters 4 to 6 profit change and its components are expressed as differences, in monetary units. Second, and not at all obviously, the decomposition of profit change is more informative than the decomposition of profitability change, since there can be as many as four identifiable components of profit change, two relating to changes in quantities and two relating to changes in prices. Changes in quantities are not necessarily attributable entirely to productivity change, and changes in prices are not necessarily attributable exclusively to price recovery change. We provide a brief insight into the richness of the decomposition of profit change in Section 4.5, although we defer a thorough analysis of the decomposition to Chapter 5.

We discuss the *generation* of profit change by decomposing profit change into the sum of a quantity effect, which allows changes in quantities to influence profit while holding prices fixed, and a price effect, which allows changes in prices to influence profit while holding quantities fixed. We also decompose the quantity effect into a productivity effect and a second effect that allows changes in quantities to contribute to profit change even in the absence of productivity change. We defer to Chapter 5 a similar decomposition of the price effect into a price recovery effect and another effect. When discussing *distribution* we isolate the quantity effect, which is allocated via the price effect and profit change itself. Thus, the price effect plays two roles in the analysis: as the set of variables responsible for the impact of price change on profit change, and as a subset of variables receiving the financial impacts of quantity change. This dual focus on generation and distribution permeates the book, and is a direct reflection of the influence of the work of Davis (1955), Kendrick and Creamer (1961), and a host of French writers beginning in the 1960s. We review the literature on profit change and its decomposition in this chapter, and we develop an analytical framework within which to extend the decomposition in Chapters 5 and 6.

In Section 4.2 we review the rich and diverse literature concerned with the use of profit as a performance indicator, and as an objective of business. In Section 4.3 we initiate an empirical decomposition of profit change. This exercise is largely historical, and relies heavily on the work of Davis and Kendrick and Creamer, and also on subsequent work of those who were influenced by them. Terminology varies but, generally speaking, profit change is attributed to quantity change and price change. Whether or not quantity change can be attributed exclusively to productivity change depends on the assumptions underlying the analysis. In Section 4.3.1 relatively strong assumptions enable quantity change to be attributed exclusively to productivity change. In Section 4.3.2 somewhat weaker assumptions drive a wedge between the two, allowing quantity change to contribute to profit change even in the absence of productivity change. In Section 4.4 we analyze the distribution of the financial impacts of quantity change. As in Section 4.3, these impacts vary with the assumptions underlying the analysis. In Section 4.4.1 relatively strong assumptions lead to the distribution of the productivity effect, while in Section 4.4.2 somewhat weaker assumptions allow for choice in what is to be distributed. In Section 4.5 we provide a numerical illustration that highlights the structural similarities and differences between the relatively straightforward ratio-based approach to the analysis of profitability change we examined in

Chapters 2 and 3 and the more complex difference-based approach to profit change we consider in Chapters 4 to 6. This numerical illustration highlights the need for a more analytical approach to the generation and distribution of profit change than this chapter offers, and we develop such an approach in Chapter 5, where we introduce empirical indicators, difference analogues to the ratio-based empirical index numbers we used in Chapters 2 and 3.

4.2 EARLY RECOGNITION OF PROFIT AS A PERFORMANCE INDICATOR

Ever since Adam Smith noted the social consequences of the pursuit of profit, the economics literature has treated profit as a natural business objective, and consequently as a natural financial performance indicator. The business literature is less likely to think of profit as a "natural," or even the sole, objective of business, and has a large portfolio of financial performance indicators. Nonetheless, profit is one measuring rod common to both literatures.

Interest in profit change, its generation, and its distribution, has a long history. As a general rule, the authors we cite make it clear that, while they consider profit to be a useful business performance indicator, they do not necessarily consider profit as the (or even a) business objective to be maximized.

Scott (1950; 3ff) treats profit as a performance indicator, a measure of what he calls business efficiency, and he claims, carefully, that "in a competitive market, no adequate substitute seems to have been found for 'net profit' and its relation to various elements." He sees net profit as being generated by a combination of designing efficiency, acquiring efficiency, production efficiency, selling efficiency, and financial efficiency. Scott distinguishes net profit from gross profit, observing that much of gross profit can be absorbed by way of increased wages or decreased selling prices before reaching the net profit stage. Subsequently, net profit is distributed to shareholders and to retained earnings to increase the stock of productive assets. Scott's explanation for the distinction between gross and net profit anticipates our dual interest in prices as influences on financial performance and also as distributional indicators.

However, Scott adds an important qualification to the claim that net profit is an adequate indicator of business efficiency. He mentions market power, periods of scarcity and easy access to raw materials as potential sources of pricing power that would weaken the link between net profit and business efficiency. Davis cites Scott's qualification with approval, and motivates his development of productivity accounting with the observation that a period of inflation following World War II "has focused attention on the short-comings of money profits as a measure of the economic performance of a business enterprise." Davis sees productivity accounting as "a method for measuring the productivity of a business enterprise that is as useful in periods of rapidly changing as in periods of stable prices" (pp. 1–2).

Penrose (1959; 27) proposes a theory capable of explaining the growth of firms, and asserts that "the growth of firms can best be explained if we can assume that investment decisions are guided by opportunities to make money." She thus treats profit as the objective of the firm. However, firms do not seek profit to raise dividends of owners, or to raise wages of employees or payments to suppliers, or to lower product prices to customers, any more than circumstances dictate. Subject to circumstances, firms seek profit in order to increase retained earnings, which subsequently generate even more profit through expansion. Penrose concludes that, in the long term, profit and growth are synonymous expressions for the objective of the firm.

Kendrick and Creamer acknowledge the primacy of profit as a measure of management success, and they address the issue of the generation of profit change by asking, rhetorically, "why measure productivity when that ulti-mate measure, profit, is available from the usual accounting records? For one thing, other forces such as favorable shifts in demand, special purchas-ing economies, or financial arrangements may obscure the effect of below-average productivity gains in the short run" (pp. 6–7). There is more to profit change than productivity change, particularly in the short term. They emphasize this point with reference to interfirm and interplant comparisons published frequently at the time by the Organization for European Economic Cooperation in *Productivity Measurement Review.*

Kendrick (1984; 47, 58) takes a longer view when he notes that "the ultimate justification of productivity analysis in a free enterprise setting is its contribution to the understanding and promotion of productive efficiency in the profitable operation of the firm." The significance of productivity change for business financial performance grows as the time horizon expands. Nonetheless, Kendrick is well aware of the role of price change, noting that "[t]he connecting link between profitability [profit in our terminology] analysis and productivity analysis is the relative change of input prices and output prices."

Perrin (1975; 35, 38) offers a very strong commentary on the appropriate objective, and performance indicator, of a public firm. He claims that "la recherché du profit maximum ne pouvait constituer ni un objectif en soi, ni un critère satisfaisant de performance." Later he appears to extend his philosophy beyond the public sector by proposing "de substituer à la recherche du bénéfice comptable ... la maximisation du surplus, c'est-à-dire, la recherche de l'avantage commun à l'ensemble des parties prenantes de la coalition ... tandis que la maximisation du bénéfice ne vise que l'une d'entre elle."

Perrin follows a tradition promoted by CERC by proposing to broaden the maximand to include not just profit but also the returns to all direct stakeholders in the company's operations. The "surplus" Perrin advocates distributing has slightly varying interpretations, but generally speaking it corresponds to the quantity effect rather than the productivity effect, both of which are defined below.

Nickell (1995; ch. 1) takes a nuanced position, by distinguishing profit as a business objective from profit as a measure of business performance. He accepts that not all businesses seek to maximize profit, and he acknowledges that some businesses that do seek to maximize profit fail to do so, for a variety of reasons. Nonetheless, he takes profit as a "sensible" measure of business performance. Consistent with our analysis, he notes that profit varies both because quantities vary and because prices vary, and he emphasizes that price changes are not necessarily exogenous. Consistent with the concerns of Davis, he acknowledges the need to account for changing price levels when using profit as a performance indicator. Consistent with the observation of Kendrick, he notes that in the long term sustained good business financial performance is likely to be attributable more to strong productivity performance than to continued favorable price performance. Perhaps most interestingly, Nickell asks, rhetorically, "Performance from whose point of view?" His response distinguishes the shareholders' point of view from that of society, and represents a modern version of Scott's similar rhetorical question "Who wants to measure efficiency?"

We reiterate that we do not assume that firms seek to maximize profit, because our analysis does not rely on any specific business objective, and despite our acknowledgement that in a market economy firms need profit to survive and grow. We use profit as we use profitability, as a financial performance indicator. The use of profit to represent financial performance has certain advantages, as well as some disadvantages:

(i) The business community may be more comfortable with differences expressed in monetary units than with ratios, as Miller (1984) and others assert;

(ii) Profit is widely and regularly reported in the business and financial press, although its revenue and cost components are less widely reported, which impedes the calculation of profitability;

(iii) Profit is not independent of the size of the organization, which limits its value in a benchmarking exercise but provides one motive for normalizing profit, which we do when we analyze return on assets (ROA) in Chapter 8;

(iv) Profit (and profit change) can take on negative values, although this complicates a difference-based analysis far less than it complicates a ratio-based analysis (Davis discusses problems and possible solutions when base period profit is negative);

(v) Profit change decomposes into quantity and price effects that can be represented using empirical indicators that we introduce in Chapter 5;

(vi) Quantity and price effects each decompose further, using empirical indicators, which enriches the analytical framework and sheds additional light on the sources of profit change; and

(vii) Unlike profitability, profit itself is the centerpiece of much business financial ratio analysis, as we discuss in Chapter 8.

4.3 EMPIRICAL DECOMPOSITION OF PROFIT CHANGE

In this section we discuss the pioneering contributions of Davis and Kendrick and Creamer, and subsequent contributions of a few later writers, some of whom, such as Vincent, clearly were inspired by the pioneers, and others who seem to be unaware of the work of the pioneers.

We define profit π as the difference between the revenue generated by outputs and the cost of employing the inputs used to produce those outputs, where revenue $R = p^T y = \sum p_m y_m$ and cost $C = w^T x = \sum w_n x_n$. Because capital plays such a prominent role in the discussion, we emphasize that the Nth component of cost is the cost of capital, $w_N x_N = w_N K$, with w_N being the unit cost of capital and K the quantity of capital. Some writers, including Davis and Kendrick and Creamer, define the cost of capital narrowly as depreciation expense, while others, including Puiseux and Bernard (1965) and

Kendrick define it more broadly to include depreciation expense and interest expense. A more inclusive measure often used in regulatory proceedings is the sum of depreciation expense and the weighted average cost of capital (WACC), which incorporates the implicit cost of equity as well as the interest cost of debt. Regardless of how it is defined, however, the cost of capital is an expense, and like other expenses, it can be decomposed into its quantity and price components. However, the cost of capital is defined, there is no requirement that profit be zero.

Profit goes by a number of names and is treated in different ways. Davis calls it both gross (i.e., pre-tax) investor input and gross return on investment, Kendrick and Creamer call it investor input, Kendrick (1961) calls it capital compensation, Eldor and Sudit (1981) call it both capital input and capital return, the French writers call it "bénéfice", and Lawrence, Diewert, and Fox (2006) call it gross operating surplus. Whatever it is called, profit is a return, positive or negative, to investors who provide capital to the business. The important point is that profit is a measure of the *return* to capital, as distinct from the *cost* of capital. This distinction suggests the notation $R - C \equiv rK \gtrless 0$, and like other monetary values rK can be decomposed into a price component r, which Davis calls the gross rate of return on investment, and a quantity component K, the quantity of capital.

Two analytical approaches to the treatment of profit, and consequently to the decomposition of profit change, have developed in the literature. One approach, pioneered by Davis, adds the return to capital to cost and redefines profit as $\check{\pi} = R - (C + rK) = R - \check{C} \equiv 0$, with $\check{C} = \check{w}^T x = w_1 x_1 + \cdots + w_{N-1} x_{N-1} + (w_N + r)K$ and $\check{w}$ coincides with w apart from the final component. An alternative approach does not expense the return to capital, and is based on the original definition of profit $\pi = R - C \gtrless 0$. It is important to note that the two approaches use exactly the same information, but they allocate this information in different ways. For example, Davis includes depreciation expense in w_N, and includes interest expense and profit in r. We use Davis's term "investor input" to describe rK, whatever (in addition to profit) is included in r. Expensing investor input makes profit zero. In the alternative approach profit appears explicitly as the difference between revenue and cost, however defined. In the approach pioneered by Davis profit is renamed investor input (or return to capital or operating surplus), given a new notation rK, and relocated together with cost to form $\check{C} = \check{w}^T x$. However, although the two approaches use the same information, they do not generate the same results. We analyze the approach pioneered by Davis in Section 4.3.1 and the alternative approach in Section 4.3.2.[1]

4.3.1 Models with investor input or a similar device

Models with investor input define profit as $\tilde{\pi} = R - (C + rK) = R - \check{C} \equiv 0$, with the return to capital grouped with cost to form $\check{C}$. Because it makes little sense to expense the return to capital in the base period but not in the comparison period, we expense the return to capital in both periods. In this model revenue is exhausted, not by cost but by the sum of cost and the return to capital.

Adding the return to capital to cost, the change in profit from base period to comparison period is

$$0 = (p^{1T}y^1 - p^{0T}y^0) - [(w^{1T}x^1 + r^1 K_0^1) - (w^{0T}x^0 + r^0 K^0)], \qquad (4.1)$$

in which K_0^1 is deflated comparison period capital. Unlike other quantities, capital is expressed in monetary units, and so its comparison period nominal value K^1 can differ from its base period value K^0 due to both quantity change and price change. Consequently, its comparison period nominal value must be deflated, and we write real comparison period capital K_0^1.

Rearranging terms and using base period prices to weight quantity changes and comparison period quantities to weight price changes yields the following expression for profit change

$$\begin{aligned} 0 = {} & [p^{0T}(y^1 - y^0) - w^{0T}(x^1 - x^0) - r^0(K_0^1 - K^0)] \\ & + [y^{1T}(p^1 - p^0) - x^{1T}(w^1 - w^0) - K_0^1(r^1 - r^0)]. \end{aligned} \qquad (4.2)$$

The first term on the right side of expression (4.2) is the quantity effect, which shows the impact of quantity changes, and the second term is the price effect, which shows the impact of price changes. The quantity effect has Laspeyres form, with quantity changes weighted by base period prices (one of which is the base period rate of return on investment r^0), and the price

---

[1] Some French writers, to whom we refer below, expense profit without giving it a name in its new location and without assigning price and quantity components to it. Davis and Kendrick expense profit in an economically meaningful way, calling it gross return to capital with gross rate of return and capital components. In addition to its economic logic, this practice has the virtue of adding no new quantity variables to the analytical framework. Proponents of labor management might propose an alternative, in which profit is called gross return to labor, with gross rate of return and labor components. In this setting labor's income, or dividend, would be $D = (w_L L + \pi) = (w_L + r)L$. Such a framework is analytically similar to the Illyrian firm model of Ward (1958) and the producer cooperative model of Domar (1966). Grifell-Tatjé and Lovell (2004) analyze these two models of labor management, using a framework similar to that we develop in Chapters 4 to 6.

Table 4.1 Productivity change and its value with zero nominal profit

	Base Period	Comparison Period, Nominal	Comparison Period, Real
R	4,800.00	5,923.08	5,592.00
Y_L		1.165	
P_P		1.059	
C	3,932.25	4,546.46	4,455.84
rK	867.75	1,376.62	943.94
$\check{X}_L$		1.125	
$\check{W}_P$		1.097	
$\check{\pi} = R - \check{C}$	0.00	0.00	192.22
$\check{\Pi}$	1.000	1.000	1.036
$Y_L/\check{X}_L$			1.036

effect has Paasche form, with price changes weighted by comparison period quantities (one of which is deflated comparison period capital K_0^1). In the quantity effect change in capital is weighted twice, by the base period cost of capital w_N^0 and also by the base period rate of return on investment r^0.

The quantity effect measures the financial impact of changes in output and input quantities, but it has deeper economic significance. Table 4.1 is inspired by a similar table in Davis, and provides a small numerical illustration designed to provide an economic interpretation of the quantity effect. The data describe the performance of a hypothetical business in two periods. The table reports nominal revenue R, with R^1/R^0 being the product of a Laspeyres output quantity index Y_L and a Paasche output price index P_P and nominal cost plus investor input $\check{C}$, with $\check{C}^1/\check{C}^0$ being the product of a Laspeyres input quantity index $\check{X}_L = \check{w}^{0T}x^1/\check{w}^{0T}x^0$ (including capital) and a Paasche input price index $\check{W}_p = x^{1T}\check{w}^1/x^{1T}\check{w}^0$ (including the rate of return to capital as well as the cost of capital). It also reports nominal profit $\check{\pi} = R - \check{C}$, profitability $\check{\Pi} = R/\check{C}$, and productivity $Y_L/\check{X}_L$. Nominal data appear in base period (column (2)) and comparison period (column (3)). Columns (3) and (4) contain nominal and real comparison period data. Davis's practice of expensing investor input makes nominal profit $\check{\pi}$ zero and nominal profitability $\check{\Pi}$ unitary in both periods.[2]

---

[2] Tables 4.1 and 4.2 are based on the following disaggregate information. The business uses three inputs to produce two outputs. In the base period $p_1^0 = 16$, $p_2^0 = 20$, $y_1^0 = 150$, $y_2^0 = 120$ and $w_1^0 = 4$, $w_2^0 = 1.75$, $w_3^0 = 0.023$, $x_1^0 = 750$, $x_2^0 = 375$, $K^0 = 12,000$. In the comparison period

The product test is satisfied since $R^1/R^0 = P_P Y_L$ and $\check{C}^1/\check{C}^0 = \check{W}_P \check{X}_L$. Solving the first equality for Y_P and the second for $\check{X}_L$ and taking the ratio of the two yields $Y_L/\check{X}_L = [(R^1/P_P)/(\check{C}^1/\check{W}_P)]/(R^0/\check{C}^0) = (R^1/P_P)/(\check{C}^1/\check{W}_P)$ because base period profitability is unitary by construction. It follows that, when investor input is expensed, a productivity index can be expressed as the ratio of real comparison period revenue to real comparison period cost, inclusive of investor input. However, real comparison period profitability $\check{\Pi}_0^1$ is also defined as the ratio of real comparison period revenue to real comparison period cost, inclusive of investor input, and so $\check{\Pi}_0^1$ is the same productivity index. The fact that $(R^1/P_P)/(\check{C}^1/\check{W}_P)$ and $\check{\Pi}_0^1$ are equivalent productivity indexes repeats the analysis of Section 2.8 in Chapter 2, with $\check{C}$ and $\check{W}$ replacing C and W. In addition, the condition $R^1 = \check{C}^1$ generates $Y_L/\check{X}_L = \check{W}_P/P_P$ a dual productivity index analogous to the dual productivity index in Section 2.9 of Chapter 2.

The investor input practice makes nominal comparison period profit zero and nominal comparison period profitability unitary, but the practice does not constrain their real values. Real comparison period profit $\check{\pi}_0^1 = R_0^1 - \check{C}_0^1 = p^{0T}y^1 - w^{0T}x^1 - r^0 K_0^1$, and since real comparison period profitability $\check{\Pi}_0^1 = R_0^1/\check{C}_0^1$ is a productivity index, real comparison period profit can be expressed as $\check{\pi}_0^1 = (\check{\Pi}_0^1 - 1)\check{C}_0^1$. This leads us to call $\check{\pi}_0^1$ the productivity effect because it measures the monetary value of productivity change, with $\check{\pi}_0^1 \gtrless 0$ as $Y_L/\check{X}_L = \check{\Pi}_0^1 \gtrless 1$. Moreover, when investor input is expensed, the quantity effect in expression (4.2) simplifies to $\check{\pi}_0^1$, so that, under Davis's practice, the quantity effect collapses to a productivity effect. The interpretation of $\check{\Pi}_0^1$ and $\check{\pi}_0^1$ as a productivity index and the monetary value of productivity change respectively is one of Davis's many fundamental insights.

In Table 4.1 real comparison period profitability $\check{\Pi}_0^1 = 1.036$, which coincides with the comparison period productivity index $Y_L/\check{X}_L = 1.036$.

$p_1^1 = 16.69, p_2^1 = 21.5, y_1^1 = 173, y_2^1 = 142$ and $w_1^1 = 4.08, w_2^1 = 1.785, w_3^1 = 0.024, x_1^1 = 855$, $x_2^1 = 420$, $K^1 = 13{,}080$. Investor input is the product of $r^0 = 0.07231$ and $K^0 = 12{,}000$ in the base period and the product of $r^1 = 0.10546$ and $K_0^1 = 13{,}054$ in the comparison period. Cost is allocated proportionately to output quantities, so that $uc_1^0 = 14.56$, $uc_2^0 = 14.56$, $uc_1^1 = 14.47$, $uc_2^1 = 14.47$. Quantities and prices are aggregated using Laspeyres and Paasche indexes, respectively.

By either measure, productivity has increased between base and comparison periods by 3.6%. The monetary value of this productivity growth is $\check{\pi}_0^1 = 192.22$. Because nominal profit remains unchanged at zero, this productivity dividend is distributed to consumers, input suppliers, and suppliers of the investor input. We examine distributional issues in more detail in Section 4.4 and in Chapter 5.

This simple numerical example illustrates an important principle. If one has access to company financial statements and appropriate price indexes, and if one is comfortable expensing investor input, it is possible to measure productivity change and to assess its financial impact simply by calculating $\check{\Pi}_0^1$ and $\check{\pi}_0^1$. This simple yet elegant procedure is called "productivity accounting" by Davis. However, Davis cautions that "the difference between the given-year output and input re-valued to base-period prices will equal the total dollar value of the productivity change only when the base-period output/input ratio is one dollar or unity" (p. 7). The procedure outlined above is valid only when base period profitability is unitary, and this condition is achieved by expensing investor input. If investor input is not expensed, the procedure must be modified using strategies we develop in Section 4.3.2.

We now explore the explanations offered by Davis and subsequent writers for expensing investor input.

Davis (1955)

Using actual data from the X manufacturing company, Davis defines a productivity index as "the change in output value per dollar of input between given and base periods after price changes have been eliminated" (p. 8). This phrase is a verbal description of $\check{\Pi}_0^1 = R_0^1/\check{C}_0^1$. Davis then converts productivity change to a monetary value by means of $\check{\pi}_0^1 = (\check{\Pi}_0^1 - 1)\check{C}_0^1$.

As we have related, Davis imposes the condition that nominal profit be zero by introducing the concept of "investor input." Investors provide the business with financial capital, some of which is used to acquire physical capital. Conceptually, Davis defines investor input as follows: "Company X incurred a cost for the purchasing power tied up in these capital goods and in the inventories and other current assets required to operate the business. This cost could be thought of as the alternative uses or returns and satisfactions which had to be foregone" (p. 19). Later he describes investor input similarly as the cost of "forgoing of alternative uses of the funds invested in the company's operations" (p. 68). Davis clearly conceives of investor input as the opportunity cost of capital, as distinct from the unit cost of capital.

As a practical matter, however, Davis measures investor input residually as the difference between revenue and cost, the latter defined by Davis as payments to labor and management, for materials, supplies, and business services, and for depreciation of capital goods. Davis refers to this difference as "gross return on investment," which, like other monetary values, has quantity and price components. Davis defines the quantity component, investment, as "the total of the funds made available for use in the business, which would include not only original investment by stockholders and reinvestment of earnings made on behalf of the stockholders by the directors and long-term loans provided by bondholders but also the short-term credits advanced by suppliers of materials and by banks" (p. 20). The price component, the gross rate of return r, is the ratio of gross return on investment rK to the quantity component K.

Expensing investor input, or gross return on investment, as an opportunity cost, or as forgone returns, makes *nominal* profit zero in base and comparison periods. However, *real* comparison period profit is not zero unless prices do not change between base and comparison periods, because real comparison period values are obtained by deflating their nominal comparison period counterparts by their base period prices. With respect to investor input, Davis reckons that: "The problem at hand, however, was not just a measure of investor input alone but a measure at prices contemporary with those of all of the other inputs. The only tangible available 'price' which met this test was the rate of return earned in the base year" (p. 20).

Davis acknowledges arguments for and against the practice of expensing investor input. He allows that disregarding investor input, wholly or in part, is not incompatible with productivity accounting, and he ponders whether the decision to expense profit or not will have an appreciable impact on productivity measurement. He asserts that the impact "depends upon the importance of ... 'investor input,' and how it moves from year to year in relation to the total of all other input" (p. 69). And later, "[a]s a practical matter, then, it does not make very much difference whether productivity computations are based on total input excluding or including gross investor input, unless the investor input is both moving over time in a different direction than other input and is relatively important in relation to this input" (pp. 70–71).

Summarizing, Davis sets forth an economic *conception* of investor input as the opportunity cost of capital. He makes this concept operational with a *definition* of investor input as gross return on investment defined as the difference between revenue and cost (which includes depreciation and excludes interest expense). The practical challenge confronting Davis and subsequent writers is the extraction of a measure of capital investment from company financial statements or other records. All writers meet this challenge, albeit with varying degrees of sophistication.[3]

Kendrick and Creamer (1961)

Greatly influenced by Davis, Kendrick and Creamer follow essentially the same procedures. They depart from Davis only in being less interested in the conceptual foundations than in the operational details, and they devote considerable attention to the construction of a measure of capital from company accounts. They invoke the investor input concept, which they define residually as the difference between revenue and cost, and they expense investor input. They divide base period investor input by base period capital to obtain a rate of return. Applying this rate of return r^0 to comparison period real capital K_0^1 yields real comparison period investor input $r^0 K_0^1$.

Kendrick and Creamer summarize the procedure succinctly. "In the base period, the sum of the inputs in base-period prices, by design, equals the output in base-period prices. In the measured period, the difference, if any, between the sum of inputs in base-period prices and output in base-period prices is the productivity gain (or loss). The total productivity index is calculated by dividing measured-period output in base-period prices by measured-period inputs in base-period prices" (p. 44). This summary illustrates the proclivity of Kendrick and Creamer for expressing productivity change both in difference form as a real monetary value and in index number form as a ratio. These two forms coincide with Davis's two forms $\check{\pi}_0^1$ and $\check{\Pi}_0^1$.

Kendrick and Creamer have a clear conception of the two sources of profit change. "The absolute productivity gains, in conjunction with the net gains (or losses) of revenue owing to relative changes in prices received for outputs and in prices paid for inputs, can also be used to analyze changes

---

[3] Davis's definition of investor input coincides with the OECD definition of gross operating surplus: "Gross operating surplus is the surplus generated by operating activities after the labor factor input has been recompensed. It can be calculated from the value added at factor cost less the personnel costs. It is the balance available to the unit which allows it to recompense the providers of own funds and debt, to pay taxes and eventually to finance all or a part of its investment." (http://stats.oecd.org/glossary/detail.asp?ID=1178)

in profit from one period to the next" (p. 45). In our parlance, profit change is attributable to productivity change and price change, conditioned of course on the practice of expensing investor input.[4]

In an updated revision of Kendrick and Creamer, Kendrick (1984) devotes special care to the development of value, quantity, and price data for all variables, particularly for investor input. It is worth quoting Kendrick in some detail. "The APC Performance Measurement System includes as an input not only lease expense and the depreciation of fixed assets but also a return component (opportunity cost) that arises from forgoing that capital's alternative use. Thus, included in capital input is a factor that represents either a profit 'standard' for that entity or simply the actual base-period profit level for that entity. If the latter approach is used, the total base-period output value will equal the total input value (by definition) and there will be no residual. If a fixed 'standard' approach is taken to capital, then little expectation remains that the profit level specified will exactly equal the actual profit level in the base year. Thus, there will be a residual between output and input viewed as 'profit above (or below) standard', or 'economic' profit. In year two, there will be a residual regardless of approach. *The difference between these residuals represents the year-to-year change in profitability, and that becomes the number the rest of the exercise aims at explaining*" (pp. 61–62, emphasis added). Kendrick uses a numerical example, developed at the American Productivity Center, to illustrate the methodology. He reports $\breve{\Pi}^1 / \breve{\Pi}^0 = (Y/\breve{X}) \times (P/\breve{W})$ as we do in Chapters 2 and 3 (but without expensing investor input), and he also reports $\breve{\Pi}_0^1 = R_0^1/\breve{C}_0^1 = Y_L/\breve{X}_L$ as an index of productivity change, and $\breve{\pi}_0^1 = R_0^1 - \breve{C}_0^1 = (\breve{\Pi}_0^1 - 1)\breve{C}_0^1$ as a measure of the contribution of productivity change to profit change.

Kendrick and Creamer and Kendrick (1984) provide a number of case studies of real companies. These case studies address a range of data issues and illustrate alternative treatments of nominal profit. One case study in Kendrick and Creamer, repeated in Kendrick, analyzes a situation in which the base period rate of return is constructed as a three-year moving average

---

[4] The framework developed by Davis and Kendrick and Creamer is based on the gross output concept, and is designed to evaluate total productivity. Kendrick and Creamer modify the framework to accommodate the value added concept, which is appropriate for the evaluation of total factor productivity, and they compare the gross output and value added approaches in two case studies. Kendrick (1961; ch. 5) provides an empirical application of the value added framework to evaluate total factor productivity in the US private domestic economy in the first half of the twentieth century. Kendrick and Grossman (1980) repeat the exercise for various aggregate sectors of the US economy over various time periods.

starting at the base period. This definition of investor input leaves nominal profit nonzero, and so the procedures outlined above require modification, although neither Kendrick and Creamer nor Kendrick do so. We develop the required modification in Section 4.3.2.

Eldor and Sudit (1981) adopt a strict interpretation of the investor input concept, in which nominal revenue is exhausted by nominal cost and investor input. They apply this framework to "a major corporation." Their treatment of the capital input is worth quoting in detail. "Each individual capital equipment account was re-priced at base year prices, according to engineering estimates of the age distribution of surviving plant, by applying the appropriate capital plant price indexes. Consequently, all capital inputs were stated in terms of replacement costs at base year prices" (p. 608). In our notation this procedure converts nominal comparison period capital K^1 to real comparison period capital K_0^1, and applying the base period rate of return r^0 yields real comparison period return to capital $r^0 K_0^1$. They calculate a productivity index by means of $\check{\Pi}_0^1 = R_0^1 / \check{C}_0^1$, and they calculate the productivity gain as $\check{\pi}_0^1 = R_0^1 - \check{C}_0^1$.

Vincent (1965, 1968), Méraud (1966), and CERC (1969a)

These writers share a common objective of developing a measure of productivity change and analyzing its relation to profit change and the distribution of the surplus. Influenced by Kendrick, Vincent proposes a model in which nominal profit is zero, a situation he refers to as "accounting equilibrium." Vincent's reasoning differs from that of Davis and Kendrick and Creamer, who invoke the concept of investor input. Vincent (1965) adds bénéfice, the difference between revenue and cost, to cost to achieve accounting equilibrium. Subsequently Vincent (1968) notes the possibility "en principe" of dividing bénéfice into quantity and price components, but bénéfice remains an additional expense. Influenced by Vincent, Méraud begins by extending Vincent's analysis, after which he develops an alternative model. He adds bénéfice to cost, but without treating it as an additional expense. He considers bénéfice to be the remuneration of capital, and he decomposes this value into "le taux de profit (ou le 'prix' correspondent)" and "volume de capital," a practice he notes Vincent thinks "audacieuse." CERC also associates bénéfice with the provision of capital, and claims that it is possible, although unnecessary for the objective at hand, to decompose bénéfice into price and quantity components. Because Méraud offers the clearest exposition, we follow his analysis.[5]

It is not clear whether Méraud distinguishes the cost of capital from the rate of return to capital in his capital price. To avoid introducing new notation, and because it makes no difference analytically, we assume that he does. Thus, augmented operating cost remains $\check{C} = \check{w}^T x = w_1 x_1 + \cdots + w_{N-1} x_{N-1} + (w_N + r)K$, and $\check{\pi} = R - \check{C} \equiv 0$. Méraud writes a productivity index in Laspeyres form as

$$
\begin{aligned}
Y_L / \check{X}_L &= (p^{0T} y^1 / p^{0T} y^0) \, / \, (\check{w}^{0T} x^1 / \check{w}^{0T} x^0) \\
&= p^{0T} y^1 / \check{w}^{0T} x^1 \quad [\text{since } \check{\pi}^0 = 0] \\
&= R_0^1 / \check{C}_0^1 \\
&= \check{\Pi}_0^1,
\end{aligned}
\tag{4.3}
$$

which confirms that real comparison period profitability is a productivity index. Méraud next derives

$$
[(Y_L / \check{X}_L) - 1] = (p^{0T} y^1 - \check{w}^{0T} x^1) / \check{w}^{0T} x^1,
$$

which we rewrite as

$$
\check{w}^{0T} x^1 [(Y_L / \check{X}_L) - 1] = p^{0T} y^1 - \check{w}^{0T} x^1
$$

and again as

$$
\check{\pi}_0^1 = R_0^1 - \check{C}_0^1 = \check{C}_0^1 (\check{\Pi}_0^1 - 1),
\tag{4.4}
$$

which confirms that real comparison period profit is the monetary value of productivity change. All three authors obtain the same productivity index and the same measure of the monetary value of productivity change, although they devote less attention than Davis and Kendrick and Creamer to the empirical issues involved in constructing measures of r and K.

Summary

Subsequent writers have managed to add little value either to Davis's opportunity cost justification for introducing investor input or to his

---

[5] Méraud (1966) is a document circulated internally at CERC and published as an appendix to CERC (1969a).

derivation and economic interpretation of $\breve{\Pi}_0^1$ and $\breve{\pi}_0^1$. The main subsequent contribution comes from Vincent, who is the first to make it clear that the results are conditioned not just on accounting equilibrium, but also on the assumption that quantity indexes have Laspeyres form and price indexes have Paasche form, an assumption that is implicit in the writings of Davis and Kendrick and Creamer and explicit in the French contributions. We expand on Vincent's point in Chapter 5, where we show that alternative index number pairings generate different expressions for productivity change and its monetary impact, although these differences are minor.[6]

We return to expression (4.2), which is expressed in difference form with a Laspeyres/Paasche structure. We wish to analyze the relationship between $\breve{\Pi}_0^1$ and $\breve{\pi}_0^1$ a bit more rigorously. Davis derives $\breve{\pi}_0^1$ from $\breve{\Pi}_0^1$, simply by subtracting the denominator from the numerator of $\breve{\Pi}_0^1$. Here we begin at the other end, with $\breve{\pi}_0^1$, by writing the profit change decomposition expression (4.2) as

$$
\begin{aligned}
0 &= \breve{\pi}_0^1 + [y^{1T}(p^1 - p^0) - x^{1T}(\breve{w}^1 - \breve{w}^0)] \\
&= \breve{C}_0^1[(Y_L/\breve{X}_L) - 1] + [y^{1T}(p^1 - p^0) - x^{1T}(\breve{w}^1 - \breve{w}^0)] \\
&= \breve{C}_0^1(\breve{\Pi}_0^1 - 1) + [y^{1T}(p^1 - p^0) - x^{1T}(\breve{w}^1 - \breve{w}^0)],
\end{aligned} \tag{4.5}
$$

in which the quantity effect in expression (4.2) is redefined as $[p^{0T}(y^1 - y^0) - w^{0T}(x^1 - x^0) - r^0(K_0^1 - K^0)] = R_0^1 - \breve{C}_0^1 = \breve{\pi}_0^1$, real comparison period profit under accounting equilibrium. The second equality manipulates $\breve{\pi}_0^1$ to redefine real comparison period profit as the Laspeyres rate of productivity growth scaled by real comparison period cost. The final equality redefines real comparison period profit as real comparison period profitability scaled by real comparison period cost. It follows that $\breve{\pi}_0^1 = \breve{C}_0^1(\breve{\Pi}_0^1 - 1) \Leftrightarrow \breve{\Pi}_0^1 = 1 + (\breve{\pi}_0^1/\breve{C}_0^1)$, so that either one can be derived from the other. Expression (4.5) almost completes the relationship between $\breve{\Pi}_0^1$

---

[6] Davis and Kendrick and Creamer are aware of the Laspeyres/Paasche distinction. Davis (1955) discusses the "base period problem," and calculates different rates, and financial impacts, of productivity change, applying Laspeyres and Paasche quantity indexes to data from Company X. Kendrick and Creamer discuss the "weighting system" and the "index number problem," and they recommend that the base period be a "recent, relatively normal, high-level production year" in which "the profit rate is close to the average over one or more business cycles."

and $\check{\pi}_0^1$ initiated by Davis, "almost" because all three equalities can be rearranged to analyze the distribution of the productivity bonus $\check{C}_0^1(\check{\Pi}_0^1 - 1)$. We conduct the analysis in Section 4.4.1.

Summarizing, in a model with investor input or a similar device,

   (i) Real comparison period profitability $\check{\Pi}_0^1 = R_0^1/\check{C}_0^1$ is a productivity index, and $\check{\Pi}_0^1 - 1$ is the rate of productivity change. This is explicit throughout Davis; and

   (ii) Real comparison period profit $\check{\pi}_0^1 = \check{C}_0^1(\check{\Pi}_0^1 - 1)$ is the monetary value of productivity change. This also is explicit throughout Davis.

These results are conditioned on the incorporation of investor input, and also on the pairing of Laspeyres quantity indexes with Paasche price indexes. All the writers we discuss obtain $\check{\Pi}_0^1$ and $\check{\pi}_0^1$, and all attach the same interpretations to the two terms. Consequently, all would reach the same conclusions from the data in Table 4.1. However, if we consider alternative index number pairings, both analytical and numerical results are modified, as we show in Chapter 5.

4.3.2 Models without investor input

Recalling that $\pi^1 = r^1 K_0^1$ and $\pi^0 = r^0 K^0$, solving expression (4.2) for $r^1 K_0^1 - r^0 K^0$, and changing notation yields

$$\pi^1 - \pi^0 = [p^{0T}(y^1 - y^0) - w^{0T}(x^1 - x^0)] + [y^{1T}(p^1 - p^0) - x^{1T}(w^1 - w^0)],$$

$$(4.6)$$

which decomposes profit change into a quantity effect (the first term on the right side) and a price effect (the second term). The significance of the absence of investor input is that it drives a wedge between the quantity effect and the productivity effect, allowing quantity change to contribute to profit change even in the absence of productivity change. We identify the productivity change component of the quantity effect below.

Table 4.2 is designed to illustrate the distinction between the quantity effect and the productivity effect. Table 4.2 replicates Table 4.1, with the single exception that investor input does not appear, making nominal profit nonzero and nominal profitability non-unitary in the base period and the comparison period. However, this modification changes the storyline significantly.

Applying the entries in Table 4.2 to the profit change decomposition in expression (4.6) generates a nominal profit increase of 508.87, a positive

Table 4.2 Productivity change and its value with nonzero nominal profit

	Base Period	Comparison Period, Nominal	Comparison Period, Real
R	4,800.00	5,923.08	5,592.00
Y_L		1.165	
P_P		1.059	
C	3,932.25	4,546.46	4,455.84
X_L		1.133	
W_P		1.020	
π	867.75	1,376.62	1,136.16
Π	1.221	1.303	1.255
Y_L/X_L			1.028

quantity effect of 268.41 and a positive price effect of 240.46 (neither of which is reported in Table 4.2). In Table 4.2 real comparison period profit $\pi_0^1 = 1{,}136.16$ differs from the quantity effect and has no apparent interpretation as the monetary value of productivity change. In addition, real comparison period profitability $\Pi_0^1 = 1.255$ differs from the real comparison period productivity index $Y_L/X_L = [(R^1/P_P)/(C^1/W_P)]/(R^0/C^0) = 1.028$. It follows that, in the absence of investor input, Π_0^1 is no longer a productivity index and π_0^1 no longer measures the monetary contribution of productivity change to profit change.

We have already quoted Davis's warning that the simplicity of Table 4.1 is based on the practice of expensing investor input, and does not survive otherwise. Table 4.2 confirms Davis's warning, and signals the need for an expanded analytical framework that decomposes the quantity effect so as to isolate the productivity bonus. This expanded analytical framework has been developed over time by a number of writers, and it greatly enriches the analysis of the sources of profit change.

Méraud (1966) and CERC (1969a)

Méraud and CERC appear to lack a strongly held opinion concerning the need for accounting equilibrium. In Section 4.3.1 we examined their analysis with accounting equilibrium, and here we discuss their analysis without it.

Méraud explores the relationship between the quantity effect (which he calls "surplus" and CERC calls "surplus de productivité globale") and a

Laspeyres productivity index (which Méraud attributes to Vincent and calls "productivité globale des facteurs"). He derives

$$(Y_L/X_L) - 1 = \{[p^{0T}(y^1 - y^0) - w^{0T}(x^1 - x^0)] - \pi^0(Y_L - 1)\} / w^{0T}x^1,$$

which we rewrite as

$$p^{0T}(y^1 - y^0) - w^{0T}(x^1 - x^0) = w^{0T}x^1[(Y_L/X_L) - 1] + \pi^0(Y_L - 1), \quad (4.7)$$

which is Méraud's desired relationship between the surplus (the quantity effect on the left side) and the productivity index (Y_L/X_L on the right side). Expression (4.7) states that the quantity effect has two components, a component related to productivity change and another component. The first is indeed a productivity effect because (i) it is greater than, equal to, or less than zero according as the Laspeyres productivity index $Y_L/X_L \gtreqless 1$, and (ii) the rate of productivity change $[(Y_L/X_L) - 1]$ is converted to monetary units through scaling by real comparison period cost $w^{0T}x^1$. Méraud calls the second component "bénéfice × taux d'accroissement de l'indice de production." The second component makes no contribution to profit change if $Y_L = 1$, i.e., if the firm's size does not change as measured by Y_L. Alternatively, this effect makes no contribution to profit change if $\pi^0 = 0$. Thus, a sufficient, but not necessary, condition for the quantity effect to collapse to a productivity effect is that base period profit be zero. This condition can result from expense exhausting revenue, or, as in Section 4.3.1, from the practice of expensing investor input.

It is instructive to rewrite the second component on the right side of expression (4.7) as

$$\begin{aligned}\pi^0(Y_L - 1) &= [1 - (\Pi^0)^{-1}][p^{0T}(y^1 - y^0)] \\ &= (\pi^0/R^0)[p^{0T}(y^1 - y^0)],\end{aligned} \quad (4.8)$$

the product of the base period profit margin π^0/R^0 applied to a Laspeyres measure of output quantity change expressed in difference form. This formulation suggests a size interpretation, since it makes no contribution to profit change if the firm's size does not change in the sense that $p^{0T}(y^1 - y^0) = 0 \Leftrightarrow Y_L = 1$. However, it also suggests a margin interpretation, since it makes no contribution to profit change if the base period profit margin $\pi^0/R^0 = 0$. We refer to $\pi^0(Y_L - 1)$ as a (quantity) margin effect.

The margin effect is new, and significant. It drives a wedge between the quantity effect and the productivity effect. In Section 4.3.1 the practice of expensing investor input eliminates the margin effect, and the quantity effect coincides with a productivity effect. This simplification of the model makes the interpretation of $\breve{\varPi}_0^1$ and $\breve{\pi}_0^1$ relatively straightforward in Table 4.1. In Section 4.3.2 the absence of an investor input introduces a margin effect, which enriches the analysis of the sources of profit change, although it temporarily complicates the search for a productivity index and its monetary value in Table 4.2.

Kurosawa (1975, 1991)

In Section 3.2.1 of Chapter 3 we provided a critical evaluation of Kurosawa's "relative value system" for decomposing *profitability* change. Here we consider Kurosawa's "absolute value system," which decomposes *profit* change, initially into a quantity effect ("total effect of the productivity change") and a price effect ("effect of relative price") as in expression (4.6). Kurosawa continues by decomposing the quantity effect as follows

$$
\begin{aligned}
p^{0T}(y^1 &- y^0) - w^{0T}(x^1 - x^0) \\
&= (p^{0T}y^1 - \varPi^0 w^{0T}x^1) + [(\varPi^0 w^{0T}x^1 - p^{0T}y^0) - (w^{0T}x^1 - w^{0T}x^0)],
\end{aligned} \tag{4.9}
$$

in which $\varPi^0$ is base period profitability ("rentability"). Kurosawa calls the first term on the right side of expression (4.9) the "effect of technical progress," and the second term the "effect of the scale of production." If $\varPi^0 = 1$, the second term disappears and the first term simplifies. If $\varPi^0 \neq 1$, matters are more complicated.

Kurosawa interprets the first term as follows: "$\varPi^0$ indicates productivity at the base year. Accordingly, the term $\varPi^0 w^{0T}x^1$ indicates the output volume that should be generated by real input at the comparative year when assuming that productivity remains the same as at the base year. Therefore, its difference from the real output volume $p^{0T}y^1$ at the comparative year will indicate the increase in real net output value caused by improvement of productivity proper, or the effect of technical progress" (p. 163). Despite its appearance, the expression actually has a straightforward economic interpretation, since

$$
p^{0T}y^1 - \varPi^0 w^{0T}x^1 = p^{0T}y^1[1 - (Y_L/X_L)^{-1}], \tag{4.10}
$$

which is a productivity effect, for the same two reasons that the first term on the right side of Méraud's expression (4.7) is a productivity effect, although the two productivity effects differ.

Kurosawa interprets the second term as a scale effect because "the term $\varPi^0 w^{0T}x^1$, which indicates the gross effects of scale, represents the output volume that should be generated by the real input volume at the comparative year under the assumption that the productivity was identical to that at the base year" (p. 164). Kurosawa rewrites the second term as the first equality below

$$[\Pi^0 w^{0T} x^1 - p^{0T} y^0] - [w^{0T} x^1 - w^{0T} x^0] = w^{0T}(x^1 - x^0)(\Pi^0 - 1)$$
$$= \pi^0(X_L - 1), \tag{4.11}$$

and we have added the second equality. This effect is also a margin effect, for the same reasons that we have interpreted Méraud's second term as a margin effect, although its structure lends support to Kurosawa's "scale of production" characterization and his subsequent (1991; 308) "quantitative expansion of input resources" interpretation. Kurosawa's margin effect also differs from Méraud's, and it can be rewritten as

$$\pi^0(X_L - 1) = (\pi^0/C^0)[w^{0T}(x^1 - x^0)], \tag{4.12}$$

the product of the base period profit margin π^0/C^0 applied to a Laspeyres measure of input quantity change expressed in difference form. Like expression (4.8), this expression suggests both size and margin interpretations, and we refer to $\pi^0(X_L - 1)$ as a (quantity) margin effect. The margin effects in expressions (4.8) and (4.12) have similar structure but different orientation.

Substituting expressions (4.10) and (4.11) into expression (4.9) yields

$$p^{0T}(y^1 - y^0) - w^{0T}(x^1 - x^0) = p^{0T} y^1 [1 - (Y_L/X_L)^{-1}] + \pi^0(X_L - 1), \tag{4.13}$$

which decomposes the quantity effect into a productivity effect and a margin effect. Summarizing, although Kurosawa made no progress in decomposing the productivity change component of profitability change in Chapter 3, he has considerably more success decomposing the more complex quantity effect component of profit change here. Expression (4.13) provides an economically plausible decomposition of the quantity effect in the absence of investor input, although both components of expression (4.13) differ from the corresponding components of expression (4.7).

Miller (1984)

Miller's work has been influential, partly for its catchy title and partly for its distinguished placement. Whereas many writers move back and forth between profit ratios and profit differences, Miller works exclusively with profit differences, largely because "the APC approach suffers from the fact that its results are developed through indices and ratios rather than through common financial terms and relationships. Consequently ... managers ... may have difficulty understanding and accepting its findings" (p. 146).

In Miller's analytical framework profit change is defined not as the difference between comparison period profit and base period profit $\pi^1 - \pi^0$, but rather as the difference between comparison period profit and profit *anticipated* in the comparison period $\pi^1 - \pi^{1A}$. Anticipated profit $\pi^{1A} = (\pi^0/R^0)R^1$, the base period profit margin π^0/R^0 applied to nominal comparison period revenue R^1. "The profit anticipated at the base period's margin constitutes a standard that is used to judge how well income has grown" (p. 147). Profit change becomes

$$\begin{aligned}
\pi^1 - \pi^{1A} &= R^1[(\pi^1/R^1) - (\pi^0/R^0)] \\
&= \pi^1 - (\pi^0/R^0)R^1 \\
&= C^1[(\Pi^1/\Pi^0) - 1].
\end{aligned} \qquad (4.14)$$

The presumed objective of Miller's manager is to earn sufficient profit in the comparison period to meet or exceed the target profit π^{1A}. This objective can be met through an increase in revenue or an increase in the profit margin or some combination of the two. Our objective is different: to decompose the deviation between actual and anticipated comparison period profit, using a strategy similar to that we use to decompose $\pi^1 - \pi^0$. To that end, we have added the third equality, which links Miller's profit change model with the APC model he denigrates.

Miller measures the contribution of productivity change to profit change by deflating all comparison period values in the first equality in expression (4.14). This procedure strips profit change of the impact of price changes. The contribution of productivity change to profit change is given by

$$\begin{aligned}
\text{productivity effect} &= R_0^1[(\pi_0^1/R_0^1) - (\pi^0/R^0)] \\
&= w^{0T}x^1[(Y_L/X_L) - 1].
\end{aligned} \qquad (4.15)$$

Miller defines the productivity effect as the first equality in expression (4.15), in which deflated margin change is applied to deflated comparison period revenue, thereby stripping $\pi^1 - \pi^{1A}$ of the impact of price changes. We derive the second equality from Miller's definition to show that Miller's framework generates a productivity effect identical to that of Méraud and CERC in expression (4.7), but different from that of Kurosawa in expression (4.13).

Although Miller's analysis is based on the notion of a profit margin π/R, his analysis does not contain a margin effect $\pi^0(Y_L - 1) = (\pi^0/R^0)[p^{0T}(y^1 - y^0)]$.

Miller measures the contribution of price change to profit change by comparing "the revenue generated by unit sales price changes" with "the dollars generated by inflation in labor rates, energy prices, and so forth" in an effort to "calculate the efficiency with which sales price increases recover the effects of inflation and contribute to profits" (p. 150). The contribution of price change to profit change is evaluated by netting out the impact of productivity change (the first equality in expression (4.15)) from profit change (the first equality in expression (4.14)), leaving

$$\text{price effect} = (R^1 - R_0^1) \times \left[\{[(R^1 - R_0^1) - (C^1 - C_0^1)]/(R^1 - R_0^1)\} - \pi^0/R^0\right]$$
$$= [(R^1 - R_0^1)/\Pi^0] - (C^1 - C_0^1). \tag{4.16}$$

Once again, Miller defines the contribution of price change to profit change as the first equality, and goes no further. The first term in the first equality is what Miller calls price-generated comparison period revenue (the difference between nominal and real comparison period revenues), and measures the contribution of output price changes to comparison period revenue. The second term is the difference between the price-generated comparison period margin (the difference between nominal and real comparison period margins) and the base period margin.

The second equality in expression (4.16) is ours, and shows that Miller's price effect is almost the difference between price generated comparison period revenue and price generated comparison period cost, "almost" because price-generated comparison period revenue is scaled by $1/\Pi^0$. Miller does not assume that $\Pi^0 = 1$, but if $\Pi^0 = 1$, Miller's price effect simplifies to the Paasche price effect in expression (4.6). Thus, $\Pi^0 = 1$ is a sufficient (but not necessary) condition for equality between Miller's price effect and a Paasche price effect, and hence for $\pi^{1A} = \pi^0$. It follows that Miller's analysis adds value only if $\Pi^0 \neq 1$, in which case Miller's expression for the contribution of price change to profit change does not coincide with a Paasche price effect. This is because Miller's conception of profit change differs from $\pi^1 - \pi^0$.

Combining expressions (4.15) and (4.16), Miller's decomposition of profit change becomes

$$\pi^1 - \pi^{1A} = w^{0T}x^1[(Y_L/X_L) - 1] + [(R^1 - R_0^1)(C^0/R^0) - (C^1 - C_0^1)], \tag{4.17}$$

which the title of his paper describes as "profitability = productivity + price recovery". The first term on the right side captures the contribution of productivity change and the second reflects the contribution of price change. These are the two sources of $\pi^1 - \pi^{1A}$; Miller has no concept of a quantity effect, and hence no concept of a margin effect, even though his analysis is based on the concept of maintaining the base period margin.[7]

Genescà and Grifell-Tatjé (1992) explore the relationship between the conventional notion of profit change and Miller's by writing

$$\pi^1 - \pi^0 = (\pi^0/R^0)(R^1 - R^0) + R^1[(\pi^1/R^1) - (\pi^0/R^0)]$$
$$= \pi^0[(R^1/R^0) - 1] + (\pi^1 - \pi^{1A}).$$

$$(4.18)$$

The first equality in expression (4.18) redefines conventional profit change as the sum of revenue change weighted by the base period profit margin and profit margin change weighted by comparison period revenue. The second equality rearranges terms to identify the difference between Miller's notion of profit change and the conventional notion as $\pi^{1A} - \pi^0 = \pi^0[(R^1/R^0) - 1]$, which looks very much like the margin effect in expression (4.7); the difference vanishes if either $\pi^0 = 0$ or if the firm's size does not change as measured by R^1/R^0. In all other cases Miller decomposes a new notion of profit change into a conventional productivity effect and a new price effect.[8]

Genescà and Grifell-Tatjé (1992)

We noted in Section 2.6 of Chapter 2 that prices can be distorted, for example, by cross-subsidies, market power, and regulation, and that

---

[7] Rao (2000, 2002) provides simple spreadsheet illustrations of Miller's profit change model, defining profit change as $\pi^1 - \pi^{1A}$ with $\pi^{1A} \neq \pi^0$, and Rao (2006) has an interesting empirical application to a municipal water utility over five periods, complete with several "what if" exercises. Miller and Rao (1989) analyze data from an anonymous firm in an effort to compare Miller's model of profit change with the ratio model of profitability change we analyzed in Chapter 3. In addition to the obvious differences between profitability ratios and profit differences, and between π^0 and π^{1A}, they trace the different results obtained from the two models to different methods of deflation, cumulative and period-to-period, which disappear when analysis is based on just two adjacent time periods. Hansen, Mowen, and Hammer (1992) use a simple numerical example to compare the performance of these two models, a similar model proposed by Banker, Datar, and Kaplan (1989), and a model of their own. They attribute the superiority of their model to its use of comparison, rather than base, period prices in the measurement of real quantities and productivity change. We discuss more substantive differences between models of profitability change and profit change in Chapter 5.

[8] Fisher (1990) proposes an alternative definition of "goal" profit based on a target after-tax return on equity. He embeds goal profit in a profitability model we considered in Chapters 2 and 3, and he expenses goal profit. This prevents $\Pi \equiv 1$ unless $\pi = \pi^A$.

distorted prices distort productivity effects, and hence productivity indexes. Genescà and Grifell-Tatjé propose a strategy for dealing with distorted prices that is similar to that of Caves, Christensen, and Swanson (1980). To see their strategy, rewrite the quantity effect decomposition in expression (4.7) as

$$p^{0T}(y^1 - y^0) - w^{0T}(x^1 - x^0) = (Y_L w^{0T} x^0 - w^{0T} x^1) + \pi^0 (Y_L - 1).$$

In the case of a single output, $Y_L = y^1 / y^0$ and the quantity effect becomes

$$p^0(y^1 - y^0) - w^{0T}(x^1 - x^0) = (c^0 y^1 - w^{0T} x^1) + (p^0 - c^0)(y^1 - y^0), \quad (4.19)$$

in which $c^0 = w^{0T} x^0 / y^0$, the base period unit cost. The productivity effect is real comparison period profit, with revenue deflation achieved with c^0 rather than p^0. The margin effect is output quantity change weighted by the base period margin of price above (or below) unit cost. With $M = 1$ no cost allocation is required.

Now consider the multiple output case, in which cost allocation is required. Cost allocation is a contentious issue that Shubik (2011) calls an open problem in economic theory and accounting. Allocating total cost requires creating a unit cost vector c satisfying $c^T y = w^T x$, so that all cost is assigned to outputs, and $c^T y \neq p^T y$ is likely without the investor input convention. The cost variance analysis we introduce in Section 7.2 of Chapter 7 provides a popular cost allocation procedure. Allocating variable cost is less challenging, and requires a unit variable cost vector c_v satisfying $c_v^T y = w_v^T x_v$. Estache and Grifell-Tatjé (2013) provide an example of the latter.[9]

Returning to expression (4.19) and replacing output prices with allocated unit costs in Y_L makes $c^{0T} y^0 = w^{0T} x^0$ and generates the quantity effect decomposition

$$
\begin{aligned}
p^{0T}(y^1 - y^0) - w^{0T}(x^1 - x^0) &= [c^{0T} y^1 - w^{0T} x^1] + [(p^0 - c^0)^T (y^1 - y^0)] \\
&= c^{0T}(y^1 - y^0) - w^{0T}(x^1 - x^0) + [(p^0 - c^0)^T (y^1 - y^0)] \\
&= w^{0T} x^1 [(Y_L^c / X_L) - 1] + [(p^0 - c^0)^T (y^1 - y^0)],
\end{aligned}
$$

$$(4.20)$$

in which $c = (c_1, \ldots, c_M)$, $c_m = $ (expenditure on output m)$/y_m$, $\sum c_m y_m = C$, and $Y_L^c = c^{0T} y^1 / c^{0T} y^0$ is a Laspeyres output quantity index with distorted output

[9] Cost allocation may be an "open problem in economic theory and accounting," but Johnson (1972) describes in great detail its use for internal management control at a mid-nineteenth century American cotton textile mill.

prices replaced by allocated unit costs. The decomposition is identical to that in expression (4.7), apart from the replacement of distorted base period output prices with base period allocated unit costs. This model requires cost allocation, but it has three virtues: (i) it purges the productivity effect, and the productivity index, of distorted prices; (ii) it allows distorted prices to influence the margin effect; and (iii) the first equality decomposes profit change without converting differences to a form that uses index numbers. The third virtue is of great value in Chapter 6, in which it facilitates decomposition of the productivity effect.

Genescà and Grifell-Tatjé also apply this strategy to Miller's profit change decomposition in expression (4.17), which, following the procedures we use above, we rewrite as

$$
\begin{aligned}
\pi^1 - \pi^{1A} &= (Y_L w^{0T} x^0 - w^{0T} x^1) + [(R^1/R^0) w^{0T} x^0 - Y_L w^{0T} x^0 - (w^{1T} x^1 - w^{0T} x^1)] \\
&= [c^{0T} y^1 - w^{0T} x^1] + [(R^1/R^0) w^{0T} x^0 - c^{0T} y^1 - (w^{1T} x^1 - w^{0T} x^1)] \\
&= w^{0T} x^1 [(Y_L^c/X_L) - 1] + [(R^1/R^0) w^{0T} x^0 - c^{0T} y^1 - (w^{1T} x^1 - w^{0T} x^1)].
\end{aligned}
$$
(4.21)

The first term on the right side is the modified productivity effect (which coincides with that in expression (4.20)), and the second reflects the impact of Miller's conception of price change.

Summary

The absence of an investor input or similar device that would absorb the difference between nominal revenue and nominal cost drives a wedge between the quantity effect and a productivity effect. Méraud and CERC decompose a quantity effect of Laspeyres form, as do Kurosawa, Miller, and Genescà and Grifell-Tatjé. Despite the structural similarity, the decompositions differ. The Méraud/CERC and Miller decompositions use real comparison period *cost* to convert a Laspeyres productivity index to a monetary value, whereas in Kurosawa's decomposition conversion is achieved with real comparison period *revenue*. The Genescà and Grifell-Tatjé decomposition uses real comparison period cost to convert a modified Laspeyres productivity index to a monetary value. The margin effect in the Méraud/CERC decomposition uses a Laspeyres measure of *output* quantity change to scale a revenue-based profit margin, whereas Kurosawa uses a Laspeyres measure of *input* quantity change to scale a cost-based profit margin. Genescà and Grifell-Tatjé follow the Méraud/CERC approach, apart from their replacement of Y_L with Y_L^c to measure size change in the productivity effect and their use of c^0 in the margin effect. Miller has no margin effect, and his price effect is unique because his definition of profit change is unique.

In Section 4.3.1 all writers define productivity change and its contribution to profit change the same way, so there is no need to compare their findings using the data in Table 4.1. All get the same answers. The situation is different in Section 4.3.2. Writers define the contribution of productivity change and its contribution to profit change differently. Consequently, it is worth comparing their findings using the data in Table 4.2. Calculated productivity effects vary from 118.68 (Genescà and Grifell-Tatjé) to 125.23 (Méraud/CERC) to 152.87 (Kurosawa). Since all three use the same quantity effect, their margin effects vary by offsetting magnitudes. Miller's model has no quantity effect, and he defines profit change differently, but his productivity effect coincides, in orientation and magnitude, with that of Méraud/CERC. We explore the causes and nature of these and other differences in Chapter 5.

4.4 DISTRIBUTION OF THE FINANCIAL IMPACTS OF QUANTITY CHANGE

Davis (1947) devotes a chapter to "sharing" the benefits of increased "productive efficiency." He identifies six possible participants in the distribution exercise: consumers, employees, suppliers, "enterprisers and investors," the business itself, and the government. He discusses prevailing views on "the disposition which *should* be made of the gains from productive efficiency in the interests of continued economic progress" (p. 97, emphasis added). He discusses measurement problems, and comments on empirical procedures proposed by Mills (1937) and Bell (1940). Finally, he mentions planned industry studies of the distribution exercise.

Davis (1955) implements the planned studies, but at Company X rather than at the industry level. In this section we evaluate his analytical model and those of several subsequent writers. We divide this section along the same lines as we divided Section 4.3. In Section 4.4.1 we consider models with an investor input or a similar device. In these models there is no distinction between the quantity effect and the productivity effect, so with one important exception it is the monetary impact of productivity change that is to be distributed. Davis, Kendrick, and others associated with the AT&T framework appear in this section. In Section 4.4.2 we consider models that do not expense investor input. In these models the quantity effect contains a productivity effect and a margin effect, allowing for choice in what is to be distributed. We discuss early French analyses in this section. Subsequent contributions add value not by extending the analytical framework, but by providing empirical applications of the technique. Although the framework was developed for use in public agencies, many of the subsequent empirical applications are to private firms and to aggregate sectors of the French economy.

4.4.1 Models with investor input or a similar device

This section shares the practice of expensing investor input with Section 4.3.1, and changes the emphasis from productivity to distribution.

Davis (1955)

Davis's practice of expensing investor input ensures that the quantity effect coincides with a productivity effect, and the productivity bonus to be distributed is given in expression (4.4) by $\check{\pi}_0^1 = R_0^1 - \check{C}_0^1 = \check{C}_0^1(\check{\Pi}_0^1 - 1)$. This bonus is distributed by means of

$$\check{\pi}_0^1 = -y^{1T}(p^1 - p^0) + x^{1T}(w^1 - w^0) + K_0^1(r^1 - r^0). \tag{4.22}$$

The right side of expression (4.22) is the negative of the price effect in expression (4.5). It identifies three groups of recipients of the fruits of productivity change: consumers, suppliers of inputs (including capital), and investors. Productivity growth, for example, allows the firm to reduce (or absorb reduced) output prices that benefit consumers, to increase (or absorb increased) input prices that benefit suppliers of inputs, and to earn a higher rate of return on its real capital investment, which benefits investors. (Of course not all output prices have to decline, not all input prices have to increase, and rates of return can decline as well as increase.) In particular, $K_0^1(r^1 - r^0)$ is the difference between nominal and real investor income in the comparison period. Investor income $r^0 K_0^1$ consists of taxes and net investor income, which is allocated to dividends and interest, debt retirement, retained earnings, and so on. In his application to Company X Davis allocates the productivity bonus in value terms and in terms of shares of the bonus being distributed.

Kendrick (1984) largely ignores the distribution of the fruits of productivity change in his analysis of productivity measurement. However, one of his case studies is particularly relevant because it illustrates the inspiration of Davis, by focusing on the distribution of the financial impacts of productivity change as embodied in the price effect. In this case study he expresses the productivity bonus to be distributed via the price effect as $\check{\pi}_0^1$ in expression (4.22). He distributes this surplus, in both monetary and percent change terms, to customers, suppliers of inputs (including capital), employees, stockholders as a higher return on investment, and the federal government as taxes on the higher return.

Eldor and Sudit (1981)

Eldor and Sudit employ the AT&T approach we summarized in Chapter 1. In so doing they reorient the distributional framework of Davis toward a management information framework. The analytical structure is similar, but the orientation is different. Eldor and Sudit seek to establish "the precise relationship between total factor productivity performance and key aspects of financial performance" (p. 605). Using data from "a major corporation," they obtain numerical expressions for the productivity bonus $\check{\pi}_0^1 = R_0^1 - \check{C}_0^1$ and the productivity index $\check{\Pi}_0^1 = R_0^1 / \check{C}_0^1$. From this point their analysis deviates from that of Davis.

Davis distributes the productivity bonus; Eldor and Sudit do not. They augment the productivity bonus with what they call "capital input increase" and Chaudry, Burnside, and Eldor (1985) more usefully call "earnings on capital expansion" (on the assumption that $K_0^1 - K^0 > 0$). Their distribution expression becomes

$$\check{\pi}_0^1 + r^0(K_0^1 - K^0) = -y^{1T}(p^1 - p^0) + x^{1T}(w^1 - w^0) + (r^1 K_0^1 - r^0 K^0).$$

$$(4.23)$$

Distribution of the augmented bonus to consumers and suppliers of inputs (including capital) is similar to that in expression (4.22). In Davis's model the final recipient of the productivity bonus is investors, whose income changes by means of a change in the rate of return to capital (but not the quantity of capital, which is fixed at its real comparison period value). In the Eldor and Sudit model the final recipient of the augmented bonus is also investors, whose income changes by means of a change in investor input (which allows both the rate of return to capital and the real quantity of capital to change). This final term on the right side of expression (4.23) is profit change.[10]

---

[10] Lawrence et al. (2006) distribute the augmented productivity bonus in expression (4.23) of Telstra, Australia's largest telecommunications company, during a period when Telstra was moving from a government-owned monopoly to a government-owned company facing its first competition. All participants, labor, consumers, and Telstra's owners, shared in the augmented bonus.

Expression (4.23) distributes an augmented bonus to consumers, input suppliers, and investors. This model of distribution differs only marginally from that of Davis. However, Eldor and Sudit are interested primarily in what might be called a managerial control issue, that of quantifying the sources of profit change. They identify "operating factors" that generally augment profit, and "inflationary factors" that, despite their name, affect profit in either direction. Profit change is obtained by rearranging expression (4.23) to obtain

$$r^1 K_0^1 - r^0 K^0 = \check{\pi}_0^1 + r^0(K_0^1 - K^0) + y^{1T}(p^1 - p^0) - x^{1T}(w^1 - w^0). \quad (4.24)$$

Eldor and Sudit interpret this expression as a framework for quantifying the *sources* of profit change, which are operating factors (the productivity bonus and the real value of capital change) and inflationary factors (output and input price changes). This expression establishes the "precise relationship" that is the objective of the study, and reinforces the operational importance, so eloquently stressed by Kendrick and reiterated by Eldor and Sudit, of separating prices from quantities in value data.[11]

Eldor and Sudit call their analytical framework "productivity-based financial net income analysis." Subsequently, Chaudry (1982) and Chaudry et al. (1985) modify the nomenclature to "net income and productivity analysis (NIPA)" and expand the analytical framework to incorporate additional income augmenting factors and income absorbing factors. The framework is similar in structure, but not in orientation, to those of Méraud, CERC, and other French writers who augment the productivity dividend with operating factors they call "héritages." We discuss these models in Section 4.4.2.

Summary

The model developed and implemented by Davis, and subsequently implemented by Kendrick, is a pure distribution model in which the productivity bonus is absorbed by consumers, input suppliers, and investors, by way of changes in prices paid, prices received, and rates of return. Eldor and Sudit adapt the model to serve their own objective of quantifying the sources of

---

[11] Since $r^1 K_0^1 - r^0 K^0 = \pi^1 - \pi^0$, expression (4.22) can be interpreted as providing an alternative decomposition of profit change in a model without investor input. The Paasche price effect is the same as in equation (4.6), but the Laspeyres quantity effect has a different productivity effect unless $\check{\pi}_0^1 = \check{w}^{0T} x^1 [(Y_L/\check{X}_L) - 1]$ and a different margin effect unless $r^0(K_0^1 - K^0) = \pi^0(Y_L - 1)$.

change in net income. The sources include operating factors and inflationary factors, and investor income has two sources.

4.4.2 Models without investor input

This section shares the feature of Section 4.3.2 of not expensing investor input, and changes the emphasis from productivity to distribution.

Méraud (1966) and CERC (1969a)

Méraud actually begins with a model of distribution and transforms it to a model of production, which illustrates the primacy the French writers accord to distributional issues. We obtain Méraud's distribution model by solving expression (4.6) for the quantity effect to obtain

$$p^{0T}(y^1 - y^0) - w^{0T}(x^1 - x^0) = -y^{1T}(p^1 - p^0) + x^{1T}(w^1 - w^0) + (\pi^1 - \pi^0).$$

$$(4.25)$$

Méraud calls the quantity effect the "surplus" to be distributed to consumers, suppliers of inputs (including capital), and the firm itself for allocation to taxes, dividends, retained earnings, and the like. Méraud identifies two components of the surplus: the productivity effect $w^{0T}x^1[(Y_L/X_L) - 1]$ and the margin effect $\pi^0(Y_L - 1)$ given in expression (4.7). In our terminology the surplus to be distributed is the entire quantity effect, not just the productivity effect. In the view of Méraud (and the majority of French writers), both components of the quantity effect are potential sources of funds, and both are available for distribution among the various claimants.

Méraud converts this surplus distribution expression into one in which discrete changes are converted to rates of change, using base period revenue share and cost share weights. This growth formulation anticipates the influential macroeconomic growth accounting framework of Jorgenson and Griliches (1967), although Méraud does not require cost to exhaust revenue, as Jorgenson and Griliches do.

CERC repeats the Laspeyres/Paasche analysis of Méraud, and also reverses the index numbers by pairing Paasche quantity indexes with Laspeyres price indexes, noting that, while the two decompositions are not the same, they cannot be very different. CERC also considers pairing Laspeyres quantity indexes with Laspeyres price indexes, a procedure we commented on critically in Section 2.4 of Chapter 2. In a profit change framework this procedure leads to

$$p^{0T}(y^1 - y^0) - w^{0T}(x^1 - x^0) = [-y^{0T}(p^1 - p^0) + x^{0T}(w^1 - w^0) + (\pi^1 - \pi^0)]$$
$$+ [(p^1 - p^0)^T (y^1 - y^0) - (w^1 - w^0)^T (x^1 - x^0)],$$
(4.26)

which distributes the Laspeyres productivity surplus in Laspeyres rather than Paasche form to consumers, input suppliers, the firm itself, and a term CERC calls "ajustement." This inconvenient term is dismissed as being a second-order term of negligible magnitude. It is easy to show that expression (4.26) can be rewritten as[12]

$$p^{1T}(y^1 - y^0) - w^{0T}(x^1 - x^0) = -y^{0T}(p^1 - p^0) + x^{1T}(w^1 - w^0) + (\pi^1 - \pi^0),$$
(4.27)

which eliminates the inconvenient "ajustement" term. It has conventional structure, but unconventional pairings of a Paasche measure of output quantity change with a Laspeyres measure of input quantity change, and a Laspeyres measure of output price change with a Paasche measure of input price change. (It can be rewritten by reversing Laspeyres and Paasche weights.)

Returning to expression (4.25), CERC recognizes that price changes on the right side can be positive for some variables and negative for others. Moving profit-enhancing price movements to the left side and decomposing the quantity effect using expression (4.7) generates

$$w^{0T}x^1[(Y_L/X_L) - 1] + \pi^0(Y_L - 1) + y^{1T}(p^1 - p^0) - x^{1T}(w^1 - w^0) - (\pi^1 - \pi^0)$$
$$p^1 > p^0 \qquad w^1 < w^0 \qquad \pi^1 < \pi^0$$
$$= -y^{1T}(p^1 - p^0) + x^{1T}(w^1 - w^0) + (\pi^1 - \pi^0),$$
$$p^1 < p^0 \qquad w^1 > w^0 \qquad \pi^1 > \pi^0$$
(4.28)

in which the surplus is augmented by the value of any product price increases and the value of any input price decreases. These additional

---

[12] The CERC "ajustement" term is the difference analogue of Houéry's adaptation indexes I_Y and I_X we discussed in Section 3.2.1 of Chapter 3. As an interesting footnote to the Laspeyres/Paasche issue, CERC (1980; 191–95) proposes replacing both Laspeyres base period weights and Paasche comparison period weights with arithmetic mean weights. Later Arruñada Sanchez (1987; 154–55) implements CERC's proposal in an empirical analysis of the distribution of the surplus in a panel of Spanish private banks. This is well before arithmetic mean weights were popularized by Balk and Diewert. We analyze arithmetic mean weights, which were actually first proposed by Bennet (1920), in Chapter 5.

sources of surplus are called "héritages," and CERC calls the augmented surplus "surplus total." The augmented surplus is allocated to consumers of products whose prices decline, and to suppliers of inputs (including capital) whose prices increase. Although profit change is either positive or negative, changes in the various uses to which profit is put can be positive for some uses and negative for others, and so profit change appears twice in expression (4.28). This allocation process is called "emplois," or "répartition de surplus total."

Empirical applications

Méraud and CERC develop the surplus distribution model given in expressions (4.25) and (4.28). The important concept of "héritages" and "emplois", which Vincent (1969) attributes to Puiseux and Bernard (1965), is incorporated into the surplus distribution model by CERC (1969a). Later CERC (1969b, 1970, 1971, 1972) and Roger-Machart (1969) provide detailed empirical applications of the model to the French public firms Société Nationale Chemins de Fer France (SNCF), Gaz de France, Charbonnages de France, and Electricité de France. CERC (1980) summarizes the analytical method and its empirical applications, and provides an extensive bibliography.

Findings vary across agencies and through time, but some empirical regularities emerge. The studies do not exploit Méraud's decomposition of the quantity effect, and so do not attempt to quantify the two sources of the surplus to be distributed. Most results are obtained from expression (4.28) incorporating "héritages". "Héritages" are important, for two reasons. First, employees and consumers often receive more than the quantity effect, requiring "héritages" if equality between the quantity effect and the price effect is to be maintained. Second, equality frequently involves negative profit, requiring government subsidy to cover losses, and subsidy change is a source of "héritage" external to the formal model. The big winners, across all agencies and through all time periods, are consumers (with the sole exception of SNCF in two of three time periods) and employees (with no exceptions). Suppliers of inputs (including capital) fare less well, and their gains or losses tend to be small compared to the gains of consumers and employees.

Table 4.3 summarizes the findings of CERC (1969b) for SNCF. The surplus to be distributed is the quantity effect. In the initial sub-period the surplus is augmented by declines in the prices of capital and materials, and the augmented surplus is distributed among employees, passengers, and

Table 4.3 Distribution at SNCF

Period	Quantity Effect	Output Price Change	Capital Price Change	Material Price Change	Profit Change	=	Labor Price Change	Output Price Change	Material Price Change	Profit Change
1952–1957	305		5	10		=	243	10		67
1958–1962	126	1	5	15			112			35
1963–1966	12	59	2		217		281		9	
1952–1966	157	4	4	9	62		207	4	3	36

Mean results by period (millions of 1962 francs)

recipients of increased profit. The second and third sub-period distributions are interpreted similarly. On average over the entire period employees receive more than the total surplus (the quantity effect), requiring sacrifice on the part of all other agents.

A related public sector study warrants mention. Geels (1988) applies the Méraud/CERC model to six Belgian urban transit systems during 1962–85. The pattern of the surplus distribution varies across cities and through time, although in most cities the surplus distribution involves a transfer from commuters to employees. The Brussels transit system is particularly interesting, because in 1978 the system changed ownership from a public/private partnership to purely public ownership. Labor gained through both ownership forms, but ironically commuters, who gained from real rate reductions under mixed ownership, became losers under public ownership. Another consistent loser was the governments that subsidize losses.

Among private sector studies at the microeconomic level, Mevellec (1977) applies the model to a sample of French agricultural cooperatives, Arruñada Sanchez (1987) applies the model to a panel of Spanish private banks, and Grifell-Tatjé (2011) applies the model to a panel of Spanish banks having three types of ownership. At the sectoral level, Courbis and Templé (1975) and Templé (1971, 1976) apply the model to several sectors of the French economy. At the macroeconomic level, Chapron and Geffroy (1984) apply the model to five advanced economies. Although these studies vary by level of aggregation and type of ownership, labor emerges as a consistent winner. The fate of consumers, governments, and other agents varies across studies.

Table 4.4 summarizes the findings of Grifell-Tatjé and Lovell (2008), who apply the model to the United States Postal Service (USPS) through a long period of time during which large losses eventually trended to small profits. Unlike other studies, they decompose the quantity effect. They find the productivity effect to exceed the quantity effect by about 2% over the entire period. The implied small negative margin effect suggests that postal prices have failed to cover unit costs. They distribute the quantity effect in accordance with expression (4.28), and they find the distribution exercise to be almost exclusively a huge (relative to the size of the quantity effect) transfer from consumers to employees. Other agents, including the government, participate in the surplus distribution exercise, but to a far smaller degree.[13]

---

[13] The economic situation has deteriorated dramatically at USPS since 2004. From 2004 to 2012 both mail volume and employment declined by 25%, and small profits turned to large losses that cumulated to nearly $40 billion (nominal) over the period.

Table 4.4 Distribution at USPS

Period	Quantity Effect	Output Price Change	Capital Price Change	Profit Change	=	Labor Price Change	Material Price Change	Capital Price Change	Profit Change
1972–1982	27.52	1,433.02				1,068.39	178.82	76.70	136.62
1982–1992	63.59	1,624.23				1,474.71	96.19	42.83	74.09
1992–2001	296.37	1,144.03	12.97	101.99		1,338.57	216.79		
2001–2004	1,145.15	1,317.04	219.92			1,649.86	152.51		879.73
1972–2004	219.18	1,400.62	66.27	101.99		1,325.86	161.21	54.66	187.74

Mean results by period (millions of current USD)

Summary

The basic model of income distribution is that of Méraud given in expression (4.25). CERC (1969a) provides a useful extension of the basic model by introducing "héritages" and "emplois" to generate the distribution model given in expression (4.28). However, even though the French writers refer to the "surplus de productivité," what they are distributing is the quantity effect, not the productivity effect. Of all the empirical applications we discuss, only Grifell-Tatjé and Lovell bother to decompose the quantity effect, and even they distribute the quantity effect. Regardless of what is distributed, we view the distribution exercise as an integral component of productivity accounting. Productivity improvements create wealth, and the distribution exercise quantifies the gains and losses of each participating agent.

4.5 A NUMERICAL ILLUSTRATION

The objective of this section is to provide a simple numerical illustration that highlights the structural similarities and differences between a ratio-based model of profitability change and a difference-based model of profit change. We adopt the APC approach to performance measurement, in which profitability change Π^1/Π^0 is the product of productivity change Y/X and price recovery change P/W. We then convert this ratio framework to a difference framework, and we express profit change $\pi^1 - \pi^0$ as the sum of a quantity effect $w^{0T}x^1[(Y_L/X_L) - 1] + \pi^0(Y_L - 1)$ (which itself is the sum of a productivity effect $w^{0T}x^1[(Y_L/X_L) - 1]$ and a margin effect $\pi^0(Y_L - 1)$) and a price effect $y^{1T}(p^1 - p^0) - x^{1T}(w^1 - w^0)$. We base the analysis of profit change on expressions (4.6) and (4.7). The numerical analysis is contained in Tables 4.5 and 4.6.

Table 4.5 contains artificially generated data on 30 producers for a base period and a comparison period. In the base period profitability is constant, with $\Pi^0 = 1.1$ for all producers. Between the base period and the comparison period prices and quantities change in such a way that profitability remains unchanged at $\Pi^1 = 1.1$ for all producers. However, despite constant profitability across producers and between periods, profit varies across producers within each period, and increases for every producer from the base period to the comparison period. Constant profitability does not imply constant profit.[14]

---

[14] The data are generated by a factor requirement frontier $lnx = (1/\beta)[lny + \theta y]$ with parameter values $\theta = 0.0091$, $\beta = 1.2$, and pre-specified variables (y, w, Π) in each period. The data exhibit regions of increasing, constant, and decreasing returns to scale in each period, with constant returns to scale occurring at output ranges [22, 40] and [23, 40.5] in the two periods.

Table 4.5 Example with artificial data

Producer	p^0	y^0	R^0	w^0	x^0	C^0	Π^0	π^0	p^1	y^1	R^1	w^1	x^1	C^1	Π^1	π^1
01	9.95	2.00	19.90	10.00	1.81	18.09	1.10	1.81	9.75	3.00	29.24	10.40	2.56	26.58	1.10	2.66
02	9.00	4.00	36.00	10.00	3.27	32.73	1.10	3.27	8.98	5.50	49.38	10.40	4.32	44.89	1.10	4.49
03	8.54	6.00	51.24	10.00	4.66	46.58	1.10	4.66	8.60	8.00	68.76	10.40	6.01	62.51	1.10	6.25
04	8.26	8.00	66.12	10.00	6.01	60.11	1.10	6.01	8.37	10.50	87.90	10.40	7.68	79.91	1.10	7.99
05	8.08	10.00	80.85	10.00	7.35	73.50	1.10	7.35	8.23	13.00	107.04	10.40	9.36	97.30	1.10	9.73
06	7.96	12.00	95.55	10.00	8.69	86.86	1.10	8.69	8.15	15.50	126.30	10.40	11.04	114.82	1.10	11.48
07	7.88	14.00	110.31	10.00	10.03	100.28	1.10	10.03	8.10	18.00	145.80	10.40	12.75	132.55	1.10	13.25
08	7.82	16.00	125.18	10.00	11.38	113.80	1.10	11.38	8.08	20.50	165.60	10.40	14.48	150.55	1.10	15.05
09	7.79	18.00	140.20	10.00	12.75	127.45	1.10	12.75	8.08	23.00	185.73	10.40	16.23	168.84	1.10	16.88
10	7.77	20.00	155.40	10.00	14.13	141.27	1.10	14.13	8.08	25.50	205.91	10.40	18.00	187.19	1.10	18.72
11	7.76	22.00	170.82	10.00	15.53	155.29	1.10	15.53	8.08	28.00	226.10	10.40	19.76	205.55	1.10	20.55
12	7.76	24.00	186.35	10.00	16.94	169.41	1.10	16.94	8.08	30.50	246.29	10.40	21.53	223.90	1.10	22.39
13	7.76	26.00	201.88	10.00	18.35	183.52	1.10	18.35	8.08	33.00	266.48	10.40	23.29	242.25	1.10	24.23
14	7.76	28.00	217.40	10.00	19.76	197.64	1.10	19.76	8.08	35.50	286.66	10.40	25.06	260.60	1.10	26.06
15	7.76	30.00	232.93	10.00	21.18	211.76	1.10	21.18	8.08	38.00	306.85	10.40	26.82	278.96	1.10	27.90
16	7.76	32.00	248.46	10.00	22.59	225.87	1.10	22.59	8.08	40.50	327.04	10.40	28.59	297.31	1.10	29.73
17	7.76	34.00	263.99	10.00	24.00	239.99	1.10	24.00	8.10	43.00	348.20	10.40	30.44	316.55	1.10	31.65
18	7.76	36.00	279.52	10.00	25.41	254.11	1.10	25.41	8.11	45.50	368.79	10.40	32.24	335.27	1.10	33.53
19	7.76	38.00	295.05	10.00	26.82	268.23	1.10	26.82	8.12	48.00	389.57	10.40	34.05	354.16	1.10	35.42
20	7.76	40.00	310.58	10.00	28.23	282.34	1.10	28.23	8.13	50.50	410.56	10.40	35.89	373.23	1.10	37.32
21	7.78	42.00	326.94	10.00	29.72	297.22	1.10	29.72	8.15	53.00	431.74	10.40	37.74	392.49	1.10	39.25
22	7.79	44.00	342.71	10.00	31.16	311.55	1.10	31.16	8.16	55.50	453.15	10.40	39.61	411.95	1.10	41.20

Table 4.5 (cont.)

Producer	p^0	y^0	R^0	w^0	x^0	C^0	Π^0	π^0	p^1	y^1	R^1	w^1	x^1	C^1	Π^1	π^1
23	7.80	46.00	358.59	10.00	32.60	325.99	1.10	32.60	8.19	58.00	474.77	10.40	41.50	431.61	1.10	43.16
24	7.80	48.00	374.59	10.00	34.05	340.54	1.10	34.05	8.21	60.50	496.62	10.40	43.41	451.47	1.10	45.15
25	7.81	50.00	390.71	10.00	35.52	355.19	1.10	35.52	8.23	63.00	518.70	10.40	45.34	471.55	1.10	47.15
26	7.83	52.00	406.96	10.00	37.00	369.97	1.10	37.00	8.26	65.50	541.03	10.40	47.29	491.84	1.10	49.18
27	7.84	54.00	423.34	10.00	38.49	384.86	1.10	38.49	8.29	68.00	563.60	10.40	49.27	512.36	1.10	51.24
28	7.85	56.00	439.86	10.00	39.99	399.87	1.10	39.99	8.32	70.50	586.42	10.40	51.26	533.11	1.10	53.31
29	7.87	58.00	456.51	10.00	41.50	415.01	1.10	41.50	8.35	73.00	609.49	10.40	53.28	554.08	1.10	55.41
30	7.89	60.00	473.30	10.00	43.03	430.27	1.10	43.03	8.38	75.50	632.83	10.40	55.32	575.30	1.10	57.53

Table 4.6 Profitability vs. profit decomposition

Producer	Π^1/Π^0	$=$ Y/X	$\times$ P/W	$\pi^1 - \pi^0$	$=$ Productivity Effect	$+$ Margin Effect	$+$ Price Effect
[1]	[2]	[3]	[4]	[5]	[6]	[7]	[8]
01	1.00	1.06	0.94	0.85	1.58	0.90	−1.64
02	1.00	1.04	0.96	1.22	1.84	1.23	−1.85
03	1.00	1.03	0.97	1.59	2.00	1.55	−1.96
04	1.00	1.03	0.97	1.98	2.05	1.88	−1.95
05	1.00	1.02	0.98	2.38	1.98	2.20	−1.81
06	1.00	1.02	0.98	2.80	1.79	2.53	−1.53
07	1.00	1.01	0.99	3.23	1.48	2.87	−1.12
08	1.00	1.01	0.99	3.68	1.04	3.20	−0.57
09	1.00	1.00	1.00	4.14	0.51	3.54	0.09
10	1.00	1.00	1.00	4.59	0.13	3.89	0.58
11	1.00	1.00	1.00	5.03	0.00	4.24	0.79
12	1.00	1.00	1.00	5.45	0.00	4.59	0.86
13	1.00	1.00	1.00	5.87	0.00	4.94	0.93
14	1.00	1.00	1.00	6.30	0.00	5.29	1.00
15	1.00	1.00	1.00	6.72	0.00	5.65	1.07
16	1.00	1.00	1.00	7.14	0.00	6.00	1.14
17	1.00	1.00	1.00	7.66	−0.85	6.35	2.16
18	1.00	1.00	1.00	8.12	−1.21	6.71	2.62
19	1.00	0.99	1.01	8.59	−1.72	7.06	3.26
20	1.00	0.99	1.01	9.09	−2.42	7.41	4.10
21	1.00	0.99	1.01	9.53	−2.34	7.78	4.08
22	1.00	0.99	1.01	10.04	−3.13	8.14	5.02
23	1.00	0.99	1.01	10.56	−3.98	8.50	6.03
24	1.00	0.99	1.01	11.09	−4.89	8.87	7.11
25	1.00	0.99	1.01	11.64	−5.87	9.24	8.27
26	1.00	0.99	1.01	12.19	−6.91	9.60	9.49
27	1.00	0.98	1.02	12.75	−8.02	9.98	10.79
28	1.00	0.98	1.02	13.32	−9.19	10.35	12.16
29	1.00	0.98	1.02	13.91	−10.43	10.73	13.61
30	1.00	0.98	1.02	14.50	−11.75	11.12	15.13

Table 4.6 explores the causes and consequences of the simultaneous occurrence of constant profitability and varying profit documented in Table 4.5. Columns (2) to (4) analyze profitability, and attribute unchanged profitability to offsetting rates of productivity change Y/X and price recovery change P/W. We first encountered this phenomenon, for which W/P provides a dual measure of productivity change, in Section 2.9 of Chapter 2. Columns

(5) to (8) analyze profit. Column (5) shows profit increasing from base period to comparison period for every producer, and by an amount that increases with producer size. Columns (6) to (8) provide a partial explanation for the observed pattern of profit change, an explanation that we flesh out in Chapter 5. Columns (6) and (7) are calculated using expression (4.6) and the decomposition in expression (4.7), and column (8) is calculated using expression (4.6).

Table 4.6 illustrates an important feature of expression (4.7). The quantity effect is not synonymous with the productivity effect. A variable but substantial portion of the contribution of quantity change to profit change comes from the margin effect, reflecting the financial benefits of expansion with a positive base period margin $\pi^0/R^0 = 1 - (\Pi^0)^{-1} = 0.091$.

The margin effect constitutes an important distinction between the ratio-based profitability model in columns (2) to (4) of Table 4.6 and the difference-based profit model in columns (5) to (8). In the former model productivity change and price recovery change tell the whole story about profitability change. In the latter model they tell only part of the story about profit change. Provided $\Pi \neq 1$, profit can change despite constant productivity and constant prices, as rows (9) to (18) of Table 4.6 illustrate. If the operating environment allows $R > C$, then expansion in the absence of productivity growth, defined as $Y = X > 0$, can be profitable, even in the presence of unchanging or deteriorating price recovery, as expression (4.7) demonstrates.

Table 4.6 also confirms that, although constant profitability generates a dual productivity *index* $(P/W)^{-1} = Y/X$, it does not generate a dual productivity *indicator*, since the productivity effect is not the negative of the price effect; the margin effect intrudes.

In Chapter 5 we develop an analogous decomposition of the price effect. This decomposition shows that the price effect is not synonymous with the price recovery effect. A second component of the price effect, analogous to the margin effect component of the quantity effect, can contribute to profit change even in the absence of price recovery. Assuming $\Pi \neq 1$, and defining inflation analogously to our definition of expansion as $P = W > 0$, we show that inflation can be profitable even in the absence of price recovery and quantity change. We also show that constant profitability is sufficient to generate a dual productivity effect; the price recovery effect is equal in value, and opposite in sign, to the productivity effect. We thus identify four distinct sources of profit change, a pair of quantity change sources and an analogous pair of price change sources. The $\Pi \neq 1$ proviso is important, because some writers adopt an accounting convention that imposes either $\Pi^0 = 1$ or $\Pi^0 = \Pi^1 = 1$. The weaker assumption eliminates the margin effect in some model specifications, and the stronger assumption eliminates it altogether.

The existence of a margin effect (together with an analogous price-related margin effect) makes the difference-based model of profit change richer than the ratio-based model of profitability change. It is of course possible to move back and forth between the two models, as many writers do, but the profit change model we explore in Chapters 4 to 6 provides more insight into business financial performance than does the profitability change model. Thus, the margin effect serves a dual purpose: it enriches an analysis of business financial performance, and it provides a strong incentive for business expansion, either organically or through M&A activity, provided only that a positive margin can be maintained.[15]

---

[15] Grifell-Tatjé (2011) emphasizes the motivating role the margin effect plays in the growth of financial institutions.

5 Decomposing the Quantity Change and Price Change Components of Profit Change

5.1 INTRODUCTION

This is the second of three chapters dealing with the generation and distribution of profit and its change. In Chapter 4 we provided an introduction, largely historical, to the subject. In this chapter we take a somewhat more analytical approach based on empirical indicators, the difference analogues to empirical indexes that are expressed in ratio form. As in Chapter 4, we attribute profit change to change in quantities (the quantity effect) and change in prices (the price effect), and we explore the distribution of the financial impacts of quantity change. However, the introduction of empirical indicators enables us to identify and characterize two components of the quantity effect and two components of the price effect. An analysis of these two decompositions forms the core of Chapter 5. In Chapter 6 we consider various approaches to the search for the economic drivers of productivity change. In all three chapters profit change is expressed in monetary units. Consequently, the impacts of productivity change and its economic drivers are expressed in monetary units.

The primary issue in this chapter concerns whether or not, and if so under what conditions, the quantity effect measures the contribution of productivity change to profit change. Our discussion in Section 4.3 of Chapter 4 suggested that it does not, except under restrictive conditions involving the presence of investor input in the model, a suggestion that was confirmed by the numerical illustration in Section 4.5. A closely related issue concerns the economic

202

interpretation of any deviation between the quantity effect and the productivity effect. In Chapter 4 we referred to the complement of the productivity effect in the quantity effect as a (quantity) margin effect, a nomenclature we retain in this chapter. A second, and equally important, pair of issues concerns whether or not, and if so under what conditions, the price effect measures the contribution of price recovery change to profit change, together with an economic interpretation of any deviation between the price effect and the price recovery effect. We adopt similar terminology to characterize any deviation between the two as a (price) margin effect. We explore the conditions that generate the two margin effects, and the economic interpretation of each, in Section 5.3. It is the possible presence of quantity and price margin effects that distinguishes the difference-based model of profit change in Chapters 4 to 6 from the ratio-based model of profitability change in Chapters 2 and 3.

In Section 5.2 we introduce empirical indicators of quantity change and price change. Indicators are aggregator functions, in the sense that they aggregate individual quantity changes (or price changes). Indicators are analogous to the empirical indexes introduced in Chapter 2, in that they use prices to weight quantity changes, and quantities to weight price changes, although indexes are expressed in ratio form and indicators are expressed in difference form. Indicators provide a convenient framework within which to investigate the decomposition issues raised in the previous paragraph. We use indicators to provide an initial decomposition of profit change into a quantity effect and a price effect. It turns out that the functional forms specified for these indicators have a significant impact on the structure of the two effects. In Section 5.3 we use indicators to decompose both the quantity effect and the price effect. In Section 5.3.1 we use relatively simple indicators, and we obtain conditions under which the quantity effect coincides with a productivity effect, and a similar set of conditions under which the price effect coincides with a price recovery effect. The economic interpretations of these conditions involve assumptions concerning the value of profit in base and comparison periods, change in the size of the business between base and comparison periods, and the functional form specified for the indicators of quantity change and price change. The role played by the value of profit in base and comparison periods parallels our discussion of the role of investor input that was so prominent in Chapter 4. We repeat this exercise in Section 5.3.2, using a more sophisticated functional form for the indicators. In Section 5.3.3 we discuss some applications of the use of empirical indicators to decompose profit change. Section 5.3.4

provides a summary of Section 5.3. A distinguishing feature of Sections 5.2 and 5.3 is the absence of investor input. There we mention the possibility that nominal profit might be zero, but without explicitly incorporating investor input. We introduce investor input in Section 5.4, and we show how incorporating investor input influences the decomposition of the quantity effect. In Section 5.5 we discuss the conditions under which a dual productivity indicator exists, and we refer to some studies that have used a dual productivity indicator. In Section 5.6 we return to the numerical illustration introduced in Section 4.5 of Chapter 4 to illustrate the use of indicators to decompose profit change.

5.2 EMPIRICAL INDICATORS OF QUANTITY CHANGE AND PRICE CHANGE

Basic notation is the same as in previous chapters, although we introduce new notation to accommodate the introduction of empirical indicators. Profit is expressed as $\pi = R - C = p^T y - w^T x$, and profit change from base period to comparison period is expressed in difference form as $\pi^1 - \pi^0 = (R^1 - C^1) - (R^0 - C^0) = (R^1 - R^0) - (C^1 - C^0)$. We are interested in decomposing profit change from base period to comparison period, recalling that "base" and "comparison" can also refer to firms.

We write the expression for profit change as

$$\pi^1 - \pi^0 = (R^1 - R^0) - (C^1 - C^0)$$
$$= [\mathbb{Y}(p^1,p^0,y^1,y^0) + \mathbb{P}(y^1,y^0,p^1,p^0)] - [\mathbb{X}(w^1,w^0,x^1,x^0) + \mathbb{W}(x^1,x^0,w^1,w^0)]$$
$$= [\mathbb{Y}(p^1,p^0,y^1,y^0) - \mathbb{X}(w^1,w^0,x^1,x^0)] + [\mathbb{P}(y^1,y^0,p^1,p^0) - \mathbb{W}(x^1,x^0,w^1,w^0)],$$

$$(5.1)$$

in which $\mathbb{Y}(p^1,p^0,y^1,y^0)$ and $\mathbb{X}(w^1,w^0,x^1,x^0)$ are empirical indicators of output quantity change and input quantity change, and $\mathbb{P}(y^1,y^0,p^1,p^0)$ and $\mathbb{W}(x^1,x^0,w^1,w^0)$ are empirical indicators of output price change and input price change. The output indicators $\mathbb{Y}(p^1,p^0,y^1,y^0)$ and $\mathbb{P}(y^1,y^0,p^1,p^0)$ are interpreted as follows. $\mathbb{Y}(p^1,p^0,y^1,y^0)$ is the monetary value of a change in output quantities from base period to comparison period, and is a function of output prices in the two periods, which provide weights for the quantity changes, and output quantities in the two periods. $\mathbb{P}(y^1,y^0,p^1,p^0)$ is the monetary value of a change in output prices from base period to comparison period, and it is a function of output quantities in the two periods, which provide weights for the price changes, and output prices in the two periods. The input indicators $\mathbb{X}(w^1, w^0, x^1, x^0)$ and $\mathbb{W}(x^1, x^0, w^1, w^0)$ are interpreted in exactly the same way.

The second equality in expression (5.1) states that profit change can be expressed as the difference between revenue change and cost change. Revenue change is expressed as the sum of an empirical indicator of output quantity change and an empirical indicator of output price change. Cost change is similarly expressed as the sum of an empirical indicator of input quantity change and an empirical indicator of input price change. The third equality rearranges terms to state that profit change can be expressed as the sum of a quantity effect and a price effect. The quantity effect is the difference between an empirical indicator of output quantity change and an empirical indicator of input quantity change. The price effect is similarly expressed as the difference between an empirical indicator of output price change and an empirical indicator of input price change. Much of the analysis in this chapter is based on the third equality.

We want these indicators to satisfy an additive analogue to the product test for index numbers, which we call the sum test, that is, we want quantity indicators and price indicators to sum to value changes, so that

$$
\begin{aligned}
R^1 - R^0 &= [\mathbb{Y}(p^1, p^0, y^1, y^0) + \mathbb{P}(y^1, y^0, p^1, p^0)], \\
C^1 - C^0 &= [\mathbb{X}(w^1, w^0, x^1, x^0) + \mathbb{W}(x^1, x^0, w^1, w^0)],
\end{aligned}
\tag{5.2}
$$

and we also want each indicator to decompose by individual variable, so that

$$
\begin{aligned}
\mathbb{Y}(p^1, p^0, y^1, y^0) &= \sum_m \mathbb{Y}_m(p_m^1, p_m^0, y_m^1, y_m^0), \\
\mathbb{P}(y^1, y^0, p^1, p^0) &= \sum_m \mathbb{P}_m(y_m^1, y_m^0, p_m^1, p_m^0), \\
\mathbb{X}(w^1, w^0, x^1, x^0) &= \sum_n \mathbb{X}_n(w_n^1, w_n^0, x_n^1, x_n^0), \\
\mathbb{W}(x^1, x^0, w^1, w^0) &= \sum_n \mathbb{W}_n(x_n^1, x_n^0, w_n^1, w_n^0).
\end{aligned}
\tag{5.3}
$$

Thus far empirical indicators have been asked to satisfy the sum test and to decompose by variable, but they have not been assigned a functional form.[1] Suppose now that the quantity indicators have Laspeyres form, so that

---

[1] Diewert (2005) lists a number of tests that empirical indicators might be asked to satisfy. Using the output price indicator $\mathbb{P}(y^1, y^0, p^1, p^0)$ to illustrate, foremost among these tests are invariance to changes in units of measurement $[\mathbb{P}(\lambda y^1, \lambda y^0, \lambda^{-1} p^1, \lambda^{-1} p^0) = \mathbb{P}(y^1, y^0, p^1, p^0), \lambda > 0]$, linear homogeneity in prices $[\mathbb{P}(y^1, y^0, \lambda p^1, \lambda p^0) = \lambda \mathbb{P}(y^1, y^0, p^1, p^0), \lambda > 0]$, linear homogeneity in quantities $[\mathbb{P}(\lambda y^1, \lambda y^0, p^1, p^0) = \lambda \mathbb{P}(y^1, y^0, p^1, p^0), \lambda > 0]$, and time reversal $[\mathbb{P}(y^1, y^0, p^1, p^0) + \mathbb{P}(y^0, y^1, p^0, p^1) = 0]$.

$$\mathbb{Y}_L(p^1,p^0,y^1,y^0) = \sum_m p_m^0(y_m^1 - y_m^0) = p^{0T}(y^1 - y^0),$$
$$\mathbb{X}_L(w^1,w^0,x^1,x^0) = \sum_n w_n^0(x_n^1 - x_n^0) = w^{0T}(x^1 - x^0),$$

(5.4)

and that the price indicators have Paasche form, so that

$$\mathbb{P}_P(y^1,y^0,p^1,p^0) = \sum_m y_m^1(p_m^1 - p_m^0) = y^{1T}(p^1 - p^0),$$
$$\mathbb{W}_P(x^1,x^0,w^1,w^0) = \sum_n x_n^1(w_n^1 - w_n^0) = x^{1T}(w^1 - w^0).$$

(5.5)

Substituting expressions (5.4) and (5.5) into expression (5.1) yields the profit change decomposition

$$\pi^1 - \pi^0 = [\mathbb{Y}_L(p^1,p^0,y^1,y^0) - \mathbb{X}_L(w^1,w^0,x^1,x^0)] + [\mathbb{P}_P(y^1,y^0,p^1,p^0)$$
$$- \mathbb{W}_P(x^1,x^0,w^1,w^0)]$$
$$= [p^{0T}(y^1 - y^0) - w^{0T}(x^1 - x^0)] + [y^{1T}(p^1 - p^0) - x^{1T}(w^1 - w^0)],$$

(5.6)

which is the sum of a Laspeyres quantity effect and a Paasche price effect. The former shows the impact on profit change of changes in quantities, using base period prices to weight quantity changes, and the latter shows the impact on profit change of changes in prices, using comparison period quantities to weight price changes. It is easily verified that $\mathbb{Y}_L(p^1,p^0,y^1,y^0) + \mathbb{P}_P(y^1,y^0,p^1,p^0) = R^1 - R^0$ and that $\mathbb{X}_L(w^1,w^0,x^1,x^0) + \mathbb{W}_P(x^1,x^0,w^1,w^0) = C^1 - C^0$, so that this pairing satisfies the sum test for outputs and for inputs.

Switching roles, pairing Paasche quantity indicators

$$\mathbb{Y}_P(p^1,p^0,y^1,y^0) = p^{1T}(y^1 - y^0),$$
$$\mathbb{X}_P(w^1,w^0,x^1,x^0) = w^{1T}(x^1 - x^0),$$

(5.7)

with Laspeyres price indicators

$$\mathbb{P}_L(y^1,y^0,p^1,p^0) = y^{0T}(p^1 - p^0),$$
$$\mathbb{W}_L(x^1,x^0,w^1,w^0) = x^{0T}(w^1 - w^0),$$

(5.8)

generates an alternative profit change decomposition

$$\pi^1 - \pi^0 = [\mathbb{Y}_P(p^1,p^0,y^1,y^0) - \mathbb{X}_P(w^1,w^0,x^1,x^0)] + [\mathbb{P}_L(y^1,y^0,p^1,p^0)$$
$$- \mathbb{W}_L(x^1,x^0,w^1,w^0)]$$
$$= [p^{1T}(y^1 - y^0) - w^{1T}(x^1 - x^0)] + [y^{0T}(p^1 - p^0) - x^{0T}(w^1 - w^0)],$$

(5.9)

which is the sum of a Paasche quantity effect that uses comparison period price weights and a Laspeyres price effect that uses base period quantity weights. It is easily verified that this pairing also satisfies the sum test for outputs and for inputs.

Laspeyres indicators use base period weights to evaluate change, and Paasche indicators use comparison period weights to evaluate change. Bennet (1920) advocates using the *arithmetic mean* of Laspeyres and Paasche *indicators* to evaluate change, a strategy analogous to that of Fisher (1922), who recommends the use of the *geometric mean* of Laspeyres and Paasche *indexes* to evaluate change. This leads to what are now known as Bennet quantity and price indicators. Our final decomposition of profit change is based on Bennet indicators, and is expressed as

$$
\begin{aligned}
\pi^1 - \pi^0 &= [\mathbb{Y}_B(p^1,p^0,y^1,y^0) - \mathbb{X}_B(w^1,w^0,x^1,x^0)] + [\mathbb{P}_B(y^1,y^0,p^1,p^0) \\
&\quad - \mathbb{W}_B(x^1,x^0,w^1,w^0)] \\
&= \tfrac{1}{2}[\mathbb{Y}_L(p^1,p^0,y^1,y^0) + \mathbb{Y}_P(p^1,p^0,y^1,y^0)] - \tfrac{1}{2}[\mathbb{X}_L(w^1,w^0,x^1,x^0) \\
&\quad + \mathbb{X}_P(w^1,w^0,x^1,x^0)] \\
&\quad + \tfrac{1}{2}[\mathbb{P}_L(y^1,y^0,p^1,p^0) + \mathbb{P}_P(y^1,y^0,p^1,p^0)] - \tfrac{1}{2}[\mathbb{W}_L(x^1,x^0,w^1,w^0) \\
&\quad + \mathbb{W}_P(x^1,x^0,w^1,w^0)] \\
&= [\bar{p}^T(y^1-y^0) - \bar{w}^T(x^1-x^0)] + [\bar{y}^T(p^1-p^0) - \bar{x}^T(w^1-w^0)],
\end{aligned}
$$
(5.10)

in which $\bar{p} = \tfrac{1}{2}(p^0+p^1)$, $\bar{y} = \tfrac{1}{2}(y^0+y^1)$ and so on. Expression (5.10) decomposes profit change into a Bennet quantity effect that uses arithmetic mean price weights and a Bennet price effect that uses arithmetic mean quantity weights.[2] Because the two previous pairings satisfy the sum test, so does their arithmetic mean, and consequently $\mathbb{Y}_B(p^1,p^0,y^1,y^0) + \mathbb{P}_B(y^1,y^0,p^1,p^0) = R^1 - R^0$ and $\mathbb{X}_B(w^1,w^0,x^1,x^0) + \mathbb{W}_B(x^1,x^0,w^1,w^0) = C^1 - C^0$.[3]

---

[2] Bennet *indicators* introduced here and EM *indexes* introduced in Section 2.4 of Chapter 2 have arithmetic mean weights in common, but they differ because the former are expressed in difference form and the latter are expressed in ratio form. To illustrate, a Bennet output price indicator is expressed as the monetary value $\bar{y}^T(p^1-p^0)$. An EM output price index is expressed as the pure number $\bar{y}^Tp^1/\bar{y}^Tp^0$. Bowley (1928; 223) also proposed the index $\bar{y}^Tp^1/\bar{y}^Tp^0$. Nonetheless, the phrase "Bennet–Bowley" appears frequently, despite the fact that one is an indicator and the other an index. However, we show in Section 5.3.2 that there exists a useful relationship between Bennet indicators and EM indexes. ·

[3] Diewert (2005) proves that Bennet quantity and price indicators satisfy 18 tests, and that Laspeyres and Paasche indicators fail some of the tests that Bennet indicators satisfy, including the important time reversal test. This leads Diewert to characterize Laspeyres and Paasche indicators as "good" indicators and the Bennet indicator as the "best" indicator from the test approach perspective.

We now have three structurally equivalent, but generally numerically different, decompositions of profit change into a quantity effect (the first term on the right side of expressions (5.6), (5.9), and (5.10)) and a price effect (the second term in each expression). The first decomposition pairs Laspeyres quantity indicators with Paasche price indicators. Quantity and price indicators are reversed in the second decomposition, while the third decomposition pairs Bennet quantity and price indicators. All three pairings satisfy the sum test and decompose by variable, making it easy to identify the contributions of individual quantity changes and price changes to profit change.[4]

At this stage we do not associate the quantity effect with a productivity effect, and we do not associate the price effect with a price recovery effect. In the ratio-based profitability change model in Chapters 2 and 3, there is no distinction between a quantity effect and a productivity effect, or between a price effect and a price recovery effect. However, as we indicated in Chapter 4, in the difference-based profit change model, it is necessary to distinguish between quantity and productivity effects, and between price and price recovery effects. In some model specifications there are no differences, and in other specifications there are. The model specifications involve both the choice of indicator and the value of base period and/or comparison period profit. We consider alternative model specifications in Section 5.3.

5.3 THE ANALYTICAL FRAMEWORK

We showed in Section 5.2 that profit change decomposes into the sum of a quantity effect and a price effect. Our objective in this section is to demonstrate that the quantity effect decomposes into the sum of a productivity effect and a (quantity) margin effect, and that the price effect decomposes into the sum of a price recovery effect and a (price) margin effect. The first decomposition is significant because many writers, apparently unaware of the (quantity) margin effect, mistakenly equate the quantity effect with a productivity

---

[4] Laspeyres quantity and price indicator pairs, and Paasche quantity and price indicator pairs, fail the sum test. On the revenue side,

$$\mathbb{Y}_L(p^1,p^0,y^1,y^0) + \mathbb{P}_L(y^1,y^0,p^1,p^0) = R^1 - R^0 - [(p^1-p^0)^T(y^1-y^0)],$$
$$\mathbb{Y}_P(p^1,p^0,y^1,y^0) + \mathbb{P}_P(y^1,y^0,p^1,p^0) = R^1 - R^0 + [(p^1-p^0)^T(y^1-y^0)],$$

in which the covariance terms $[(p^1 - p^0)^T(y^1 - y^0)]$ quantify the failure. A similar result holds on the cost side. The same problem occurs with incompatible pairs of index numbers; we provide some background in footnote 10 in Chapter 2.

effect. The second decomposition is significant because all writers seem to overlook the (price) margin effect, and so erroneously equate the price effect with a price recovery effect. This oversight is unfortunate because both margin effects can make substantial contributions to profit change.[5]

In Section 5.3.1 we decompose profit change using Laspeyres quantity indicators and Paasche price indicators, as in expression (5.6), and we also decompose profit change using Paasche quantity indicators and Laspeyres price indicators, as in expression (5.9). It turns out that neither decomposition is unique, and we end up with eight different decompositions of profit change. In Section 5.3.2 we decompose profit change using Bennet quantity and price indicators, as in expression (5.10). Because Bennet weights are arithmetic means of Laspeyres and Paasche weights, we end up with four additional decompositions of profit change. In Section 5.3.3 we discuss empirical applications of the various decompositions, and in Section 5.3.4 we summarize the analytical framework.

5.3.1 Laspeyres and Paasche decompositions of profit change

We consider two profit change decompositions that satisfy the sum test. In the first the quantity effect has Laspeyres form and the price effect has Paasche form, and in the second the quantity effect has Paasche form and the price effect has Laspeyres form.

Laspeyres quantity indicators and Paasche price indicators

We begin by decomposing the Laspeyres quantity effect, the first term on the right side of expression (5.6). Since Laspeyres quantity indicators use base period prices to weight quantity changes, we assume, temporarily and for analytical purposes only, that base period profit $\pi^0 = 0$. This simplifies the Laspeyres quantity effect to $p^{0T}y^1 - w^{0T}x^1$. We take an output orientation by isolating $p^{0T}y^1$ in the simplified quantity effect to obtain

$$p^{0T}y^1 - w^{0T}x^1 = p^{0T}y^1[1 - (w^{0T}x^1/w^{0T}x^0)(p^{0T}y^0/p^{0T}y^1)] \quad (\text{since } \pi^0 = 0)$$
$$= p^{0T}y^1[1 - (Y_L/X_L)^{-1}].$$

This is a Laspeyres productivity effect. It is also the Laspeyres quantity effect, under the simplifying assumption that $\pi^0 = 0$. It is not the Laspeyres quantity effect otherwise, and so something must be missing. Call this

---

[5] Henceforth, we dispense with the quantity and price qualifiers of the two margin effects, on the assumption that the context makes it obvious which one we refer to.

something Z. Then this Laspeyres productivity effect plus Z must equal the Laspeyres quantity effect $p^{0T}(y^1 - y^0) - w^{0T}(x^1 - x^0)$, and so

$$p^{0T}y^1[1 - (Y_L/X_L)^{-1}] \; + \; Z = p^{0T}y^1 - w^{0T}x^1 - \pi^0,$$

in which the right side is the Laspeyres quantity effect $[p^{0T}(y^1 - y^0) - w^{0T}(x^1 - x^0)]$. Solving for Z yields

$$\begin{aligned} Z &= p^{0T}y^1 - w^{0T}x^1 - \pi^0 - p^{0T}y^1 + p^{0T}y^1(w^{0T}x^1/w^{0T}x^0)(p^{0T}y^0/p^{0T}y^1) \\ &= \pi^0[X_L - 1], \end{aligned}$$

and so the Laspeyres quantity effect decomposes as

$$p^{0T}(y^1 - y^0) \; - \; w^{0T}(x^1 - x^0) = p^{0T}y^1[1 - (Y_L/X_L)^{-1}] + \pi^0[X_L - 1]. \quad (5.11)$$

The first term on the right side of expression (5.11) is an output-oriented Laspeyres productivity effect, and the second is the corresponding input-oriented Laspeyres margin effect. The productivity effect consists of a Laspeyres productivity index $[1 - (Y_L/X_L)^{-1}]$ scaled by real comparison period revenue $p^{0T}y^1$ to convert a pure number to monetary terms. The productivity effect $p^{0T}y^1[1 - (Y_L/X_L)^{-1}] \gtreqless 0$ as $Y_L \gtreqless X_L$. The productivity effect coincides with the quantity effect if, and only if, the margin effect is zero. The margin effect $\pi^0[X_L - 1] = 0$ if $\pi^0 = 0$ (the temporary assumption that base period profit is zero is actually correct) or if $X_L = 1$ (there is no change in firm size, as measured by a Laspeyres input quantity index). In all other circumstances the margin effect makes an independent contribution to profit change.

We call the second term a margin effect because, as we showed in Chapter 4 in expression (4.12), it can be rewritten as a function of the base period profit margin π^0/C^0, since $\pi^0(X_L - 1) = (\pi^0/C^0)[w^{0T}(x^1 - x^0)]$. The margin effect can be viewed in another light. Suppose that output quantities and input quantities vary in proportion, in the sense that that $y^1 = \lambda y^0$, $x^1 = \lambda x^0$, $\lambda \neq 1$, so that $Y_L = X_L \neq 1$, and there is no productivity change. However, the quantity effect is still nonzero, provided the base period profit margin $\pi^0/C^0 \neq 0$. If the base period profit margin is positive, and if, for example, output quantities and input quantities increase in proportion, the quantity effect makes a positive contribution to profit change, even in the absence of productivity growth. This feature of the quantity effect is not well known, even though actual profit $\pi = p^Ty - w^Tx$ is homogeneous of degree $+1$ in (y, x).

We return to the Laspeyres quantity effect, the first term on the right side of expression (5.6). We now take an input orientation by isolating $w^{0T}x^1$ in the simplified quantity effect to obtain

$$p^{0T}y^1 - w^{0T}x^1 = w^{0T}x^1[(p^{0T}y^1/p^{0T}y^0)(w^{0T}x^0/w^{0T}x^1) - 1] \quad \text{(since } \pi^0 = 0\text{)}$$
$$= w^{0T}x^1[(Y_L/X_L) - 1].$$

This is an alternative Laspeyres productivity effect. It is also the Laspeyres quantity effect, under the same simplifying assumption that $\pi^0 = 0$. We therefore let $\pi \neq 0$ and, following the strategy utilized above, we write

$$w^{0T}x^1[(Y_L/X_L) - 1] + Z = p^{0T}y^1 - w^{0T}x^1 - \pi^0,$$

and solving for Z yields

$$Z = p^{0T}y^1 - w^{0T}x^1 - \pi^0 + w^{0T}x^1 - w^{0T}x^1(p^{0T}y^1/p^{0T}y^0)(w^{0T}x^0/w^{0T}x^1)$$
$$= \pi^0[Y_L - 1],$$

and so the Laspeyres quantity effect also decomposes as

$$p^{0T}(y^1 - y^0) - w^{0T}(x^1 - x^0) = w^{0T}x^1[(Y_L/X_L) - 1] + \pi^0[Y_L - 1]. \quad (5.12)$$

The first term on the right side of expression (5.12) is an input-oriented Laspeyres productivity effect, and the second is the corresponding output-oriented Laspeyres margin effect. The productivity effect is a Laspeyres productivity index $[(Y_L/X_L) - 1]$ scaled by real comparison period cost $w^{0T}x^1$, with $w^{0T}x^1[(Y_L/X_L) - 1] \gtreqless 0$ as $Y_L \gtreqless X_L$. The productivity effect coincides with the quantity effect if, and only if, the margin effect is zero. We showed in Chapter 4 in expression (4.8) that the margin effect can be rewritten as a function of the base period profit margin π^0/R^0, since $\pi^0(Y_L - 1) = (\pi^0/R^0)[p^{0T}(y^1 - y^0)]$. The margin effect is zero if the base period profit margin $\pi^0/R^0 = 0$ or if there is no change in firm size, as measured here by a Laspeyres output quantity indicator.

The two decompositions of the Laspeyres quantity effect in expressions (5.11) and (5.12) are different. The two Laspeyres productivity effects are equal if $\pi^0 = 0$ (base period profit is zero, in which case the quantity effect simplifies to a unique productivity effect), or if $Y_L = X_L$ (there is no productivity change as measured by a Laspeyres productivity index, in which case the quantity effect simplifies to a unique margin effect). In all other circumstances the two productivity effects differ, even though they share a Laspeyres structure. The two Laspeyres margin effects also differ, and coincide only under either of the same two conditions.

We continue by decomposing the Paasche price effect, the second term on the right side of expression (5.6). We follow the same procedures we use to decompose the Laspeyres quantity effect, with the sole exception being that because Paasche price indicators use comparison period quantities to weight price changes, we temporarily assume that comparison period profit $\pi^1 = 0$, which simplifies the Paasche price effect to $-y^{1T}p^0 + x^{1T}w^0$. We take an output orientation by isolating $-y^{1T}p^0$ in the simplified price effect to obtain the decomposition

$$y^{1T}(p^1-p^0)-x^{1T}(w^1-w^0)= y^{1T}p^0[(P_P/W_P) - 1] + \pi^1[1 - W_P^{-1}]. \quad (5.13)$$

The first term on the right side of expression (5.13) is an output-oriented Paasche price recovery effect, and the second term is the corresponding input-oriented Paasche margin effect. The price recovery effect is a Paasche price recovery index $[(P_P/W_P) - 1]$ scaled by real comparison period revenue $y^{1T}p^0$, with $y^{1T}p^0[(P_P/W_P)-1] \gtreqless 0$ as $P_P \gtreqless W_P$. The price recovery effect coincides with the price effect if, and only if, the margin effect is zero, which occurs if $\pi^1 = 0$ or if $W_P = 1$ (there is no input price change as measured by a Paasche input price index). In all other circumstances the margin effect makes an independent contribution to profit change.

We call the second term a margin effect because it can be rewritten as a function of the comparison period profit margin π^1/C^1, since $\pi^1[1 - W_P^{-1}] = (\pi^1/C^1)[x^{1T}(w^1 - w^0)]$. Suppose that output prices and input prices vary in proportion, in the sense that $p^1 = \lambda p^0$, $w^1 = \lambda w^0$, $\lambda \neq 1$, so that $P_P = W_P \neq 1$, and there is no price recovery as defined by Paasche price indexes. However, the price effect is still nonzero provided $\pi^1 \neq 0$. If comparison period profit is positive, and if output prices and input prices increase in proportion, the price effect makes a positive contribution to profit change, even in the absence of positive price recovery. This feature of the price effect appears to be unknown, even though it is a consequence of actual profit $\pi = p^Ty - w^Tx$ being homogeneous of degree +1 in (p, w).

Taking an input orientation by isolating $x^{1T}w^0$ in the simplified price effect generates an alternative decomposition of the Paasche price effect given by

$$y^{1T}(p^1-p^0)-x^{1T}(w^1-w^0)= x^{1T}w^0[1 - (P_P/W_P)^{-1}] + \pi^1[1 - P_P^{-1}], \quad (5.14)$$

in which the first term on the right side is an input-oriented Paasche price recovery effect and the second term is the corresponding output-oriented Paasche margin effect. The latter can be rewritten as a function of the comparison period profit margin π^1/R^1 since $\pi^1[1 - P_P^{-1}] = (\pi^1/R^1)[y^{1T}(p^1 - p^0)]$. The price margin effect is zero if the comparison period profit margin $\pi^1/R^1 = 0$ or if there is no price change as measured by a Paasche output price indicator. The two effects in expression (5.14) have the same interpretations as the two effects in expression (5.13), with appropriate modifications.

The two decompositions of the Paasche price effect in expressions (5.13) and (5.14) differ. The two Paasche price recovery effects are equal if $\pi^1 = 0$ (comparison period profit is zero, in which case the price effect simplifies to a unique price recovery effect), or if $P_P = W_P$ (there is no price recovery change as measured by Paasche price indexes, in which case the price effect collapses to a unique margin effect). In all other circumstances the two price recovery effects differ, even though they share a Paasche structure. The two Paasche margin effects also differ, and coincide only under either of the same two conditions.

We have two Laspeyres quantity effects in expressions (5.11) and (5.12), and two Paasche price effects in expressions (5.13) and (5.14). This generates four Laspeyres/Paasche profit change decompositions that satisfy the sum test.

Paasche quantity indicators and Laspeyres price indicators

We now turn to the Paasche quantity effect, the first term on the right side of expression (5.9). We follow the same procedures as we used to decompose the Paasche price effect, reversing the roles of quantities and prices, temporarily assuming that comparison period profit $\pi^1 = 0$ so that the Paasche quantity effect simplifies to $-p^{1T}y^0 + w^{1T}x^0$. Taking an output orientation by isolating $-p^{1T}y^0$ in the simplified quantity effect, we obtain the decomposition

$$p^{1T}(y^1 - y^0) - w^{1T}(x^1 - x^0) = p^{1T}y^0[(Y_P/X_P) - 1] + \pi^1[1 - X_P^{-1}], \quad (5.15)$$

in which the first component is an output-oriented Paasche productivity indicator and the second is an input-oriented Paasche margin effect that can be rewritten as $\pi^1[1 - X_P^{-1}] = (\pi^1/C^1)[w^{1T}(x^1 - x^0)]$. Taking an input orientation by isolating $w^{1T}x^0$ in the simplified quantity effect generates the alternative decomposition

$$p^{1T}(y^1 - y^0) - w^{1T}(x^1 - x^0) = w^{1T}x^0[1 - (Y_P/X_P)^{-1}] + \pi^1[1 - Y_P^{-1}], \quad (5.16)$$

in which the first component is an input-oriented Paasche productivity indicator and the second is an output-oriented Paasche quantity margin effect that can be rewritten as $\pi^1[1 - Y_P^{-1}] = (\pi^1/R^1)[p^{1T}(y^1 - y^0)]$.

The two decompositions of the Paasche quantity effect in expressions (5.15) and (5.16) differ. The two Paasche productivity effects are equal if $\pi^1 = 0$

(comparison period profit is zero, in which case the quantity effect simplifies to a unique productivity effect), or if $Y_P = X_P$ (there is no productivity change as measured by Paasche quantity indexes, in which case the quantity effect simplifies to a unique margin effect). In all other circumstances the two productivity effects differ, even though they share a Paasche structure. The two Paasche margin effects also differ in general, and coincide if $Y_P = X_P$, or if $\pi^1 = 0$, in which case the two margin effects are zero.

We finally turn to the Laspeyres price effect, the second term on the right side of expression (5.9). This term decomposes in the same mathematical fashion as the Laspeyres quantity effect, reversing the roles of quantities and prices. Consequently, the Laspeyres price effect decomposes as

$$y^{0T}(p^1 - p^0) - x^{0T}(w^1 - w^0) = y^{0T}p^1[1 - (P_L/W_L)^{-1}] + \pi^0[W_L - 1], \quad (5.17)$$

with $\pi^0[W_L - 1] = (\pi^0/C^0)[x^{0T}(w^1 - w^0)]$, and alternatively as

$$y^{0T}(p^1 - p^0) - x^{0T}(w^1 - w^0) = x^{0T}w^1[(P_L/W_L) - 1] + \pi^0[P_L - 1], \quad (5.18)$$

with $\pi^0[P_L - 1] = (\pi^0/R^0)[y^{0T}(p^1 - p^0)]$. Interpretations of the two Laspeyres price effects in expressions (5.17) and (5.18) parallel those of the two Paasche price effects in expressions (5.13) and (5.14), with appropriate modifications.

We have two Paasche quantity effects in expressions (5.15) and (5.16), and two Laspeyres price effects in expressions (5.17) and (5.18). This generates four Paasche/Laspeyres decompositions of profit change that satisfy the sum test.

Table 5.1 collects all eight profit change decompositions. The four Laspeyres/Paasche decompositions appear in the first four rows, and the four Paasche/Laspeyres decompositions appear in the next four rows. Several features of Table 5.1 are noteworthy:

(i) Two functional forms, Laspeyres and Paasche, generate eight profit change decompositions, and these eight decompositions differ except under restrictive conditions;

(ii) All eight decompositions express Laspeyres and Paasche *indicators* as functions of Laspeyres and Paasche *indexes*;

(iii) The condition $\pi^0 = 0$ is sufficient for the Laspeyres quantity margin effects and the Laspeyres price margin effects to disappear; in this case the Laspeyres productivity effects coincide with the Laspeyres quantity effect, and the Laspeyres price recovery effects coincide with the Laspeyres price effect;

Table 5.1 Decompositions of profit change derived from Laspeyres and Paasche indicators

		Laspeyres and Paasche Decompositions of Profit Change		
	Quantity Effect		Price Effect	
Index Numbers	Productivity Effect	Quantity Margin Effect	Price Recovery Effect	Price Margin Effect
[1] Y_L, X_L, P_P, W_P	$p^{0T}y^1[1-(Y_L/X_L)^{-1}]$	$\pi^0[X_L-1]$	$y^{1T}p^0[(P_P/W_P)-1]$	$\pi^1[1-W_P^{-1}]$
[2] Y_L, X_L, P_P, W_P	$w^{0T}x^1[(Y_L/X_L)-1]$	$\pi^0[Y_L-1]$	$x^{1T}w^0[1-(P_P/W_P)^{-1}]$	$\pi^1[1-P_P^{-1}]$
[3] Y_L, X_L, P_P, W_P	$p^{0T}y^1[1-(Y_L/X_L)^{-1}]$	$\pi^0[X_L-1]$	$x^{1T}w^0[1-(P_P/W_P)^{-1}]$	$\pi^1[1-P_P^{-1}]$
[4] Y_L, X_L, P_P, W_P	$w^{0T}x^1[(Y_L/X_L)-1]$	$\pi^0[Y_L-1]$	$y^{1T}p^0[(P_P/W_P)-1]$	$\pi^1[1-W_P^{-1}]$
[5] Y_P, X_P, P_L, W_L	$p^{1T}y^0[(Y_P/X_P)-1]$	$\pi^1[1-X_P^{-1}]$	$y^{0T}p^1[1-(P_L/W_L)^{-1}]$	$\pi^0[W_L-1]$
[6] Y_P, X_P, P_L, W_L	$w^{1T}x^0[(1-(Y_P/X_P)^{-1}]$	$\pi^1[1-Y_P^{-1}]$	$x^{0T}w^1[(P_L/W_L)-1]$	$\pi^0[P_L-1]$
[7] Y_P, X_P, P_L, W_L	$p^{1T}y^0[(Y_P/X_P)-1]$	$\pi^1[1-X_P^{-1}]$	$x^{0T}w^1[(P_L/W_L)-1]$	$\pi^0[P_L-1]$
[8] Y_P, X_P, P_L, W_L	$w^{1T}x^0[(1-(Y_P/X_P)^{-1}]$	$\pi^1[1-Y_P^{-1}]$	$y^{0T}p^1[1-(P_L/W_L)^{-1}]$	$\pi^0[W_L-1]$

(iv) The alternative condition $\pi^1=0$ is sufficient for the Paasche quantity margin effects and the Paasche price margin effects to disappear; in this case the Paasche productivity effects coincide with the Paasche quantity effect, and the Paasche price recovery effects coincide with the Paasche price effect;

(v) $\pi^0=\pi^1=0$, a condition imposed by many writers, is sufficient for both margin effects to disappear in all eight decompositions; in this case all productivity effects coincide with their corresponding quantity effects, and all price recovery effects coincide with their corresponding price effects; and

(vi) If neither $\pi^0=0$ nor $\pi^1=0$, productivity effects coincide with corresponding quantity effects only if appropriate quantity indexes are unitary, and price recovery effects coincide with corresponding price effects only if appropriate price indexes are unitary.

(vii) All eight decompositions express productivity, price recovery, and margin effects in terms of index numbers. We develop indicator form expressions for these four effects in Chapter 6.

5.3.2 Bennet decompositions of profit change

In this section we decompose the Bennet profit change expression (5.10), which we reproduce for convenience as

$$\pi^1 - \pi^0 = [\overline{p}^T(y^1 - y^0) - \overline{w}^T(x^1 - x^0)] + [\overline{y}^T(p^1 - p^0) - \overline{x}^T(w^1 - w^0)].$$

The first term on the right side of this expression is the Bennet quantity effect, with arithmetic mean price weights, and the second term is the Bennet price effect, with arithmetic mean quantity weights.

We follow two different decomposition strategies. The first replicates the strategy we followed to decompose profit change using Laspeyres and Paasche indicators in Section 5.3.1. This strategy generates four Bennet decompositions of profit change. These Bennet decompositions are functions of Edgeworth-Marshall (EM) quantity and price indexes, and so we refer to decompositions generated by the first strategy as Bennet/EM decompositions. In the second strategy we calculate the arithmetic mean of a Laspeyres/Paasche profit change decomposition and a Paasche/Laspeyres profit change decomposition. There being four of each in Table 5.1, this strategy generates 16 decompositions of profit change. We refer to these decompositions as Bennet/LP decompositions. The advantage of the first strategy is that it generates closed form expressions for all four effects, whereas the second strategy does not. The second strategy has the virtue that each of its four effects is bounded by the corresponding Laspeyres/Paasche effects and Paasche/Laspeyres effects, whereas the first strategy does not.

Our first decomposition strategy is methodologically the same as the strategy we employed in Section 5.3.1. We decompose the Bennet quantity effect in three steps. In the first step we simplify the quantity effect by temporarily assuming either $(\overline{p}^T y^0 - \overline{w}^T x^0) = 0$ (profit is zero evaluated at arithmetic mean prices and base period quantities) or $(\overline{p}^T y^1 - \overline{w}^T x^1) = 0$ (profit is zero evaluated at arithmetic mean prices and comparison period quantities). In the second step we choose an orientation, either an output orientation by isolating one of $(\overline{p}^T y^1, \overline{p}^T y^0)$, or an input orientation by isolating one of $(\overline{w}^T x^1, \overline{w}^T x^0)$. In the third step we relax the simplifying assumption. We decompose the Bennet price effect following the same three steps. Because Bennet quantity and price indicators use arithmetic mean price weights and quantity weights, respectively, we end up with four distinct decompositions of profit change.

We illustrate the procedure by deriving one of the four decompositions. We decompose the quantity effect first, on the assumption that $(\overline{p}^T y^0 - \overline{w}^T x^0) = 0$. Isolating $\overline{p}^T y^1$, the simplified quantity effect decomposes as

$$\overline{p}^T y^1 - \overline{w}^T x^1 = \overline{p}^T y^1 [1 - (\overline{w}^T x^1 / \overline{p}^T y^1)(\overline{p}^T y^0 / \overline{w}^T x^0)] \quad (\text{since } \overline{p}^T y^0 - \overline{w}^T x^0 = 0)$$
$$= \overline{p}^T y^1 [1 - (Y_{EM}/X_{EM})^{-1}],$$

in which $Y_{EM} = \overline{p}^T y^1 / \overline{p}^T y^0$ and $X_{EM} = \overline{w}^T x^1 / \overline{w}^T x^0$ are EM quantity indexes. This is a Bennet productivity effect, expressed as a function of an EM productivity index. The corresponding Bennet margin effect is obtained by dropping the simplifying assumption that $(\overline{p}^T y^0 - \overline{w}^T x^0 = 0)$ and subtracting the Bennet productivity effect from the Bennet quantity effect. This generates the corresponding Bennet margin effect

$$[(\overline{p}^T y^1 - \overline{w}^T x^1) - (\overline{p}^T y^0 - \overline{w}^T x^0)] - \overline{p}^T y^1 [1 - (Y_{EM}/X_{EM})^{-1}]$$
$$= (\overline{p}^T y^0 - \overline{w}^T x^0)[X_{EM} - 1],$$

and so one decomposition of the Bennet quantity effect is

$$\overline{p}^T (y^1 - y^0) - \overline{w}^T (x^1 - x^0) = \overline{p}^T y^1 [1 - (Y_{EM}/X_{EM})^{-1}] + (\overline{p}^T y^0 - \overline{w}^T x^0)[X_{EM} - 1].$$
$$(5.19)$$

In this decomposition the Bennet productivity effect is expressed in terms of an EM productivity index and the corresponding Bennet margin effect is expressed in terms of an EM input quantity index. The interpretation of the latter as a margin effect is clarified by rewriting it as $[(\overline{p}^T y^0 - \overline{w}^T x^0)/ \overline{w}^T x^0][\overline{w}^T(x^1 - x^0)]$, in which the margin uses base period quantities and Bennet prices and firm size change is measured using a Bennet input quantity indicator.

Turning to the price effect and assuming that $(\overline{y}^T p^1 - \overline{x}^T w^1) = 0$ and isolating $\overline{y}^T p^0$, the simplified Bennet price effect decomposes as

$$-\overline{y}^T p^0 + \overline{x}^T w^0 = \overline{y}^T p^0 [(\overline{x}^T w^0 / \overline{y}^T p^0)(\overline{y}^T p^1 / \overline{x}^T w^1) - 1] \quad (\text{since } \overline{y}^T p^1 - \overline{x}^T w^1 = 0)$$
$$= \overline{y}^T p^0 [(P_{EM}/W_{EM}) - 1],$$

in which $P_{EM} = \overline{y}^T p^1 / \overline{y}^T p^0$ and $W_{EM} = \overline{x}^T w^1 / \overline{x}^T w^0$ are EM price indexes. This is a Bennet price recovery effect, expressed as a function of an EM price recovery index. The corresponding Bennet price margin effect is obtained by dropping the simplifying assumption that $(\overline{y}^T p^1 - \overline{x}^T w^1) = 0$ and subtracting the Bennet price recovery effect from the Bennet price effect. This generates the corresponding Bennet price margin effect

$$[(-\overline{y}^T p^0 + \overline{x}^T w^0) - (\overline{y}^T p^1 - \overline{x}^T w^1)] - \overline{y}^T p^0 [(P_{EM}/W_{EM}) - 1] = (\overline{y}^T p^1 - \overline{x}^T w^1)[1 - W_{EM}^{-1}],$$

and so one decomposition of the Bennet price effect is

$$\bar{y}^T(p^1-p^0)-\bar{x}^T(w^1-w^0) = \bar{y}^T p^0[(P_{EM}/W_{EM})-1] + (\bar{y}^T p^1-\bar{x}^T w^1)[1-W_{EM}^{-1}].$$

$$(5.20)$$

In this decomposition the Bennet price effect is expressed in terms of an EM price recovery index and the corresponding Bennet margin effect is expressed in terms of an EM input price index. The margin effect can be written as $[(\bar{y}^T p^1-\bar{x}^T w^1)/\bar{x}^T w^1)][\bar{x}^T(w^1-w^0)]$, the product of a margin that uses comparison period quantities and Bennet prices and a Bennet input price indicator. Combining expressions (5.19) and (5.20) generates a Bennet/EM profit change decomposition.

All four Bennet/EM decompositions of profit change are collected in Table 5.2. Each feature of Table 5.2 is analogous to a corresponding feature of Table 5.1, with appropriate changes in definitions of quantity indexes, price indexes, and profit. Thus:

(i) The use of Bennet indicators generates four profit change decompositions;

(ii) All four decompositions express Bennet *indicators* as functions of EM *indexes*;

(iii) A sufficient condition for equality of all four Bennet productivity indicators is that outputs and inputs vary in the same proportion, in the EM sense that $Y_{EM}=X_{EM}$, but this condition also makes all four Bennet productivity effects zero;

(iv) A sufficient condition for equality of all four Bennet price recovery indicators is that output prices and input prices vary in the same proportion, in the EM sense that $P_{EM}=W_{EM}$, but this condition makes all four Bennet price recovery effects zero;

(v) A sufficient condition for all four quantity margin effects to disappear is that $(\bar{p}^T y^0 - \bar{w}^T x^0) = (\bar{p}^T y^1 - \bar{w}^T x^1) = 0$, but this condition also makes the Bennet quantity effect, and all four Bennet productivity effects, zero;

(vi) A sufficient condition for all four price margin effects to disappear is that $(\bar{y}^T p^0 - \bar{x}^T w^0) = (\bar{y}^T p^1 - \bar{x}^T w^1) = 0$, but this condition makes the Bennet price effect, and all four Bennet price recovery effects, zero;

(vii) Although Bennet margin effects have the same structure as Laspeyres and Paasche margin effects, their use of base period,

Table 5.2 Decompositions of profit change derived from Bennet indicators

Index Numbers	Bennet/EM Decompositions of Profit Change			
	Quantity Effect		Price Effect	
	Productivity Effect	Quantity Margin Effect	Price Recovery Effect	Price Margin Effect
[1] Y_B, X_B, P_B, W_B	$\bar{p}^T y^1 [1 - (Y_{EM}/X_{EM})^{-1}]$	$(\bar{p}^T y^0 - \bar{w}^T x^0)[X_{EM} - 1]$	$\bar{y}^T p^0 [(P_{EM}/W_{EM}) - 1]$	$(\bar{y}^T p^1 - \bar{x}^T w^1)[1 - W_{EM}^{-1}]$
[2] Y_B, X_B, P_B, W_B	$\bar{w}^T x^1 [(Y_{EM}/X_{EM}) - 1]$	$(\bar{p}^T y^0 - \bar{w}^T x^0)[Y_{EM} - 1]$	$\bar{x}^T w^0 [1 - (P_{EM}/W_{EM})^{-1}]$	$(\bar{y}^T p^1 - \bar{x}^T w^1)[1 - P_{EM}^{-1}]$
[3] Y_B, X_B, P_B, W_B	$\bar{p}^T y^0 [(Y_{EM}/X_{EM}) - 1]$	$(\bar{p}^T y^1 - \bar{w}^T x^1)[1 - X_{EM}^{-1}]$	$\bar{y}^T p^1 [1 - (P_{EM}/W_{EM})^{-1}]$	$(\bar{y}^T p^0 - \bar{x}^T w^0)[W_{EM} - 1]$
[4] Y_B, X_B, P_B, W_B	$\bar{w}^T x^0 [1 - (Y_{EM}/X_{EM})^{-1}]$	$(\bar{p}^T y^1 - \bar{w}^T x^1)[1 - Y_{EM}^{-1}]$	$\bar{x}^T w^1 [(P_{EM}/W_{EM}) - 1]$	$(\bar{y}^T p^0 - \bar{x}^T w^0)[P_{EM} - 1]$

comparison period, and arithmetic mean data sacrifices clarity of interpretation; and

(viii) All four decompositions express productivity, price recovery, and margin effects in terms of EM index numbers.

The second strategy for generating Bennet decompositions of profit change is based on the following logic. A Bennet indicator is the arithmetic mean of Laspeyres and Paasche indicators. Consequently, a Bennet/LP profit change decomposition can be obtained as the arithmetic mean of Laspeyres/Paasche and Paasche/Laspeyres profit change decompositions. There being four of each in Table 5.1, a total of 16 Bennet/LP profit change decompositions emerge from this strategy. Using rows (1) and (5) of Table 5.1 to illustrate the strategy, one Bennet/LP productivity effect can be calculated as

$$\text{Bennet/LP productivity indicator}_{1,5} = \tfrac{1}{2}\{p^{0T}y^1\,[1 - (Y_L/X_L)^{-1}] + p^{1T}y^0\,[(Y_P/X_P) - 1]\},$$

and the corresponding Bennet/LP margin effect is

$$\text{Bennet/LP margin indicator}_{1,5} = \tfrac{1}{2}[\pi^0(X_L - 1) + \pi^1(1 - X_P^{-1})].$$

This effect is easy to calculate, and it is bounded by its two components. We provide a numerical illustration that compares the two Bennet strategies in Section 5.6.

5.3.3 Empirical applications

Applications based on Laspeyres and Paasche indicators are numerous, and we discussed several in Sections 4.3 and 4.4 of Chapter 4. Most writers focus on the quantity effect and ignore the price effect, and virtually all writers use Laspeyres quantity indicators and Paasche price indicators. Davis (1955), Kendrick and Creamer (1961), Vincent (1965, 1968), and Eldor and Sudit (1981) introduce an investor input or similar device to derive input-oriented productivity effects given in rows (2) and (4) of Table 5.1. Because the practice of expensing investor input eliminates the margin effect, the productivity effects these authors obtain are quantity effects. Méraud (1966), CERC (1969a), Kurosawa (1975, 1991), and Miller (1984) allow nominal profit to be nonzero and, with some generous interpretive assistance, decompose the quantity effect into productivity effects and margin effects given in the first four rows of Table 5.1. Among the writers we discuss, the French writers also study distribution, but they are content to leave the price effect in indicator form, which serves their objective of identifying individual agents who gain or lose in the distribution exercise. Eldor and Sudit also study distribution, but primarily as a managerial tool to evaluate the "total economic health" of a business rather than as a way of identifying gainers and losers in the distribution exercise. No writer we know of is interested in decomposing the price effect into a price recovery effect and a margin effect.

Applications based on Bennet indicators are rare.

New South Wales Treasury (1999)

The New South Wales Treasury develops a "Profit Composition Analysis" framework for tracking the productivity and financial performance of government-owned businesses, particularly those possessing market power and subject to price regulation. Their decomposition of profit change can be expressed as

$$
\pi^1 - \pi^0 = (\bar{p}^T y^1)[(\bar{w}^T x^0 / \bar{p}^T y^0) - (\bar{w}^T x^1 / \bar{p}^T y^1)]
$$
$$
+ (\bar{p}^T y^1 - \bar{p}^T y^0)[1 - (\bar{w}^T x^0 / \bar{p}^T y^0)] + \bar{y}^T (p^1 - p^0) - \bar{x}^T (w^1 - w^0).
$$
$$(5.21)$$

The third term on the right side of expression (5.21), called "total price performance," is the Bennet price effect given by the second term on the right side of expression (5.10). Consequently, the sum of the first two terms on the right side, called "net TFP," must coincide with the Bennet quantity effect. The first term on the right side, called "gross TFP," coincides with the Bennet productivity effect appearing in row (2) of Table 5.2, since

$$
(\bar{p}^T y^1)[(\bar{w}^T x^0 / \bar{p}^T y^0) - (\bar{w}^T x^1 / \bar{p}^T y^1)] = (\bar{w}^T x^0)(\bar{p}^T y^1 / \bar{p}^T y^0) - \bar{w}^T x^1
$$
$$
= \bar{w}^T x^1 [(Y_{EM} / X_{EM}) - 1].
$$

Consequently, the second term on the right side, called "scale adjustment," coincides with the Bennet quantity margin effect also given in row (2) of Table 5.2, since

$$
(\bar{p}^T y^1 - \bar{p}^T y^0)[1 - (\bar{w}^T x^0 / \bar{p}^T y^0)] = [(\bar{p}^T y^1 / \bar{p}^T y^0) - 1](\bar{p}^T y^0)(\bar{p}^T y^0 - \bar{w}^T x^0)
$$
$$
\times (1 / \bar{p}^T y^0)
$$
$$
= (\bar{p}^T y^0 - \bar{w}^T x^0)[Y_{EM} - 1],
$$

which generates the Bennet quantity change decomposition

$$\bar{p}^T(y^1-y^0)-\bar{w}^T(x^1-x^0) = \bar{w}^T x^1[(Y_{EM}/X_{EM}) - 1]+(\bar{p}^T y^0 - \bar{w}^T x^0)[Y_{EM} - 1]$$
(5.22)

in row (2) of Table 5.2.

The authors emphasize that, while the productivity effect and the margin effect are converted from indicator form to index number form, the price effect is left in indicator form. This dual structure is intended to assist management in isolating the two quantity drivers (productivity change and size/margin change) of profit change, and also to assist the regulator in setting output price(s) in a manner that balances the interests of consumers and the business. The workings of the model are illustrated with a pilot study of a government business subject to price regulation.

Lee, Park, and Kim (1999)

Lee et al. also analyze the Bennet profit change decomposition given in expression (5.10). They call the quantity effect a "superficial productivity difference" because it can be decomposed into a "true productivity difference" and the effect of "scale difference." Their decomposition of the quantity effect can be expressed as

$$\bar{p}^T(y^1-y^0)-\bar{w}^T(x^1-x^0) = \bar{w}^T x^0[(\bar{p}^T y^1/\bar{w}^T x^1) - (\bar{p}^T y^0/\bar{w}^T x^0)]$$
$$+ \bar{w}^T(x^1-x^0)[(\bar{p}^T y^1/\bar{w}^T x^1) - 1],$$
(5.23)

in which the $\bar{p}^T y^t/\bar{w}^T x^t$ are productivity levels of EM form in base and comparison periods. The first term on the right side of expression (5.23), "true productivity difference," makes no contribution to profit change if, and only if, the productivity level does not change, and the second term, "scale difference," makes no contribution to profit change if input use does not change in a Bennet sense or if the comparison period EM productivity level is unitary.

The authors do not do so, but their "superficial productivity difference" can be rewritten as

$$\bar{p}^T(y^1-y^0)-\bar{w}^T(x^1-x^0) = \bar{p}^T y^0[(Y_{EM}/X_{EM}) - 1]+(\bar{p}^T y^1 - \bar{w}^T x^1)[1-X_{EM}^{-1}],$$
(5.24)

which is the quantity change decomposition in row (3) of Table 5.2.

The authors apply a model given by expressions (5.10) and (5.23) to evaluate managerial performance in an international panel of natural gas transportation companies. Thus, base and comparison situations refer to both companies and time periods, and the authors convert bilateral indicators and indexes to multilateral form. Because variation in firm size is extensive, the authors subtract the quantity margin effect from both sides of expression (5.10), and so they attribute scale-adjusted profit variation to productivity variation independent of scale and to price variation. The objective of adjusting performance evaluation for size variation is sensible, particularly in an international panel. However, the authors' scale adjusted profit variation remains sensitive to firm size because the size-independent productivity index $[(Y_{EM}/X_{EM}) - 1]$ is scaled by a size-dependent revenue measure $\bar{p}^T y^0$.

The New South Wales Treasury and Lee et al. use different terminology, but they have a common objective of separating the financial impacts of productivity variation from those of size variation. To this end both decompose a Bennet quantity effect into productivity and margin effects, in the process transforming Bennet quantity indicators into EM quantity indexes. However, they obtain different decompositions. The two productivity effects differ, as do the two margin effects, except under restrictive conditions. Both studies leave the Bennet price effect in indicator form.[6]

5.3.4 Summary

Change in profit from one situation to another decomposes into the separate impacts of changes in quantities and changes in prices. We show that the quantity effect decomposes into a productivity effect and a margin effect. This result is not new, but it is not widely appreciated either. We also show that the price effect decomposes into a price recovery effect and a margin effect. This result appears to be new, and we emphasize the significance of the price margin effect. We also show that the conditions under which the productivity effect coincides with the quantity effect, and the conditions under which the price recovery effect coincides with the price effect, both depend on the functional form specified for the quantity and price indicators. This result also appears to be new.

---

[6] Grifell-Tatjé and Lovell (2008) decompose the quantity effect in the Bennet profit change expression (5.10). They obtain a productivity effect and a quantity margin effect very similar to those in Table 5.2. The differences arise from the replacement of observed input vectors with unobserved cost-efficient input vectors that play an important role in decomposing the productivity effect into its economic drivers. Lim and Lovell (2009) follow the same strategy, and they augment expression (5.10) with a term capturing the financial impact of variation in quasi-fixed inputs.

The majority of profit change models is based on Laspeyres quantity indicators and Paasche price indicators. We show that there exist four generally different decompositions of profit change using this pairing, and four additional generally different decompositions using the reverse pairing. As yet very few profit change models are based on Bennet quantity and price indicators, and we show that there exist four generally different decompositions using Bennet indicators. Bennet indicators use arithmetic mean price and quantity weights. We suggest a variant on Bennet's idea by applying the arithmetic mean operator to the effects themselves rather than to prices and quantities. Since we have four Laspeyres/Paasche decompositions and four Paasche/Laspeyres decompositions, this strategy generates 16 Bennet decompositions. We provide a numerical illustration of the various profit change decompositions in Section 5.6.

5.4 INCORPORATING INVESTOR INPUT INTO THE ANALYTICAL FRAMEWORK

The concept of investor input played an important role in Chapter 4, but the analytical framework in Section 5.3 does not incorporate the concept. In this section we incorporate investor input in the model by explicitly incorporating capital and its rate of return. Doing so generates somewhat different decompositions of profit change. We decompose the quantity effect, but we leave the price effect in its original form, partly because the strategy for decomposing the price effect is the same as that for decomposing the quantity effect and partly because its original form is well suited to identifying individual price changes most responsible for profit change. Our findings remain sensitive to the choice of functional form for empirical indicators, but much less so than in Section 5.3.

Recall that $R - C \gtreqless 0$, and that $R - (C + rK) = R - \check{C} = R - \check{w}^T x = \pi - rK = 0 \Rightarrow \pi = rK$. In the presence of investor input, $p^{0T}y^0 - w^{0T}x^0 - r^0K^0 = p^{1T}y^1 - w^{1T}x^1 - r^1K_0^1 = 0$.

We begin with an expression for profit change based on a Laspeyres quantity effect and a Paasche price effect

$$\pi^1 - \pi^0 = [p^{0T}(y^1 - y^0) - w^{0T}(x^1 - x^0)] + [y^{1T}(p^1 - p^0) - x^{1T}(w^1 - w^0)],$$

and adding $r^0(K_0^1 - K^0) - r^0(K_0^1 - K^0)$ to the right side generates

$$\pi^1 - \pi^0 = [p^{0T}(y^1 - y^0) - w^{0T}(x^1 - x^0) - r^0(K_0^1 - K^0)] \tag{5.25}$$
$$+ r^0(K_0^1 - K^0) + [y^{1T}(p^1 - p^0) - x^{1T}(w^1 - w^0)].$$

Expression (5.25) decomposes profit change into three parts, each in indicator form. The first is a productivity effect with modified capital weight $w_N^0 + r^0$, the second is an earning on capital expansion effect, and the third is the price effect. Recalling that $p^{0T}y^0 - w^{0T}x^0 - r^0K^0 = 0$, expression (5.25) becomes

$$\pi^1 - \pi^0 = [p^{0T}y^1 - w^{0T}x^1 - r^0K_0^1] + r^0(K_0^1 - K^0) + [y^{1T}(p^1 - p^0) - x^{1T}(w^1 - w^0)]$$
$$= \check{\pi}_0^1 + r^0(K_0^1 - K^0) + [y^{1T}(p^1 - p^0) - x^{1T}(w^1 - w^0)],$$

$$(5.26)$$

in which $\check{\pi}_0^1 = p^{0T}y^1 - w^{0T}x^1 - r^0K_0^1 = \check{w}^{0T}x^1[(Y_L/\check{X}_L) - 1]$ is the productivity effect in expression (4.4) in Chapter 4. Replacing $\pi^1 - \pi^0$ with $r^1K_0^1 - r^0K^0$ yields the Eldor and Sudit profit change decomposition in expression (4.24) in Chapter 4.

Expression (5.26) is the Laspeyres/Paasche decomposition of profit change with investor input incorporated and the price effect left in its original form. The productivity change component has an input orientation in expression (4.4) in Chapter 4, which generates the profit change decomposition in expression (5.26). If the productivity change component is given an output orientation by means of $\check{\pi}_0^1 = p^{0T}y^1[1 - (Y_L/\check{X}_L)^{-1}]$, the profit change decomposition becomes

$$\pi^1 - \pi^0 = p^{0T}y^1[1 - (Y_L/\check{X}_L)^{-1}] + r^0(K_0^1 - K^0) + [y^{1T}(p^1 - p^0) - x^{1T}(w^1 - w^0)].$$

$$(5.27)$$

The input- and output-oriented productivity change components are equal, which does not happen in the absence of investor input.

Expressions (5.26) and (5.27) convert the productivity effect from its indicator form in expression (5.25) to index number form. They appear to provide different profit change decompositions, but they are the same. They share a common price effect and a common earnings on capital expansion effect, which implies that their productivity effects have the same value, despite their differing orientation. There exists just a single Laspeyres/Paasche profit change decomposition when investor input is incorporated in the model, that decomposition being given by expression (5.26), with input-oriented productivity effect, or by expression (5.27), with output-oriented productivity effect.

We continue with an expression for profit change based on a Paasche quantity effect and a Laspeyres price effect. Following the same procedures as above, and recalling that $p^{1T}y^1 - w^{1T}x^1 - r^1K_0^1 = 0$, yields

$$\pi^1 - \pi^0 = -\check{\pi}_1^0 + r^1(K_0^1 - K^0) + [y^{0T}(p^1 - p^0) - x^{0T}(w^1 - w^0)], \quad (5.28)$$

in which $-\check{\pi}_1^0 = -(p^{1T}y^0 - w^{1T}x^0 - r^1K^0)$ is the Paasche productivity effect and $r^1(K_0^1 - K^0)$ is the Paasche earnings on capital expansion effect. As before, the productivity effect can be given an input orientation by defining

$$-\check{\pi}_1^0 = (w^{1T}x^0 + r^1K^0)[1 - (Y_p/\check{X}_p)^{-1}]$$
$$= \check{w}^{1T}x^0 [1 - (Y_p/\check{X}_p)^{-1}] \quad (5.29)$$

or an output orientation by defining

$$-\check{\pi}_1^0 = p^{1T}y^0[(Y_P/\check{X}_P) - 1]. \quad (5.30)$$

Also as before, and for the same reason, the two orientations generate the same profit change decomposition. Expression (5.28), incorporating either expression (5.29) or expression (5.30), is the Paasche/Laspeyres profit change decomposition when investor input is incorporated in the model.

There being one Laspeyres/Paasche decomposition and one Paasche/Laspeyres decomposition, there exists a single Bennet profit change decomposition when investor input is incorporated in the model. This decomposition is given by

$$\pi^1 - \pi^0 = \tfrac{1}{2}(\check{\pi}_0^1 - \check{\pi}_1^0) + \bar{r}(K_0^1 - K^0) + [\bar{y}^T(p^1 - p^0) - \bar{x}^T(w^1 - w^0)], \quad (5.31)$$

in which $\bar{r} = 1/2(r^1 + r^0)$ and all other terms are defined above. Expression (5.31) does not define the productivity effect $1/2(\check{\pi}_0^1 - \check{\pi}_1^0)$ as a function of an EM productivity index, as we do in Section 5.3.2. However, it can be given an appealing interpretation by rewriting it to obtain

$$\tfrac{1}{2}(\check{\pi}_0^1 - \check{\pi}_1^0) = [\bar{p}^T(y^1 - y^0) - \tilde{w}^T(x^1 - x^0)], \quad (5.32)$$

in which $\tilde{w} = [\bar{w}_1, ..., \bar{w}_{N-1}, (\bar{w}_N + \bar{r})]$. Expression (5.32) defines the Bennet productivity effect as the Bennet quantity effect appearing in expression (5.10), but with capital change assigned a weight $(\bar{w}_N + \bar{r})$ instead of $\bar{w}_N$.[7]

---

[7] A similar interpretation can be applied to the two previous decompositions, and so

In this section we incorporate investor input by explicitly introducing capital and its rate of return. Doing so has an impact. Most significantly, it alters the explanation of profit change by replacing a quantity margin effect with a return on capital expansion effect that acknowledges the contribution to profit growth of investment that generates a positive rate of return. It reduces the number of profit change decompositions from twelve in Section 5.3 to just three, a reduction that occurs because orientation of the productivity effect no longer matters. The three decompositions differ because they assign different weights to changes. Each productivity effect differs from its analogues in Section 5.3 because capital is assigned a different weight (the sum of its unit cost and its rate of return). Each return on capital expansion effect differs from its corresponding quantity margin effect in Section 5.3.

Finally, in Section 5.3 we are unable to express productivity, price recovery, and margin effects in indicator form. Here in Section 5.4 the practice of expensing investor input allows us to do so. Expressions (5.26) and (5.27) illustrate our ability to express the productivity effect in indicator form. Similar results apply for the Paasche/Laspeyres and Bennet decompositions. The key is the fact that profit is expensed in Section 5.4, but not in Section 5.3.

5.5 A FAMILY OF DUAL PRODUCTIVITY INDICATORS

In Chapter 2 we explored the generation of profitability change, a procedure that we formalized in expression (2.19). This expression states that profitability change is the product of an index of productivity change and an index of price recovery change. In Section 2.9 we supposed that profitability remains unchanged from base period to comparison period, so that $\Pi^1 = \Pi^0$. In this case, provided that the product test is satisfied, $Y/X = W/P$, and the reciprocal of the index of price recovery change provides a dual index of productivity change. We also noted in Section 2.9 that several writers have obtained the same dual productivity index under the

$$\check{\pi}_0^1 = p^{0T}(y^1 - y^0) - \check{w}^{0T}(x^1 - x^0)$$

for the Laspeyres/Paasche decomposition and

$$-\check{\pi}_1^0 = p^{1T}(y^1 - y^0) - \check{w}^{1T}(x^1 - x^0)$$

for the Paasche/Laspeyres decomposition. Both expressions define a productivity effect as a quantity effect with capital assigned a weight equal to its unit cost plus its rate of return.

much stronger supposition that $\pi^1 = \pi^0 = 0$. In this section we explore the conditions under which a dual productivity indicator exists. Existence implies that a price recovery effect is equal in magnitude, and opposite in sign, to its corresponding productivity effect. This property is the indicator analogue to the index property $Y/X = W/P$. We explore conditions for the existence of a dual productivity indicator with the assistance of the profit change decompositions appearing in Tables 5.1 and 5.2.

Laspeyres/Paasche, Paasche/Laspeyres, and Bennet/LP
decompositions

Profit change decompositions based on Laspeyres and Paasche indicators, and expressed in Laspeyres and Paasche index number form, appear in Table 5.1.

The condition $\Pi^1 = \Pi^0 = 1$ (which is equivalent to the condition $\pi^1 = \pi^0 = 0$) is sufficient to eliminate both margin effects from all eight decompositions of profit change, which itself is zero since $\pi^1 = \pi^0 = 0$. Every row of Table 5.1 collapses to an expression of the form "0 = productivity effect + price recovery effect." Consequently, all eight productivity effects have a corresponding dual productivity effect given by the negative of the corresponding price recovery effect. The monetary value of a Laspeyres (Paasche) productivity effect is the negative of the monetary value of the corresponding Paasche (Laspeyres) price recovery effect when $\pi^1 = \pi^0 = 0$. Under this condition the financial impacts of productivity change are fully distributed to consumers and resource suppliers.

Because Bennet/LP decompositions are component-by-component arithmetic means of Laspeyres/Paasche and Paasche/Laspeyres decompositions, the condition $\Pi^1 = \Pi^0 = 1$ also generates 16 Bennet/LP dual productivity indicators.

The weaker condition $\Pi^1 = \Pi^0$ (which does not require that $\pi^1 = \pi^0 = 0$) suffices for the existence of a dual productivity indicator in four of eight decompositions in Table 5.1. This condition equates the productivity effect with (minus) the price recovery effect in the decompositions in rows (1), (2), (5), and (6). In these four rows the price recovery effect provides a dual productivity indicator, *even though profit change is not zero and neither margin effect disappears*. In the remaining four decompositions the productivity effect and the price recovery effect have different absolute values, and the price recovery effect is not a dual productivity effect. The key is orientation. In rows (1), (2), (5), and (6) the productivity effect and the price recovery effect have the same orientation, while in the remaining rows they have opposite orientations. The fact that the decompositions in rows (1), (2), (5), and (6) have dual productivity indicators under weaker assumptions than the remaining four decompositions that rely on $\pi^1 = \pi^0 = 0$ leads to a preference for them.

The existence of four dual productivity indicators has interesting implications. Since the productivity effect and the price recovery effect sum to zero in these four cases, profit change is the nonzero sum of the quantity margin effect and the price margin effect. Using the relationship $\pi = C(\Pi - 1)$ in output-oriented rows (1) and (5), it follows that the condition $\Pi^1 = \Pi^0$ implies that $\pi^1/\pi^0 = C^1/C^0$. Using the relationship $\pi = R(1 - \Pi^{-1})$ in input-oriented rows (2) and (6), it follows that the condition $\Pi^1 = \Pi^0$ implies that $\pi^1/\pi^0 = R^1/R^0$.

Because Bennet/LP profit change decompositions are arithmetic means of Laspeyres/Paasche and Paasche/Laspeyres profit change decompositions, the condition $\Pi^1 = \Pi^0$ also generates four Bennet/LP dual productivity indicators (from row pairs (1) and (5), (1) and (6), (2) and (5), and (2) and (6) in Table 5.1). Only two of these decompositions share the implications in the previous paragraph (output-oriented row pair (1) and (5), for which $\pi^1/\pi^0 = C^1/C^0$, and input-oriented row pairs (2) and (6), for which $\pi^1/\pi^0 = R^1/R^0$).

No other plausible condition, including $\pi^1 = \pi^0$, generates a dual productivity indicator when indicators have Laspeyres and Paasche, and therefore Bennet/LP, form.

Bennet/EM decompositions

Profit change decompositions based on Bennet indicators, and expressed in EM index number form, appear in Table 5.2.

Unlike the Laspeyres/Paasche and Bennet/LP case, the condition $\Pi^1 = \Pi^0 = 1$ ($\pi^1 = \pi^0 = 0$) is not sufficient to generate a dual productivity indicator for any of the four Bennet/EM profit change decompositions appearing in Table 5.2. This is because, even though profit change is zero, neither π^0 nor π^1 appears in the Bennet/EM margin effects, and so none of the Bennet/EM profit change decompositions collapses to the form "0 = productivity effect + price recovery effect." Since this condition fails to generate a dual productivity indicator, the weaker condition $\Pi^1 = \Pi^0$ also fails.

The condition $(\bar{p}^T y^0 - \bar{w}^T x^0) = (\bar{y}^T p^1 - \bar{x}^T w^1) = 0$ eliminates both margin effects in rows (1) and (2) of Table 5.2, and would appear to generate a pair of dual productivity indicators. However, this condition also implies that $\pi^1 = \pi^0 = 0$, making both dual productivity indicators zero. The alternative condition $(\bar{p}^T y^1 - \bar{w}^T x^1) = (\bar{y}^T p^0 - \bar{x}^T w^0) = 0$ generates the same meaningless result in rows (3) and (4) for the same reasons.

When profit change decompositions are based on EM indexes derived from Bennet indicators, there appear to be no conditions under which a price recovery indicator provides a dual productivity indicator.

Summary

We conclude that dual productivity indicators are unlikely to exist, at least not exactly, regardless of functional form. When profit change decompositions are based on Laspeyres and Paasche indexes derived from Laspeyres and Paasche indicators (which includes Bennet/LP profit change decompositions), dual productivity indicators are guaranteed to exist in the unlikely event that $\Pi^1 = \Pi^0 = 1$, and can exist if $\Pi^1 = \Pi^0$. We have demonstrated that six index number pairs (four Laspeyres/Paasche pairs and two Bennet/LP pairs) generate dual productivity indicators. Importantly, existence of these dual productivity indicators does not require zero profit in either period. This finding provides compelling evidence contradicting those who claim in Section 2.9 of Chapter 2 that zero profit in both periods is required for the existence of a dual productivity index.

5.6 A NUMERICAL ILLUSTRATION

In this section we provide a numerical example to illustrate some prominent features of the profit change decompositions in Section 5.3. The example is based on data contained in Table 4.5 in Section 4.5 of Chapter 4. We arbitrarily select producer #5, whose data we use to decompose profit change. Producer #5 has $\Pi^0 = \Pi^1 = 1.10$ and $\pi^0 = 7.35, \pi^1 = 9.73$. We conduct a total of 16 decompositions, eight based on Laspeyres and Paasche decompositions in Table 5.1, four based on Bennet/EM decompositions in Table 5.2, and four based on Bennet/LP decompositions. The profit change decompositions appear in Table 5.3. These decompositions illustrate a number of points:

(i)   No two decompositions are the same
(ii) Both types of Bennet quantity and price effects are bounded by Laspeyres and Paasche quantity and price effects

Table 5.3 Alternative decompositions of profit change

		Decompositions of Profit Change					
					Quantity Effect	Price Effect	
		Quantity Effect	Price Effect	Productivity	Quantity Margin Effect	Price Recovery	Price Margin Effect
Laspeyres and Paasche							
[1]	Y_L, X_L, P_P, W_P	4.19	−1.81	2.18	2.01	−2.18	0.37
[2]	Y_L, X_L, P_P, W_P	4.19	−1.81	1.98	2.20	−1.98	0.18
[3]	Y_L, X_L, P_P, W_P	4.19	−1.81	2.18	2.01	−1.98	0.18
[4]	Y_L, X_L, P_P, W_P	4.19	−1.81	1.98	2.20	−2.18	0.37
[5]	Y_P, X_P, P_L, W_L	3.83	−1.45	1.75	2.09	−1.75	0.29
[6]	Y_P, X_P, P_L, W_L	3.83	−1.45	1.59	2.25	-1.59	0.14
[7]	Y_P, X_P, P_L, W_L	3.83	−1.45	1.75	2.09	−1.59	0.14
[8]	Y_P, X_P, P_L, W_L	3.83	−1.45	1.59	2.25	−1.75	0.29
Bennet/EM							
[1]	Y_B, X_B, P_B, W_B	4.01	−1.63	2.20	1.81	−1.93	0.30
[2]	Y_B, X_B, P_B, W_B	4.01	−1.63	2.02	1.99	−1.77	0.14
[3]	Y_B, X_B, P_B, W_B	4.01	−1.63	1.73	2.28	−2.01	0.38
[4]	Y_B, X_B, P_B, W_B	4.01	−1.63	1.56	2.45	−1.80	0.17
Bennet/LP							
1/2([1]+[5])	Y_B, X_B, P_B, W_B	4.01	−1.63	1.96	2.05	−1.96	0.33
1/2([1]+[6])	Y_B, X_B, P_B, W_B	4.01	−1.63	1.88	2.13	−1.88	0.25
1/2([2]+[5])	Y_B, X_B, P_B, W_B	4.01	−1.63	1.86	2.15	−1.86	0.23
1/2([2]+[6])	Y_B, X_B, P_B, W_B	4.01	−1.63	1.79	2.23	−1.79	0.16

(iii) Bennet/LP productivity and margin effects are bounded by their Laspeyres and Paasche counterparts, but Bennet/EM productivity and margin effects are not;

(iv) Bennet/LP price recovery and margin effects are bounded by their Paasche and Laspeyres counterparts, but Bennet/EM price recovery and margin effects are not;

(v) Two Laspeyres/Paasche decompositions and two Paasche/ Laspeyres decompositions have dual productivity indicators, because $\Pi^1 = \Pi^0$ and orientation is the same for each pair;

(vi) No Bennet/EM decomposition has a dual productivity indicator; and

(vii) Bennet/LP decompositions do not necessarily have a dual productivity indicator, but the four we specify do have a dual productivity indicator because they are arithmetic means of Laspeyres/Paasche and Paasche/Laspeyres decompositions that have a dual productivity indicator because they have the same orientation.

All decompositions of profit change have the same basic structure, with each component having an intuitive economic interpretation. However, despite this similarity, the profit change decompositions differ quantitatively, depending on functional forms selected for indicators and, in the Bennet case, on the strategy used to define a Bennet profit change decomposition.

6 Decomposing the Productivity Change Component of Profit Change

6.1 INTRODUCTION

The research objective in this chapter is the same as in the ratio-oriented Chapter 3: to tell a story about the economic drivers of the productivity change component of change in financial performance. The models developed in Chapters 4 and 5 do not meet this objective. They are constructed solely from accounting information, and they generate valuable information on productivity change and its financial impact, but not on the economic drivers of productivity change and their financial impacts.

We introduce best practice technology and varying degrees of optimization in order to identify the economic drivers of productivity change and to quantify their contributions to profit change. Because best practice technology is unknown, it must be estimated, and this, together with a sufficiently large sample to make estimation feasible, is the price to be paid for gaining insight into the economic drivers of productivity change. The analytical framework we develop in this chapter has similarities with and differences with the framework we developed in Chapter 3. The analytical techniques we use to decompose the productivity effect are similar, but reliance on optimization to establish best practice benchmarks is new. Although optimization is used to establish benchmarks, we do not assume that firms are successful optimizers. Indeed change in the ability to optimize is a key driver of productivity change. A significant difference between the two analytical frameworks is the appearance of an effect that drives a wedge between the quantity effect and the

233

productivity effect. The analytical framework in Section 6.2 incorporates investor input, and the effect is an earnings on capital expansion effect. The analytical frameworks in Sections 6.3 and 6.4 do not incorporate investor input. In Section 6.3 the effect is a margin effect. The earnings on capital expansion effect and the margin effect appeared in Chapters 4 and 5. In Section 6.4 the effect is an activity effect, which is new. All three effects complement the productivity effect in the quantity effect, but in different ways, and as we demonstrate with empirical applications, each of these effects can be large relative to the productivity effect.

In Section 6.2 we explore alternative ways of decomposing the productivity effect when the analytical framework incorporates investor input. This analysis extends developments in Section 4.3.1 of Chapter 4 and Section 5.4 of Chapter 5. The presence of investor input is signalled by the presence of a return to capital, in addition to the cost of capital, and creates what we call an earnings on capital expansion effect. In Sections 6.3 and 6.4 we explore decomposition when the analytical framework ignores investor input. This exploration extends analyses initiated in Section 4.3.2 of Chapter 4 and Section 5.3 of Chapter 5. The analytical framework in Section 6.3 contains a productivity effect and a margin effect, and the productivity effect has three drivers. The analytical framework in Section 6.4 contains a productivity effect and an activity effect, and the productivity effect has two drivers. In Section 6.5 we relate the analytical frameworks in the two previous sections. A distinguishing feature of this section is that it is not dogmatic about the forces that drive productivity change. Productivity change can have three drivers, as in Section 6.3, or two, as in Section 6.4, or more or less as circumstances warrant. Section 6.6 provides a summary and conclusion of the analysis of profit change appearing in Chapters 4 to 6.

6.2 DECOMPOSING PRODUCTIVITY CHANGE WITH INVESTOR INPUT INCORPORATED

We begin with a notational refresher. If we expense investor input, as Davis and others do, we add the return to capital to operating cost and redefine profit as $\check{\pi} = R - (C + rK) = R - \check{C} \equiv 0$, with $\check{C} = \check{w}^T x = w_1 x_1 + \cdots + w_{N-1} x_{N-1} + (w_N + r)K$, so that $\check{w}$ coincides with w apart from the final component. We show in Section 4.3.1 of Chapter 4 and in Section 5.4 of Chapter 5 that deflated comparison period productivity $\check{\Pi}_0^1 = R_0^1 / \check{C}_0^1 = Y_L / \check{X}_L$ is a Laspeyres productivity index with monetary value

$\check{\pi}_0^1 = p^{0T}y^1 - \check{w}^{0T}x^1 = \check{w}^{0T}x^1[(Y_L/\check{X}_L) - 1] = p^{0T}y^1[1 - (Y_L/\check{X}_L)^{-1}]$. A Paasche productivity index is expressed similarly as $(\check{\Pi}_1^0)^{-1} = \check{C}_1^0/R_1^0 = Y_P/\check{X}_P$ with monetary value $-\check{\pi}_1^0 = -(p^{1T}y^0 - \check{w}^{1T}x^0) = \check{w}^{1T}x^0[1 - (Y_P/\check{X}_P)^{-1}] = p^{1T}y^0[(Y_P/\check{X}_P) - 1]$.

If we expense investor input we do not have a Bennet expression for productivity change in EM form, but we can construct an alternative Bennet expression for the value of productivity change by taking the arithmetic mean of the Laspeyres and Paasche expressions. The Bennet expression (5.32) for productivity change in indicator form is

$$\tfrac{1}{2}(\check{\pi}_0^1 - \check{\pi}_1^0) = \bar{p}^T(y^1 - y^0) - \bar{\check{w}}^T(x^1 - x^0), \tag{6.1}$$

which becomes, in Laspeyres/Paasche index number form,

$$\bar{p}^T(y^1 - y^0) - \bar{\check{w}}^T(x^1 - x^0) = \tfrac{1}{2}\{\check{w}^{0T}x^1[(Y_L/\check{X}_L) - 1] + \check{w}^{1T}x^0[1 - (Y_P/\check{X}_P)^{-1}]\}$$
$$= \tfrac{1}{2}\{p^{0T}y^1[1 - (Y_L/\check{X}_L)^{-1}] + p^{1T}y^0[(Y_P/\check{X}_P) - 1]\}, \tag{6.2}$$

the first equality having an input orientation and the second having an output orientation. Each index number formulation in expression (6.2) is equal to the indicator formulation in expression (6.1), which allows us to use either one, depending on the context.

Although $\check{\Pi}_0^1, \check{\pi}_0^1, (\check{\Pi}_1^0)^{-1}, -\check{\pi}_1^0$, and $\tfrac{1}{2}(\check{\pi}_0^1 - \check{\pi}_1^0)$ provide useful information, they do not quantify or value the drivers of productivity change. In this section we suggest two strategies that do provide information on the drivers of productivity change. Information is not free, however, and both strategies require estimation of the technology that generates the quantity data. Neither strategy requires an assumption of optimizing behavior, successful or not. Neither strategy uses price information in the estimation stage, which is based on quantity information only, but both strategies use price information after estimation to value the contribution of each driver. The outcome of both strategies is a set of estimates of the magnitudes and financial impacts of the drivers of productivity change.

The two strategies extend analyses initiated in Section 4.3.1 of Chapter 4 and continued in Section 5.4 of Chapter 5. Both strategies decompose the productivity effect into its economic drivers, although they have contrasting features. The first strategy is based on the Bennet indicator form of the productivity effect given in expression (6.1), and generates a decomposition that satisfies the sum test with the other sources of profit change, but it weights capital change in a conceptually different way ($w_N + r$) than it weights other quantity changes. However, this weighting issue is a natural consequence of expensing investor input; it arises only in the valuation stage, not in the estimation stage, and its impact is likely to be minor, particularly in competitive environments that drive the rate of return to capital toward zero. The second strategy is based on the Bennet/LP index number form of the productivity effect given in either orientation in expression (6.2). The estimation stage generates a decomposition of productivity change into its economic drivers, but at the cost of failing the sum test with the other sources of profit change, although satisfaction can be treated as a hypothesis to be tested. The valuation stage remains dependent on $(w_N + r)$.

6.2.1 A productivity indicator approach

The first strategy is based on the indicator form of the Bennet profit change decomposition in expression (6.1). We substitute this expression into expression (5.31) in Chapter 5 and rearrange terms to obtain

$$
\begin{aligned}
\pi^1 - \pi^0 = {} & [\bar{p}^T(y^1 - y^0) - \breve{w}^T(x^1 - x^0)] + \bar{r}(K_0^1 - K^0) \\
& + [\bar{y}^T(p^1 - p^0) - \bar{x}^T(w^1 - w^0)],
\end{aligned}
\tag{6.3}
$$

which states that profit change consists of the value of productivity change, $[\bar{p}^T(y^1 - y^0) - \breve{w}^T(x^1 - x^0)]$, plus the earnings on capital expansion effect and the price effect. We want to decompose the productivity effect. The expression for the productivity effect is identical to those we decompose in Section 6.3, apart from $\breve{w}_N \gtreqless \bar{w}_N$. The productivity effect does not specify an orientation, so we are free to take either orientation. In Section 6.3.1 we take an input orientation, and in Section 6.3.2 we take an output orientation. Because we provide detailed decompositions there, and because the decomposition strategy is independent of the different capital weights, we postpone decomposing a Bennet productivity indicator to Section 6.3. Even without decomposing the productivity effect, expression (6.3) provides the basis for an interesting story, as the following empirical application demonstrates.

An empirical application

Brea-Solís, Casadesus-Masanell, and Grifell-Tatjé (in press) trace the financial performance of Walmart (Wal-Mart prior to 2008), the world's largest public company by revenue, through three successive CEO eras spanning 1977 to 2008. We use their data to construct Table 6.1, which summarizes the profit change decomposition in expression (6.3) under the assumption

Table 6.1 Components of profit change at Walmart
Millions of cumulative 1970 USD, by era

	Chief Executive Officers at Walmart from 1977 to 2008			
	Sam Walton (1977–88)	David Glass (1988–2000)	Scott Lee (2000–08)	1977–2008
Profit Change	368.6	1,487.8	1,102.3	2,958.6
Productivity effect	44.5	−324.6	−661.6	−948.5
Capital expansion effect	371.4	2,070.9	2,027.5	4,469.9
Change in number of outlets	1,045.0	2,786.0	2,141.0	5,972.0
Domestic	1,045.0	1,787.0	871.0	3,703.0
Overseas	–	999.0	1,270.0	2,269.0
Price effect	−47.3	−258.5	−263.6	−569.4
Input price effect	−144.3	32.5	913.1	801.3
Capital	−3.6	−121.5	−214.2	−339.4
Labor	−140.6	154.1	1,127.3	1,140.7
Output price effect	−191.6	−225.9	649.4	231.9
Output 1 (Walmart)	−132.5	−132.1	671.2	406.6
Output 2 (Sam's Club)	−59.1	−93.8	−21.8	−174.7

that investor input is expensed. Table 6.1 goes a bit further, by decomposing the price effect, although not the productivity effect. Strong profit growth throughout the three managerial eras is more than fully accounted for by the capital expansion effect; productivity change and price change actually detracted from profit growth. The capital expansion effect reflects increasing capital investment, primarily in the form of a rapid expansion in the number of outlets, multiplied by a large and declining rate of return to capital. After growing at a moderate pace under Sam Walton, productivity levels declined thereafter, perhaps reflecting the difficulties in managing such rapid growth, particularly the growth in the number of overseas outlets.

The price effect was negative throughout the study period, although its composition varies by era. In the Sam Walton era the negative price effect reflects the value of real output price *declines* exceeding the value of real input price *declines* that were dominated by real wage reductions. In the David Glass era the negative price effect reflects continued output price declines and essentially flat input prices. Both patterns are consistent with the one-time Walmart slogan "Always low prices, always." However, in the Scott Lee era the negative price effect story reversed itself, reflecting the value of real output price *increases* falling short of the value of real input price *increases* that were dominated by rising real wages. It appears that management strategy has adapted, or has been forced to adapt, to a dramatically altered operating environment, although company annual reports do not admit to a change in business strategy.

6.2.2 A productivity index approach

The second strategy is based on the index number forms of the Bennet/LP profit change decompositions in expression (6.2). We choose an output orientation because $p^{0T}y^1$ and $p^{1T}y^0$ are independent of the return to capital (although $\check{X}_L$ and $\check{X}_P$ are not). We combine the output-oriented formulation of expressions (6.1) and (6.2) as

$$\tfrac{1}{2}\,(\tilde{\pi}_0^1 - \tilde{\pi}_0^1) = \tfrac{1}{2}\{p^{0T}y^1[1 - (Y_L/\check{X}_L)^{-1}] + p^{1T}y^0[(Y_P/\check{X}_P) - 1]\}.$$

This Bennet/LP productivity effect contains two explicit productivity indexes, and this motivates our second strategy. We can calculate Y_L, $\check{X}_L$, Y_P and $\check{X}_P$ to generate a pair of productivity indexes and the productivity effect, but this procedure does not generate information on the drivers of productivity change. Instead, we apply procedures set out in Chapter 3 to estimate and decompose a Malmquist productivity index, which does contain information on the drivers of productivity change.

We know that both the Laspeyres productivity index $Y_L/\check{X}_L$ and the Paasche productivity index $Y_P/\check{X}_P$ provide empirical approximations to their theoretical Malmquist counterpart. Consequently, our strategy is to estimate a geometric mean Malmquist productivity index, and decompose the index using the geometric mean version of expression (3.47) in Chapter 3. The result is an attribution of productivity change to technical efficiency change, technical change, and size change. Since a Malmquist productivity index is independent of prices, the dependence of $\check{X}_L$ and $\check{X}_P$ on $(w_N + r)$ is no longer relevant. The financial contribution of productivity change is approximated by substituting the estimated Malmquist productivity index twice into the Bennet productivity effect to yield

$$\tfrac{1}{2}\,(\tilde{\pi}_0^1 - \check{\pi}_1^0) \approx \tfrac{1}{2}\{p^{0T}y^1[1 - M(y^1,y^0,x^1,x^0)^{-1}] + p^{1T}y^0[M(y^1,y^0,x^1,x^0) - 1]\}.$$

$$(6.4)$$

The financial contribution is only approximated, however, because the two empirical productivity indexes have been replaced by estimates of their theoretical counterpart. This leads to a failure of the sum test when expression (6.4) replaces the first term on the right side of expression (6.3). We expect the failure to be "small," and it can be tested for its statistical significance. Whatever the cost of the approximation in the index number form expression (6.4) relative to the equality in the indicator form expression (6.1), it is more than offset by the ability to incorporate the Malmquist productivity index and its three economic drivers of productivity change.[1]

This strategy is conducted within a Bennet framework, to preserve the framework initiated in Section 6.2.1. It is possible to simplify the analysis by conducting it within either a Laspeyres or a Paasche framework, which would simplify expression (6.4), although at the cost of a likely increase in approximation error. Regardless of the index framework, the procedure continues to be independent of prices in the estimation stage, and independent of the rate of return to capital in the valuation stage (because productivity change is valued with $p^{0T}y^1$ and $p^{1T}y^0$). Also, regardless of the index framework, the procedure continues to fail the sum test, and failure is likely to be more serious in a single firm benchmarking exercise than in a large panel such as the one we examined in Section 3.4 of Chapter 3.

6.3 DECOMPOSING PRODUCTIVITY CHANGE WITHOUT INVESTOR INPUT: A MARGIN EFFECT APPROACH

If investor input is not incorporated into the analytical framework, the difference between revenue and cost is unconstrained. Profit change is $\pi^1 - \pi^0 = [p^T(y^1 - y^0) - w^T(x^1 - x^0)] + [y^T(p^1 - p^0) - x^T(w^1 - w^0)]$. The quantity effect $[p^T(y^1 - y^0) - w^T(x^1 - x^0)]$ decomposes into the sum of a productivity effect and a margin effect, familiar from Section 5.3 of Chapter 5. Orientation is unconstrained, and we adopt an input orientation

---

[1] The right side of expression (6.4) attaches value to an estimated Malmquist productivity index, and this value approximates the Bennet/LP productivity effect. The Malmquist productivity index decomposes into the product of three drivers, each expressed as an index. The next step is to allocate the value of an estimated Malmquist productivity index to each driver, so that we can say, for example, that improvements in technical efficiency have contributed a certain amount to the bottom line.

in Section 6.3.1 and an output orientation in Section 6.3.2. In both sections we estimate a production frontier in order to estimate and decompose the productivity effect. This production frontier framework also enables us to provide the promised productivity effect decomposition in Section 6.2.1. In Sections 6.3.1 and 6.3.2 we use Laspeyres quantity indicators, and so in Section 6.3.3 we briefly examine Paasche and Bennet quantity indicators. In Section 6.3.4 we use the same analytical framework as in Sections 6.3.1 and 6.3.2, although we estimate either a productivity index or a quantity index, and so this approach shares features with the strategy in Section 6.2.2. This framework can also have either orientation. It also offers a preview of Chapter 7 because it analyzes only the cost change (or revenue change) component of profit change.

6.3.1 An input-oriented margin effect model

Our strategy begins with the quantity effect, expressed in indicator form. We exploit Tables 5.1 and 5.2 of Chapter 5 to decompose the quantity effect into a productivity effect and a margin effect, both expressed in index number form. We then convert the productivity effect and the margin effect back from index number form to modified indicator form. This allows us to decompose the productivity indicator into the values of the drivers of productivity change. We use a Laspeyres framework throughout because it enhances contact with Chapters 4 and 5, but Paasche and Bennet frameworks generate analogous results, as we demonstrate in Section 6.3.3.

Méraud (1966) and CERC (1969a) first decomposed the Laspeyres quantity effect $[p^{0T}(y^1 - y^0) - w^{0T}(x^1 - x^0)]$, using an input orientation. This decomposition, which appears in expression (4.7) in Chapter 4 and in expression (5.12) and rows (2) and (4) in Table 5.1 in Chapter 5, is

$$[p^{0T}(y^1 - y^0) - w^{0T}(x^1 - x^0)] = w^{0T}x^1[(Y_L/X_L) - 1] + \pi^0[Y_L - 1],$$

with input-oriented productivity effect $w^{0T}x^1[(Y_L/X_L) - 1]$ and output-oriented margin effect $\pi^0[Y_L - 1]$, both expressed in index number form. We extend expression (4.8) in Chapter 4 to rewrite the margin effect in indicator form as $\pi^0[Y_L - 1] = (\pi^0/R^0)p^{0T}(y^1 - y^0) = [1 - (\Pi^0)^{-1}]p^{0T}(y^1 - y^0)$. Moving the new margin effect to the left side enables us to rewrite the productivity effect as

$$w^{0T}x^1[(Y_L/X_L) - 1] = (p^0/\Pi^0)^T(y^1 - y^0) - w^{0T}(x^1 - x^0), \qquad (6.5)$$

which converts the Laspeyres productivity effect from index number form to indicator form, with scaled output price vector p^0/Π^0. Since $(p^0/\Pi^0)^T y^0 = w^{0T} x^0$, the productivity effect simplifies to $(p^0/\Pi^0)^T y^1 - w^{0T} x^1$. The advantage of writing the productivity effect in indicator form is computational, not analytical.

Having both productivity and margin effects in indicator form in and above expression (6.5) enables us to decompose the quantity effect in indicator form as

$$
\begin{aligned}
w^{0T} x^1 [(Y_L/X_L) - 1] + \pi^0 [Y_L - 1] & \\
= (p^0/\Pi^0)^T (y^1 - y^0) - w^{0T} (x^1 - x^0) & \quad \text{productivity effect} \\
+ [p^0 - (p^0/\Pi^0)]^T (y^1 - y^0). & \quad \text{margin effect}
\end{aligned}
$$

(6.6)

If competitive pressures force $\Pi^0 = 1$, the margin effect is zero and the productivity effect coincides with the quantity effect. If $\Pi^0 \neq 1$, the margin effect is positive ($\Pi^0 > 1$) or negative ($\Pi^0 < 1$) and the productivity effect is smaller or larger than the quantity effect, respectively.

The transformation of the Laspeyres productivity index to indicator form in expression (6.5) allows us to easily decompose the indicator form. Referring to Figure 6.1, the structure of the decomposition is

$$
\begin{aligned}
w^{0T} x^1 [(Y_L/X_L) - 1] & \\
= [w^{0T} (x^0 - x^A) - w^{0T} (x^1 - x^C)] & \quad \text{technical efficiency effect} \\
+ [w^{0T} (x^A - x^B)] & \quad \text{technology effect} \\
+ [(p^0/\Pi^0)^T (y^1 - y^0) - w^{0T} (x^C - x^B)]. & \quad \text{size effect}
\end{aligned}
$$

(6.7)

The technical efficiency effect values the change in technical inefficiency. If the value of comparison period technical inefficiency is less than the value of base period technical inefficiency, the technical efficiency effect is positive. The technology effect values the change in technology, measured at base period output. Technical progress creates a positive technology effect. The size effect values the movement along the surface of the comparison period production frontier from (x^B, y^0) to (x^C, y^1). The productivity effect is the sum of these three values.[2]

---

[2] It is also possible to measure the size effect along the surface of T^0 and the technology effect at y^1, and to calculate the productivity effect and its components as the arithmetic mean of the two decompositions.

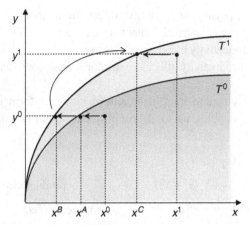

Figure 6.1 Input-oriented productivity effect decomposition

Quantity vectors y^1, y^0, x^1, and x^0, and scalar Π^0, are observed, but input quantity vectors x^A, x^B, and x^C are not, and must be estimated. However, each is located on a production frontier (the surface of either T^0 or T^1) and each is a radial contraction of an observed input quantity vector. Consequently, each can be defined in terms of the input distance functions we introduced in Section 1.6 of Chapter 1. The technically efficient base period input quantity vector $x^A = x^0/D_i^0(y^0, x^0)$ on the boundary of T^0, and the technically efficient comparison period input quantity vector $x^C = x^1/D_i^1(y^1, x^1)$ on the boundary of T^1. Like x^A, $x^B = x^0/D_i^1(y^0, x^0)$ is a radial contraction of x^0, but to the boundary of T^1. Estimates of x^A, x^B, and x^C can be inserted into expression (6.7) to generate a complete decomposition of the productivity effect. The margin effect depends only on observed variables.

We return to expression (6.6), which decomposes the quantity effect in what we call modified indicator form, the modification consisting of scaling p^0 by Π^0. We now provide intuition behind the modification. Suppose $M = 1$. In this single output case $p^0/\Pi^0 = w^{0T}x^0/y^0$, base period unit cost, and the productivity effect becomes $(w^{0T}x^0/y^0)(y^1 - y^0) - w^{0T}(x^1 - x^0)$ and the margin effect becomes $[p^0 - (w^{0T}x^0/y^0)](y^1 - y^0)$, which we derived in expression (4.19) in Chapter 4. The contribution of the scaling factor Π^0 is to replace the base period output price p^0 with base period unit cost C^0/y^0. In essence, the productivity effect now reflects what the output costs to produce rather than the price it commands. The margin effect simply collects the difference $[p^0 - (w^{0T}x^0/y^0)]$, a positive margin reflecting a product price in excess of unit cost.

The single output exercise does not require cost allocation, there being just one output. It is possible to extend the analysis to $M > 1$, simply by leaving expressions (6.5) to (6.7) as they are, with the unfortunate consequence that, since Π^0 is a scalar, all output prices are scaled equivalently in the creation and decomposition of the productivity effect, and all products have the same margin of price over (or under) allocated unit cost. Avoiding this consequence requires cost allocation.

Suppose a company receives prices for its products that do not reflect their relative costs, perhaps reflecting company monopoly power or buyer monopsony power. Then output prices differ from their marginal costs, by magnitudes reflecting product supply and demand elasticities. If scale economies are not "too" important, marginal costs are approximated by their allocated unit costs $c_m = \sum_n w_n x_{nm}/y_m$, with $\sum_m c_m y_m = C$. In measuring productivity change for this company it is theoretically desirable to replace prices with marginal costs, but using allocated unit costs has the analytical advantage of exhausting total cost and the enormous practical advantage of requiring information on allocated unit costs rather than on marginal costs.

Prices serve as weights in empirical productivity indexes. As we reported in Section 2.6 of Chapter 2, Caves, Christensen, and Swanson (1980) found railroad rates to be distorted by cross-subsidy, and they replaced observed revenue shares with estimated cost elasticities in a Törnqvist productivity index. Our strategy here is similar. If we suspect output prices of being influenced by market power, and we want to avoid market power influencing a productivity index, we replace observed output prices with their calculated unit costs. Return to expression (6.6), and replace observed output prices p_m^0 with their allocated unit costs $c_m^0, m = 1, \ldots, M$, in the Laspeyres output quantity index Y_L on the left side. This converts Y_L to $Y_L^c = c^{0T} y^1 / c^{0T} y^0$, a Laspeyres output quantity index with output prices replaced by their allocated unit costs. The resulting quantity effect decomposes as

$$[p^{0T}(y^1 - y^0) - w^{0T}(x^1 - x^0)] = [c^{0T}(y^1 - y^0) - w^{0T}(x^1 - x^0)]$$
$$+ [(p^0 - c^0)^T(y^1 - y^0)], \qquad (6.8)$$

with productivity effect $[c^{0T}(y^1 - y^0) - w^{0T}(x^1 - x^0)] = w^{0T} x^1 [(Y_L^c/X_L) - 1]$ and margin effect $[(p^0 - c^0)^T(y^1 - y^0)] = \pi^0 [Y_L^c - 1]$. Expression (6.8) repeats expression (4.20) in Chapter 4. The productivity effect and the margin effect both have index number and indicator forms.

A nice feature of expression (6.8) is that output prices appear in the margin effect but not in the productivity effect. This allows output prices to influence the aggregate margin, as they should, while ensuring that they have no impact on the productivity effect. With $M > 1$ the interpretation of the margin effect is altered slightly; increasing production of outputs whose price exceeds their allocated unit cost, and reducing production of outputs whose allocated unit cost exceeds their price, are profitable strategies. We anticipate that $c_m^0 < p_m^0$ for most outputs, and that $c_m^0/p_m^0 \neq c_q^0/p_q^0$ for outputs y_m and y_q. That is, we anticipate positive margins over allocated unit costs, and we anticipate that these margins are not uniform across outputs.

Under cost allocation the productivity effect again is expressed in indicator form, is independent of p^0, and decomposes as

$$
\begin{aligned}
c^{0T}(y^1 - y^0) - w^{0T}(x^1 - x^0) \\
= [w^{0T}(x^0 - x^A) - w^{0T}(x^1 - x^C)] & \quad \text{technical efficiency effect} \\
+ [w^{0T}(x^A - x^B)] & \quad \text{technology effect} \\
+ [c^{0T}(y^1 - y^0) - w^{0T}(x^C - x^B)]. & \quad \text{size effect}
\end{aligned}
$$

$$(6.9)$$

It is instructive to compare the initial decompositions in expressions (6.6) and (6.7) with the final decompositions in expressions (6.8) and (6.9). The two structures are identical, and both decompositions require estimation of unobserved input quantity vectors x^A, x^B, and x^C. The difference lies in the weights attached to the output changes $(y^1 - y^0)$. In the initial decompositions output changes are weighted by (p^0/Π^0), and so all output prices are scaled equally. In the final decompositions output changes are weighted by their allocated unit costs. The initial decompositions are easy to implement, since Π^0 is observed. The final decompositions involve the difficult task of cost allocation, but offer the offsetting benefit of a more accurate valuation of productivity change and its size change component.

We conclude with an observation on motivation. Our intuition behind the appearance of the output price scaling factor Π in expression (6.5) eventually led us to a scenario in which output prices thought to be distorted by market power are replaced by their allocated unit costs. An even more appealing scenario is one in which prices are missing altogether, rather than just distorted, and are replaced by their allocated unit costs. Service provision in the public sector is a prominent case in point, a case highlighted by the Atkinson Review (2005), which discusses the relative merits of marginal costs, marginal valuations, and allocated unit costs as weights in public sector productivity measurement. Diewert (2011, 2012) continues the discussion.

Empirical applications

Grifell-Tatjé and Lovell (2008) apply a model similar to the decompositions in expressions (6.8) and (6.9). In their model $M = 1$, so they do not need to allocate cost, but the likelihood of market power induces them to replace product price with unit cost. In a twist on the model in expressions (6.8) and (6.9), they use *cost-efficient* unit cost in place of observed unit cost, and they use Bennet weights. This has the considerable benefit of allowing for cost inefficiency and the possibility of resource misallocation in an input-oriented evaluation of financial performance. This comes at the cost of having to estimate a cost frontier, and at the further cost of breaking the equality between the index number formulation and the indicator formulation of the productivity effect, since $C_{CE}^0 \leq C^0$. They use the model to evaluate the performance of the United States Postal Service (USPS) subsequent to its reorganization as an independent government agency in 1971. A summary of their findings appears in Table 6.2, which complements Table 4.4 in Chapter 4. A positive quantity effect indicates that output growth has contributed to profit growth at USPS (which for much of the period took the form of reductions in losses), and more than all of the contribution of output growth has been due to productivity growth. The contribution of the margin effect has been very small, indicating that output prices have hovered near cost-efficient unit costs. The composition of the productivity effect is striking. Improvements in technology, much heralded in USPS annual reports, have driven productivity growth and its contribution to profit growth. There has been virtually no improvement in the efficiency of resource allocation, and the behavior of the size effect suggests that expansion prior to 2001 and contraction since then have occurred in the region of decreasing returns to scale.

Arocena, Blázquez, and Grifell-Tatjé (2011) provide a similar empirical application. They study the financial performance of four utilities that dominate the Spanish electric power sector before (1991–97) and after (1998–2004) a restructuring of the industry brought on by a regulatory change. The change replaced a system featuring substantial public

Table 6.2 Quantity effect and its decomposition at USPS
Mean results by period (millions of current dollars)

Period	Quantity Effect	Margin Effect +	Productivity Effect	Productivity Effect Technical Efficiency Effect	Technology Effect	Size Effect
1972–1982	27.52	−5.6	33.1	−39.6	101.1	−28.4
1982–1992	63.59	−26.2	89.8	47.6	324.2	−282.0
1992–2001	296.37	13.4	282.9	0.0	541.3	−258.3
2001–2004	1,145.15	10.6	1,134.6	0.0	680.1	454.5
1972–2004	219.18	−5.2	224.3	2.5	348.9	−127.0

ownership, vertical integration, uniform tariffs, and incentive regulation with one that reduced public ownership, unbundled generation from distribution, and created a wholesale electricity market, although all four utilities retained their generation and distribution businesses, and both markets remained highly concentrated. Their analytical model has two outputs, and they replace output prices with allocated cost-efficient unit costs (rather than allocated unit costs), expressed in Bennet form, in both productivity and margin effects. As in the USPS example, this replacement has the effect of increasing the margin effect and reducing the productivity effect. Their findings are summarized in Table 6.3. In both periods the quantity effect was dominated by the productivity effect. The primary differences between the two periods are (i) the quantity effect tripled after restructuring, (ii) the share attributable to productivity growth doubled after restructuring, and (iii) the contribution of the margin effect changed from negative to positive, accounting for 15% of the post-restructuring quantity effect. The primary drivers of the productivity effect have been improvements in technology and changes in the output mix (a component of the size effect in expression (6.9)), the latter reflecting increases in the ratio of power distributed to power generated. The authors also conduct a distribution exercise in which they distribute what they call value creation, which they define, following Méraud and CERC (Section 4.4.2 of Chapter 4), as the quantity effect plus héritages. The main beneficiaries of value creation have been consumers, in the form of reduced real electricity prices, but to a lesser extent than producers have benefitted, in the form of increased profits, reflecting a continuing lack of competition.

Table 6.3 Quantity effect and its decomposition by company in the Spanish electricity industry
Millions of cumulative 2004 €

Period	Company	Quantity Effect	Margin Effect	Productivity + Effect	Productivity Effect		
					Cost Efficiency Effect	Technology Effect	Size Effect
Pre-restructuring	Iberdrola	1,991.9	82.2	1,909.7	0.1	333.7	1,576.0
(1991–1997)	Unión Fenosa	378.9	30.7	348.2	−249.8	633.3	−35.3
	Hidrocantábrico	−40.1	−9.0	−31.1	−66.0	35.0	0.0
	Endesa	−676.4	−403.1	−273.2	0.1	716.5	−989.9
	Total	1,654.4	−299.2	1,953.6	−315.6	1,718.5	550.7
Post-restructuring	Iberdrola	1,250.9	316.1	934.8	0.1	1,177.4	−242.6
(1998–2004)	Unión Fenosa	703.8	111.7	592.1	139.5	456.4	−3.8
	Hidrocantábrico	302.6	104.5	198.1	37.5	116.5	44.1
	Endesa	2,477.6	177.5	2,300.2	−0.1	1,954.8	345.5
	Total	4,734.9	709.7	4,025.2	177.0	3,705.1	143.1
Industry (1991–2004)		1,597.3	102.6	1,494.7	−34.7	1,355.9	173.5

6.3.2 An output-oriented margin effect model

We now reverse the orientation and consider a situation in which the input prices a company pays are, or are expected to be, distorted, perhaps by company monopsony power or input supplier monopoly power. Because the use of distorted input prices in an input quantity index would confuse monopsony- or monopoly-induced input price change with input quantity change, we replace input prices with their allocated unit revenues. The strategy is the same as that in Section 6.3.1, albeit with the opposite orientation. We begin with a quantity effect expressed in indicator form, which we then decompose into a productivity effect and a margin effect expressed in index number form, which we finally convert back to modified indicator form. This allows us to decompose the productivity effect into the values of the drivers of productivity change.

Kurosawa (1975) first decomposed the Laspeyres quantity effect, using an output orientation. This decomposition appears in expression (4.13) in Chapter 4, and again in expression (5.11) and rows (1) and (3) in Table 5.1 in Chapter 5. This decomposition is

$$[p^{0T}(y^1 - y^0) - w^{0T}(x^1 - x^0)] = p^{0T}y^1[1 - (Y_L/X_L)^{-1}] + \pi^0[X_L - 1],$$

with output-oriented productivity effect $p^{0T}y^1[1 - (Y_L/X_L)^{-1}]$ and input-oriented margin effect $\pi^0[X_L - 1]$. We extend expression (4.12) in Chapter 4 by converting the margin effect to indicator form as $\pi^0[X_L - 1] = (\pi^0/C^0)$ $w^{0T}(x^1 - x^0) = (\Pi^0 - 1)w^{0T}(x^1 - x^0)$ and isolating the productivity effect to convert it to indicator form as

$$p^{0T}y^1[1 - (Y_L/X_L)^{-1}] = p^{0T}(y^1 - y^0) - \Pi^0 w^{0T}(x^1 - x^0), \tag{6.10}$$

in which the input price vector is scaled to $\Pi^0 w^0$. Expression (6.10) is the same as expression (4.10) in Chapter 4, which exploits the equality $p^{0T}y^0 = \Pi^0 w^{0T}x^0$.

Using expression (6.10), the quantity effect decomposes as

$$
\begin{aligned}
p^{0T}y^1[1 - (Y_L/X_L)^{-1}] &+ \pi^0[X_L - 1] \\
&= p^{0T}(y^1 - y^0) - \Pi^0 w^{0T}(x^1 - x^0) \qquad \text{productivity effect} \\
&+ (\Pi^0 w^0 - w^0)^T(x^1 - x^0). \qquad \text{margin effect}
\end{aligned}
\tag{6.11}
$$

The index number and indicator forms of the productivity effect are equal, as are the index number and indicator forms of the margin effect. As in Section 6.3.1, if $\Pi^0 \gtreqless 1$ the margin effect is greater than, equal to, or less

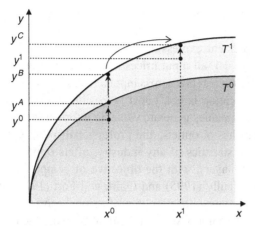

Figure 6.2 Output-oriented productivity effect decomposition

than zero and the productivity effect is correspondingly less than, equal to, or larger than the quantity effect.

Referring to Figure 6.2, the productivity effect decomposes into its drivers as

$$p^{0T}y^1\left[1-(Y_L/X_L)^{-1}\right]$$

$$= \left[p^{0T}(y^A-y^0)-p^{0T}(y^C-y^1)\right] \qquad \text{technical efficiency effect}$$

$$+ \left[p^{0T}(y^B-y^A)\right] \qquad \text{technology effect}$$

$$+ \left[p^{0T}(y^C-y^B)\right] - \Pi^0 w^{0T}(x^1-x^0)\right]. \qquad \text{size effect}$$

$$(6.12)$$

Expressions (6.11) and (6.12) and Figure 6.2 tell the same story as expressions (6.6) and (6.7) and Figure 6.1, with the opposite orientation and with scaled input prices rather than scaled output prices.

The quantity vectors $y^1, y^0, x^1,$ and x^0 are observed, as is the scalar Π^0, but $y^A, y^B,$ and y^C must be estimated. Each is located on the boundary of either T^0 or T^1 and each is a radial expansion of either y^1 or y^0 and can be defined in terms of output distance functions as $y^A = y^0/D_o^0(x^0, y^0),$ $y^B = y^0/D_o^1(x^0, y^0)$ and $y^C = y^1/D_o^1(x^1, y^1).$

If $N=1$ in expression (6.11), the productivity effect becomes $p^{0T}(y^1 - y^0)-(p^{0T}y^0/x^0)(x^1-x^0)$ and the margin effect becomes $[(p^{0T}y^0/x^0)-w^0](x^1-x^0)$. The base period input price w^0 is replaced with its base period unit revenue R^0/x^0. The productivity effect now reflects what the input is worth rather than what it is paid, and the margin effect collects the difference

$[(p^{0T}y^0/x^0) - w^0]$, a positive margin reflecting a wage less than the value of the input's contribution.

It is possible to implement expressions (6.11) and (6.12) with $N > 1$, although since Π^0 is a scalar, all input prices become equivalently scaled. The alternative is to allocate revenue across inputs. Although cost allocation is common, revenue allocation is not, but it is feasible in certain circumstances. For example, companies generate valuable information by allocating revenue across branches or outlets, and professional sport, with by far the most comprehensive statistics of any industry, offers opportunities to allocate revenue across players, with the objective of comparing salaries with revenue products. Scully (1995) and Quirk and Fort (1997) provide extensive evidence on revenue allocation in professional sport.

Suppose a company does not pay its input suppliers what their services are worth, either because of company monopsony power or input supplier monopoly power. Then input prices differ from the value of their marginal products by magnitudes reflecting input supply and demand elasticities. If demands for and supplies of the company's products are not "too" inelastic, then the values of input marginal products are approximated by their allocated unit revenues $v_n = $ (revenue generated by input n)$/x_n = \sum_m p_m y_{mn}/x_n$ with $\sum v_n x_n = R$. In measuring productivity for this company it is theoretically desirable to replace input prices with the values of their marginal products, but using allocated unit revenues has the analytical advantage of exhausting total revenue, although it requires revenue allocation across inputs. However, if the revenue allocation exercise is feasible, it becomes possible to implement the decomposition exercise in expressions (6.11) and (6.12) without resorting to Π^0.

Because we do not want distorted input prices to influence an input quantity index, we replace them. In expression (6.11) we replace input prices w_n^0 with their allocated unit revenues v_n^0, $n = 1,...,N$, in the Laspeyres input quantity index. This converts X_L to $X_L^v = v^{0T}x^1/v^{0T}x^0$, a Laspeyres input quantity index with input prices replaced by their allocated unit revenues. This substitution generates the decomposition

$$[p^{0T}(y^1 - y^0) - w^{0T}(x^1 - x^0)] = [p^{0T}(y^1 - y^0) - v^{0T}(x^1 - x^0)]$$
$$+ [(v^0 - w^0)^T(x^1 - x^0)], \qquad (6.13)$$

with productivity effect $[p^{0T}(y^1 - y^0) - v^{0T}(x^1 - x^0)] = p^{0T}y^1[1 - (Y_L/X_L^v)^{-1}]$ and margin effect $[(v^0 - w^0)^T(x^1 - x^0)] = \pi^0[X_L^v - 1]$. The productivity effect and the margin effect have equivalent index number and indicator expressions. Input prices w^0 appear in the margin effect, where they belong, but not in the productivity effect, where they are replaced by allocated unit revenues. The margin effect is enhanced by increasing the use of inputs having value in excess of their price, and by contracting the use of inputs having price in excess of their value.

Referring to Figure 6.2, the productivity effect decomposes as

$$
\begin{aligned}
[p^{0T}(y^1 - y^0) &- v^{0T}(x^1 - x^0)] \\
&= [p^{0T}(y^A - y^0) - p^{0T}(y^C - y^1)] \qquad \text{technical efficiency effect} \\
&\quad + [p^{0T}(y^B - y^A)] \qquad\qquad\qquad \text{technology effect} \\
&\quad + [p^{0T}(y^C - y^B) - v^{0T}(x^1 - x^0)], \qquad \text{size effect}
\end{aligned}
$$

$$(6.14)$$

which has the same structure, but opposite orientation, as decomposition (6.9). Because the analysis is output-oriented, the values of technical efficiency change and technical change are independent of input quantities, and immune to input price distortion. Only the size effect involves change in input quantities, and this is where w^0 is replaced by v^0.

The underlying theme of this section is to quantify the contribution of productivity change and its drivers to profit change in a way that is not adversely influenced by potentially distorted input prices. The analytical framework is also appropriate in a situation in which one or more input prices are missing, rather than distorted. Potential examples include public infrastructure, which provides an unpriced input to private businesses, household service provision, which is frequently unpriced, and fish stocks, which provide an unpriced input to the fishery production process.

6.3.3 Paasche and Bennet decompositions

Sections 6.3.1 and 6.3.2 have Laspeyres structure. It is possible to replace this structure with Paasche or Bennet structure, based on results in Sections 5.3.1 and 5.3.2 in Chapter 5.

A Paasche quantity indicator with input orientation appears in expression (5.16) and rows (6) and (8) in Table 5.1 in Chapter 5 as

$$[p^{1T}(y^1 - y^0) - w^{1T}(x^1 - x^0)] = w^{1T}x^0[1 - (Y_P/X_P)^{-1}] + \pi^1[1 - Y_P^{-1}].$$

Subsequent analysis proceeds as in expressions (6.5) to (6.9) in Section 6.3.1, replacing base period weights $(p^0, p^0/\Pi^0, w^0, c^0)$ with comparison period weights $(p^1, p^1/\Pi^1, w^1)$ in expressions (6.5) to (6.7), and (p^1, c^1, w^1) in expressions (6.8) and (6.9). Reversing orientation, an output-oriented Paasche quantity indicator appears in expression (5.15) and rows (5) and (7) in Table 5.1 in Chapter 5 as

$$[p^{1T}(y^1 - y^0) - w^{1T}(x^1 - x^0)] = p^{1T}y^0[(Y_P/X_P) - 1] + \pi^1[1 - X_P^{-1}].$$

Subsequent analysis proceeds as in expressions (6.10) to (6.14) in Section 6.3.2, replacing base period weights $(p^0, \Pi^0 w^0, w^0, v^0)$ with comparison period weights $(p^1, \Pi^1 w^1, w^1)$ in expressions (6.10) to (6.12), and (p^1, v^1, w^1) in expressions (6.13) and (6.14).

In Section 5.3.2 of Chapter 5 we developed a pair of Bennet approaches to decomposing the quantity effect. The Bennet/LP approach simply calculates the arithmetic mean of similarly oriented Laspeyres and Paasche decompositions. This approach generates arithmetic mean weights $(\bar{p}, \overline{p/\Pi}, \bar{w}, \bar{c})$ in an input-oriented approach and $(\bar{p}, \overline{\Pi w}, \bar{w}, \bar{v})$ in an output-oriented approach.

The Bennet/EM approach decomposes the quantity effect using EM quantity indexes. An input-oriented Bennet/EM decomposition of the quantity effect appears in expression (5.22) and row (2) in Table 5.2 in Chapter 5 as

$$[\bar{p}^T(y^1 - y^0) - \bar{w}^T(x^1 - x^0)] = \bar{w}^T x^1 [(Y_{EM}/X_{EM}) - 1] + (\bar{p}^T y^0 - \bar{w}^T x^0)[Y_{EM} - 1].$$

We proceed exactly as in expressions (6.5) to (6.7), replacing $(p^0, p^0/\Pi^0, w^0)$ with either $(\bar{p}, \overline{p/\Pi}^0 = \bar{p}/(\bar{p}^T y^0/\bar{w}^T x^0), \bar{w})$ or $(\bar{p}, \overline{p/\Pi}^1 = \bar{p}/(\bar{p}^T y^1/ \bar{w}^T x^1), \bar{w})$. It is not possible to convert expressions (6.8) and (6.9) to Bennet/EM form by replacing either $\overline{p/\Pi}^0$ or $\overline{p/\Pi}^1$ with $\bar{c}$ because $\bar{w}^T x^1 [(Y_{EM}^c/X_{EM}) - 1] \neq [\bar{c}^T(y^1 - y^0) - \bar{w}^T(x^1 - x^0)]$.

An output-oriented Bennet/EM decomposition appears in expression (5.19) and row (1) in Table 5.2 in Chapter 5 as

$$[\bar{p}^T(y^1 - y^0) - \bar{w}^T(x^1 - x^0)] = \bar{p}^T y^1 [1 - (Y_{EM}/X_{EM})^{-1}] + (\bar{p}^T y^0 - \bar{w}^T x^0)[X_{EM} - 1].$$

We proceed as in expressions (6.10) to (6.12), replacing $(p^0, \Pi^0 w^0, w^0)$ with either $(\bar{p}, \overline{\Pi w}^0, \bar{w})$ or $(\bar{p}, \overline{\Pi w}^1, \bar{w})$. It is not possible to convert expressions (6.13) and (6.14) to Bennet/EM form by replacing either $\overline{\Pi w}^0$ or $\overline{\Pi w}^1$ with $\bar{v}$ because $\bar{p}^T y^1 [1 - (Y_{EM}/X_{EM}^v)^{-1}] \neq [\bar{p}^T(y^1 - y^0) - \bar{v}^T(x^1 - x^0)]$.

Table 6.4 Quantity effect decompositions

		Quantity Effect	
	Generalizes	Productivity Indicator	Quantity Margin Effect
[1]	Expression (6.6)	$(p/\Pi)^T(y^1 - y^0) - w^T(x^1 - x^0)$	$[p - (p/\Pi)]^T(y^1 - y^0)$
[2]	Expression (6.8)	$c^T(y^1 - y^0) - w^T(x^1 - x^0)$	$[p - c]^T(y^1 - y^0)$
[3]	Expression (6.11)	$p^T(y^1 - y^0) - \Pi w^T(x^1 - x^0)$	$(\Pi w - w)^T(x^1 - x^0)$
[4]	Expression (6.13)	$p^T(y^1 - y^0) - v^T(x^1 - x^0)$	$(v - w)^T(x^1 - x^0)$

Laspeyres, Paasche, Bennet/LP, and Bennet/EM decompositions of the quantity effect share a common structure, although their different weights generate numerically different decompositions, as we showed in Table 5.3 in Chapter 5. Their common structure is illustrated in Table 6.4, in which the four quantity effect decompositions do not indicate the weights attached to quantity changes. The weights in rows (1) and (3), which are based on either p/Π or Πw, as in expressions (6.6) and (6.11), can be Laspeyres, Paasche, Bennet/LP, or Bennet/EM. Decompositions in rows (2) and (4) are more general, being based on allocated unit cost c or allocated unit revenue v, as in expressions (6.8) and (6.13), and can be Laspeyres, Paasche, or Bennet/LP, but not Bennet/EM for reasons mentioned previously. Decompositions in rows (1) and (2) are input-oriented, and those in rows (3) and (4) are output-oriented. All quantity effect decompositions have the same structure, and all productivity indicators decompose into the same three drivers; only the weights vary.

We conclude by noting that Tables 5.1 and 5.2 in Chapter 5 decompose both the quantity effect and the price effect, whereas here we decompose only the quantity effect. However, the procedures for decomposing the price effect parallel those developed above for decomposing the quantity effect, and the intuition underlying both decompositions is similar.

6.3.4 A productivity index or a quantity index

In Sections 6.3.1 and 6.3.2 we converted index number expressions for a productivity effect to indicator expressions, which we then decomposed. Here we analyze the index number expressions themselves, and we concentrate on the productivity effect, ignoring the margin effect. We take a primal approach based on the Bennet productivity indicators in Table 5.2 in Chapter 5. These indicators are functions of an EM productivity index. We arbitrarily select the input-oriented second row of Table 5.2. Our first strategy is simple; we estimate a Malmquist productivity index, which we substitute into the Bennet productivity indicator to obtain

$$\overline{w}^T x^1 [(Y_{EM}/X_{EM}) - 1] \approx \overline{w}^T x^1 [M(y^1, y^0, x^1, x^0) - 1], \tag{6.15}$$

in which $M(y^1, y^0, x^1, x^0)$ decomposes into three drivers of productivity change. The value of productivity change $\overline{w}^T x^1 [(Y_{EM}/X_{EM}) - 1]$ satisfies the sum test with the remaining components of profit change appearing in the second row of Table 5.2. However, $M(y^1, y^0, x^1, x^0)$ only approximates Y_{EM}/X_{EM}, and so our procedure fails the sum test with the remaining components of profit change, although satisfaction of the sum test is a testable hypothesis.

Our second strategy is not as simple. We continue to focus on the input-oriented productivity effect in the second row of Table 5.2, but we ignore output change as represented by Y_{EM}. Potential reasons for doing so include (i) $y^1 = y^0$ or, somewhat less restrictively, $Y_{EM} = 1$, or (ii) one or more output prices is missing or thought to be distorted, combined with an unwillingness to allocate unit costs. Profit change simplifies to cost change, which we write in Bennet form as $w^{1T} x^1 - w^{0T} x^0 = \overline{w}^T (x^1 - x^0) + \overline{x}^T (w^1 - w^0)$, and the productivity effect simplifies to

$$\begin{aligned} \overline{w}^T (x^1 - x^0) &= \overline{w}^T x^0 (X_{EM} - 1) \\ &= \overline{w}^T x^1 (1 - X_{EM}^{-1}), \end{aligned} \tag{6.16}$$

in which X_{EM} is an EM input quantity index. Our strategy is to replace X_{EM} with an estimate of a Malmquist input quantity index $X_M(y, x^1, x^0)$. We specify a comparison period index $X_M^1 (y^1, x^1, x^0)$, which decomposes as

$$X_M^1(y^1, x^1, x^0) = \Delta TE_i(y^1, y^0, x^1, x^0) \times \Delta T_i(y^0, x^0) \times [D_i^1(y^0, x^0)/D_i^1(y^1, x^0)]. \tag{6.17}$$

$\Delta TE_i(y^1, y^0, x^1, x^0)$ is an input-oriented measure of technical efficiency change, $\Delta T_i(y^0, x^0)$ is an input-oriented measure of technical change, and because the only thing that varies in the third term is the output quantity vector, we call it an output effect.

Replacing X_{EM} in expression (6.16) with $X_M^1 (y^1, x^1, x^0)$ in expression (6.17) yields

$$\begin{aligned} \overline{w}^T (x^1 - x^0) &\approx \overline{w}^T x^0 \{\Delta TE_i(y^1, y^0, x^1, x^0) \times \Delta T_i(y^0, x^0) \\ &\times [D_i^1(y^0, x^0)/D_i^1(y^1, x^0)] - 1\}, \end{aligned} \tag{6.18}$$

which decomposes the productivity effect into the sum of the values of the contributions of technical efficiency change, technical change, and output change. This relationship is only approximate because an estimated Malmquist input quantity index approximates a calculated EM input quantity index. Consequently, expression (6.18) fails the sum test with the remaining components of profit change appearing in the second row of Table 5.2, although the hypothesis that the sum test is satisfied is testable, and the benefits offered by the ability to tell a story about the drivers of productivity change are considerable.

This section is input-oriented. It is straightforward to reverse its orientation, simply by starting with an odd-numbered output-oriented row in Table 5.2, and ignoring input change X_{EM}. The procedure can be motivated by (i) $X_{EM} = 1$, or (ii) one or more input prices is missing or distorted, combined with an unwillingness to allocate unit revenues. Profit change simplifies to revenue change $p^{1T}y^1 - p^{0T}y^0 = \bar{p}^T(y^1 - y^0) + \bar{y}^T(p^1 - p^0)$, and the productivity effect simplifies to $\bar{p}^T(y^1 - y^0) = \bar{p}^T y^0[Y_{EM} - 1] = \bar{p}^T y^1[1 - Y_{EM}^{-1}]$. We replace Y_{EM} with a Malmquist output quantity index $Y_M(x, y^1, y^0)$, which decomposes, and proceed as above to tell an approximate story about the drivers of output-oriented productivity change.

Sections 6.3.1 and 6.3.2 begin with an expression for the quantity effect component of profit change and end with a story about the economic drivers of productivity change. In both sections the margin effect component of the quantity effect decomposes by variable, but not by economic driver. Section 6.3.4 begins with the productivity effect, ignores the margin effect, and ends with a decomposition of the productivity effect. An important implication of Section 6.3.4 is that it is also possible to begin with a less inclusive expression for cost change or revenue change, and still end up with a nearly identical story about the drivers of productivity change. This provides a brief introduction to Chapter 7, which is devoted to the study of productivity change within a cost change framework.

6.4 DECOMPOSING PRODUCTIVITY CHANGE WITHOUT INVESTOR INPUT: AN ACTIVITY EFFECT APPROACH

We continue to exclude investor input from the analytical framework, and so profit can take any value. Using Bennet quantity and price indicators, profit change is $\pi^1 - \pi^0 = [\bar{p}^T(y^1 - y^0) - \bar{w}^T(x^1 - x^0)] + [\bar{y}^T(p^1 - p^0) - \bar{x}^T(w^T - w^0)]$. As in Section 6.3, the quantity effect $[\bar{p}^T(y^1 - y^0) - $

$\overline{w}^T(x^1 - x^0)\big]$ decomposes into the sum of a productivity effect and a second effect. In this section the second effect is an activity effect. The activity effect and the margin effect are closely related, 'as we explain in Section 6.5. In Sections 6.4.1 and 6.4.2 we estimated a production frontier to decompose the quantity effect and its productivity effect component. Only orientation differs in these two sections. In Section 6.4.3 we relate the productivity effect to a CCD Malmquist productivity index.

6.4.1 An input-oriented activity effect model

Grifell-Tatjé and Lovell (1999b) develop a profit change decomposition in which the quantity effect decomposes into a productivity effect and an activity effect. They use base period prices to weight quantity changes, and they adopt an output orientation. Here we reverse the orientation and we use Bennet price weights. The strategy we follow is structurally similar to the strategy we used in Section 6.3.1, although the concept of productivity differs from the one defined in Section 6.3.1. Nonetheless, Figure 6.1 illustrates this strategy as well, when augmented by Figures 6.3 and 6.4. The quantity effect in the Bennet profit change expression above decomposes as

$$
\begin{aligned}
[\overline{p}^T(y^1 - y^0) &- \overline{w}^T(x^1 - x^0)] \\
&= [\overline{w}^T(x^0 - x^B) - \overline{w}^T(x^1 - x^C)] \qquad \text{productivity effect} \\
&\quad + [\overline{p}^T(y^1 - y^0) - \overline{w}^T(x^C - x^B)]. \qquad \text{activity effect}
\end{aligned}
$$

$$(6.19)$$

The first term on the right side of expression (6.19) measures the contribution of productivity change, and the second term measures the contribution of size change from (x^B, y^0) to (x^C, y^1) on the surface of T^1, with $x^B = x^0/D_i^1(y^0, x^0) \in IL^1(y^0)$ and $x^C = x^1/D_i^1(y^1, x^1) \in IL^1(y^1)$. If there is no productivity change, $x^0 = x^B$ and $x^1 = x^C$. The activity effect is unaffected by the absence of productivity change, however, and measures the financial impact of a change in the size of the business from (x^B, y^0) to (x^C, y^1).

Expression (6.19) and Figure 6.1 suggest that the productivity effect includes the contributions of efficiency change and technical change, and nothing else. We formalize this suggestion by decomposing the productivity effect as

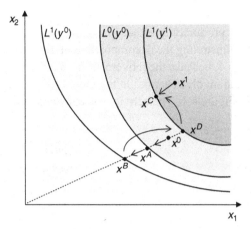

Figure 6.3 Input-oriented productivity effect decomposition ($N = 2$)

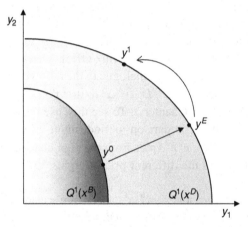

Figure 6.4 Input-oriented productivity effect decomposition ($M = 2$)

$$[\overline{w}^T(x^0 - x^B) - \overline{w}^T(x^1 - x^C)]$$
$$= [\overline{w}^T(x^0 - x^A) - \overline{w}^T(x^1 - x^C)] \qquad \text{technical efficiency effect}$$
$$+ [\overline{w}^T(x^A - x^B)]. \qquad\qquad\qquad \text{technology effect}$$

$$(6.20)$$

The first term on the right side of expression (6.20) measures the contribution of a change in technical efficiency relative to the two technologies, with $x^A = x^0/D_i^0(y^0, x^0) \in IL^0(y^0)$, and the second term measures the contribution of a change in technology. Both are input-oriented, and together they exhaust the productivity effect.

If $M > 1$ and/or $N > 1$, illustrating the decomposition of the activity effect requires Figures 6.3 and 6.4, because the movement from (x^B, y^0) to (x^C, y^1) along the surface of T^1 can involve changes in the input mix and the output mix that are invisible in Figure 6.1. The activity effect decomposes as

$$[\bar{p}^T(y^1 - y^0) - \bar{w}^T(x^C - x^B)]$$
$$= \bar{w}^T(x^D - x^C) \qquad\qquad\qquad \text{input mix effect}$$
$$+ \bar{p}^T(y^1 - y^E) \qquad\qquad\qquad \text{output mix effect}$$
$$+ [\bar{p}^T(y^E - y^0) - \bar{w}^T(x^D - x^B)]. \qquad \text{radial activity effect}$$

$$(6.21)$$

The vector $x^D = x^0/D_i^1(y^1, x^0) \in IL^1(y^1)$ is used to define $y^E = y^0/D_o^1(x^D, y^0) \in IQ^1(x^D)$. In Figures 6.3 and 6.4 the movement from (x^B, y^0) to (x^D, y^E), when weighted by $\bar{p}$ and $\bar{w}$ respectively, is the radial activity effect. The movement from (x^D, y^1) to (x^C, y^1), when weighted by $\bar{w}$, is the input mix effect, and the movement from (x^D, y^E) to (x^D, y^1) in Figure 6.4, when weighted by $\bar{p}$, is the output mix effect.

The input mix effect is the difference analogue to the ratio version of the input mix effect given by $[w^{1T}x^1/D_i^1(y^1, x^1)]/[w^{1T}x^0/D_i^1(y^1, x^0)]$ in expressions (3.59) and (3.60) in Chapter 3. To see this, use the definitions of x^D and x^C to write the comparison period input mix effect as $\bar{w}^T x^0/D_i^1(y^1, x^0) - \bar{w}^T x^1/D_i^1(y^1, x^1)$. Apart from the sign change to reflect the change in orientation and the different price weights, the two effects are the same.

Unobserved input quantity vectors x^A, x^B, x^C, and x^D are scalar multiples of observed input quantity vectors, and can be recovered by estimating input distance functions, as in Section 6.3.1. The single unobserved output quantity vector y^E can be recovered by estimating an output distance function, as in Section 6.3.2. With estimates of these vectors in hand, the contributions to profit change of productivity change and its two components, and the activity effect and its three components, can be calculated using expressions (6.20) and (6.21).

This decomposition differs from the decomposition provided in Section 6.3.1. The price weights differ, but the substantive difference is attributable to the presence of a size effect in the productivity effect decomposition in expressions (6.7) and (6.9), and its absence from the productivity effect decomposition in expression (6.20). Isolating the activity effect from the productivity effect, as we do in expression (6.20), is consistent with the notion that efficiency and technology are under the control of management, whereas firm size is less likely to be endogenous. Even if firm size is controllable, management may wish to isolate it from productivity to explore the impacts of size change reflected in the activity effect, as in developing alternative strategies for efficient downsizing, for example. We emphasize that the technical efficiency effect and the technology effect in expression (6.20) are identical to those in expressions (6.7) and (6.9). Our conception of the value of technical efficiency change and the value of technical change does not vary across model formulations, although the value of size change does. We explore the issue of what drivers are, and are not, likely to be under management control, in Section 6.5.[3]

An empirical application

De Witte and Saal (2010) illustrate the insights that can be gained from applying a profit change decomposition model in an incentive regulation context. They apply the model in expressions (6.19) to (6.21), with a Laspeyres quantity effect and a Paasche price effect, to evaluate the impacts of a 1997 transition to light-handed sunshine regulation on productivity and profit in the Dutch drinking water sector. Their findings are summarized in Table 6.5. They find substantially different profit decompositions before and after the transition, with profit growth shrinking by 60% as even light-handed regulation took effect. The diminished profit growth is a consequence of an 80% shrinkage in the price effect partially offset by a strong turnaround in the quantity effect. The diminished price effect is primarily due to a large reversal in the output price effect, which is to be expected. The turnaround in the quantity effect is primarily due to a large increase in both components of the productivity effect, which is to be desired, nearly offset by a large decline in the activity effect. Technical progress dominates the

---

[3] Sahoo and Tone (2009) apply the profit change decomposition in expressions (6.19) to (6.21) to the Indian banking sector. They implement both radial and nonradial decompositions, and they use Laspeyres, Paasche, and Bennet prices to weight changes. Hadley and Irz (2008) apply the same decomposition to a panel of cereal farms in England and Wales. A distinguishing feature of their panel is that profit is negative, on average and for the majority of observations, which rules out a ratio-based analysis of profit change. Asaftei (2008) applies the same decomposition to four size-based groups of US commercial banks, with a twist. He divides π, y, and x by assets to generate a decomposition of return on assets. We propose an alternative approach to decomposing ROA in Chapter 8.

Table 6.5 Cumulative effect of regulatory change in the Dutch drinking water sector
Millions of cumulative 1995 € by period

	1992–1997	1997–2006
Profit Change	237.1	95.6
Quantity effect	−76.6	40.4
Productivity effect	−100.9	227.9
Technical change effect	12.3	214.0
Efficiency change effect	−113.1	13.9
Activity effect	24.3	−187.5
Product mix effect	22.0	17.6
Resource mix effect	0.7	−254.3
Radial activity effect	1.5	49.2
Price effect	313.7	54.2
Input price effect	29.5	158.1
Capital	49.1	183.2
Labor	−25.2	−17.4
Other inputs	5.6	−7.7
Output price effect	284.1	−103.9
Domestic consumers	185.2	−43.1
Nondomestic consumers	99.0	−60.9

productivity effect, and the negative resource mix effect, which the authors attribute to excessive capitalization intended to enhance security of water supply, dominates the activity effect. It appears that the transition to sunshine regulation has had its desired effect: productivity decline has turned to productivity growth, the benefits of which have accrued primarily, but not entirely, to consumers.

6.4.2 An output-oriented activity effect model

In this section we adopt an output orientation to the same activity effect model. The expressions for profit change and its quantity and price effects are unchanged. With an output orientation and the assistance of Figure 6.2, the quantity effect decomposes as

$$
\begin{aligned}
[\bar{p}^T(y^1 - y^0) &- \bar{w}^T(x^1 - x^0)] \\
&= [\bar{p}^T(y^B - y^0) - \bar{p}^T(y^C - y^1)] && \text{productivity effect} \\
&+ [\bar{p}^T(y^C - y^B) - \bar{w}^T(x^1 - x^0)]. && \text{activity effect}
\end{aligned}
\tag{6.22}
$$

The first term on the right side of expression (6.22) measures the value of productivity change, and the second term measures the financial impact of a change in the size of the business from (x^0, y^B) to (x^1, y^C), where $y^B = y^0/D_o^1(x^0, y^0)$ on the boundary of T^1 and $y^C = y^1/D_o^1(x^1, y^1)$ on the boundary of T^1.

Expression (6.22) and Figure 6.2 suggest that the productivity effect includes the contributions of efficiency change and technical change, and so

$$
\begin{aligned}
& [\bar{p}^T(y^B - y^0) - \bar{p}^T(y^C - y^1)] \\
& = [\bar{p}^T(y^A - y^0) - \bar{p}^T(y^C - y^1)] \qquad \text{technical efficiency effect} \\
& + [\bar{p}^T(y^B - y^A)]. \qquad \text{technology effect}
\end{aligned}
\tag{6.23}
$$

Since the activity effect may involve nonradial changes, an illustration of the decomposition of the activity effect is provided by Figures 6.5 and 6.6. The activity effect decomposes as

$$
\begin{aligned}
& [\bar{p}^T(y^C - y^B) - \bar{w}^T(x^1 - x^0)] \\
& = \bar{p}^T(y^C - y^D) \qquad \text{output mix effect} \\
& - \bar{w}^T(x^1 - x^E) \qquad \text{input mix effect} \\
& + [\bar{p}^T(y^D - y^B) - \bar{w}^T(x^E - x^0)]. \qquad \text{radial activity effect}
\end{aligned}
\tag{6.24}
$$

The output mix effect values the move from (x^1, y^D) to (x^1, y^C) in Figure 6.5. The input mix effect values the move from (x^E, y^D) to (x^1, y^D) in Figure 6.6, where $y^D = y^0/D_o^1(x^1, y^0) \in IQ^1(x^1)$ is used to define $x^E = x^0/D_i^1(y^D, x^0) \in IL^1(y^D)$. The radial activity effect values the move from (x^0, y^B) in Figure 6.5 to (x^E, y^D) in Figure 6.6.

It is straightforward to use the definitions of y^C and y^D to show that the output mix effect is the difference analogue to the ratio version of the comparison period output mix effect given by $[p^{1T}y^1/D_o^1(x^1, y^1)]/[p^{1T}y^0/D_o^1(x^1, y^0)]$ in expressions (3.52) and (3.53) in Chapter 3. The only difference between the two output mix effects is the price weights.

As in Section 6.4.1, unobserved quantity vectors are scalar multiples of observed quantity vectors, and can be recovered by estimating distance functions. With estimates of these vectors in hand, the contributions to profit change of productivity change and its two components, and the activity

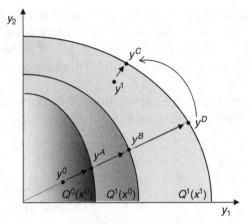

Figure 6.5 Output-oriented productivity effect decomposition ($M=2$)

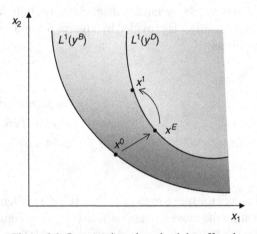

Figure 6.6 Output-oriented productivity effect decomposition ($N=2$)

effect and its three components, can be calculated using expressions (6.23) and (6.24).

Once again the productivity effect consists of the impacts of technical change and technical efficiency change, this time both output-oriented. These two components are identical to their counterparts in expressions (6.12) and (6.14) in the margin effect model. The impact of size change is captured by the activity effect, which has no orientation, but which may involve changes in input and output mixes.

6.4.3 Relating the productivity effect to a CCD Malmquist productivity index

In Section 2.3.2 of Chapter 2 we introduced a CCD Malmquist productivity index developed by Caves, Christensen, and Diewert (1982). This version cannot be expressed as the ratio of an output quantity index to an input quantity index, which breaks the structural similarity with empirical productivity indexes, but it can be assigned an output orientation or an input orientation. In either orientation it decomposes into separate indexes of technical change and technical efficiency change, which makes it analytically consistent with profit change decompositions that include an activity effect. In this section we assign an input orientation to the CCD Malmquist productivity index, and we relate it to the productivity change decomposition in Section 6.4.1. It is a straightforward exercise to reverse the orientation and relate it to the productivity change decomposition in Section 6.4.2, and for completeness we include it in a footnote.

An output-oriented CCD Malmquist productivity index is defined in expression (2.5) in Chapter 2. An input-oriented comparison period Malmquist productivity index is defined similarly, using input distance functions, as

$$
\begin{aligned}
M_{i\,\mathrm{CCD}}^1(y^1,y^0,x^1,x^0) &= \frac{D_i^1(y^0,x^0)}{D_i^1(y^1,x^1)} \\
&= \frac{D_i^1(y^0,x^0)}{D_i^0(y^0,x^0)} \times \frac{D_i^0(y^0,x^0)}{D_i^1(y^1,x^1)}.
\end{aligned}
$$

This productivity index decomposes into the product of a technical change index $D_i^1(y^0,x^0)/D_i^0(y^0,x^0)$ and a technical efficiency change index $D_i^0(y^0,x^0)/D_i^1(y^1,x^1)$, with both indexes being input-oriented. Similar results can be obtained with the base period technology. A value of either index greater (less) than unity contributes to productivity growth (decline).

We revisit the profit change decomposition in Section 6.4.1, with the assistance of Figure 6.1 and the objective of relating the productivity effect to $M_{i\,\mathrm{CCD}}^1(y^1,y^0,x^1,x^0)$. The productivity effect in expression (6.20) is input-oriented, and can be expressed in terms of input distance functions as

$$[\overline{w}^T(x^0 - x^B) - \overline{w}^T(x^1 - x^C)]$$
$$= [\overline{w}^T x^0(1 - (1/D_i^0(y^0,x^0))) - \overline{w}^T x^1(1 - (1/D_i^1(y^1,x^1)))] \qquad (6.25)$$
$$+\overline{w}^T x^A[1 - (D_i^1(y^0,x^0)/D_i^0(y^0,x^0))^{-1}].$$

It is not difficult to show that the first term on the right side of expression (6.25) can be written as $\overline{w}^T(x^0 - x^A) - \overline{w}^T(x^1 - x^C)$, the technical efficiency effect in expression (6.20), and that the second term can be written as $\overline{w}^T(x^A - x^B)$, the technology effect in expression (6.20). Thus, the first term on the right side of expression (6.25) is the technical efficiency effect and the second is the technology effect, expressed not in terms of Figure 6.1, but in terms of the input distance functions used to define and decompose the CCD Malmquist productivity index. The technical change component remains in its original ratio form in the productivity effect, and consequently the absence of technical change $[D_i^1(y^0,x^0)/D_i^0(y^0,x^0) = 1]$ implies, and is implied by, a zero technology effect. Moreover, $D_i^1(y^0,x^0)/D_i^0(y^0,x^0) \gtrless 1 \Leftrightarrow$ $\overline{w}^T x^A[1 - (D_i^1(y^0,x^0)/D_i^0(y^0,x^0))^{-1}] \gtrless 0$, so that technical progress, for example, adds value. However, the efficiency change component is transformed to difference form, and the absence of technical efficiency change $[D_i^0(y^0,x^0)/D_i^1(y^1,x^1) = 1]$ neither implies nor is implied by a zero technical efficiency effect. Also, $D_i^0(y^0,x^0)/D_i^1(y^1,x^1) \gtrless 1$ neither implies nor is implied by $[\overline{w}^T x^0(1 - (1/D_i^0(y^0,x^0))) - \overline{w}^T x^1(1 - (1/D_i^1(y^1,x^1)))] \gtrless 0$, so that an improvement in technical efficiency, for example, can (not must) subtract value. It follows that $M_{iCCD}^1(y^1,y^0,x^1,x^0) \gtrless 1$ neither implies nor is implied by $\overline{w}^T(x^0 - x^B) - \overline{w}^T(x^1 - x^C) \gtrless 0$, so that productivity growth, if it comes via technical efficiency improvement, can (again not must) subtract value.

The explanation for this apparent paradox lies in the difference form of the technical efficiency effect. A constant degree of technical efficiency applied to different expenditures $\overline{w}^T x^0$ and $\overline{w}^T x^1$ generates a nonzero technical efficiency effect, and an improvement in efficiency, applied to a sufficiently large expenditure, can subtract value. Or, wasting 10% of a large budget can be more costly than wasting 15% of a smaller budget.

Two options are available. One is to understand that the paradox is only apparent, and to accept the lack of a one-to-one correspondence between technical efficiency change, as defined in the CCD Malmquist productivity index, and the technical efficiency effect, as defined in this chapter. The other is to seek conditions under which the apparent paradox is resolved, and there is a one-to-one correspondence.

One such condition is technical efficiency in the comparison period only. In this case the productivity effect in expression (6.25) becomes

$$[\overline{w}^T(x^0 - x^B) - \overline{w}^T(x^1 - x^C)] = \overline{w}^T x^0 \{1 - [M^1_{i\,CCD}(y^1, y^0, x^1, x^0)]^{-1}\},$$

$$(6.26)$$

which establishes the desired exact linkage between the productivity effect and $M^1_{i\,CCD}(y^1, y^0, x^1, x^0)$. Comparison period technical efficiency suffices for $M^1_{i\,CCD}(y^1, y^0, x^1, x^0) \gtreqless 1 \Leftrightarrow \overline{w}^T(x^0 - x^B) - \overline{w}^T(x^1 - x^C) \gtreqless 0$. In this case the productivity effect is a scaled normalized CCD Malmquist productivity index, and the scaling factor $\overline{w}^T x^0$ can be very large, as we demonstrate in the empirical application below.[4]

An analogous strategy of combining a base period CCD Malmquist productivity index $M^0_{i\,CCD}(y^1, y^0, x^1, x^0)$ with an assumption of base period technical efficiency generates a second exact decomposition. Alternative economically plausible restrictions do not appear to generate expressions having the same structure as expression (6.26).[5]

---

[4] Proof of (6.26): if $D^1_i(y^1, x^1) = 1$, expression (6.26) becomes

$$\overline{w}^T(x^0 - x^B) - \overline{w}^T(x^1 - x^C) = \overline{w}^T x^A \left(1 - \frac{D^0_i(y^0, x^0)}{D^1_i(y^0, x^0)}\right) + \overline{w}^T x^A \left(\frac{D^0_i(y^0, x^0)}{D^1_i(y^1, x^1)} - 1\right)$$

$$= \overline{w}^T x^0 \left(1 - \frac{1}{D^1_i(y^0, x^0)}\right) \qquad [\text{since } x^A = x^0/D^0_i(y^0, x^0)]$$

$$= \overline{w}^T x^0 \left(1 - \frac{D^1_i(y^1, x^1) D^0_i(y^0, x^0)}{D^0_i(y^0, x^0) D^1_i(y^0, x^0)}\right) \qquad [\text{since } D^1_i(y^1, x^1) = 1]$$

$$= \overline{w}^T x^0 (1 - [M^1_{i\,CCD}(y^1, y^0, x^1, x^0)]^{-1}).$$

[5] Output-oriented results are essentially the same. An output-oriented comparison period CCD Malmquist productivity index is

$$M^1_{o\,CCD}(x^1, x^0, y^1, y^0) = \frac{D^1_o(x^1, y^1)}{D^1_o(x^0, y^0)} = \frac{D^0_o(x^0, y^0)}{D^1_o(x^0, y^0)} \times \frac{D^1_o(x^1, y^1)}{D^0_o(x^0, y^0)},$$

and given technical efficiency in the comparison period $[D^1_o(x^1, y^1) = 1]$, the productivity effect in expression (6.20) becomes

$$\overline{p}^T(y^B - y^0) - \overline{p}^T(y^C - y^1) = \overline{p}^T y^0 [M^1_{o\,CCD}(x^1, x^0, y^1, y^0) - 1].$$

Analogous results hold for a base period CCD Malmquist productivity index of either orientation.

An empirical application

We return to the Walmart experience, relying again on Brea-Solís et al. (in press). We illustrate the profit change decompositions in expression (6.3) and surrounding expressions (6.19) to (6.20), although we do not decompose the activity effect.

Our first objective is to contrast the activity effect model in Section 6.4.1, in which investor input is not expensed, with the model in Section 6.2.1, in which investor input is expensed, using a common data set. Results when investor input is expensed appear in Table 6.1 and results when it is not appear in Table 6.6, which summarizes results of Brea-Solís et al. The two price effects are independent of the treatment of investor input, and they are equal and they detract from profit growth. Consequently, the productivity effect and the capital expansion effect in the investor input model sum to the

Table 6.6 Profit change decomposition by CEO era at Walmart
Millions of cumulative 1970 USD, by era

	Chief Executive Officers at Walmart from 1977 to 2008			
	Sam Walton (1977–88)	David Glass (1988–2000)	Scott Lee (2000–08)	1977–2008
Profit Change	368.6	1,487.8	1,102.3	2,958.6
Quantity effect	415.8	1,746.3	1,365.9	3,528.0
Productivity effect	247.8	215.0	528.3	991.1
Technical change effect	242.0	215.0	528.3	985.3
Efficiency change effect	5.8	0.0	0.0	5.8
Activity effect	168.0	1,531.3	837.6	2,536.9
Price effect	−47.3	−258.5	−263.6	−569.4
Input price effect	−144.3	32.5	913.1	801.3
Capital	−3.6	−121.5	−214.2	−339.4
Labor	−140.6	154.1	1,127.3	1,140.7
Output price effect	−191.6	−225.9	649.4	231.9
Output 1 (Walmart)	−132.5	−132.1	671.2	406.6
Output 2 (Sam's Club)	−59.1	−93.8	−21.8	−174.7

quantity effect in the activity effect model. However, the activity effect differs from the capital expansion effect, and consequently the two productivity effects differ. Only if the activity effect equals the capital expansion effect can the two productivity effects coincide, but the capital expansion effect involves change in the capital input only, while the activity effect incorporates change in all inputs, and K has grown faster than x. Thus, the capital expansion effect in expression (6.3) and Table 6.1 is larger than the activity effect in expression (6.19) and Table 6.6, and the contribution of productivity change to profit change correspondingly smaller. Summarizing, if investor input is expensed, the productivity effect actually detracts from profit growth, which is attributable exclusively to capital expansion combined with a large rate of return to capital. If investor input is not expensed, the productivity effect accounts for a third of profit growth, with the remainder attributable to the activity effect.

Our second objective is to illustrate expression (6.26), in which a Malmquist productivity index is scaled up to a productivity effect. A sufficient condition for expression (6.25) to collapse to expression (6.26) is comparison period technical efficiency, a condition that holds for Walmart in every year since 1984. Figure 6.7 illustrates the power of the scaling factor in expression (6.26), with rates of productivity change on the left axis converted to the productivity

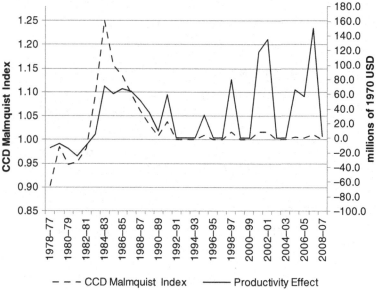

Figure 6.7 Productivity growth and its value at Walmart

effect expressed in 1970 USD on the right axis. In a few years $M_{i\,\mathrm{CCD}}^1(y^1, y^0, x^1, x^0) = 1$ and so there is no productivity change, making the scaling factor irrelevant. In most post-1988 years estimated productivity change is positive, but less than 2% per annum. However, the scaling factor translates modest productivity growth rates into many millions of 1970 USD. For one example, in 2007 $D_i^1(y^1, x^1) = 1$ and $M_{i\,\mathrm{CCD}}^1(y^1, y^0, x^1, x^0) = 1.012$, but the scaling factor converts this into over 150 million 1970 USD.

6.5 RELATING THE MARGIN EFFECT APPROACH AND THE ACTIVITY EFFECT APPROACH

In Section 6.3 we decomposed the quantity effect into a productivity effect and a margin effect. In Section 6.4 we decomposed the quantity effect into a productivity effect and an activity effect. The two productivity effects differ because activity effects differ from margin effects. Figure 6.8 links the decompositions in Sections 6.3 and 6.4. The former productivity effect has a size effect, and the latter does not. Expressions (6.12) and (6.23) demonstrate that, apart from the different price weights, the two productivity effects share a common technical efficiency effect and a common technology effect; this is clear in Figure 6.8. Consequently, the activity effect in expression (6.22) is the sum of the margin effect and the size effect in expressions (6.11) and (6.12); this is also clear in Figure 6.8.

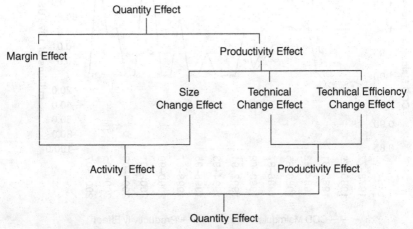

Figure 6.8 The structure of two quantity effect decompositions

It is straightforward to verify this relationship, with the assistance of Figures 6.2 and 6.8. To enhance comparability, we express both decompositions in Laspeyres form, and we take an output orientation. We decompose the activity effect in expression (6.22) as

$$
\begin{aligned}
[p^{0T}(y^C - y^B) - w^{0T}(x^1 - x^0)] & \\
= (\Pi^0 w^0 - w^0)^T(x^1 - x^0) & \qquad \text{margin effect} \\
+ [p^{0T}(y^C - y^B) - \Pi^0 w^{0T}(x^1 - x^0)], & \qquad \text{size effect}
\end{aligned}
$$

$$(6.27)$$

in which the margin effect coincides with the margin effect in expression (6.11) and the size effect coincides with the size effect in expression (6.12).

The relationship in expression (6.27) and Figure 6.8 is general. It holds for output-oriented and input-oriented decompositions, and for decompositions having Laspeyres, Paasche, and Bennet/LP structure. Regardless of orientation and structure, the difference between a model containing an activity effect and a model containing a margin effect is the placement of the size effect. If size change is considered to be a controllable driver of productivity change, it is located within the productivity effect in a model containing a margin effect. If, on the other hand, the time frame is considered sufficiently short to make size change exogenous, it is located outside the productivity effect in a model containing an activity effect. The quantity effect in a margin effect model is decomposed in the top half of Figure 6.8, and the quantity effect in an activity effect model is decomposed in the bottom half of Figure 6.8.

A logical corollary to the foregoing analysis concerns the two Malmquist productivity indexes. The Malmquist productivity index has three drivers: technical change, technical efficiency change, and size change. The CCD Malmquist productivity index has two drivers: technical change and technical efficiency change. A choice between the two productivity indexes can be based on whether the time frame or other circumstances allow managerial control over firm size. The choice can be based on more than just managerial control. The profit change decomposition for Walmart in Table 6.6 is based on an activity effect model in order to isolate the impact of a growth strategy of the company, and the activity effect has been the largest source of profit growth. Incentive regulation is frequently based on a model of productivity change that is independent of size, which is largely exogenous, and it is important to separate variation in demand from variation in productivity. Still other examples can be introduced to illustrate the point that the choice between the two frameworks depends on the circumstances and the objective of the exercise.

As we noted in Section 6.4, the activity effect itself decomposes. This makes the margin effect model and the activity effect model extreme cases. Depending on the nature of the operating environment, it may be appropriate to move one or two components of the activity effect into the productivity effect, or to move a component of the productivity effect into the activity effect.

Suppose, for example and as seems reasonable, that the output mix is under the control of management. Management accounting textbooks incorporate a product mix variance in their treatments of variance analysis, and automobile manufacturers adjust their product lines in accordance with changing consumer demands, both suggesting that changes in the product mix are endogenous, perhaps with a lag, and so contribute to productivity change. This suggestion is not new. Davis (1955; 3, 11–12) mentions changes in the product mix as a potential source of productivity change, and shows how to incorporate changes in the product mix into a profit change decomposition. More recently, a large theoretical literature on endogenous product selection has developed. Schoar (2002) and Bernard, Redding, and Schott (2010) exploit this literature to examine the impacts of corporate diversification and product switching on firm performance. Based on different data sets, they find a generally positive impact on productivity and an uncertain impact on profitability. Schoar's explanation for the muted impact on profitability is that highly diversified firms tend to "dissipate rents in the form of higher wages." O'Donnell (2012a, b) has developed a profitability and productivity decomposition framework in which changes in the output mix and the input mix play a prominent role.

Moving the output mix effect from the activity effect to the productivity effect alters the output-oriented decomposition (6.22) to (6.24) as follows. Using Figures 6.2, 6.5, and 6.6 to illustrate, the quantity effect decomposes as

$$[\bar{p}^T(y^1 - y^0) - \bar{w}^T(x^1 - x^0)]$$
$$= [\bar{p}^T(y^B - y^0) - \bar{p}^T(y^D - y^1)] \qquad \text{productivity effect}$$
$$+ [\bar{p}^T(y^D - y^B) - \bar{w}^T(x^1 - x^0)]. \qquad \text{activity effect}$$
$$(6.28)$$

The productivity effect decomposes as

$$[\bar{p}^T(y^B - y^0) - \bar{p}^T(y^D - y^1)]$$

$$= [\bar{p}^T(y^B - y^A)] \qquad\qquad \text{technology effect}$$
$$+ [\bar{p}^T(y^A - y^0) - \bar{p}^T(y^C - y^1)] \qquad \text{technical efficiency effect}$$
$$+ [\bar{p}^T(y^C - y^D)] \qquad\qquad \text{output mix effect}$$

$$(6.29)$$

and the activity effect decomposes as

$$[\bar{p}^T(y^D - y^B) - \bar{w}^T(x^1 - x^0)]$$

$$= [\bar{p}^T(y^D - y^B) - \bar{w}^T(x^E - x^0)] \qquad \text{radial activity effect}$$
$$- \bar{w}^T(x^1 - x^E). \qquad\qquad \text{input mix effect}$$

$$(6.30)$$

In this decomposition change in the output mix joins changes in technical efficiency and technology as drivers of productivity change. Depending on the circumstances, any of the components of the original activity effect in expression (6.24) can be reallocated to the productivity effect. The input mix effect is a likely candidate, particularly if the analysis is input-oriented, and is consistent with the inclusion of "reallocation of resources" as a driver of productivity change recommended by Denison (1962, 1974), BLS, and OECD, among others. Alternatively, a component can be moved from the productivity effect in expression (6.23) to the activity effect in expression (6.24). The likely candidate is the technology effect. Although characteristics of technology are popular drivers of productivity change, in some circumstances characteristics of technology may not be under management control, at least not in the short term.

Summarizing, the margin effect model contains three drivers of productivity change, and the activity effect model has two drivers, one of which has three components. However, the relationship between the two models allows one to move individual effects into or out of the productivity effect, as circumstances dictate. This flexibility is an attractive feature of the analytical framework. It also suggests that there are new productivity indexes (based on distance functions) and indicators to be developed, as circumstances warrant.

6.6 CONCLUSIONS ON DIFFERENCE MODELS OF PROFIT CHANGE

In Chapters 4 to 6 we measure business financial performance with profit, the difference between revenue and cost. The difference approach provides insights into financial performance that are unavailable in the ratio approach we developed in Chapters 2 and 3.

In Chapter 4 we began our investigation of the sources of profit change and the distribution of its financial impacts. We introduced two analytical frameworks. One, associated with Davis (1955) and Kendrick and Creamer (1961) expenses profit, which is called investor input, so that the difference between revenue and augmented cost is identically zero. This approach is consistent with the structure of the national accounts. The second framework dispenses with investor input, allowing the difference between revenue and cost to reclaim its original name, and to take any value.

Within the investor input framework, the fundamental findings reported in Sections 4.3.1 and 4.4.1 are (i) there is no distinction between a quantity effect and a productivity effect; (ii) real comparison period profitability $\check{\Pi}_0^1 = R_0^1/\check{C}_0^1$ is a productivity index, and $\check{\Pi}_0^1 - 1$ is the rate of productivity change; (iii) real comparison period profit $\check{\pi}_0^1 = \check{C}_0^1(\check{\Pi}_0^1 - 1)$ is the monetary value of productivity change; and (iv) the productivity bonus $\check{\pi}_0^1 = -y^{1T}(p^1 - p^0) + x^{1T}(w^1 - w^0) + K_0^1(r^1 - r^0)$ is distributed to consumers, input suppliers, and investors by way of change in prices paid and received and change in the rate of return.

When profit is allowed to take any value, the fundamental findings reported in Sections 4.3.2 and 4.4.2 are (i) the productivity effect differs from the quantity effect; (ii) real comparison period profitability π_0^1 differs from the real comparison period productivity index $Y_L/X_L = [(R^1/P_P)/(C^1/W_P)]/(R^0/C^0)$ unless $R^0 = C^0$, which would result from investor input or a similar device; (iii) real comparison period profit π_0^1 differs from the quantity effect and has no apparent interpretation as the monetary value of productivity change; and (iv) in most cases the bonus being distributed is not the productivity effect but the quantity effect, which is distributed to consumers, input suppliers, and the business itself through profit change rather than through change in the rate of return as in the investor input model.

In Chapter 5 we introduced empirical indicators, the difference analogue to empirical index numbers. We used these indicators to decompose profit change into a quantity effect and a price effect, to decompose the quantity effect into a productivity effect and a quantity margin effect, and to decompose the price effect into a price recovery effect and a price margin effect. We expressed all four effects in both indicator form and index number form. We also set out conditions under which quantity and productivity effects coincide, and under which price and price recovery effects coincide. When investor input is incorporated, profit change decomposes somewhat differently, into a productivity effect, an earnings on capital expansion effect that reflects the contribution to profit change of investment having a nonzero rate of return, and a price effect that we can, but choose not to, decompose. Finally, we introduced a family of dual productivity indicators, the difference analogue of dual productivity indexes we introduced in Chapter 2.

In Chapter 6 we decompose the productivity effect with and without investor input. Since the only difference between the two productivity effects is their different price weights, we devote most of the chapter to decomposing the productivity effect in the absence of investor input. We began by continuing the analysis initiated in Chapter 5. In this framework the quantity effect includes a productivity effect and a margin effect, and the productivity effect decomposes into the product of three drivers: technical efficiency change, technical change, and size change. We then considered an alternative framework in which the quantity effect includes a productivity effect and an activity effect, and the productivity effect decomposes into the product of two drivers, technical efficiency change and technical change. The essential difference between the two frameworks is that in the former framework size change is a productivity driver under management control, while in the latter size change is removed from the productivity effect under the supposition that it is not under management control. For example, under incentive regulation the regulator must determine whether or not size, as measured by output, is demand driven, largely beyond management control, and is not a proper component of a productivity effect. This distinction leads naturally to alternative frameworks within which drivers of the activity effect, such as change in the product mix, can be moved into the productivity effect, making the placement of alternative drivers depend on the circumstances. To cite another example, the empirical application to Walmart is based on an activity effect model because we want to explore the financial impact of the company's growth strategy.

PART III

Productivity, Cost, and Return on Assets

7 Productivity and Cost

7.1 INTRODUCTION

Subsequent to the global economic downturn that began in 2008, firms responded in various ways, but primarily through efforts to match declining revenues with cost reductions. Examples culled from media reporting include, and are not limited to, workforce reductions, rewriting labor contracts to reduce real wages and benefits, increasing reliance on outsourcing and offshoring, undertaking "transformative" changes to the cost structure, adopting cost-saving new technologies, and reducing service quality. Some of these actions are attempts to reduce waste, others are attempts to reduce the levels of efficient costs, and others involve downsizing. Borenstein and Farrell (2000) assign these and more examples to either of two categories: (i) trimming fat, and (ii) re-optimizing in response to changes in exogenous factors.

In Section 6.3.4 of Chapter 6 we introduced the notion that we might wish to measure and decompose productivity change within a cost change framework, ignoring the contribution of revenue change to profit change. In this chapter we follow up on that notion by exploring the relationship between financial performance and productivity performance in an environment that ignores the revenue half of the picture. In such an environment financial performance depends on cost, and productivity performance depends on output and input quantities, and also on input prices. We begin in Section 7.2 with a brief discussion of variance analysis as it is presented in cost

277

accounting textbooks. Variance analysis identifies essentially the same cost drivers as economic analysis does, although from a different perspective and under different assumptions. Indeed, a central tenet of variance analysis is that input-oriented productivity change is a key driver of cost change. This discussion helps motivate subsequent analyses in Sections 7.3 and 7.4, where we use a cost frontier to estimate and decompose the contribution of productivity change to cost change. In Section 7.5 we change the financial performance indicator from cost to unit cost, a widely used performance indicator. In Section 7.6 we focus on partial factor productivities, which we relate to total factor productivity and unit cost. In Section 7.7 we narrow the indicator from unit cost to unit labor cost, another widely used performance indicator, particularly in international comparisons. Throughout the chapter we use a mixture of ratio (Chapters 2 and 3) and difference (Chapters 4 to 6) models to conduct our analyses. Section 7.8 concludes.[1]

The terminology of variance analysis suggests that output quantities and input prices are not entirely under management control. Economic analysis concurs, and is more explicit: reliance on a cost frontier $c(y, w)$ is appropriate when firms treat output quantities and input prices as exogenous. If some input quantities are also fixed, at least temporarily, the relevant frontier becomes a variable cost frontier $c_v(y, w_v, x_f)$, w_v being a vector of variable input prices and x_f a vector of fixed input quantities. The appropriateness of a cost frontier is enhanced if firms seek to adjust endogenous inputs in an effort to minimize cost, total or variable. Scholars have been using cost functions to estimate, and occasionally to decompose, productivity change for decades, and it is a short but potentially informative step from a cost *function* to a cost *frontier*, a step we take throughout this chapter.[2]

The primal approaches we developed in Chapter 6 are based on quantity data (x, y), using price data only in the evaluation stage of the exercise. They introduce technical efficiency change as a potential driver of productivity

---

[1] Chapter 7 can be reoriented from measuring and decomposing productivity change within a cost frontier context to a revenue frontier context. Conditions under which reliance on a revenue frontier is appropriate are analogous; exogeneity of input quantities and output prices, combined with flexibility in the choice of product mix and possible fixity of some outputs due to contractual commitments. Estimation of revenue frontiers for the purpose of estimating and decomposing the contribution of productivity change to revenue change is not widespread, but the presence of relatively inflexible input markets and highly capital-intensive technologies encourage increased reliance on the use of revenue frontiers.

[2] Dean (1941) was one of the first to estimate a cost function, and he attributed divergence of empirical from theoretical cost functions (i.e., $w^T x \geq c(y, w)$) to managerial inertia and other rigidities. He also argued, wrongly, that divergence cannot be removed by statistical methods.

change, and hence change in financial performance. The dual approaches we develop in this chapter are based on both quantity and price data, with a cost frontier being based on (y, w). An advantage of cost frontiers is that, being based on price as well as quantity data, they introduce change in the efficiency with which inputs are allocated as a new potential driver of productivity change. Thus, emphasis expands from technical efficiency to cost efficiency, which has technical and allocative components.

Focusing analysis on the cost half of the picture is easily motivated and widely practiced.

(i) In Section 4.3.2 of Chapter 4, and again in Section 6.3.1 of Chapter 6, we replaced potentially distorted output prices with allocated unit costs. Depending on the difficulties surrounding the cost allocation exercise, it may be preferable to ignore the revenue half of the picture.

(ii) In variance analysis it is typical to do both: ignore the revenue half of the picture and allocate cost.

(iii) In some sectors output prices are missing, particularly in services such as health care, police services, court administration, corrective services, and emergency management. In these sectors the analysis of financial and productivity performance necessarily takes on a cost perspective.

(iv) In some sectors firms have limited control over output quantities, and therefore over revenue. When output quantities are largely uncontrollable, it is appropriate to analyze performance from a cost perspective.

(v) In other sectors firms lack control over output quantities and output prices. This occurs under incentive regulation, in which firms must satisfy demand and the regulator sets prices so as to provide firms with an incentive to increase productivity in order to contain or reduce cost. In this context performance analysis naturally focuses on the cost half of the picture.

(vi) Unit cost and unit labor cost are widely reported performance indicators, particularly in international competitiveness comparisons. In some circumstances unit labor cost, despite its obvious drawback, is the best available indicator.

We suggest five strategies for analyzing financial and productivity performance from a cost perspective. The first is variance analysis. The next two are based on a cost frontier, the dual to the production frontier supporting the strategies in Chapter 6. The fourth is a variant of the third, and is based on a unit cost frontier. It has the same theoretical foundation as a cost frontier, and it decomposes similarly. The fifth is based on a unit labor cost frontier, and is appropriate when labor is the only variable input, in which case unit labor cost is unit variable cost, or when labor is the only input for which reliable comparable data are available.

7.2 VARIANCE ANALYSIS

Throughout most of the book situations "^{1}" and "^{0}" refer to comparison period and base period, although there are exceptions, Miller (1984) being one in Section 4.3.2 of Chapter 4. In variance analysis situations "^{1}" and "^{0}" refer to actual and budgeted. The objective of variance analysis is to explain the deviation, or variance, of actual from budgeted cost, which we write $w^{1T}x^1 - w^{0T}x^0$. Three drivers come to mind. Output quantities can differ from their budgeted amounts; this is referred to as a sales activity (or volume) variance. Input quantities can differ from their budgeted amounts, independently of the sales activity variance; this is referred to as a productivity (or efficiency) variance. Finally, input prices can differ from their budgeted values; this is referred to as a price variance.

An important feature of variance analysis is the procedure by which budgeted input quantities are determined. Input requirements are determined by fixed input/output ratios $x_n/y_m = \alpha_{nm}$, $n = 1, \ldots, N$, $m = 1, \ldots, M$, and so a Leontief technology underlies the budget. Thus, if the budgeted amounts of outputs y_m are y_m^0, the budgeted amount of input x_n is $x_n^0 = \sum_m x_{nm}^0 = \alpha_{n1}y_1^0 + \cdots + \alpha_{nm}y_m^0 + \cdots + \alpha_{nM}y_M^0 = \sum_m \alpha_{nm}y_m^0$. If the budgeted prices of inputs x_n are w_n^0, the cost budgeted for the production of output y_m is $C_m^0 = w_1^0\alpha_{1m}y_m^0 + \cdots + w_n^0\alpha_{nm}y_m^0 + \cdots + w_N^0\alpha_{Nm}y_m^0 = y_m^0\sum_n w_n^0\alpha_{nm}$, and the unit cost budgeted for output y_m is $c_m^0 = C_m^0/y_m^0 = \sum_n w_n^0\alpha_{nm} = \sum_n w_n^0 x_{nm}^0/y_m^0$. We introduced cost allocation in Chapter 4, and we made extensive use of it in Chapter 6, but we did not explain how it is implemented. Variance analysis offers one procedure. Although variance analysis allocates budgeted cost, and in Chapters 4 and 6 we allocated actual cost, the Leontief procedure adopted in variance analysis can also be used to allocate actual cost.

We can now decompose the cost variance $w^{1T}x^1 - w^{0T}x^0$ into its three drivers by means of

$$w^{1T}x^1 - w^{0T}x^0$$

$$= \sum_m \sum_n w_n^0 \alpha_{nm}(y_m^1 - y_m^0) \qquad \text{sales activity variance}$$

$$+ \sum_n w_n^0 [x_n^1 - \sum_m \alpha_{nm} y_m^1] \qquad \text{productivity variance}$$

$$+ \sum_n x_n^1 (w_n^1 - w_n^0). \qquad \text{price variance} \qquad (7.1)$$

The sales activity variance is the sum of M individual output activity variances, and measures the cost impact of a departure of the actual output vector from what was originally budgeted. It can be rewritten as $\sum_m c_m^0(y_m^1 - y_m^0) = c^{0T}(y^1 - y^0)$, which is a Laspeyres output quantity indicator that values output variances at their budgeted unit costs. It appears in expression (4.20) in Chapter 4 and in expression (6.8) in Chapter 6 as half of the margin effect. The productivity variance is the sum of N individual input productivity variances, and measures the cost impact of a departure of actual input use from budgeted input use *for the output vector actually produced.* It can be simplified to $\sum_n w_n^0 x_n^1 - \sum_m c_m^0 y_m^1 = w^{0T}x^1 - c^{0T}y^1$, which is the negative of the productivity effect in expressions (4.20) and (6.8) (since $c^{0T}y^0 = w^{0T}x^0$). The productivity variance thus values actual inputs by their budgeted prices and values actual outputs by their budgeted unit costs. The price variance is the sum of N individual input price variances, and measures the cost impact of a departure of actual input prices from their budgeted values, *for the input vector actually used.* The price variance is a Paasche input price indicator $x^{1T}(w^1 - w^0)$, using actual input quantities to weight input price variances. The sales activity variance, the productivity variance, and the price variance sum to the cost variance. Each variance is said to be favorable if it reduces the cost variance.[3]

The information required to implement variance analysis is minimal: budgeted quantities y^0, x^0 and input prices w^0, and actual quantities y^1, x^1 and input prices w^1. However, the fixed proportions assumption that generates budgeted input quantities x^0 is hardly innocuous. It is often criticized for not allowing varying input proportions in response to changes in input prices, and consequently for providing the wrong incentives to management. Variance analysis models with totally flexible budgets, flexible with respect to output quantities as in traditional variance analysis, and also,

---

[3] Banker, Datar, and Kaplan (1989) add budgeted and actual output prices to generate a profit variance analysis. Their model of profit change has the same sales activity variance and the same input-oriented productivity variance as expression (7.1), and converts the input price variance to a price recovery variance.

inspired by economic theory, with respect to input prices, have been proposed by Mensah (1982), Darrough (1988), and Callen (1988) among others, on the grounds that management should be held responsible for adjusting the input mix to changing relative input prices, but the fixed proportions assumption survives. In Sections 7.3 and 7.4 we develop a pair of economic alternatives to variance analysis. Both frameworks allow, even encourage, input substitution. However, dispensing with the fixed proportions assumption comes at a cost: the need to estimate the structure of the underlying technology. Management can conduct an informative variance analysis with a sample of size one, while estimating the structure of technology requires a somewhat larger sample. Thus, variance analysis *assumes* a fixed proportions technology, and economic analysis *estimates* the structure of the technology.

7.3 A COST FRONTIER: A KONÜS FRAMEWORK

Recall from Section 2.3.3 of Chapter 2 that a Konüs input price index is expressed as the ratio of two cost frontiers $c(y, w^1)/c(y, w^0)$, where w^1 and w^0 are comparison period and base period input price vectors. The Konüs concept can be extended to generate a decomposition of cost change between base and comparison periods expressed in ratio form. This decomposition begins with

$$\frac{w^{1T}x^1}{w^{0T}x^0} = \frac{c^1(y^1, w^1)}{c^1(y^1, w^0)} \times \frac{w^{1T}x^1/c^1(y^1, w^1)}{w^{0T}x^0/c^1(y^1, w^0)}. \tag{7.2}$$

The first term on the right side of expression (7.2) is a Konüs input price index that holds technology and output quantities fixed at comparison period levels in order to measure the impact of the input price change from w^0 to w^1; $c^1(y^1, w^1)/c^1(y^1, w^0) \lesseqgtr 1$ as input prices decline, remain unchanged, or increase, which does not require $w_n^1 \lesseqgtr w_n^0 \ \forall n$. The second term is a Konüs implicit input quantity index $XI_K(y^1, w^1, w^0, x^1, x^0)$, which decomposes as

$$\frac{w^{1T}x^1/c^1(y^1, w^1)}{w^{0T}x^0/c^1(y^1, w^0)} = \frac{w^{1T}x^1/c^1(y^1, w^1)}{w^{0T}x^0/c^0(y^0, w^0)} \times \frac{c^1(y^0, w^0)}{c^0(y^0, w^0)} \times \frac{c^1(y^1, w^0)}{c^1(y^0, w^0)}. \tag{7.3}$$

The first component of the implicit input quantity index is a cost efficiency index that allows technology, output quantities, and input prices to vary between periods and compares actual with minimum feasible expenditure in the two periods. $[w^{1T}x^1/c^1(y^1, w^1)]/[w^{0T}x^0/c^0(y^0, w^0)] \lessgtr 1$ as cost efficiency improves, remains unchanged, or declines. The second component is a Konüs type of technical change index that holds output quantities and input prices fixed at base period levels to measure the impact of a change in technology, with $c^1(y^0, w^0)/c^0(y^0, w^0) \lessgtr 1$ as technical change is progress, stagnation, or regress. The final component is an activity index that holds technology fixed at its comparison period level and input prices fixed at base period levels in order to measure the impact of the output change from y^0 to y^1; $c^1(y^1, w^0)/c^1(y^0, w^0) \lessgtr 1$ as output quantities decline, remain unchanged, or increase, which does not require $y_m^1 \lessgtr y_m^0 \forall m$. An improvement in cost efficiency, technical progress, and a reduction in output produced all reduce the implicit input quantity index, and therefore $w^{1T}x^1/w^{0T}x^0$.

Expressions (7.2) and (7.3) decompose cost change from a comparison period perspective, the cost frontiers being of the form $c^1(y, w)$. There exists a similar decomposition of cost change from a base period perspective with cost frontiers of the form $c^0(y, w)$. The geometric mean of the two generates the following decomposition of cost change

$$\frac{w^{1T}x^1}{w^{0T}x^0}$$

$$= \left[\frac{c^1(y^1, w^1)}{c^1(y^1, w^0)} \times \frac{c^0(y^0, w^1)}{c^0(y^0, w^0)} \right]^{1/2} \qquad \text{input price effect}$$

$$\times \left[\frac{w^{1T}x^1/c^1(y^1, w^1)}{w^{0T}x^0/c^0(y^0, w^0)} \right] \qquad \text{cost efficiency effect}$$

$$\times \left[\frac{c^1(y^0, w^0)}{c^0(y^0, w^0)} \times \frac{c^1(y^1, w^1)}{c^0(y^1, w^1)} \right]^{1/2} \qquad \text{technology effect}$$

$$\times \left[\frac{c^1(y^1, w^0)}{c^1(y^0, w^0)} \times \frac{c^0(y^1, w^1)}{c^0(y^0, w^1)} \right]^{1/2}. \qquad \text{activity effect}$$

$$(7.4)$$

The Konüs framework identifies four drivers of cost change, two of which (the activity effect and the cost efficiency effect) can be further decomposed. It also is possible to create a dual cost-oriented productivity index from expression (7.4). Throughout much of Chapters 2 to 6 we defined a productivity effect as including a size component. However in Chapter 6, especially in Section 6.5 and Figure 6.8, we developed a margin effect framework in which output is under management control, and an activity effect framework in which output is not under management control. Here in Chapter 7 reliance on a cost frontier implies that input prices and output quantities are exogenous. Under this assumption a dual cost-oriented productivity index becomes that part of cost change not accounted for by input price change and output quantity change, and we have from expression (7.4)[4]

$$\left[\frac{w^{1T}x^1}{w^{0T}x^0}\right] \Big/ \left[\frac{c^1(y^1,w^1)}{c^1(y^1,w^0)} \times \frac{c^0(y^0,w^1)}{c^0(y^0,w^0)} \times \frac{c^1(y^1,w^0)}{c^1(y^0,w^0)} \times \frac{c^0(y^1,w^1)}{c^0(y^0,w^1)}\right]^{1/2}$$

$$= \left[\frac{w^{1T}x^1/c^1(y^1,w^1)}{w^{0T}x^0/c^0(y^0,w^0)}\right] \qquad \text{cost efficiency effect}$$

$$\times \left[\frac{c^1(y^0,w^0)}{c^0(y^0,w^0)} \times \frac{c^1(y^1,w^1)}{c^0(y^1,w^1)}\right]^{1/2}. \qquad \text{technology effect}$$

$$(7.5)$$

We now convert the Konüs cost decomposition from ratio form to the difference form introduced by Grifell-Tatjé and Lovell (2003). In the process we clarify the relationship between the ratio form and the difference form. The difference form analogue to expressions (7.2) and (7.3) begins with

$$w^{1T}x^1 - w^{0T}x^0$$
$$= c^1(y^1,w^1) - c^1(y^1,w^0) \qquad \text{input price effect}$$
$$+ [w^{1T}x^1 - c^1(y^1,w^1)] - [w^{0T}x^0 - c^1(y^1,w^0)]. \qquad \text{input quantity effect}$$

$$(7.6)$$

The Konüs input quantity effect decomposes as

$$[w^{1T}x^1 - c^1(y^1,w^1)] - [w^{0T}x^0 - c^1(y^1,w^0)]$$
$$= [w^{1T}x^1 - c^1(y^1,w^1)] - [w^{0T}x^0 - c^0(y^0,w^0)] \qquad \text{cost efficiency effect}$$
$$+ [c^1(y^0,w^0) - c^0(y^0,w^0)] \qquad \text{technology effect}$$
$$+ [c^1(y^1,w^0) - c^1(y^0,w^0)]. \qquad \text{activity effect} \quad (7.7)$$

If the monetary value of cost inefficiency declines from base period to comparison period, the cost efficiency effect is negative. The cost efficiency effect decomposes into its technical efficiency and allocative efficiency components, a decomposition we implement in Section 7.4. If technical change is progress, the cost frontier shifts downward and the technology effect is also negative. A negative activity effect signals a decrease in output

---

[4] Diewert (2014) derives our expressions (7.4) and (7.5), with one minor exception. Our size effect and his technical change effect contain mixed-period variables.

quantities, even if $y^1 \not< y^0$. As in the index expressions (7.2) and (7.3), it is possible to base the analysis in expressions (7.6) and (7.7) on $c^0(y^0, w)$, or on the arithmetic mean of $c^1(y^1, w)$ and $c^0(y^0, w)$. Either would require offsetting adjustments to the input quantity effect and its components that appear below.[5]

A comparison of expressions (7.6) and (7.7) with expression (7.1) in Section 7.2 shows that, despite their different methodologies and terminologies, variance analysis and economic analysis identify the same drivers of cost change/variance. The only difference is that expression (7.1) contains a productivity variance and expression (7.7) contains a dual cost-oriented productivity variance consisting of a cost efficiency effect and a technology effect.

Now recall the fixed proportions assumption used to determine x^0 in variance analysis. If the fixed proportions are set not just by engineers but also by managers with w^0 in mind, then we expect that the budgeted cost $w^{0T}x^0 \approx c^0(y^0, w^0)$. If there is a price variance, $w^1 \neq w^0$ and we expect management to substitute inputs in an effort to minimize $[w^{1T}x^1 - c^1(y^1, w^1)]$. This effort puts downward pressure on the cost efficiency effect in expression (7.7), but it is penalized in expression (7.1), where the productivity variance values $[x_n^1 - \sum_m \alpha_{nm} y_m^1]$ at $w_n^0 \, \forall n$. An unfavorable productivity variance is built into variance analysis, because it penalizes input substitution in response to an input price change.

We illustrate the decomposition of cost change in expressions (7.6) and (7.7), with the assistance of Figure 7.1, in which a base period cost frontier $c^0(y, w^0)$ lies above a comparison period cost frontier $c^1(y, w^1)$, which in turn lies above a mixed-period cost frontier $c^1(y, w^0)$, all on the assumption that

---

[5] The difference and ratio forms of the cost change decompositions in expressions (7.6) and (7.2) are related by means of

$$w^{1T}x^1 - w^{0T}x^0 = c^1(y^1, w^0)\{[c^1(y^1, w^1)/c^1(y^1, w^0)] - 1\}$$
$$+ [c^1(y^1, w^1)\{[w^{1T}x^1/c^1(y^1, w^1)] - 1\} - c^1(y^1, w^0)\{[w^{0T}x^0/c^1(y^1, w^0)] - 1\}],$$

and the difference and ratio forms of the quantity effect decompositions in expressions (7.7) and (7.3) are related by

$$[w^{1T}x^1 - c^1(y^1, w^1)] - [w^{0T}x^0 - c^1(y^1, w^0)]$$
$$= c^1(y^1, w^1)\{[w^{1T}x^1/c^1(y^1, w^1)] - 1\} - c^0(y^0, w^0)\{[w^{0T}x^0/c^0(y^0, w^0)] - 1\}$$
$$+ c^0(y^0, w^0)\{[c^1(y^0, w^0)/c^0(y^0, w^0)] - 1\}$$
$$+ c^1(y^0, w^0)\{[c^1(y^1, w^0)/c^1(y^0, w^0)] - 1\}.$$

All subsequent difference and ratio expressions can be related in a similar manner.

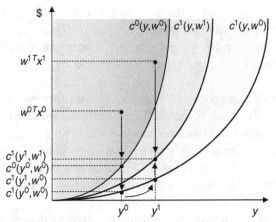

Figure 7.1 A Konüs cost-oriented productivity effect decomposition

the cost-reducing benefits of technical progress are partly offset by an increase in input prices.

A firm's expenditure increases from $w^{0T}x^0$ to $w^{1T}x^1$. Part of cost change is attributable to change in cost efficiency, as indicated by the two arrows pointing down from $w^{0T}x^0$ to $c^0(y^0, w^0)$, and from $w^{1T}x^1$ to $c^1(y^1, w^1)$. A second part of the cost change is due to technical progress, as measured by the arrow pointing down from $c^0(y^0, w^0)$ to $c^1(y^0, w^0)$. A third part of the cost change is attributable to expansion, as indicated by the arrow from $c^1(y^0, w^0)$ to $c^1(y^1, w^0)$. This completes the decomposition of the quantity effect. The remaining source of cost change appears as the vertical distance between $c^1(y^1, w^0)$ and $c^1(y^1, w^1)$. This is the Konüs price effect. Each source of cost change has its ratio counterpart in expressions (7.2) and (7.3). The structure of these dual cost change decompositions corresponds to the primal quantity change decomposition in the bottom half of Figure 6.8 in Chapter 6.

The activity effect captures the cost impact of moving from y^0 to y^1, a move that has radial and nonradial components. In the primal Section 6.4 of Chapter 6 we decomposed the activity effect into radial and mix components. Here the decomposition becomes

$$
\begin{aligned}
[c^1(y^1, w^0) &- c^1(y^0, w^0)] \\
&= [c^1(\varphi y^0, w^0) - c^1(y^0, w^0)] && \text{radial activity effect} \\
&+ [c^1(y^1, w^0) - c^1(\varphi y^0, w^0)], && \text{output mix effect}
\end{aligned}
$$

(7.8)

in which $\varphi y^0 \in IQ^1(x^1)$, with $\varphi = 1/D_o^1(x^1, y^0)$, belongs to the same output isoquant as y^1. In Section 6.4 of Chapter 6 the two decompositions of the activity effect have radial, output mix, and input mix components. Decomposition (7.8) of the cost-based activity effect has no input mix effect because the drivers of cost change include output quantities, input prices, and technology, but not input quantities. Changes in the input mix do appear, indirectly, as components of the cost efficiency effect in decomposition (7.7).

Summarizing the decomposition of cost change, the Konüs framework can be expressed in either ratio or difference form. In both forms it uses a cost frontier to decompose cost change into four drivers. The four drivers are input price change (the input price effect in expressions (7.2) and (7.6)), output quantity change (the activity effect in expressions (7.3) and (7.7)), and cost efficiency change and technical change (the cost efficiency and technology effects in expressions (7.3) and (7.7)), the latter two effects constituting the impact of productivity change on cost change. It is also possible to disentangle the radial and output mix components of the activity effect, as we do in expression (7.8).

The Konüs approach to decomposing cost change can be extended to a decomposition of profit change that is quite different from those we developed in Chapters 5 and 6. We begin by decomposing profit change in a new way as

$$\pi^1 - \pi^0 = (p^{1T}y^1 - w^{1T}x^1) - (p^{0T}y^0 - w^{0T}x^0)$$
$$= (p^{1T}y^1 - p^{0T}y^0) - (w^{1T}x^1 - w^{0T}x^0)$$
$$= [p^{0T}(y^1 - y^0) + y^{1T}(p^1 - p^0)] - (w^{1T}x^1 - w^{0T}x^0). \quad (7.9)$$

The first component of profit change combines a Laspeyres output quantity indicator with a Paasche output price indicator to generate a revenue change indicator. The second component is cost change. We use expressions (7.6) and (7.7) to develop a Konüs type of decomposition of the cost change component of profit change as

$w^{1T}x^1 - w^{0T}x^0$

$\begin{aligned} = &[c^1(y^1, w^1) - c^1(y^1, w^0)] &&\text{input price effect} \\ &+ [c^1(y^1, w^0) - c^1(y^0, w^0)] &&\text{activity effect} \\ &+ [w^{1T}x^1 - c^1(y^1, w^1)] - [w^{0T}x^0 - c^0(y^0, w^0)] &&\text{cost efficiency effect} \\ &+ [c^1(y^0, w^0) - c^0(y^0, w^0)]. &&\text{technology effect} \end{aligned}$

$$(7.10)$$

Merging expressions (7.9) and (7.10) generates a new cost-oriented decomposition of profit change

$$\pi^1 - \pi^0$$

$$
\begin{aligned}
&= y^{1T}(p^1 - p^0) & \text{output price effect} \\
&+ [c^1(y^1, w^0) - c^1(y^1, w^1)] & \text{input price effect} \\
&+ p^{0T}(y^1 - y^0) - [c^1(y^1, w^0) - c^1(y^0, w^0)] & \text{profit activity effect} \\
&+ \{[w^{0T}x^0 - c^0(y^0, w^0)] - [w^{1T}x^1 - c^1(y^1, w^1)]\} & \text{cost efficiency effect} \\
&+ [c^0(y^0, w^0) - c^1(y^0, w^0)]. & \text{technology effect}
\end{aligned}
$$

$$(7.11)$$

The revenue change indicator is divided into a Paasche output price effect and part of an augmented activity effect we call a profit activity effect because, unlike the activity effect in expressions (7.7) and (7.10), which measure the contribution of output change to cost change, the profit activity effect measures the contribution of output change to profit change. The profit activity effect is positive, zero, or negative as output change causes $p^{0T}(y^1 - y^0) \gtreqless [c^1(y^1, w^0) - c^1(y^0, w^0)]$. A second noteworthy feature of expression (7.11) is that all non-price drivers of profit change do so through the cost side, although it is a straightforward exercise to construct a revenue-oriented analogue to decomposition (7.11).

7.4 A COST FRONTIER: A BENNET FRAMEWORK

We follow Grifell-Tatjé and Lovell (2000), who use Bennet input quantity and price indicators to identify the drivers of cost change within a cost frontier framework. Observed cost change decomposes as

$$
\begin{aligned}
w^{1T}x^1 - w^{0T}x^0 &= \bar{w}^T(x^1 - x^0) + \bar{x}^T(w^1 - w^0) \\
&= \bar{w}^T x^0 (X_{EM} - 1) + \bar{x}^T w^0 (W_{EM} - 1),
\end{aligned}
$$

$$(7.12)$$

with $\bar{w} = \frac{1}{2}(w^0 + w^1)$ and $\bar{x} = \frac{1}{2}(x^0 + x^1)$. The first term on the right side is an input quantity effect and the second is an input price effect. The first equality expresses cost change using Bennet quantity and price indicators, which the second equality converts to scaled Edgeworth-Marshall (EM) quantity and price indexes. Expression (7.12) is the cost change half of profit change decompositions appearing in Section 5.3.2 of Chapter 5. It

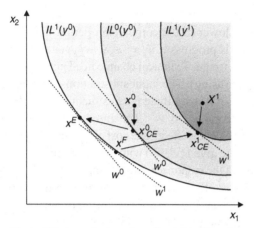

Figure 7.2 A cost-oriented productivity effect decomposition

is straightforward to replace the Bennet/EM structure of expression (7.12) with a Laspeyres/Paasche structure or a Paasche/Laspeyres structure to obtain the cost change half of profit change expressions appearing in Section 5.3.1 of Chapter 5.

We decompose the input quantity effect following a strategy suggested by Figure 7.2. Elimination of base period cost inefficiency moves x^0 to cost-efficient $x_{CE}^0 \in IL^0(y^0)$, and so $w^{0T}x_{CE}^0 = c^0(y^0, w^0)$. Elimination of comparison period cost inefficiency moves x^1 to cost-efficient $x_{CE}^1 \in IL^1(y^1)$, and so $w^{1T}x_{CE}^1 = c^1(y^1, w^1)$. Technical progress enlarges $L^0(y^0)$ to $L^1(y^0)$ and allows x_{CE}^0 to move to cost-efficient $x^E \in IL^1(y^0)$, and so $w^{0T}x^E = c^1(y^0, w^0)$. Cost-efficient input substitution in response to the input price change from w^0 to w^1 moves x^E to cost-efficient $x^F \in IL^1(y^0)$, and so $w^{1T}x^F = c^1(y^0, w^1)$. Cost-efficient expansion from $x^F \in IL^1(y^0)$ to $x_{CE}^1 \in IL^1(y^1)$ completes the decomposition of the input quantity effect.

The input quantity effect attaches values to the movements described in Figure 7.2, and decomposes as

$$
\begin{aligned}
\overline{w}^T(x^1 - x^0) \\
= [\overline{w}^T(x^1 - x_{CE}^1) - \overline{w}^T(x^0 - x_{CE}^0)] &\qquad \text{cost efficiency effect} \\
+ \overline{w}^T(x^E - x_{CE}^0) &\qquad \text{technology effect} \\
+ \overline{w}^T(x^F - x^E) &\qquad \text{input substitution effect} \\
+ \overline{w}^T(x_{CE}^1 - x^F). &\qquad \text{activity effect}
\end{aligned}
$$

$$(7.13)$$

Cost efficiency improves if $\overline{w}^T(x^1 - x^1_{CE}) < \overline{w}^T(x^0 - x^0_{CE})$, or if the cost of inefficient input usage is lower in the comparison period than in the base period. Technical change is progress if $\overline{w}^T x^E < \overline{w}^T x^0_{CE}$, or if it reduces the cost of cost-efficient input usage. Technical change need not be neutral in its impact on input saving (or using). The input substitution effect captures the cost, positive or negative, of a cost-efficient adjustment along $IL^1(y^0)$ to the change in input prices from w^0 to w^1. The input substitution effect is independent of the cost efficiency effect. The cost efficiency effect compares the efficiency of input usage given (y^1, w^1) with that given (y^0, w^0). The input substitution effect involves the response of input usage, given y^0, to a change from w^0 to w^1. The activity effect reflects the cost of moving from a cost-efficient input vector on $IL^1(y^0)$ to a cost-efficient input vector on $IL^1(y^1)$, both given comparison period technology and input prices.

The cost efficiency effect decomposes as

$$
\begin{aligned}
[\overline{w}^T(x^1 - x^1_{CE}) &- \overline{w}^T(x^0 - x^0_{CE})] \\
&= [\overline{w}^T(x^1 - x^1_{TE}) - \overline{w}^T(x^0 - x^0_{TE})] \qquad \text{technical efficiency effect} \\
&\quad + [\overline{w}^T(x^1_{TE} - x^1_{CE}) - \overline{w}^T(x^0_{TE} - x^0_{CE})], \qquad \text{allocative efficiency effect}
\end{aligned}
$$
$$(7.14)$$

where x^0_{TE} and x^1_{TE} are not depicted in Figure 7.2, but are radial contractions of x^0 and x^1, so that $x^0_{TE} = x^0/D^0_i(y^0, x^0) \in IL^0(y^0)$ and $x^1_{TE} = x^1/D^1_i(y^1, x^1) \in IL^1(y^1)$.

The input vectors $x^0_{CE}, x^1_{CE}, x^0_{TE}, x^1_{TE}, x^E$, and x^F are unobserved, and must be estimated. Once they are estimated, it is possible to implement the input quantity effect decomposition. It is worth stressing that although $\overline{w}$ is used to *value* the effects in expressions (7.12) to (7.14), w^0 is used to *estimate* x^0_{CE} and x^E, and w^1 is used to *estimate* x^1_{CE} and x^F.

The cost change models in Sections 7.3 and 7.4 are structurally similar, although they generate different decompositions. The two price effects differ, and so the two quantity effects also differ. The quantity effects decompose differently. The final difference is that effects in Section 7.3 are valued using either w^1 or w^0, while effects in Section 7.4, although they are identified using w^0 and w^1 as appropriate, are valued using $\overline{w}$.[6]

---

[6] It is straightforward to convert Sections 7.3 and 7.4 to a short-term cost change decomposition, by replacing $c(y, w)$ with $c_v(y, w_v, x_f)$ in Section 7.3, and by replacing x and w with x_v and w_v in Section 7.4. Lim and Lovell (2008) apply the Bennet framework to a study of short-term variable cost behavior and productivity change in US Class I railroads. We discuss short-term cost behavior in Chapter 8.

An empirical application

Grifell-Tatjé and Lovell (2000) use the model in expressions (7.12) to (7.14) to conduct a benchmarking exercise, a modern interfirm comparison of the sort practiced by the European Productivity Agency in the 1950s and 1960s. Suppose we observe a cross-section of producers. We convert the cost change decomposition exercise above to a cost gap decomposition exercise, the gap being the difference between the cost of a benchmarking producer (say $w^{1T}x^1$) and the cost of a target firm in the sample ($w^{0T}x^0$). We propose two ways of selecting the target firm. In one exercise firms benchmark their performance against that of the firm having the lowest unit cost in the sample. In the other exercise the target firm is a cost-efficient firm, which requires estimation of a cost frontier. In both exercises the cost gap can be decomposed into an input price effect and a quantity effect. Since the sample is a cross-section, the quantity effect contains only a cost efficiency effect and an activity effect, because in a cross-section it is possible to estimate only a single best practice technology, so there is no technology effect. In addition, Grifell-Tatjé and Lovell do not distinguish x^F from x^E, so there is no input substitution effect. Consequently, the activity effect is price-dependent, being based on x^E, which is cost-efficient for w^0, and x^1_{CE}, which is cost-efficient for w^1. The exercise can be conducted in a panel setting (with the benefit of being able to identify a technology effect), and the target firm can be selected in additional ways.

Table 7.1 summarizes the benchmarking results they obtain for a sample of 93 US electric power generating companies in 1992. Cost gaps and their components are means across the sample, and means are generally smaller than standard deviations. The low-cost benchmark has unit generating cost

Table 7.1 Benchmarking US electric power generation performance
Millions of USD

Benchmarking Utilities	Low-cost Benchmark	Cost-efficient Benchmark
Cost gap	619	−2,524
Input price effect	70	−161
Quantity effect	549	−2,363
Cost efficiency effect	265	301
Technical efficiency effect	178	203
Allocative efficiency effect	87	97
Activity effect	284	−2,664

less than half the sample mean, and so mean cost gaps are large. However, barely 10% of the mean cost gap is attributable to the input price effect, so benchmarking firms are not unduly disadvantaged by relatively high input prices. The activity effect and the cost efficiency effect each account for about 45% of the mean cost gap. The activity effect may reflect exogenous size differences over which benchmarking firms have little or no control, but the cost efficiency effect is entirely under management control, and reveals a lot of waste and misallocation. If benchmarking managements have little influence over the input prices they face, and if they cannot control the demand they face, they can direct their efforts at improving their cost efficiency. Turning to the cost-efficient benchmark, the mean cost gap is very large, and negative because the cost-efficient benchmark is one of the largest firms in the sample. Consequently, the activity effect dominates the cost gap, with benchmarking firms having a negative mean activity effect reflecting their smaller size. The negative price effect implies that the cost-efficient benchmark is disadvantaged by relatively high input prices. Once again, benchmarking firms may have little to learn from these two components of the cost gap. However, the positive cost efficiency effect suggests, once again, that benchmarking utilities can narrow the cost gap primarily, if not exclusively, through improvements in cost efficiency.[7]

7.5 A UNIT COST FRONTIER

Bliss (1923; ch. 14) advocates the use of two ratios, unit cost and the expense ratio C/R, (the reciprocal of profitability Π) to evaluate business financial performance, and he notes that unit cost information can inform product pricing decisions. He also warns that unit cost is likely to be more volatile than the expense ratio because price fluctuations influence only the numerator of unit cost but both numerator and denominator of the expense ratio. We investigated profitability in Chapters 2 and 3; here we turn our attention to Bliss's other ratio, unit cost, which Johnson (1972) claims is a useful performance indicator, particularly in competitive product markets, in

---

[7] Blázquez Gómez and Grifell-Tatjé (2008) replace the cost orientation of Section 7.4 with a revenue orientation, and take a Bennet approach to the decomposition of revenue change among Spanish electricity distribution companies operating under incentive regulation. The quantity effect decomposes into activity and productivity effects, and the latter decomposes into revenue efficiency change and technical change effects. The reimbursement (price) effect reflects the price setting behavior of the regulator.

facilitating management control of internal plant operations, that is in keeping costs down. A virtue of unit cost as a financial performance indicator is
its independence of firm size, a property it shares with unit revenue and
profitability $\Pi = (R/y)/(C/y)$; it is a meaningful way to compare financial
performance of firms of varying size. A corresponding difficulty is the
definition of "unit." This is not an issue for a single product firm, but it
does arise with a multiple product firm, for which aggregation of multiple
outputs into real output is required.

Gold (1971) analyzes total cost, unit cost, and what he calls cost proportions and we call cost shares. He expresses the belief that having timely and
accurate information on all three cost concepts is essential to all areas of
managerial decision making, including budgeting, the allocation of resources among product lines, pricing policies, and forecasting. He analyzes the
term "unit" in some detail, and discusses the construction of a "non-existent
composite product." He decomposes change in unit cost, using base period
cost proportions to weight change in individual output unit costs; this
analysis is a precursor to our analysis in Sections 7.5 and 7.6. He discusses
cost cutting and the pressure to "keep costs down," and he notes that keeping
unit costs down does not require keeping *all* unit costs down, and that unit
cost policies cannot ignore unit revenues. Finally, he echoes Davis (1955) in
viewing cost components as representing "the distribution of returns from
production," or the "proportional allocation of the change in average
product price among the unit cost (and profit) categories."

Kendrick and Grossman (1980) examine trends in unit cost (with real
value added in the denominator) in the US nonfinancial corporate sector
(and other sectors as well) over the 1948–76 period and its two sub-periods
1948–66 and 1966–76. The latter sub-period marks the early stages of the
fabled productivity slowdown and its inflationary consequences. It is worth
quoting their motivation for focusing on unit cost.

> In addition to its role as the major source of rising planes of living, productivity
> is also a potent counter-inflationary force. This is so since productivity
> increases offset to a greater or lesser degree the effect of rising factor prices
> on unit costs, which are the main element in product prices. (p. 51)

Their findings are summarized in Table 7.2, in which P and W are output and
input price indexes, respectively, VA is real value added (an implicit output
quantity index), and C/VA includes unit profit (i.e., investor input is
expensed). In the early sub-period annual productivity growth of 2.65%
held annual unit cost increase to a modest 1.62%, despite an annual input

Table 7.2 Components of price change, US
nonfinancial corporate business sector

Variable	Annual Percent Change	
	1948–66	1966–76
P	1.69	5.31
C/VA	1.62	5.30
W	4.32	6.70
TFP	2.65	1.32

price increase of 4.32%. The story changes dramatically in the later sub-period. The rate of productivity growth fell by half, and the rate of input price growth increased by half. As a consequence the rate of unit cost increase more than tripled, as did the rate of growth of the output price index. This exercise provides a vivid illustration of the counter-inflationary force productivity growth plays. It also prompts a further investigation into the sources of change in unit cost.

We develop a simple model that underlies the Kendrick and Grossman decomposition of unit cost change into the impacts of changing input prices and productivity change. We express this model in ratio form, consistent with the Kendrick and Grossman presentation and with the analysis of profitability change in Chapters 2 and 3, and also in difference form, consistent with the analysis of profit change in Chapters 4 to 6. Because output is a divisor, we aggregate output vector y^t to obtain a measure of aggregate output Y^t in period $t = 0.1$, the value of the output quantity index $Y = Y^1/Y^0$, unit cost is $UC^t = C^t/Y^t$.

The change in nominal unit cost from base period to comparison period is, in ratio form,

$$
\begin{aligned}
UC^1/UC^0 &= (C^1/Y^1)/(C^0/Y^0) \\
&= (C^1/C^0)/(Y^1/Y^0) \\
&= W/(Y/X),
\end{aligned}
\tag{7.15}
$$

in which W and X are input price and quantity indexes, Y is an output quantity index, Y/X is a productivity index, and the third equality invokes the product test, which requires $WX = C^1/C^0$. Expression (7.15) states that unit cost change is entirely determined by two drivers: input price change and productivity change. An increase in the input price index raises unit cost, and productivity growth reduces unit cost.

Solving expression (7.15) for Y/X yields

$$Y/X = UC^0/(UC^1/W), \tag{7.16}$$

which defines a dual cost-oriented productivity index as the ratio of base period nominal unit cost to comparison period real unit cost. Expressions (7.15) and (7.16) do not assign functional forms to the index numbers. However, if Y and X are given Laspeyres form, W must have Paasche form to satisfy the product test, and expression (7.16) becomes $Y_L/X_L = UC^0/UC_0^1 = (w^{0T}x^0/Y^0)/(w^{0T}x^1/Y^1)$, Y^0 and Y^1 being base period and comparison period values of the real output quantity index Y_L, a result obtained by Mme Cahen (1960).[8]

In the remainder of this section we follow a Konüs strategy analogous to the strategy we developed in Section 7.3; an advantage of this strategy is that cost efficiency change, which plays no role in the Kendrick and Grossman study, is a natural component of unit cost change.

Mme Cahen specified a comparison period $W = W_P$ and a base period $X = X_L$ to satisfy the product test. Suppose instead that we specify a comparison period Konüs input price index $W_K = c^1(y^1, w^1)/c^1(y^1, w^0)$. Then $C^1/C^0 = W_K XI_K \Rightarrow XI_K(y^1, w^1, w^0, x^1, x^0) = [C^1/C^0] / [c^1(y^1, w^1)/c^1(y^1, w^0)]$, an implicit Konüs input quantity index that also appears in expression (7.2). Substituting $XI_K(y^1, w^1, w^0, x^1, x^0)$ into expression (7.15) and rearranging terms yields a second expression for unit cost change

$$
\begin{aligned}
\frac{UC^1}{UC^0} &= \frac{c^1(y^1, w^1)}{c^1(y^1, w^0)} \times \left[\frac{w^{1T}x^1/c^1(y^1, w^1)\ Y^0}{w^{0T}x^0/c^1(y^1, w^0)\ Y^1}\right] \\
&= \frac{c^1(y^1, w^1)}{c^1(y^1, w^0)} \times \left[\frac{w^{1T}z^1/ac^1(y^1, w^1)}{w^{0T}z^0/ac^1(y^1, w^0)}\right],
\end{aligned}
\tag{7.17}
$$

in which we replace total cost $w^T x$ with unit cost $w^T z$, where $z^t = x^t/Y^t$ and $w^T z \geq ac(y, w)$, minimum unit cost. Expression (7.17) states that unit cost change is the product of a Konüs input price index and a reciprocal Konüs implicit productivity index $XI_K(y^1, w^1, w^0, x^1, x^0)/Y$. Although expression (7.17) places unit cost change in a Konüs framework, cost efficiency change

---

[8] At the time Mme Cahen was Administrateur à l'Institut National de la Statistique et des Études Économique (INSEE) in Paris. She used the Laspeyres expression for productivity change based on unit cost change in her lengthy study of productivity developments in the French coal mining sector, a study that was both analytically innovative and empirically thorough. She influenced Vincent (1968), and no doubt additional contributors to subsequent CERC studies.

plays no role. However, since $UC = w^T z \geq ac(y, w)$, it is possible to express change in unit cost as

$$UC^1/UC^0 = [ac^1(y^1, w^1)/ac^0(y^0, w^0)] \div [CE^1(y^1, w^1, x^1)/CE^0(y^0, w^0, x^0)],$$
(7.18)

which is a third expression for unit cost change, in which $CE(y, w, x) = c(y, w)/w^T x \leq 1$ is cost efficiency. Expression (7.18) states that unit cost change is the ratio of change in efficient unit cost to change in cost efficiency. A reduction in efficient unit cost and an increase in cost efficiency both reduce unit cost.

Expressions (7.17) and (7.18) are both based on the concept of a unit cost frontier $ac(y, w)$. Although they have different structures and different interpretations, both lead directly to a final decomposition of unit cost change

$$UC^1/UC^0 = [ac^1(y^1, w^1)/ac^1(y^1, w^0)] \times [ac^1(y^0, w^0)/ac^0(y^0, w^0)]$$
$$\times [ac^1(y^1, w^0)/ac^1(y^0, w^0)] \div [CE^1(y^1, w^1, x^1)/CE^0(y^0, w^0, x^0)].$$
(7.19)

Change in unit cost is driven by a shift in the unit cost frontier, attributable to either a change in input prices $ac^1(y^1, w^1)/ac^1(y^1, w^0)$ or technical change $ac^1(y^0, w^0)/ac^0(y^0, w^0)$, and by a movement along a unit cost frontier due to a change in output quantities $ac^1(y^1, w^0)/ac^1(y^0, w^0)$, and by a change in cost efficiency $CE^1(y^1, w^1, x^1)/CE^0(y^0, w^0, x^0)$. The input price effect, the technology effect, and the cost efficiency effect are identical to their cost frontier counterparts in expressions (7.2) and (7.3) in Section 7.3, although the size effect is not. The final three components of decomposition (7.19) equal the implicit Konüs productivity effect in expression (7.17) and, apart from the size effect, equal the dual cost-oriented productivity effect in Section 7.3.[9]

We now explore a difference version of the ratio expression (7.19). We adapt the theoretical cost frontier model of Section 7.3 to a unit cost context, and we replace the cost frontier $c(y, w)$ with a unit cost frontier $ac(y, w)$. We also replace total cost $w^T x$ with unit cost $w^T z$, and we write $w^T z \geq ac(y, w)$. This yields the decomposition of unit cost change

---

[9] Expression (7.19) decomposes unit cost change. It can be rewritten as

$$\frac{w^{1T} z^1}{w^{0T} z^0} = \frac{c^1(y^0, w^0)}{c^0(y^0, w^0)} \times \left[\frac{c^1(y^1, w^0)/Y^1}{c^1(y^0, w^0)/Y^0}\right] \times \frac{c^1(y^1, w^1)}{c^1(y^1, w^0)} \times \left[\frac{w^{1T} x^1/c^1(y^1, w^1)}{w^{0T} x^0/c^0(y^0, w^0)}\right].$$

Three of four components are the same as their cost change components in expressions (7.2) and (7.3) in Section 7.3 because they have a common output, either Y^0 or Y^1. The activity effect contains both Y^0 and Y^1, and differs from its counterpart in expression (7.3).

$w^{1T}z^1 - w^{0T}z^0$

$$
\begin{aligned}
&= [ac^1(y^1, w^1) - ac^1(y^1, w^0)] && \text{input price effect} \\
&\quad + [w^{1T}z^1 - ac^1(y^1, w^1)] - [w^{0T}z^0 - ac^1(y^1, w^0)], && \text{productivity effect}
\end{aligned}
\tag{7.20}
$$

in which the price effect is the difference version of a Konüs input price index and the productivity effect is the difference version of the implicit Konüs productivity effect in expression (7.17). The productivity effect decomposes as

$$
\begin{aligned}
&[w^{1T}z^1 - ac^1(y^1, w^1)] - [w^{0T}z^0 - ac^1(y^1, w^0)] \\
&= [ac^1(y^0, w^0) - ac^0(y^0, w^0)] && \text{technology effect} \\
&\quad + [ac^1(y^1, w^0) - ac^1(y^0, w^0)] && \text{size effect} \\
&\quad + [w^{1T}z^1 - ac^1(y^1, w^1)] - [w^{0T}z^0 - ac^0(y^0, w^0)]. && \text{cost efficiency effect}
\end{aligned}
\tag{7.21}
$$

The technology effect values a shift in $ac(y^0, w^0)$, the size effect values a movement along $ac^1(y, w^0)$, and the cost efficiency effect values movements toward or away from $ac^1(y^1, w^1)$ and $ac^0(y^0, w^0)$. If output is treated as being exogenous, the productivity effect can be relabeled as a quantity effect that contains a size effect and a productivity effect.

In Figure 7.3 the cost efficiency effect is given by the two arrows connecting $w^{1T}z^1$ with $ac^1(y^1, w^1)$, and $w^{0T}z^0$ with $ac^0(y^0, w^0)$, respectively.

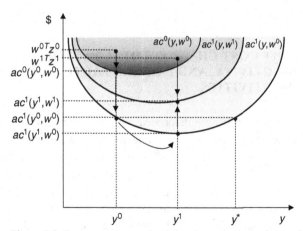

Figure 7.3 Decomposing productivity change using unit cost frontiers

The technology effect is given by the arrow connecting $ac^0(y^0, w^0)$ with $ac^1(y^0, w^0)$. The size effect is given by the arrow connecting $ac^1(y^0, w^0)$ with $ac^1(y^1, w^0)$. This completes a decomposition of the productivity effect. The decomposition of unit cost change is completed by the price effect, which is given by the arrow connecting $ac^1(y^1, w^0)$ with $ac^1(y^1, w^1)$. An improvement in cost efficiency $\{[w^{1T}z^1 - ac^1(y^1, w^1)] < [w^{0T}z^0 - ac^0(y^0, w^0)]\}$ and technical progress $[ac^1(y^0, w^0) < ac^0(y^0, w^0)]$ both increase productivity and reduce unit cost, although they reduce unit cost in different ways, the former by moving closer to a unit cost frontier and the latter by shifting a unit cost frontier downward. Sliding down a unit cost curve [in this case $ac^1(y^1, w^0) < ac^1(y^0, w^0)$] also reduces unit cost (although moving up a unit cost curve would increase unit cost). A zero size effect does not imply that the technology is characterized by locally constant returns to scale. In Figure 7.3 expansion from y^0 to y^* along $ac^1(y, w^0)$ makes the size effect zero, even in the absence of constant returns to scale. Finally, input price increases $[ac^1(y^1, w^1) > ac^1(y^1, w^0)]$ increase unit cost by shifting a unit cost frontier upward. Empirically, all that is required is the estimation of a unit cost frontier, on which the four points identified in Figure 7.3 are located. This strategy decomposes unit cost change into price and productivity effects, the latter including a size effect as well as cost efficiency and technology effects. On this interpretation, decompositions (7.20) and (7.21) are dual unit cost change versions of the quantity change decomposition in the top half of Figure 6.8 in Chapter 6. All effects have Konüs structure, expressed in indicator rather than index number form.

7.6 UNIT COST CHANGE, TOTAL FACTOR PRODUCTIVITY, AND PARTIAL FACTOR PRODUCTIVITIES

In this section we switch from a theoretical unit cost frontier $ac(y, w)$ to an empirical approach based on indicators and indexes. We express unit cost change in difference form $w^{1T}z^1 - w^{0T}z^0$, and we decompose this difference into an aggregate productivity effect and an aggregate input price effect, both expressed in index number form. This procedure returns us to expressions (7.15) and (7.16) and Mme Cahen's Laspeyres/Paasche version, although we transform unit cost change from ratio form to difference form. Table 7.3 lists

Table 7.3 Decompositions of unit cost change

	Unit Cost Change Indicators	Aggregate Productivity Effect	Aggregate Price Effect
[1]=(7.22)	$w^{0T}(z^1 - z^0) + z^{1T}(w^1 - w^0)$	$w^{0T}z^1(1 - Z_L^{-1})$	$z^{1T}w^0(W_P - 1)$
[2]=(7.22)	$w^{0T}(z^1 - z^0) + z^{1T}(w^1 - w^0)$	$w^{0T}z^0(Z_L - 1)$	$z^{1T}w^1(1 - W_P^{-1})$
[3]	$w^{1T}(z^1 - z^0) + z^{0T}(w^1 - w^0)$	$w^{1T}z^1(1 - Z_P^{-1})$	$z^{0T}w^0(W_L - 1)$
[4]	$w^{1T}(z^1 - z^0) + z^{0T}(w^1 - w^0)$	$w^{1T}z^0(Z_P - 1)$	$z^{0T}w^1(1 - W_L^{-1})$
[5]=(7.23)	$\bar{w}^T(z^1 - z^0) + \bar{z}^T(w^1 - w^0)$	$\bar{w}^Tz^1(1 - Z_{EM}^{-1})$	$\bar{z}^Tw^1(1 - W_{EM}^{-1})$
[6]=(7.23)	$\bar{w}^T(z^1 - z^0) + \bar{z}^T(w^1 - w^0)$	$\bar{w}^Tz^0(Z_{EM} - 1)$	$\bar{z}^Tw^0(W_{EM} - 1)$
[7]=½([1]+[3])	$\bar{w}^T(z^1 - z^0) + \bar{z}^T(w^1 - w^0)$	$\bar{w}^{1T}z^1(1 - Z_{EM}^{-1})$	$\bar{z}^Tw^0(W_{EM} - 1)$
[8]=½([2]+[4])	$\bar{w}^T(z^1 - z^0) + \bar{z}^T(w^1 - w^0)$	$\bar{w}^Tz^0(Z_{EM} - 1)$	$\bar{z}^Tw^1(1 - W_{EM}^{-1})$
[9]=½([1]+[4])	$\bar{w}^T(z^1 - z^0) + \bar{z}^T(w^1 - w^0)$	½([1]+[4])	½([1]+[4])
[10]=½([2]+[3])	$\bar{w}^T(z^1 - z^0) + \bar{z}^T(w^1 - w^0)$	½([2]+[3])	½([2]+[3])

ten such decompositions. The first two are Laspeyres/Paasche decompositions, the next two are Paasche/Laspeyres decompositions, the next four are Bennet/EM decompositions, and the final two are Bennet/LP decompositions that cannot be expressed in closed form. We begin by decomposing aggregate productivity and input price effects into sums of individual partial productivity and price effects. We then return to the aggregate productivity effect, which we decompose into its economic drivers.

We arbitrarily select a Laspeyres/Paasche decomposition of unit cost change in Table 7.3, and we express the first row as

$$w^{0T}(z^1 - z^0) + z^{1T}(w^1 - w^0) = w^{0T}z^1(1 - Z_L^{-1}) + z^{1T}w^0(W_P - 1)$$
$$= w^{0T}z^0(Z_L - 1) + z^{1T}w^1(1 - W_P^{-1}), \quad (7.22)$$

in which $Z_L = w^{0T}z^1/w^{0T}z^0$ is a Laspeyres quantity index and $W_P = z^{1T}w^1/z^{1T}w^0$ is a Paasche input price index. However, since the quantities in the Laspeyres quantity index are z_n, this quantity index is also a reciprocal productivity index, with $Z_L^{-1} = Y_L/X_L$. An increase in productivity ($Z_L < 1$) causes unit cost to decline, and an increase in input prices ($W_P > 1$) causes unit cost to rise. If the Laspeyres productivity index grows at the same rate as the Paasche input price index, $Z_L^{-1} = W_P$, the two effects cancel and unit cost remains unchanged.

We obtain similar results if we reverse the Laspeyres/Paasche structure of expression (7.22) by decomposing the Paasche/Laspeyres expression in row (4) in Table 7.3; in particular, if $Z_P = W_L^{-1}$ unit cost remains unchanged. However, if we use Bennet prices from either row (5) or row (6) in Table 7.3, unit cost change can be expressed as

$$\bar{w}^T(z^1 - z^0) + \bar{z}^T(w^1 - w^0) = \bar{w}^T z^1 (1 - Z_{EM}^{-1}) + \bar{z}^T w^1 (1 - W_{EM}^{-1})$$
$$= \bar{w}^T z^0 (Z_{EM} - 1) + \bar{z}^T w^0 (W_{EM} - 1), \tag{7.23}$$

in which $Z_{EM}^{-1} = Y_{EM}/X_{EM}$ is an EM productivity index and $W_{EM} = \bar{z}^T w^1 / \bar{z}^T w^0$ is an EM input price index. The Bennet productivity effect and input price effect are interpreted exactly as in the simpler Laspeyres/Paasche case, with the important exception that $Z_{EM}^{-1} = W_{EM}$ does not imply that the two effects cancel.

Expressions (7.22) and (7.23) are unit cost change decomposition analogues to a profit change decomposition we examined in Chapter 6 and illustrated with an application to Walmart in Figure 6.7. In both frameworks the productivity index and the price index are scaled to value their contributions to value (profit or unit cost) change.

Expressions (7.22) and (7.23) decompose unit cost change into an *aggregate* productivity effect and an *aggregate* input price effect. It is possible to decompose the aggregate productivity effect by variable, since in expression (7.22) $w^{0T}(z^1 - z^0) = \sum w_n^0 [(x_n^1/Y^1) - (x_n^0/Y^0)] = \sum w_n^0 z_n^1 [1 - (z_n^0/z_n^1)]$ to generate N *partial* productivity effects with partial productivities z_n^0/z_n^1. It is also possible to decompose the aggregate input price effect by variable, since in (7.22) $z^{1T}(w^1 - w^0) = \sum (x_n^1/Y^1)[w_n^1 - w_n^0] = \sum w_n^0 z_n^1 [(w_n^1/w_n^0) - 1]$ to generate N *partial* input price effects.

Suppose the nth input is labor. Labor's partial productivity change in indicator form is

$$w_L^0 [(L^1/Y^1) - (L^0/Y^0)] = (V_{L0}^1 \times UC_0^1) \times \{1 - [(Y^1/L^1)/(Y^0/L^0)]\}$$
$$= ULC_0^1 \times \{1 - [(Y^1/L^1)/(Y^0/L^0)]\}, \tag{7.24}$$

which values labor productivity change and, using $w^{0T}(z^1 - z^0)$ in expression (7.22), values the contribution of labor productivity change to unit cost change. The impact of labor productivity change on unit cost change depends on deflated comparison period values of unit cost $UC_0^1 = w^{0T}x^1/Y^1$ and labor's cost share $V_{L0}^1 = w_L^0 L^1/w^{0T}x^1$. Their product, which equals deflated comparison period unit labor cost $ULC_0^1 = w_L^0 L^1/Y^1$, acts as a multiplier that converts labor's productivity change to unit cost change.

Again focusing on labor, we express its partial price change in indicator form as

$$
\begin{aligned}
(L^1/Y^1)[w_L^1 - w_L^0] &= (V_{L0}^1 \times UC_0^1) \times [(w_L^1/w_L^0) - 1] \\
&= ULC_0^1 \times [(w_L^1/w_L^0) - 1],
\end{aligned}
\tag{7.25}
$$

which values change in labor's wage and, using $z^{1T}(w^1 - w^0)$ in expression (7.22), values the contribution of a change in labor's wage to unit cost change. The impact of a change in labor's wage on unit cost change depends on deflated comparison period values of unit cost and labor's cost share. Their product is a multiplier that converts labor's wage change to unit cost change, and this multiplier is the same as the multiplier in expression (7.24).

It is conventional to relate labor's partial productivity and wage to unit labor cost, and we do so in Section 7.7, but expressions (7.24) and (7.25) relate labor's partial productivity and wage to the broader concept of unit cost.

Adding expressions (7.24) and (7.25) yields an expression for labor's net contribution to unit cost change

$$
\begin{aligned}
w_L^0[(L^1/Y^1) - (L^0/Y^0)] &+ (L^1/Y^1)(w_L^1 - w_L^0) \\
&= (V_{L0}^1 \times UC_0^1) \times \{(w_L^1/w_L^0) - [(Y^1/L^1)/(Y^0/L^0)]\} \\
&= ULC_0^1 \times \{(w_L^1/w_L^0) - [(Y^1/L^1)/(Y^0/L^0)]\}.
\end{aligned}
\tag{7.26}
$$

Thus, labor's net contribution to unit cost change depends on the difference between labor's wage change and its partial productivity change, scaled by ULC_0^1.

Summing expressions (7.24) and (7.25) over all inputs, unit cost change can be expressed as

$$
\begin{aligned}
w^{1T}z^1 - w^{0T}z^0 &= UC_0^1 \times \sum\{V_{n0}^1 \times \{(w_n^1/w_n^0) - [(Y^1/x_n^1)/(Y^0/x_n^0)]\}\} \\
&= \sum\{UC_{n0}^1 \times \{(w_n^1/w_n^0) - [(Y^1/x_n^1)/(Y^0/x_n^0)]\}\},
\end{aligned}
\tag{7.27}
$$

in which $UC_{n0}^1 = w_n^0 x_n^1/Y^1$ is the deflated comparison period unit cost of the nth input. Expression (7.27) scales the differences between individual price changes and partial productivity changes by their deflated comparison period unit costs.

Expressions (7.22) and (7.27) provide complementary decompositions of unit cost change, the former into *aggregate* price and productivity effects and the latter into weighted sums of *partial* price and productivity effects. Neither expression quantifies the contributions of the economic drivers of productivity change. However, the fact that $w^{0T}(z^1 - z^0) = w^{0T}z^1(1 - Z_L^{-1})$ in expression (7.22), and the fact that $\overline{w}^T(z^1 - z^0) = \overline{w}^T z^1(1 - Z_{EM}^{-1})$ in expression (7.23), enables us to decompose the aggregate productivity indicator by economic driver, using either base period weights or arithmetic mean weights, by adapting procedures we developed in Section 6.3 of Chapter 6.

In Section 7.4 we decomposed cost change expressed in Bennet indicator form and EM index form, and expressions (7.12) and (7.23) are identical apart from the use of x in the former and z in the latter. One option is to follow the steps in Section 7.4, replacing x with z. Another option is to replace the Bennet/EM framework with a Laspeyres/Paasche framework and follow the same steps. The advantage of the Laspeyres/Paasche framework is that it preserves the direct comparisons between individual input price and productivity changes in expressions (7.26) and (7.27).

We return to expressions (7.22) and (7.23), and note the similarity of their structure to that of the profit change decompositions in Tables 5.1 and 5.2 in Chapter 5, which list four decompositions of Laspeyres/Paasche form, four of Paasche/Laspeyres form, and four of Bennet/EM form. We also have multiple decompositions of unit cost change in Table 7.3, which contains ten decompositions, two of Laspeyres/Paasche form, two of Paasche/Laspeyres form, four of Bennet/EM form, and two of Bennet/LP form. We note some features of Table 7.3:

(i) Each aggregate productivity effect is the sum of N partial productivity effects;

(ii) Each aggregate price effect is the sum of N partial price effects;

(iii) The two Laspeyres productivity effects in [1] and [2] have different mathematical expressions but the same value;

(iv) The two Paasche price effects in [1] and [2] have different mathematical expressions but the same value;

(v) Features (iii) and (iv) also apply to Paasche productivity effects and Laspeyres price effects in [3] and [4];

(vi) Decomposition [1] simplifies to $\sum w_n^0(z_n^1 - z_n^0) + \sum z_n^1(w_n^1 - w_n^0) = \sum w_n^0 z_n^1[W_P - (Y_L/X_L)]$ so that if the rate of productivity change matches the rate of input price change, unit cost remains unchanged;

(vii) Decomposition [4] simplifies to $\sum w_n^1(z_n^1 - z_n^0) + \sum z_n^0(w_n^1 - w_n^0) = \sum w_n^1 z_n^0 [(Y_P/X_P)^{-1} - W_L^{-1}]$ with the same implication as feature (vi);

(viii) Decompositions [2] and [3] do not have this desirable implication;

(ix) The four Bennet/EM decompositions do not have this desirable implication; and

(x) The six Bennet decompositions have different mathematical expressions but the same productivity effects and the same price effects.

We can illustrate these features, and more, with the assistance of the artificial data appearing in Table 4.5 of Chapter 4. These data underpin the profit change decompositions in Table 5.3 of Chapter 5 and, with the addition of a second input, underpin the unit cost change decomposition in Table 7.4. As we do in Chapter 5, we report results for producer #5. Rows in Table 7.4 correspond to rows in Table 7.3. The first two columns report productivity change and input price change in indicator form, and the next two columns report aggregate productivity and input price effects in index number form. The final column reports unit cost change calculated as the sum of the productivity and input price effects. Table 7.4 illustrates the first five features and the final feature. It also shows that all six Bennet quantity and input price effects are bounded by their Laspeyres/Paasche counterparts.

Table 7.4 Decompositions of unit cost change using artificial data

	Unit Cost Change Indicators		Aggregate Productivity Effect	Aggregate Price Effect	$uc^1 - uc^0$
[1]	−4.68	1.27	−4.68	1.27	−3.41
[2]	−4.68	1.27	−4.68	1.27	−3.41
[3]	−4.75	1.35	−4.75	1.35	−3.41
[4]	−4.75	1.35	−4.75	1.35	−3.41
[5]	−4.72	1.31	−4.72	1.31	−3.41
[6]	−4.72	1.31	−4.72	1.31	−3.41
[7]	−4.72	1.31	−4.72	1.31	−3.41
[8]	−4.72	1.31	−4.72	1.31	−3.41
[9]	−4.72	1.31	−4.72	1.31	−3.41
[10]	−4.72	1.31	−4.72	1.31	−3.41

7.7 A UNIT LABOR COST FRONTIER

It is easy to find both macroeconomic and microeconomic motivations for, and applications of, a focus on labor productivity and unit labor cost. To cite one example, both BLS and OECD track labor productivity, labor's wage, and unit labor cost, on both national currency basis and USD basis, across countries through time. OECD is motivated by the fact that increases in unit labor cost "may create pressure on producer prices," which presages a BLS concern with "international labor cost competitiveness."

In Section 7.5 we establish a relationship between productivity and unit cost. The relationship is comprehensive in the sense that all inputs to the production process are incorporated in cost (capital and labor if output is value added, capital, labor, and intermediate inputs if output is gross output). However, in some circumstances, particularly those involving international comparisons, information on capital and its cost is unavailable or unreliable or not comparable. In these circumstances the relationship is partial, between *labor* productivity and unit *labor* cost. Exchange rate movements are important drivers of unit labor cost in international comparisons, and we incorporate exchange rates in a unit labor cost expression at the end of this section.

Businesses engage in the practice of outsourcing, particularly of the offshoring variety, in an effort to reduce cost and enhance their competitiveness. Since most offshoring involves jobs, we anticipate that its impact works through a reduction in unit labor cost, and then unit cost, as we discuss in Section 7.6. Expression (7.26) demonstrates that if offshoring is to reduce labor's net contribution to unit cost change, it must put downward pressure on wages or raise labor productivity or both, and the magnitude of the net contribution depends on deflated comparison period unit labor cost. Limited empirical evidence suggests that offshoring does reduce unit labor cost, through both channels.[10]

---

[10] The *McKinsey Quarterly* has published several offshoring studies. Themes common to many studies include (i) the practice is beneficial to both countries, (ii) it reduces unit labor cost at offshoring companies, and (iii) the reduction in unit labor cost opens up additional opportunities to increase revenue, although these opportunities are frequently overlooked. Amiti and Wei (2009) provide evidence on the impact of offshoring on labor productivity in US manufacturing over the period 1992–2000. They find that service offshoring has contributed roughly 10% of the labor productivity growth over the period, and materials offshoring another 5%. However, *The Economist* (2013), in a Special Report on Outsourcing and Off-shoring, finds narrowing wage gaps and a growing tendency of American firms to reverse the offshoring phenomenon, a practice called "re-shoring."

We begin by acknowledging that in some circumstances unit labor cost may provide an acceptable approximation to unit cost. The relationship between the two is

$$ULC = (w_L L/C) \times (C/Y)$$
$$= V_L \times UC, \tag{7.28}$$

where ULC and UC are unit labor cost and unit cost, respectively, $w_L L$ is labor expense, and $V_L = w_L L/C$ is labor's cost share. The closer V_L is to unity, the better is the approximation of ULC to UC.

Now consider change in unit labor cost, given by

$$UCL^1/UCL^0 = (V_L^1/V_L^0) \times (UC^1/UC^0), \tag{7.29}$$

and so change in ULC provides a relatively good approximation to change in UC when labor's cost share is relatively stable. This result does not require a large cost share of labor. Although we prefer (comprehensive) unit cost to (partial) unit labor cost as a performance indicator, often we must satisfice, and expression (7.29) offers cause for optimism when we must.[11]

We now turn to the decomposition of change in unit labor cost. Substituting expression (7.19) into expression (7.29) generates the decomposition

$$ULC^1/ULC^0 = (V_L^1/V_L^0) \times \{[ac^1(y^1,w^1)/ac^1(y^1,w^0)] \times [ac^1(y^0,w^0)/ac^0(y^0,w^0)]$$
$$\times [ac^1(y^1,w^0)/ac^1(y^0,w^0)] \div CE^1(y^1,w^1,x^1)/CE^0(y^0,w^0,x^0)\}, \tag{7.30}$$

and so change in unit labor cost has the same drivers as change in unit cost (input price change, technical change, output quantity change, and change in cost efficiency), weighted by V_L^1/V_L^0. The impact of technical change is magnified if it is labor-saving, and the impact of cost efficiency change is magnified if allocative efficiency change reduces labor misallocation. Expression (7.30) compares observed ULC in two periods. A complementary within-period comparison is of cost-efficient and observed ULC $[w_L L(y,w)/Y] / [w_L L/Y] = L(y,w)/L$, with $L(y,w)$ cost-minimizing labor use.

---

[11] BLS reports that labor's cost share in the US private nonfarm business sector has averaged 63.5% since 1947, which has discouraged the use of ULC as a proxy for UC, but it has rarely moved outside a 62%–66% range until early in the twenty-first century, which, until recently, has encouraged the use of ULC^1/ULC^0 as a proxy for UC^1/UC^0. OECD reports slightly greater variability through time in labor's cost share in the manufacturing sector of OECD member countries since 1993. Variation across member countries is far larger, ranging from over 80% in the United Kingdom down to 30% in Ireland.

We continue with an alternative, more conventional, expression that converts the BLS definition of unit labor cost (hourly compensation divided by real output per hours worked) to a unit labor cost change format

$$UCL^1/UCL^0 = (w_L^1/w_L^0)/[(Y/L)^1/(Y/L)^0], \qquad (7.31)$$

which states that unit labor cost is driven up by wage increases and down by labor productivity gains. Suppose next that the production relationship can be expressed as $Y = Af(K, L)$, where $f(K, L)$ is a real value added production frontier satisfying constant returns to scale and A is a productivity index. Then $Y/L = Af(K/L)$ and, using expression (7.31),

$$ULC^1/ULC^0 = (w_L^1/w_L^0)/\{(A^1/A^0) \times [f(K/L)^1/f(K/L)^0]\}, \qquad (7.32)$$

which states that unit labor cost is raised by increases in labor's wage, and reduced by productivity growth and by capital deepening (provided $f'(K/L) > 0$). Scholars and statistical agencies alike stress the empirical significance of capital deepening as a source of labor productivity growth. An additional, increasingly popular, wrinkle is to decompose K into its IT and non-IT components, and to decompose L into its hours and composition components.[12]

We can incorporate change in technical efficiency relative to the production frontier by rewriting the production relationship as $Y = Af(K, L)\theta$, with $\theta = TE_o(K, L, Y) \leq 1$ reflecting technical inefficiency. This generates

$$ULC^1/ULC^0 = (w_L^1/w_L^0)/\{(A^1/A^0) \times [f(K/L)^1/f(K/L)^0] \times (\theta^1/\theta^0)\}, \qquad (7.33)$$

which introduces technical efficiency change as an additional driver of unit labor cost change. Increases in technical efficiency reduce unit labor cost. If we make the further assumption that $f(K, L) = K^\alpha L^{1-\alpha}$, $0 < \alpha < 1$, then

$$ULC^1/ULC^0 = (w_L^1/w_L^0)/\{(A^1/A^0) \times [(K/L)^1/(K/L)^0]^\alpha \times (\theta^1/\theta^0)\}, \qquad (7.34)$$

---

[12] BLS reports that capital deepening and multifactor productivity growth have each contributed 1% toward a 2.3% labor productivity growth in the US private business sector since 1987. BLS also reports roughly equal contributions of IT and non-IT capital to labor productivity growth in the US manufacturing sector since 1987, and equal contributions of hours and labor composition to the labor input in the private business sector since 1987.

which specifies the magnitude of the impact of capital deepening as depending on the unobserved (and presumed constant) output elasticity of capital α, which is frequently proxied by the observed cost share of capital V_K (because if K and L are allocated in a cost-efficient manner, then $\alpha = V_K$). The denominator is a familiar decomposition of labor productivity change practiced around the world, here embedded in a unit labor cost context.

Expression (7.34) decomposes change in unit labor cost in ratio form, and has a somewhat different structure than previous decompositions of cost change and unit cost change. It is easily extended from a value added framework to a gross output framework, provided the assumption of constant returns to scale is maintained.

We return to international comparisons, in which productivity is invariably defined as labor productivity and financial performance is defined as unit labor cost. Unit labor cost in, say, Spain, expressed in its domestic currency, is

$$ULC^\epsilon = w_L^\epsilon/(Y/L). \tag{7.35}$$

Spain's international competitiveness depends on its domestic wages and its labor productivity, but also on the exchange rates between the euro and other currencies. Since many traded commodities are valued in USD, we transform ULC^ϵ to ULC^{USD} to express Spain's unit labor cost in USD as

$$UCL^{USD} = [w_L^\epsilon/(Y/L)] \times E^{\epsilon/USD}, \tag{7.36}$$

where E is the exchange rate that converts euros to USD. Converting expression (7.36) to a change format, expressing change as "Δ" rather than the explicit ratio of comparison period to base period values, generates

$$\Delta ULC^{USD} = [\Delta w_L^\epsilon/\Delta(Y/L)] \times \Delta E^{\epsilon/USD}. \tag{7.37}$$

Spain's international competitiveness is enhanced by an increase in its labor productivity, and retarded by two factors: by an increase in its domestic wages, over which it presumably has some control, and also by a strengthening euro, over which it presumably has little control. The impact of exchange rate movements on international competitiveness can be dramatic. BLS usually reports several countries experiencing change in ULC in one direction when expressed in their own currency, and change in the opposite direction when converted to USD.

7.8 SUMMARY AND CONCLUSIONS

In this chapter we have largely ignored the revenue side of a firm's financial performance in order to explore the linkage between cost and productivity. We know that changes in input use and changes in input prices create changes in cost. In order to introduce productivity into the story we need to develop an analytical framework that links input use to output production.

In Section 7.2 we introduced variance analysis, in which the link is provided by a Leontief production technology that fixes $N \times M$ input–output ratios, thereby providing a vehicle for cost allocation. This framework allows cost change, or cost variance, to be attributed to input price change, output quantity change, and productivity change. This three-way attribution recurs throughout the chapter.

In Sections 7.3 and 7.4 the link is provided by a cost frontier $c(y, w) \leq w^T x$. This framework allows cost change to be attributed to input price change, output quantity change, and productivity change, as in variance analysis but without the restrictive fixed proportions assumption. This framework has the added benefit of allowing productivity change to be attributed to cost efficiency change (which itself can be decomposed into input-oriented technical change and input allocative efficiency change) and technical change. In Section 7.3 we developed a theoretical Konüs approach, in which we express cost change and its drivers in both ratio form and difference form. In Section 7.4 we developed an empirical Bennet approach, in which cost change and its drivers are expressed in difference form.

In Sections 7.5 and 7.6 the link is provided by a unit cost frontier $ac(y, w) \leq w^T z$, with $z^t = x^t/Y^t$, Y^t being aggregate output, the period t value of an output quantity index Y. The analysis largely replicates that in Sections 7.3 and 7.4, being based on Konüs and Bennet approaches. We attribute unit cost change to input price change, output quantity change, and productivity change as in Sections 7.3 and 7.4. We also decompose unit cost change into the sum of N net input contributions to unit cost change, with a net contribution being a weighted difference between an input price change and an input partial productivity change.

In Section 7.7 we narrowed the focus still further, to a unit labor cost frontier, mainly on practical data availability grounds. We related unit labor cost to the more inclusive unit cost, and we showed that unit labor cost change has the same economic drivers as unit cost change. Since unit labor cost is widely used in international competitiveness comparisons, we also introduced exchange rates as a new driver of unit labor cost.

8 Productivity, Capacity Utilization, and Return on Assets

8.1 INTRODUCTION

We established the nature of the relationship between productivity and financial performance in Chapters 2 and 3, where financial performance was measured by profitability, in Chapters 4 to 6, where financial performance was measured by profit, and in Chapter 7, where financial performance was measured by cost. In this chapter we explore the relationship when financial performance is measured by return on assets (ROA), defined generically as π/A, the ratio of profit to assets.

The four measures of financial performance are closely linked. Profitability is a ratio, and profit is a difference. ROA combines the two, with a difference ($\pi = R - C$) in the numerator of a ratio. But the difference can be related to a ratio ($\Pi = R/C$), and so ROA is related to profitability as well as to profit. Thus, this chapter links the ratio analysis of Chapters 2 and 3 with the difference analysis of Chapters 4 to 6.

We began Chapter 7 with a discussion of various forms of cost cutting firms pursued in an effort to offset declining revenues during the global economic downturn that began in 2008. We revisit the issue, this time within an ROA context and a focus on financial institutions, which suffered during the downturn (or the global financial crisis). According to the US Federal Deposit Insurance Corporation (www2.fdic.gov/qbp), ROA at US commercial banks hovered in the neighborhood of 1% for over 15 years, and quickly turned negative at the onset of the downturn. ROA finally returned to its previous levels around 2010. The history of that period, as recounted in the

310

business press, is one of extensive cost cutting and asset shedding. Since $ROA = (R - C)/A$, cost cutting, by increasing the numerator, and asset shedding, by reducing the denominator, can reduce and perhaps reverse the impact of declining revenue on ROA. Commercial banks have bolstered returns by pursuing both strategies, through extensive job cuts and also by closing branches and shedding troubled assets, primarily through the government's Troubled Assets Relief Program.

ROA is a widely used measure of financial performance. Bliss (1923; 78), in discussing ROA, claims that "[f]rom the operating point of view as distinguished from the stockholders' point of view, the real measure of the financial return earned by a business is the percentage of operating profits earned on the total capital used in the conduct of such operations ... regardless from what sources such capital may have been secured." Two duPont executives, Kline and Hessler (1952; 1599), concur, writing that "It is our considered opinion, which has been critically re-examined many times over three decades, that a manufacturing enterprise with large capital committed to the manufacture and sale of goods can best measure and judge the effectiveness of effort in terms of 'return on investment'." Gilchrist (1971; 79) asks us to accept that, for all its limitations, ROA is "the ultimate measure of managerial effectiveness." From the perspective of the analyst, ROA also levels the playing field when comparing the financial performance of firms of varying size within an industry or sector, since it normalizes profit by assets, which is likely to vary with firm size, however size is measured.

Notice that these writers treat ROA as *an indicator* of firms' financial performance, whatever their objective may be. And if the objective of firms is to maximize profit, why is ROA such a popular measure of financial performance? Amey (1969; 20) calls ROA "the key index of business 'success'," even though he acknowledges that maximizing ROA and maximizing profit in absolute terms do not generally coincide. "Throughout this monograph, therefore, maximization of profits in absolute terms will be taken as the firm's objective; this can then be *expressed* as a rate of return" (emphasis in the original). Thus, ROA is an observable consequence of the pursuit of a different (indeed, almost any) objective.

Because ROA is such a popular indicator of financial performance, it has found widespread use in empirical research. It is used as an *independent* variable in models designed to explain, or predict, executive compensation (Albuquerque 2009), default and bankruptcy (Premachandra, Chen, and Watson 2011), Duan, Sun, and Wang 2012), and earnings and stock returns (Soliman 2008; Amir, Kama, and Livnat 2011). It is a *dependent* variable in models in which financial performance is hypothesized to be a consequence of governance structure (Lehmann, Warning, and Weigand 2004), board of directors gender diversity (Lückerath-Rovers 2013), human resource management (Huselid 1995), working capital management (Baños-Caballero, Carcía-Teruel, and Martínez-Solano 2012), supply chain management and JIT adoption (Kinney and Wempe 2002; Dehning, Richardson, and Zmud 2007), the practice of total quality management and ISO 9000 certification (Corbett, Montes-Sancho, and Kirsch 2005; Benner and Veloso 2008; Corredor and Goñi 2011), corporate social responsibility (Bonini, Koller, and Mirvis 2009), environmental performance and environmental management systems (Iwata and Okada 2011; Lioui and Sharma 2012; Horváthová 2012; Lo, Yeung, and Cheng 2012), technological innovation performance (Cruz-Cázares, Bayona-Sáez, and García-Marco 2013), and management practices in general (Bloom et al. 2012; Bloom and Van Reenen 2007, 2010). ROA is even in the balanced scorecard, as a component of return on equity (ROE) (Kaplan and Norton 1992).

Both numerator and denominator of ROA are generic terms, and different writers define each differently.

(i) The duPont definition

Kline and Hessler define the denominator of ROA as the amount invested in plant and working capital rather than just stockholder-invested capital. "Operating management must turn in a profit on capital assigned to that management, regardless of how that capital was raised" (pp. 1617–18). They are less clear on the definition of the numerator, which they call gross profit before the impact of taxes, but it is easy to infer that gross profit includes both "corporate entity profit" and net interest expense.

(ii) A government definition

BEA (2011) uses ROA as a measure of profitability and defines ROA as the ratio of the net operating surplus to the net stock of produced assets. For nonfinancial corporations the net operating surplus is revenue less the cost of labor and intermediate inputs, which in turn is the sum of corporate profit, net interest, and business current transfer payments. The net stock of produced assets is the net stock of capital plus inventories, both valued at current cost. The ratio is reported both before and after tax.

(iii) The Walmart definition

In its annual reports Walmart defines the numerator of ROA as income from continuing operations (revenues less costs and expenses less interest), and the denominator as average total assets of continuing operations (the account balance at the end of the current period plus the account balance at the end of the prior period divided by 2).

(iv) A textbook definition

Palepu and Healy (2008) define ROE as net income/shareholder equity, and they consider ROE to be the key indicator of financial performance because it indicates how well management uses funds provided by shareholders to generate income. They decompose ROE = ROA × financial leverage, where ROA = net income/assets and financial leverage = assets/shareholder equity. However, they note an asymmetry: the denominator of ROA includes assets claimed by all providers of capital to the firm, and the numerator includes only the earnings available to shareholders. They prefer the ratio operating ROA = (net income + net interest expense after tax)/assets, which, by adding net interest expense after tax to net income, corrects the asymmetry. The appropriate benchmark for evaluating operating ROA is the weighted average cost of capital (WACC).

These definitions vary in their details, but they follow a common strategy. If the denominator includes equity capital only, the numerator includes profit only. The "return" in ROE is profit, the base is equity capital, and the benchmark is the cost of equity capital. If the denominator includes equity and debt capital, the numerator also incorporates net interest expense (interest paid on debt) together with earnings available to equity holders (profit), that is, earnings before interest and taxes (EBIT). The "return" in ROA is what Davis (1955) and Kendrick and Creamer (1961) call investor input, and what Davis and Kay (1990) and Nickell (1995) and others call added value, the asset base is capital employed (which excludes financial and other non-operating assets), and the benchmark is WACC. In the rest of this chapter we simply refer to ROA or ROE, without concern for the finer points in their construction.

The chapter unfolds as follows. In Section 8.2 we examine alternative decompositions of ROA, ignoring the economic concepts of productivity, price recovery, and capacity utilization. We begin with the duPont triangle, which decomposes ROA into the product of two financial ratios. We continue by exploring a literature developed under the auspices of the European Productivity Agency, which extends the triangle to a pyramid. Next we explore a literature developed by Gold, Eilon, and their associates. This literature extends the triangle by developing alternative sets of secondary drivers of the two primary drivers of ROA in the triangle; many of these secondary drivers are nonfinancial. Surprisingly, in none of these formulations does productivity appear explicitly as a driver of ROA, although some formulations come close. We conclude by identifying some challenges not adequately addressed in this literature.

In Section 8.3 we incorporate the rate of capacity utilization into the analytical framework. We begin by providing motivation for doing so. We continue by noting the wide variety of definitions of capacity we encounter in the literature, and we propose both output-oriented and input-oriented, that is, cost-based, definitions appropriate for the issue at hand. One is an engineering, or technology-based, definition that is independent of prices. The others are price-dependent, the solutions to economic optimization problems. Armed with these definitions, we confront the challenge of incorporating the rate of capacity utilization into the framework in a manner that enables it to influence ROA. We conclude Section 8.3 by addressing a second challenge not addressed in Section 8.2, the incorporation of productivity into the analytical framework. It turns out that this challenge, unlike the incorporation of the rate of capacity utilization, cannot easily be met within an atemporal context.

Accordingly, in Section 8.4 we convert the analytical framework to an intertemporal context, and we show how *change* in the rate of capacity utilization, productivity *change*, and price recovery *change* influence ROA *change*. Change in the rate of capacity utilization can influence ROA change through either or both of two avenues: through its influence on asset turnover change or through its influence on productivity change. We develop two analytical frameworks within which to decompose ROA change. In Section 8.4.1 we build the decomposition around a theoretical Malmquist productivity index, and in Section 8.4.2 we build a similar decomposition around empirical Laspeyres and Paasche quantity and price indexes.

In Section 8.5 we summarize the ROA/capacity/productivity/price recovery relationship, and we provide some conclusions on efforts to identify sources of variation in ROA.

8.2 DECOMPOSITIONS OF RETURN ON ASSETS

A large variety of models provide managerially informative decompositions of ROA. We present a few of these models in roughly chronological order. The earliest decomposition, the duPont triangle, has proved to be the most durable and influential.

8.2.1 The duPont triangle

Donaldson Brown joined duPont in 1909 as an explosives salesman. However, his financial and accounting skills quickly became evident and he was promoted to Treasurer in 1918 and appointed to the powerful Executive Committee in 1920. Soon thereafter duPont gained a controlling interest in the General Motors Corporation (GM), and Brown became GM's Vice President of Finance in 1921 and was appointed to GM's Executive Committee in 1924. Throughout this period Brown was developing, and both duPont and GM were implementing, a management accounting system based on what is now known as the duPont triangle.[1]

Johnson (1975, 1978) characterizes Brown's triangle system as the use of accounting data for management coordination, control, and compliance. Even then both duPont and GM were diversified corporations, producing a variety of products in multiple locations, and management had to decide how to allocate capital investment, as well as other resources and managerial compensation, across product lines and among plants. The allocation criterion duPont and GM used was return on investment. Brown's sophisticated management accounting system provided the requisite information, and more, for each product line and each plant, to the Executive Committee at regular intervals, thereby enabling the Committee to make informed allocation decisions. Brown also devised a product pricing formula designed to set product prices that would yield a desired return on investment when production was at standard volume, defined at GM to be two shifts per day.

The peak of the duPont triangle depicted in Figure 8.1 is return on assets, π/A. The objective of the triangle is to decompose π/A into a pair of financial

[1]   Horrigan (1968) credits Bliss, with apparent inspiration from Alfred Marshall (1892; 310–11), for the development of the triangle. However, in his discussion of the triangle, Bliss mentions duPont only in passing. Kline and Hessler (1952), Chandler (1962; ch. 2), and Johnson (1975) provide detailed historical analyses of duPont; Chandler (1962; ch. 3), and Johnson (1978) provide extensions to GM; and Kaplan (1984) puts these developments in historical perspective. None of these writers mentions Bliss, and Bliss is not mentioned in the duPont web site, which does contain a biography of Brown, "Donaldson Brown."

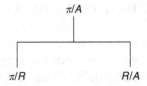

Figure 8.1 The duPont triangle

ratios that drive π/A. This in turn enables management to develop strategies to enhance either ratio, and hence π/A. The decomposition states that π/A is the product of π/R, variously called return on sales revenue and profit margin, and R/A, commonly called asset turnover. π/R indicates how much of sales revenue a firm retains as profit rather than absorbs as expense. An increase in π/R is consistent with an improvement in cost efficiency, the adoption of cost-saving technology, a reduction in input prices, or an increase in output prices. R/A indicates the (revenue) productivity of a firm's assets and, perhaps because of its productivity dimension, asset turnover plays a prominent role in the subsequent pyramids of Gold, Eilon, and their associates. An increase in R/A suggests that capital is working harder, or capital is being allocated to higher-valued uses, or output prices are increasing.

Summarizing, the duPont triangle identifies a pair of driving financial ratios, enabling management to pursue strategies that promote increases in either. Four additional points deserve mention. First, there is more to the duPont triangle than this two-way decomposition of π/A. Kline and Hessler indicate that duPont expanded the triangle by adding additional levels of explanatory variables. In the π/R leg π is defined as revenue minus cost, and cost is broken down into production cost, selling expense, transport cost, and administrative expense. Johnson (1975) claims that in the π/R leg cost is defined as the sum of costs attributable to capital, labor, and intermediates. Both decompositions are expressed as ratios of a cost component to revenue, and both are informative to management, although for different reasons. Either way the decomposition reveals what is sometimes called the firm's "cost structure," and it is informative to management in the following sense: $\pi/R = 1 - \Pi^{-1} = 1 - C/R = 1 - C_1/R - C_2/R - \cdots - C_N/R$, where C_1, C_2, and so on, can refer to departments or inputs. In the R/A leg, A is broken down into working capital and fixed capital, so that the ratio of the two influences R/A. Donaldson Brown constructed a triangle that occupies an entire page in Johnson (1978). These expansions of the triangle provide management with additional insight into drivers of trends in π/R and R/A, respectively.

Second, as Kline and Hessler emphasize, the accounting information provided to the Executive Committee was "'internal reporting', as contrasted with external reporting to the stockholders, SEC, etc." The charts provided to management "are prepared for and used by the executive committee" (pp. 1595, 1598) and do not supplant the usual financial statements. The privacy of the information provided by the duPont triangle contrasts sharply with the subsequent very public use of the triangle by the European Productivity Agency, a use we discuss in Section 8.2.2.

Third, an alternative two-way decomposition is available. Since $\pi = R - C$, basing a decomposition on the linking variable C instead of R yields $\pi/A = \pi/C \times C/A = (\Pi - 1) \times C/A$. In this variant of the triangle the interpretation of the π/C leg is straightforward; cost-cutting strategies that reduce C/R, and revenue-enhancing strategies that increase R/C, each increase π/A. Strictly speaking, this decomposition is not a duPont triangle, but it does have two nice features. First, π/C is an equally valid measure of the profit margin, or markup, and has been used by Bahiri and Martin (1970) (recall their secondary profit productivity index in Chapter 2) and Applebaum (1979), among others. Second, it provides the framework for an investigation of a firm's "revenue structure" since $\Pi = R/C = R_1/C + R_2/C + \cdots + R_M/C$, with R divided into products or markets or branches. The challenge is to provide an interpretation of the C/A leg, and perhaps for this reason we are unaware of triangle studies based on cost as the linking variable. More generally, any ratio, including π/A, can be decomposed an infinite number of ways, since $\pi/A = \pi/Z \times Z/A$, for any linking variable Z not restricted to R or C. The only constraints are the analyst's imagination and ability to provide motivation and interpretation within a business financial performance framework.

Finally, ROA clearly depends on quantities and prices, but the duPont triangle does not contain a productivity measure or a price recovery measure that drives, directly or indirectly, ROA. It does contain R/A, but R is influenced by output prices, and to the extent that A is associated with the capital input, it is far from the only input. A productivity measure is to be found in, or lurking behind, the π/R leg of the triangle, as we show in Section 8.3.5. We introduce both productivity change and price recovery change in intertemporal Section 8.4.

8.2.2 The European productivity agency pyramids

In the 1950s and 1960s a vast literature emerged from a 1956 European Productivity Agency (EPA) conference in Vienna. We call it the "interfirm comparisons" literature. Three types of comparison appear, each undertaken at the firm or plant level. One is based on productivity, principally labor productivity, and is of limited interest because it is a partial productivity indicator with scalar-valued output, variation in which is likely driven also by variation in capital intensity. However, some comparisons report firm characteristics that might provide additional insight into variation in labor productivity. Another is based on cost and its components; this exploration into a comparison of "cost structures" is of considerable interest, but rather than treat it separately we embed it in the third comparison. The third is based on financial ratios such as ROE, ROA, and π/C, and is referred to as "operating ratios."

EPA (1956) provides an extensive early survey of methods and findings. Kendrick and Creamer mention this volume, along with Davis (1955), as two books that "merit special attention." Ingham (1961, 1965) and Ingham and Harrington (1958) provide an accessible entry to this vast literature, much of which appears in *Productivity Measurement Review*. The literature is almost entirely empirical, based on confidential data collected from and shared with firms within and across industries and countries. The objective is to collect and disseminate information about the sources and magnitudes of participating firms' relative (dis) advantages as reflected in labor productivity, cost structure, and a set of financial ratios, the most important being ROA. Although most of the literature is interfirm, the EPA also encouraged within-firm comparisons through time.

Firms are compared based on a pyramid of financial ratios, a pyramid being a multilevel duPont triangle, although the origin of the pyramid is not mentioned in this literature. To provide a sense of the structure of the pyramid, the π/R leg of π/A is decomposed as $\pi/R = 1 - C/R$, and C/R is divided into various classes of expense ratios, enabling management to determine which costs are absorbing what would otherwise have been profit, a procedure developed at duPont and championed by Rostas (1943), to whom EPA (1955) is dedicated. The cost structure, which is a key feature of EPA studies, has two levels. The first level breaks down cost into production cost, selling and distribution expense, promotional expenses, and general and administrative expenses. The second level breaks down production cost, either into fixed and variable costs or into expenses associated with capital, labor, and other inputs. The other component of π/A, R/A, is divided into R/fixed assets and fixed assets/assets. Both decompositions elaborate on the original duPont triangle, and both typically are extended to create additional levels of the pyramid; the pyramids in Ingham and Harrington contain nine financial ratios.[2]

The many virtues of this interfirm comparison literature based on financial ratios do not include its incorporation of total factor (or total) productivity, which it does not do, or its pyramid structure, much of which was in use at duPont and GM four decades earlier. One virtue, which motivates much of the entire exercise, is the emphasis it places on the magnitude of interplant or interfirm variations in labor productivity, cost structure, and financial ratios. This emphasis on dispersion highlights the opportunities for improvement in each area. Another is the establishment of a uniform set of definitions of the various financial ratios, which minimizes reporting inconsistencies and encourages a sufficiently large number of firms to participate in the exercise to make the findings credible. Still another is the practice of disseminating findings to all participants. A final virtue is that it is not an academic exercise. It is a practical exercise of conducting interfirm comparisons, with confidentiality, and with an objective of enhancing firm performance by identifying strengths and weaknesses of each firm relative to a comparison set. Ingham and Harrington attribute these virtues to confidentiality, comparability, and cost.[3]

8.2.3 The pyramids of Gold, Eilon, and their associates

Starting at approximately the same time, a group of writers not associated with the EPA were constructing pyramids of their own. This literature started with Gold (1955), and is nicely summarized by Eilon (1984). The pyramids continue to be constructed from ratios, which Gold calls "management control ratios," although not all pyramids have duPont structure and not all ratios are financial ratios. The notions of productivity and capacity (and its rate of utilization) are introduced in an attempt to make both drivers of

---

[2] Amey (1960) uses the triangle system to provide a detailed comparison of what he calls the business efficiency of two similar firms operating in the same industry over 1930–55, and attributes higher ROA in one firm to higher asset turnover that more than offsets a lower profit margin. Rowan and Dunning (1968) conduct an interfirm comparison of comparable British and US firms operating in the UK, using an extended duPont triangle and various "efficiency" measures, including cost efficiency and our profitability measure Π.

[3] Johnson (1975) relates the use of monthly interplant comparisons at duPont, based on quantities and/or costs of each input per unit of each output. Results were provided to plant managers, who compared their performance with those of other managers and accounted for their performance to vice presidents. duPont also used a reciprocal profitability indicator to evaluate managers' performance. Both exercises provided incentives to improve performance, and managers received bonuses for exceeding targets.

financial performance. Gold, Eilon, and their associates have constructed some interesting pyramids and confronted, if not always resolved, some difficult analytical issues. We discuss a few models that we find interesting, either for their positive contributions or for the analytical issues they raise.[4]

We begin at the beginning, with Gold, who writes, in our notation and terminology,

$$
\begin{aligned}
\pi/A &= \pi/y \times y/A \\
&= [(R/y) - (C/y)] \times [y/A_F \times A_F/A],
\end{aligned}
\tag{8.1}
$$

in which A_F is fixed assets. The first equality is not a duPont triangle, since the linking variable is output y rather than revenue R. ROA is the product of profit per unit of output π/y and the productivity of assets y/A. Unit profit is the difference between unit revenue R/y and unit cost C/y. Asset productivity is the product of the productivity of fixed assets y/A_F and the share of fixed assets in total assets A_F/A. Gold clearly sees the distinction between $M=1$ and $M>1$, and in the latter case he proposes to aggregate outputs into scalar-valued real output and, following Fabricant (1940), he recommends use of the Edgeworth-Marshall (EM) output quantity index Y_{EM} to do so.

Gold calls the four ratios on the right side management control ratios that blend short-term and long-term perspectives, and that reflect areas of operating policy that can influence π/A. Gold views the first three as short-term drivers and A_F/A as a long-term driver involving capital investment. None of the drivers is a productivity measure, but Gold discusses in some detail how productivity change might impact on each driver, and thus π/A. For example, productivity growth may reduce C/y by reducing input requirements, and it may increase R/y by improving "the quality, durability or other attributes" of the product, which in turn would permit price increases. In the longer term productivity growth may improve ROA by enhancing the productivity of fixed assets, the more so if new investment embodies superior technology and/or requires less maintenance, both of which reduce cost.

Harper (1984) proposes an interesting variant of Gold's expression (8.1). She retains y as the linking variable, retains the unit profit leg π/y, and decomposes the y/A leg to obtain

---

[4] Gold's book is comprehensive. He begins with productivity concepts, and discusses input-oriented and output-oriented productivity measurement, the impact of price changes on output and input proportions, and the role of capacity and its rate of utilization. He then explores the impact of productivity adjustments on cost and unit cost, and on pyramids constructed from various financial ratios. Throughout the book he considers alternative managerial objectives. In terms of being ahead of its time, this book rivals Davis's book published in the same year.

$$\begin{aligned}
\pi/A &= \pi/y \times y/A \\
&= \pi/y \times [(y/L)/(K/L)] \quad [\text{assuming } K = A] \\
&= \pi/y \times [(w_L L/L)/(w_L L/y)/(K/L)] \\
&= \pi/y \times [(y/H) \times (H/L)/(K/L)],
\end{aligned} \qquad (8.2)$$

in which w_L is labor's hourly wage, L is the number of employees, H is standard hours, and the use of y again requires either $M = 1$ or aggregating the components of y into real output. The third equality is derived from the second, while the fourth is an alternative to the third. Partial productivity indexes appear in the second and fourth equalities, allowing a comparison of the contributions of y/L and y/H. The third equality introduces unit labor cost $w_L L/y = w_L/(y/L)$, and states that y/A increases if unit labor cost decreases; for example, if w_L increases by less than labor productivity increases. Harper uses the term "return on capital employed" in place of "return on assets," making the $K = A$ assumption plausible, although the association of K with A implies that capital deepening reduces y/A.[5]

The first two pyramids in this section use output as the linking variable. We now consider a duPont triangle in which revenue is the linking variable, making the distinction between $M = 1$ and $M > 1$ irrelevant. Harper revisits the duPont triangle, which she extends in two ways. In the first she retains the π/R leg and decomposes the R/A leg to yield

$$\begin{aligned}
\pi/A &= \pi/R \times R/A \\
&= \pi/R \times [(R/L)/(K/L)] \quad [\text{assuming } K = A] \\
&= \pi/R \times [(R/w_L L) \times (w_L L/L)/(K/L)],
\end{aligned} \qquad (8.3)$$

---

[5] Harper does not do so, but it is possible to transform the second equality in expression (8.2) to growth format, assuming constant returns to scale, to establish a near-direct link between $G_{\pi/A}$ and G_{TFP} given by

$$G_{\pi/A} = G_{\pi/y} + G_{y/L} - G_{K/L} = G_{\pi/y} + G_{TFP} + (\varepsilon_{yK} - 1)G_{K/L},$$

in which ε_{yK} is the partial elasticity of output with respect to capital. The second equality decomposes the asset productivity leg of the triangle into the product of a total factor productivity index and, since $K = A$ is assumed, a capital deepening term. G_{TFP} has a positive effect on $G_{\pi/A}$. $G_{K/L}$ has a negative impact on $G_{\pi/A}$ since $0 < \varepsilon_{yK} < 1$; capital deepening increases the denominator of π/A. Conditional on two assumptions, $K = A$ and constant returns to scale, this expression isolates total factor productivity as an independent driver of ROA. If input allocative efficiency is assumed, unobserved ε_{yK} can be replaced with the observed cost share of capital. We do not pursue this approach further because it does not easily generalize to non-constant returns to scale and more than two inputs.

which generates four drivers of ROA. In the second equality asset turnover is increased by improvements in R/L (driven by either a product price increase or an increase in labor productivity) and reduced by capital deepening (since $K = A$). In the third equality R/L is further decomposed into the product of two ratios, a partial profitability index and labor's wage, presumably with opposite impacts and unknown net impact on asset turnover. In both rows the association of K with A yields an inverse relationship between capital deepening and ROA, as in expression (8.2). Although R/L can be interpreted as a partial value productivity index, it is difficult to imagine a total factor productivity index emerging from expression (8.3).

Harper's second duPont triangle adopts the more promising approach of retaining the R/A leg and decomposing the π/R leg to obtain

$$
\begin{aligned}
\pi/A \;=\; &\pi/R \times R/A \\
=\; &[(\pi/w_L L) \times (w_L L/R)] \times R/A \\
=\; &[(\pi/w_L L) \times (w_L L/L) / (R/L)] \times R/A \\
=\; &\{[(\pi/w_L L) \times (w_L L)/L] / [(R/K) \times (K/L)]\} \times R/A,
\end{aligned}
\tag{8.4}
$$

which generates five drivers of ROA. Association of A with K is no longer required, but it is difficult to interpret some ratios as drivers of ROA. For example, it seems unlikely that increases in $w_L L/L$ and reductions in R/K both lead to increases in the profit margin. Once again it is difficult to imagine a total factor productivity index emerging from expression (8.4).

Gilchrist (1971) and Taussig and Shaw (1985) propose a modified duPont triangle in which revenue is replaced by added value (Gilchrist) or value added (Taussig and Shaw), defined by both as $VA = R - M$, revenue less purchased intermediate inputs. Gilchrist justifies the substitution on the ground that VA is the net income of a company, the fund out of which all operating expenses must be paid. Taussig and Shaw (an electric utility executive) justify the substitution on different grounds; VA tracks physical production more closely than R does, because VA is not distorted by volatile intermediate input prices that are passed along to consumers.

Taussig and Shaw make further use of the triangle. First, since VA tracks output closely, they track labor productivity by dividing VA by labor hours. Second, since $VA = R - M$, it must cover all remaining expenses, and they track "the distribution of value added to various participants in the organization," including wages, interest, dividends, depreciation, taxes, and retained earnings. This dual focus on productivity and distribution is reminiscent of the analyses of Davis and subsequent French writers we discussed in Chapter 4.

This provides a brief but suggestive introduction to a large literature associated with, and inspired by, Gold, Eilon, and their associates, in which the triangle (often but not invariably duPont) is expanded to a pyramid, and even into what Harper calls a set of "widely varying hierarchies." Indeed what distinguishes this literature from its predecessors is its willingness to explore unconventional non-duPont pyramids that attempt to introduce productivity, either directly or indirectly, as a determinant of ROA.[6]

Summarizing Sections 8.2.1 to 8.2.3, the duPont triangle and its extensions, and the EPA pyramids, are constructed primarily on financial ratios. Neither literature has shown much interest in incorporating physical productivity measures that might enrich the story about the drivers of change in ROA. Many interfirm comparisons conducted by the EPA do investigate variation in labor productivity, unit labor cost, unit cost, and cost–revenue ratios, but these comparisons are conducted independently of the pyramid-based comparisons. The Gold–Eilon pyramid literature augments financial ratios with a variety of management control ratios in an effort to introduce non-financial drivers of financial performance. They introduce several partial value productivity measures into their pyramids, but they are unable to incorporate a total factor (or total) productivity measure. Two promising approaches are to express the profit margin in terms of unit revenue and unit cost, analogous to what Gold does in expression (8.1), or in terms of profitability, as we suggest in expression (8.14). A virtue of both approaches is that productivity can influence unit profit and the profit margin in either an input-conserving or an output-enhancing orientation, with the latter enhancing asset turnover as well. A drawback of both expressions is that productivity remains behind, rather than among, the drivers of ROA. Its impact is apparent, but conjectural rather than explicit. We make it explicit in Section 8.4.

8.2.4 Remaining challenges

Some thorny issues remain, including

---

[6] One example of an unconventional non-duPont triangle involves a firm operating several outlets (branches, stores, etc.), each having size measured in square meters. If the firm defines its assets in terms of square meters, then

$$\pi/A = \pi/R \times R/A = \pi/R \times R/outlet \div m^2/outlet,$$

which identifies revenue per outlet and outlet size as drivers of asset turnover, and hence ROA. Market research organization RetailSails reports R/outlet and ft^2/outlet for the top 20 US chains by R/ft^2. http://www.retailsails.com/

(i) Incorporating multiple outputs

Most writers are unclear whether they are considering a single output or multiple outputs, others assume $M = 1$, or use homogeneous output data for which the $M = 1$ assumption is plausible, and a few aggregate multiple outputs into real output. Eilon and Teague (1973) suggest using average prices to aggregate outputs, a proposal Eilon, Gold, and Soesan (1975) implement by using "the Edgeworth formula" to aggregate outputs, and also to aggregate materials inputs. We discuss aggregation in Section 8.4.

(ii) Incorporating capacity utilization

Hendrickson (1961) sensibly advocates conducting interfirm comparisons at equal rates of capacity utilization, which requires a definition of capacity. Many writers, beginning with Gold, attempt to incorporate the concept of capacity into their pyramids in decompositions similar to that in expression (8.1). Gold does not define capacity precisely, although he clearly has in mind a maximum feasible output notion. He provides an empirical application, based on trends in real output and real capacity output, and therefore the trend in the rate of capacity utilization, obtained from Fabricant's aggregate output and capacity output indexes. These trends reinforce Gold's claim, which we discuss below, that real output is more volatile than real capacity output, and so provides a less reliable guide to short-term productivity change. Clarity did not improve much in ensuing years, although Hendrickson and Eilon and Teague offer useful proposals. None of the triangle/pyramid writers has considered input-oriented capacity measures based on a firm's short-term cost frontiers and, conversely, contributors to the cost-based capacity measurement literature do not explore their impact on ROA. We integrate the two literatures in Sections 8.3.2 to 8.3.4.

(iii) Introducing productivity change

Most pyramids incorporate partial productivity measures such as y/L, y/H, R/K, R/VA, $(w_L L/y)^{-1}$, and the like. duPont pyramids have a profit margin leg, which decomposes as $\pi/R = 1 - (C/R)$, and C/R is influenced by the level of productivity, although this is overlooked by all three pyramid groups. Other pyramids decompose $\pi/y = R/y - C/y$, and both unit revenue and unit cost are influenced by the level of productivity, but no writer has exploited this link in an analytical way. Perhaps more significantly, the incorporation of productivity *change* when either $M > 1$ or $N > 1$ requires the conversion of an atemporal pyramid to an intertemporal pyramid. We incorporate productivity change into an intertemporal pyramid in Section 8.4.

(iv) Introducing price recovery change

Finally, change in ROA is sensitive to price changes, and no triangle/ pyramid writer has incorporated price change among the drivers of ROA, much less change in ROA. We formalize the notion of price change with price recovery change, the ratio of an index of change in output prices to an index of change in input prices. We incorporate price recovery change into an intertemporal pyramid in Section 8.4.

8.3 INCORPORATING CAPACITY UTILIZATION INTO A DUPONT TRIANGLE

The sub-title of the Kendrick and Grossman (1980) productivity study is *Trends and Cycles*. They argue that productivity increases through time, but productivity change is pro-cyclical, and so short-term productivity growth exceeds its long-term trend during expansionary periods and falls short of its long-term trend during contractionary periods. Their primary explanation for pro-cyclical productivity involves capacity and its rate of utilization. In an expansion, "the movement from low rates of utilization of capacity back toward more efficient utilization rates" boosts productivity, and in a contraction "output falls faster than labor and capital inputs and capacity utilization rates drop," depressing productivity. Their empirical analysis of aggregate US data supports their argument. They adopt the popular macroeconomic peak-to-peak framework, a peak occurring at a time when output ceases to rise and begins to decline. Capacity utilization declines following a peak and increases as the next peak is approached. They qualify their argument in two ways: (i) they acknowledge that productivity gains taper off as a peak is approached and productivity begins to recover as a trough is approached, and (ii) they observe a great deal of heterogeneity across industries in the timing and amplitude of this pattern.[7] Pro-cyclical productivity is widely, but not unanimously, accepted at the aggregate economy level, although there are exceptions at the industry level.

---

[7] Interindustry heterogeneity in the timing and amplitude of productivity growth cycles has prompted Barnes (2011) to calculate productivity trends separately for a number of Australian industries using a peak-to-peak approach based on industry productivity peaks rather than industry output peaks.

Gold makes an interesting observation on the relationship between capacity utilization and productivity at the level of the individual firm. He contemplates measuring productivity in two ways: as the ratio of output to input and as the ratio of productive capacity to input. The former is the more variable of the two, because varying demand makes output more volatile than productive capacity, and he attributes the difference between the two measures to variation in the degree of utilization of relatively fixed inputs. He describes a scenario in which technical progress raises the productivity of inputs, but slack demand prevents a corresponding increase in output. A comparison of input with output suggests that no productivity change has occurred, while a comparison of input with productive capacity suggests that productivity growth has taken place. He concludes by writing, in our notation,

$$Y/X = Y^c/X \times Y/Y^c, \tag{8.5}$$

or, alternatively, $Y^c/X = Y/X \div Y/Y^c$, where Y, Y^c, and X are quantity indexes of output, capacity output, and input, respectively. Expression (8.5) states that productivity change is the product of potential productivity change and change in the rate of capacity utilization. The empirical challenge, which Gold does not adequately address, is that the quantity components of Y^c are unobserved, and must be estimated. We return to this relationship in Sections 8.3.2 and 8.3.3.[8]

The Kendrick and Grossman analysis can be adopted at the firm level, provided that peaks are identifiable. However, the microeconomic literature on capacity and its rate of utilization generally avoids the peak-to-peak framework, and we do also. Avoiding this peak-to-peak framework necessitates the development of an alternative definition of capacity and its rate of utilization. Several have been proposed, and we discuss some in Sections 8.3.2 and 8.3.3. A second challenge is to incorporate capacity utilization into a triangle. It is easy to expand a triangle to incorporate capacity utilization, as we show in Section 8.3.4. It is a greater challenge to incorporate capacity utilization *and* productivity into a tringle, making

---

[8] For the most part we follow Kendrick and Grossman and Gold by taking an output orientation to the capacity issue. In an input orientation attention focuses on quasi-fixed inputs, whose service flows are more volatile, and more pro-cyclical, than their measured quantities. Following Gold, and in our notation, $Y/X = Y/X^c \times X^c/X$, where X^c is a quantity index of input services. Measured productivity change Y/X is the product of productivity change based on input service flows Y/X^c and the ratio of input service flows to measured inputs X^c/X. In an expansion $X^c/X > 1$ and $Y/X > Y/X^c$, and in a contraction just the opposite occurs. The problem is that X^c is unobserved.

both the rate of capacity utilization and productivity drivers of ROA. We provide a framework for doing so in Section 8.3.5, and we implement the incorporation in intertemporal Section 8.4.

8.3.1 Capacity utilization at duPont and General Motors

According to Johnson (1978; 495), GM executives felt that "the Corporation over the long run should earn average after-tax profits equal to 20 per cent of investment while operating on average at 80 per cent of rated capacity (the so-called 'standard volume')." Standard volume is defined as the output that can be produced by operating two shifts per day, and apparently GM's output stayed within 7% of standard volume over a period of three decades. Johnson stresses that the combination of volatile demand, relatively stable prices, and high fixed costs meant that GM's short-term ROA was also volatile, depending on the rate of capacity utilization.

Three important points stand out. First, capacity is defined as the output obtainable from two shifts, when three shifts are technically feasible. Johnson argues that GM was concerned that operating more than two shifts would be less profitable than operating two shifts, increasing cost by more than revenue. This makes GM's definition of capacity an economic, rather than engineering, definition. Second, capacity is a maximal concept conditional on the number of shifts. Capacity can be expanded by moving to three shifts, but in either event the rate of capacity utilization cannot exceed unity. Third, Johnson describes how duPont and GM used capacity output to set product price sufficiently high to earn a target return on investment. In a nutshell, given an asset base, a target ROA implies a target profit. Dividing target profit by capacity output and adding unit cost evaluated at capacity output generates target revenue divided by capacity output. This ratio defines a minimum price required to achieve the target ROA. Managers were allowed to raise price above the target level, but if market forces drove price beneath the target level managers were asked to reduce cost. The sophisticated management accounting system devised by Donaldson Brown allowed duPont and GM to use this procedure to set target prices for each product.

A fourth point raises questions. Accepting the dependence of ROA on the rate of capacity utilization, how is this dependence to be modeled? Does the rate of capacity utilization influence ROA through the π/R leg or the R/A leg or both? If, as some suggest, the rate of capacity utilization influences productivity, through which leg does productivity influence ROA? We address these questions in Section 8.4.

8.3.2 Output-oriented capacity utilization measures

Gold does not offer an operationally useful definition of capacity, but he does offer some practical insights. He emphasizes "practically sustainable" output rather than "the utmost theoretically attainable" output, which gives his definition a managerial slant akin to the use of standard volume at GM. He assumes that technology, the customary number of shifts and length of work day all remain constant, and that appropriate allowances are made for break-downs, repairs, and maintenance. He also assumes that sufficient variable inputs are available "to service the full utilization of present capital facilities." Gold also considers the capacity of a plant producing more than one product, and suggests two approaches. In the first he proposes to measure capacity "for stipulated patterns of product proportions," that is, as the maximum feasible radial expansion of an existing output vector. In the second he proposes the use of "relative prices as weights" to construct a capacity output index. Gold did not develop or implement either of these ideas until some years later.

Lacking a clear definition of capacity proved to be no deterrent to the incorporation of capacity into a triangle, however, and Gold writes

$$
\begin{aligned}
\pi/A &= \pi/y \times y/A \\
&= [(R/y) - (C/y)] \times y/y^c \times y^c/A,
\end{aligned}
\tag{8.6}
$$

in which y/y^c is the rate of capacity utilization, which requires either $M = 1$ or "stipulated patterns of product proportions" or the aggregation of the components of y and y^c into real output and real capacity output, respectively, and y^c/A is a physical measure of potential asset turnover.

Gold also suggested, but did not implement, the use of price weights to aggregate multiple outputs. Doing so actually generates an augmented duPont triangle since

$$
\begin{aligned}
\pi/A &= \pi/R \times R/A \\
&= \pi/p^T y \times p^T y/p^T y^c \times p^T y^c/A,
\end{aligned}
\tag{8.7}
$$

with output price vector $p \in R_{++}^M$ (recall his earlier recommendation of arithmetic mean prices). Weighting output quantity vectors y and y^c by p allows $M > 1$. Expression (8.7) decomposes ROA into the product of three drivers: the profit margin, the rate of capacity utilization, and potential asset turnover, the turnover that would occur at full capacity output. This decomposition does not require fixed output proportions, but it does require output prices. The full capacity output vector y^c is generic, and we consider how to define y^c.

Eilon and Teague repeat Gold's pyramid (8.6), and they allow for multiple outputs. They think seriously about defining capacity in an operationally meaningful way, and it is worth quoting them in some detail. They ask "[w]hat, for instance, is precisely meant by the *capacity of a plant*? (emphasis in the original) Presumably it is the set of all product mixes that the designer and the plant manager expect the plant to produce per unit time, given the availability of material, labour and whatever other inputs are necessary." They continue "the set of all product mixes may be determined in the form of a production-possibilities curve, or a full capacity envelope as interpreted in a linear programming model through a series of constraints, provided these constraints can be defined and measured consistently and unambiguously." Their accompanying diagram is almost identical to our Figure 2.1 in Chapter 2; actual output y is a vector on the interior of an output set, and capacity output y^c belongs to a "full capacity line." Having read Farrell (1957), they measure the rate of capacity utilization radially, maintaining "stipulated patterns of product proportions," as the ratio of observed output to its radial extension on the full capacity line. This radial measure of capacity and its rate of utilization accommodates multiple outputs. They are unclear on two points. First, they are vague concerning what, if anything, is being held fixed in the exercise, although their reference to the number of shifts worked and the availability of sufficient variable inputs suggests that they are following Gold. They are also vague concerning whether their full capacity line implies that the rate of capacity utilization cannot exceed unity, although their reference to two shifts suggests that it cannot, because a full capacity line is conditioned on the number of shifts, the number of hours per shift, and the technology currently in place.

Eilon, Gold, and Soesan (1976; ch 8) clarify both points. They assume that "an adequate supply is available of labour, materials and other inputs needed to attain the productive potential of given capital facilities." Thus, the capacity measurement exercise holds capital facilities fixed and imposes no constraints on the availability and employment of other inputs. With regard to the nature of the envelope, they emphasize the managerial relevance of practically sustainable capacity rather than some theoretical maximum. This implies, for example, conditioning the fixed inputs on the customary number of shifts and the normally acceptable length of work day and work week, making standard allowances for breakdowns, repairs, and maintenance, and allowing for "moderate margins of uncertainty." Thus, under normal operating conditions the envelope constrains the rate of capacity utilization to be less than or equal to unity, although capacity can be expanded as demand conditions warrant.

Gold's triangles in expressions (8.6) and (8.7), and those of subsequent writers we have mentioned (and many others as well), have four distinguishing features. First, these triangles are not pure duPont triangles. The second is the association of capacity with an output vector, and a definition of the rate of capacity utilization as a radial or price-based comparison of actual and full capacity output vectors. The third is the introduction of the rate of capacity utilization as an additional driver of financial performance. In this model capacity utilization influences financial performance through the y/A leg in expression (8.6) and the R/A leg in expression (8.7). The final feature is a sense, growing in clarity and consistent with our interpretation of the treatment of capacity at duPont and GM, that capacity is a maximal concept, although with an economic or managerial foundation.

Johansen (1968) proposes a similar definition of capacity, which he somewhat misleadingly calls a technical (or engineering) concept. He writes: "*The capacity of existing plant and equipment* . . . is the maximum amount that can be produced per unit of time with the existing plant and equipment, *provided that the availability of variable factors of production is not restricted*" (emphasis in the original). Like Gold before him, Johansen frames his engineering definition in a managerial context in which the firm is "operating under normal conditions with respect to number of shifts, hours of work etc." Unlike Gold, he does not incorporate capacity into an ROA triangle, although many subsequent writers have done so.

Gold's main contributions to the concept of capacity utilization – defining capacity utilization as the ratio of two aggregate real output quantity levels, defining real capacity output as an aggregate of "practically sustainable" capacity output vectors, and imposing no limit on the availability of variable inputs – remain in use today. Corrado and Mattey (1997) describe the US Federal Reserve Board (FRB) industrial capacity utilization measures as the ratio of two real outputs, with real capacity output respecting the concept of sustainable practical capacity, a realistic work schedule, and sufficient availability of variable inputs to operate the fixed inputs in place. The distinguishing feature of the FRB capacity utilization series is that they are derived from detailed survey evidence collected annually from interviews with plant managers.

Figure 8.2 supports four output-oriented definitions of capacity output and its rate of utilization. We observe output vector $y \in R_+^M$ and input vector $x \in R_+^N$, with $y \in Q(x)$ and feasible set $Q(x)$ bounded above by its

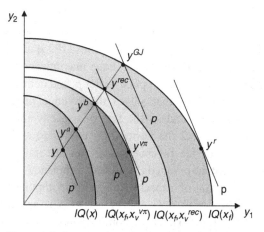

Figure 8.2 Output-oriented capacity utilization ($M=2$)

frontier $IQ(x)$. All $y \in IQ(x)$ are maximum output vectors that can be produced with x and given technology. The technically efficient output vector associated with y is $y^a = y/D_o(x,y) \in IQ(x) \subset Q(x)$, with $D_o(x,y)$ an output distance function defined in Chapter 1, and the technical efficiency of y is $y/y^a = D_o(x,y) \leq 1$. We partition x into variable input and fixed input sub-vectors, so that $x = (x_v, x_f)$. This partitioning high-lights the fact that capacity utilization is a short-term phenomenon imposing an upper bound on the ability to increase the sub-vector of fixed inputs in response to increasing product demand. We define $Q(x_f)$ as the set of feasible output vectors obtainable from x_f when no con-straints are imposed on the availability and use of x_v. $Q(x_f)$ is bounded above by its frontier $IQ(x_f) \subset Q(x_f)$, and all $y \in IQ(x_f)$ are full capacity output vectors, given x_f and technology.

Our first output-oriented definition of capacity and its rate of utilization follows Gold and Johansen, and solves an output maximization problem "for stipulated patterns of product proportions." It allows $M > 1$, it is independent of prices, and it defines capacity output as the largest feasible radial expansion of y. In Figure 8.2 $y^{GJ} = y/D_o(x_f, y) \in IQ(x_f)$ is the full capacity output vector associated with output vector y, and so the rate of capacity utilization is $CU^{GJ} = y/y^{GJ} = D_o(x_f, y) \leq 1$. The superscript "$GJ$" honors the two pioneers. CU^{GJ} is measured holding the output mix constant, and so is useful in the absence of output price information when $M > 1$. CU^{GJ} is a gross measure that can be decomposed into the product of an output-oriented technical efficiency term $y/y^a = D_o(x,y) \leq 1$ and a net capacity utilization term $y^a/y^{GJ} = D_o(x_f, y)/D_o(x, y) \leq 1$. We refer to the two components of CU^{GJ} as *wasted capacity* and *excess capacity*, respectively.[9]

Our second definition follows Segerson and Squires (1995) and Lindebo, Hoff, and Vestergaard (2007), and solves a revenue maximization problem. This definition is dependent on the output price vector p, and defines capacity output as the vector $y^r \in IQ(x_f)$ that solves the revenue maximization problem $max_y\{p^T y: y \in Q(x_f)\}$, and so the rate of capacity utilization is $CU^r = p^T y/p^T y^r \leq 1$. In Figure 8.2 the vectors $y^a = y/D_o(x, y) \in IQ(x)$ and $y^{GJ} = y/D_o(x_f, y) \in IQ(x_f)$ divide revenue-based capacity utilization into three components, an output-oriented technical efficiency term $p^T y/p^T y^a = D_o(x, y) \leq 1$ and a pair of capacity utilization components, a net capacity utilization term $p^T y^a/p^T y^{GJ} = D_o(x_f, y)/D_o(x, y) \leq 1$, and an output mix term $p^T y^{GJ}/p^T y^r \leq 1$. We refer to the three components of $CU^r = (p^T y/p^T y^a) \times (p^T y^a/p^T y^{GJ}) \times (p^T y^{GJ}/p^T y^r)$ as wasted capacity, excess capacity, and *misallocated capacity*, respectively. Wasted capacity and excess capacity have the same interpretations and magnitudes as in the output maximization problem. Misallocated capacity is new, and captures the economic value of an optimizing movement along $IQ(x_f)$ from y^{GJ} to y^r to adjust the output mix to prevailing output prices.

Our third definition solves a variable profit maximization problem, with variable profit $\pi_v = p^T y - w_v^T x_v$, w_v being the variable input price vector and $w_v^T x_v$ being variable cost. This definition is dependent on two price vectors, p and w_v. It defines capacity output as the output vector $y^{v\pi} \in Q(x_f)$ that, together with $x_v^{v\pi}$, solves the variable profit maximization problem $max_{y,x_v}\{p^T y - w_v^T x_v : y \in Q(x_f)\}$, so that maximum $\pi_v^{v\pi} = p^T y^{v\pi} - w_v^T x_v^{v\pi}$. The rate of capacity utilization is $CU^{v\pi} = p^T y/p^T y^{v\pi}$. In Figure 8.2 the vectors $y^a = y/D_o(x, y) \in IQ(x)$ and $y^b = y/D_o(x_f, x_v^{v\pi}, y) \in IQ(x_f, x_v^{v\pi})$ divide $CU^{v\pi}$ into an output-oriented technical efficiency term $p^T y/p^T y^a = D_o(x, y) \leq 1$ and a pair of capacity utilization components, a net capacity utilization term $p^T y^a/p^T y^b = D_o(x_f, x_v^{v\pi}, y)/D_o(x, y) \leq 1$, and an output mix term $p^T y^b/p^T y^{v\pi} \leq 1$. As in the revenue maximization problem we refer to the three components of $CU^{v\pi} = (y/y^a) \times (y^a/y^b) \times (y^b/y^{v\pi})$ as wasted capacity, excess capacity, and misallocated capacity, although excess capacity and

---

[9] Without adopting our terminology, the United Nations Food and Agriculture Organization (FAO 2000) has endorsed this physical measure of capacity utilization for use in fisheries, in part due to the shortage of reliable information on output and variable input prices that are required in subsequent definitions.

misallocated capacity have different magnitudes in the two problems. Unlike the two previous definitions, in which $y^{GJ} \in IQ(x_f)$ and $y' \in IQ(x_f)$, $y^{v\pi}$ is located on the interior of $Q(x_f)$.

Our final definition follows Coelli, Grifell-Tatjé, and Perelman (2002), who propose an interesting variant on the variable profit maximization problem. Their variable profit maximization problem is subject to an additional constraint requiring the solution output vector to be a radial expansion of the observed output vector, which makes it useful in the absence of output prices. In Figure 8.2 their solution output vector moves from $y^{v\pi} \in IQ(x_f, x_v^{v\pi})$ to $y^{rec} = y/D_o(x_f, x_v^{rec}, y) \in IQ(x_f, x_v^{rec})$, where $x_v^{rec} \neq x_v^{v\pi}$; y^{rec} generates the same revenue as $y^{v\pi}$, but the radial constraint causes $p^T y^{rec} - w_v^T x_v^{rec} \leq p^T y^{v\pi} - w_v^T x_v^{v\pi} \Rightarrow w_v^T x_v^{rec} \geq w_v^T x_v^{v\pi}$. However, since y^{rec} is a radial expansion of y, y^a, and y^b, this allows the replacement of output prices with output distance functions in the calculation and decomposition of capacity utilization, as in the initial output maximization problem. In this entirely radial model capacity utilization is defined as the ratio y/y^{rec}, and decomposes somewhat differently than in the variable profit maximization problem as $y/y^{GJ} = [y/y^a \times y^a/y^{rec}] \times y^{rec}/y^{GJ}$. Coelli et al. refer to the term in brackets as ray economic capacity utilization (hence "rec"), the product of technical efficiency $y/y^a = D_o(x, y) \leq 1$ and ray economic capacity utilization net of technical inefficiency $y^a/y^{rec} = D_o(x_f, x_v^{rec}, y)/D_o(x, y) \leq 1$, and they refer to y^{rec}/y^{GJ} as the optimal amount of capacity idleness, which shrinks with increases in p and decreases in w_v. There is no output mix term in this problem. As in the variable profit maximization problem, y^{rec} is located on the interior of $Q(x_f)$.

The four output-oriented CU measures are derived from an analytical framework in which x_f is a fixed input quantity vector, making fixed cost $C_f = w_f^T x_f$ fixed as well. However, it is possible to fix expenditure without fixing every element of x_f, thereby allowing one or more elements of x_f to be less than fully utilized. Machlup (1952) provided early motivation for doing so by distinguishing between indivisibility *in purchase* and divisibility *in use*. Somewhat later Maxwell (1965) emphasized the importance of allowing fixed inputs to be less than fully utilized, a distinction also emphasized by Balk (2010). These observations raise the possibility of specifying $w_f^T \bar{x}_f = \bar{C}_f$ and imposing constraints $x_f \leq \bar{x}_f$, with the weak inequalities allowing fixed inputs *in use* x_f to fall short of the amounts *in place* $\bar{x}_f$, which can be under-utilized but not expanded in the short term. In this case $\bar{x}_f$ would generate a strict engineering concept of capacity and x_f would generate a managerial concept of capacity. It follows that

$w_f^T x_f \leq \overline{C}_f \Leftrightarrow (w_f/\overline{C}_f)x_f \leq 1$. This formulation allows the construction of four "fixed cost indirect" capacity utilization measures ICU^c corresponding to the four direct measures CU^c. In this case $Q(x_f)$ is replaced by $Q(w_f/\overline{C}_f) \supseteq Q(x_f)$, and so each fixed cost indirect ICU measure is smaller than its corresponding direct CU measure. Referring to Figure 8.2, $IQ(x)$ remains unchanged, but $IQ(x_f, x_v^{v\pi})$ expands to $IQ(w_f/\overline{C}_f, x_v^{v\pi})$, $IQ(x_f, x_v^{rec})$ (which is not depicted) expands to $IQ(w_f/\overline{C}_f, x_v^{rec})$, and $IQ(x_f)$ expands to $IQ(w_f/\overline{C}_f)$. The full capacity output quantity vectors increase accordingly and each indirect CU measure is smaller than its corresponding direct CU measure.[10]

The direct and fixed cost indirect analyses are structurally similar; the only difference is the expansion of the direct output sets to the fixed cost indirect output sets, and the corresponding increases in capacity outputs and reductions in capacity utilization rates. Among the virtues of the fixed cost indirect approach are (i) at the firm level it offers flexibility in the allocation of fixed cost budgets when not all fixed input constraints are binding; (ii) at the industry level it offers managers or regulators an alternative way of managing or allocating capacity (e.g., as at duPont, where ROA considerations drove the allocation of assets among divisions, branches, and product lines), by assigning quotas to a single variable C_f rather than each element of x_f; and (iii) at the analyst level it shrinks the number of direct constraints in an optimization problem.

For subsequent use we collect and rewrite the four direct capacity utilization measures. Our rewrites are based on the fact that $p^T y / p^T y^a = D_o(x, y)$, and so

(i) Output maximizing capacity utilization

$$CU^{GJ} = p^T y / p^T y^{GJ} = (p^T y / p^T y^a)(p^T y^a / p^T y^{GJ}) \Rightarrow p^T y / p^T y^a = CU^{GJ} \times (p^T y^{GJ} / p^T y^a)$$
$$\Rightarrow D_o(x, y) = CU^{GJ} \times (p^T y^{GJ} / p^T y^a) \qquad [p^T y^{GJ} / p^T y^a = D_o(x, y) / D_o(x_f, y)]$$

(ii) Revenue maximizing capacity utilization

$$CU^r = p^T y / p^T y^r = (p^T y / p^T y^a)(p^T y^a / p^T y^r) \Rightarrow p^T y / p^T y^a = CU^r \times (p^T y^r / p^T y^a)$$
$$\Rightarrow D_o(x, y) = CU^r \times (p^T y^r / p^T y^a)$$

---

[10] Following this line of reasoning would provide a new interpretation of the theory of cost indirect production pioneered by Shephard (1974) and extended by Färe, Grosskopf, and Kirkley (2000), although it would introduce yet another component of the rate of capacity utilization. It is worth noting that our focus on capacity utilization inspires a fixed cost indirect approach, whereas an interest in "throwing money at schools" motivated Grosskopf et al. (1997, 1999) to develop a variable cost indirect approach.

(iii) Variable profit maximizing capacity utilization

$$CU^{v\pi} = p^T y / p^T y^{v\pi} = (p^T y / p^T y^a)(p^T y^a / p^T y^{v\pi}) \Rightarrow p^T y / p^T y^a = CU^{v\pi} \times (p^T y^{v\pi} / p^T y^a)$$
$$\Rightarrow D_o(x,y) = CU^{v\pi} \times (p^T y^{v\pi} / p^T y^a)$$

(iv) Ray economic variable profit maximizing capacity utilization

$$CU^{rec} = p^T y / p^T y^{rec} = (p^T y / p^T y^a)(p^T y^a / p^T y^{rec}) \Rightarrow p^T y / p^T y^a = CU^{rec} \times (p^T y^{rec} / p^T y^a)$$
$$\Rightarrow D_o(x,y) = CU^{rec} \times (p^T y^{rec} / p^T y^a).[p^T y^{rec} / p^T y^a = D_o(x,y) / D_o(x_f, x_v^{rec}, y)]$$

Each of these results states that the output distance function $D_o(x,y)$ that provides an output-oriented measure of technical efficiency can be expressed as the product of a capacity utilization measure and the reciprocal of the corresponding measure of net excess capacity. This is a general result, applicable to all four capacity utilization measures, and we write

$$D_o(x,y) = CU^c \times p^T y^c / p^T y^a, \tag{8.8}$$

in which the output price vector p is deliberately unspecified and "c" can be defined by GJ, r, $v\pi$, or rec. In each case CU^c is a gross measure, inclusive of output-oriented technical efficiency; there is disagreement about whether waste should be a component of capacity utilization, and our use of a distance function enables us to show that waste can be separated from net capacity utilization. In each case the reciprocal of the corresponding measure of net excess capacity $p^T y^c / p^T y^a \geq 1$ can be interpreted as a measure of plant availability or capacity idleness. Expression (8.8) generalizes a similar expression in Färe, Grosskopf, and Kokkelenberg (1989) by incorporating output prices, thereby allowing $c = r$ or $v\pi$ or rec in addition to $c = GJ$.

We write the ratio of comparison period to base period versions of expression (8.8) as

$$\frac{D_o^1(x^1, y^1)}{D_o^0(x^0, y^0)} = \frac{CU^{c1}}{CU^{c0}} \times \frac{(p^T y^{c1} / p^T y^{a1})}{(p^T y^{c0} / p^T y^{a0})}, \tag{8.9}$$

which states that change in technical efficiency from base period to comparison period can be expressed as the product of change in capacity utilization and change in available capacity; if the growth of available capacity outpaces the growth of capacity utilization, technical efficiency must decline. Thus, expression (8.9) provides a new framework for a structural explanation for change in technical efficiency. The significance of this result, which generalizes a similar decomposition of De Borger and Kerstens (2000), is that technical efficiency change is a core component of Malmquist productivity indexes, and so expression (8.9) provides a way of introducing change in capacity utilization as a new component of a Malmquist index of productivity change. We exploit expression (8.9) for this purpose in Section 8.4.[11]

8.3.3 Input-oriented capacity utilization measures

"From an economist's viewpoint capacity is a cost concept," wrote Hickman (1964), who defined capacity as that output that minimizes short-term average cost, "given the existing physical plant and organization of production and the prevailing factor prices." Hickman noted that CU $\gtreqless$ 1, and that CU $\neq$ 1 drives short-term average cost above minimum because x_v "is either too large or too small to make optimum use of the physical facilities." Hickman's definition is consistent with an earlier definition proposed by Klein (1960), although Klein offered a different defense of the association of capacity output with the rate of output that minimizes short-term average cost. For Klein this definition of capacity output is consistent with a zero profit competitive economy. Still other input-oriented definitions of capacity utilization have been proposed.[12]

We continue to partition the input quantity vector as $x = (x_v, x_f)$, and we partition the input price vector similarly as $w = (w_v, w_f)$, x_v and w_v being variable input quantity and price sub-vectors, and x_f and w_f being quantity and price sub-vectors of inputs that are fixed in the short term with cost $C_f = w_f^T x_f$.

Figure 8.3 contains a conventional $\cup$ – shaped long-term average cost frontier $LAC(y, w)$ together with one of its $\cup$ – shaped short-term average cost frontiers $SAC(y, w_v, x_f, w_f) = SAC_v(y, w_v, x_f) + w_f^T x_f$ and its short-term marginal cost frontier $SMC(y, w_v, x_f)$, and marginal revenue $MR(y, p)$. All writers mentioned above and below assume, explicitly or implicitly, that $M = 1$ and that the firm allocates variable inputs in a cost-efficient manner, so that $(w_v^T x_v / y) + C_f / y = SAC(y, w_v, x_f, w_f)$, and for the moment we retain these two assumptions.

---

[11] Solving expression (8.9) for CU^{c1}/CU^{c0} and merging the two remaining terms generates $CU^{c1}/CU^{c0} = (p^T y^1 / p^T y^0)/(p^T y^{c1} / p^T y^{c0})$, which coincides with Gold's capacity utilization index Y/Y^c in expression (8.5).

[12] Paul (1999) provides a good introduction to the input-oriented approach to the measurement of capacity utilization and its relation to the measurement of productivity change.

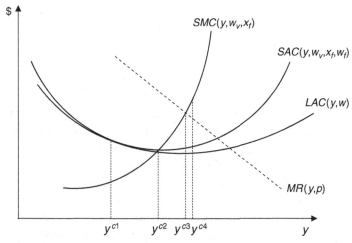

Figure 8.3 Input-oriented capacity utilization

Figure 8.3 depicts four input-oriented definitions of capacity output. Output y^{c1} has been attributed to Klein, who did not propose it.[13] However, it can be recommended on the grounds that it equates short-term and long-term average (and so total) cost; for any other output $y \neq y^{c1}$, $SAC(y,w_v,x_f,w_f) > LAC(y,w)$. Output y^{c2} has been recommended by Klein, Hickman, and Berndt and Morrison (1981), among others, on the grounds that it minimizes $SAC(y,w_v, x_f,w_f)$; for any other output $y \neq y^{c2}$, $SAC(y,w_v,x_f,w_f) > SAC(y^{c2},w_v,x_f,w_f)$. Output y^{c3} has been recommended on the grounds that it maximizes short-term variable profit; any $y \neq y^{c3}$ would sacrifice profit, and in this sense capacity output y^{c3} in Figure 8.3 is analogous to capacity output $y^{v\pi}$ in Figure 8.2. Our favorite capacity output is y^{c4}, recommended by de Leeuw (1962; 83–4); at y^{c4} short-term marginal cost exceeds short-term minimum average cost "by some given percentage . . . and we would therefore expect a high rate of capacity utilization to represent appreciable upward price pressure and a high level of investment demand." de Leeuw goes on to discuss, and defend, the arbitrariness of the percentage, noting that it is situation-dependent. Our candidate for the percentage would be the most appropriate producer price index, in which case y^{c4} would equate $SMC(y,w_v,x_f)$ with the

[13] Klein proposed an entirely different tangency solution, one of Chamberlinian excess capacity brought on by imperfect competition. In this situation actual output at the tangency solution must fall short of capacity output at the minimum point on the short-term average cost frontier, and so CU < 1.

producer price index. It should be apparent from Figure 8.3 that each of these input-oriented definitions allows the rate of capacity utilization to exceed unity, in sharp contrast to the output-oriented measures, which treat capacity as a maximal concept.

Writers have generally noted that these alternative definitions of y^c are conditioned on the assumption of normal operating conditions. Thus, Smithies (1957) writes "[b]y full capacity output I mean the output that the existing stock of equipment is intended to produce under normal working conditions with respect to hours of work, number of shifts, and so forth," a view repeated by de Leeuw, Hickman, and others.

We return to the two assumptions. Suppose first that $w^T x > c(y, w)$ or that $w_v^T x_v > c_v(y, w_v, x_f)$, that is, the firm fails to solve the two optimization problems above and allocates x inefficiently in the long term or allocates x_v inefficiently the short term. It is straightforward to eliminate cost inefficiency before embarking on the CU exercise by replacing $w^T x > c(y, w)$ with $w^T x_{CE} = c(y, w)$ and $w_v^T x_v > c_v(y, w_v, x_f)$ with $w_v^T x_{vCE} = c_v(y, w_v, x_f)$, x_{CE} and x_{vCE} being cost-efficient input quantity vectors. As for the $M = 1$ assumption, in an aggregate environment considered by the writers cited earlier "output" is the value of a real output quantity index. At the firm level the problem caused by $M > 1$ is not the measurement of capacity utilization, but rather the definition of "average" cost from which capacity vectors $y^{c1} - y^{c4}$ are derived. We define a long-term average cost frontier as $LAC^t(y^t, w^t) = c^t(y^t, w^t)/Y^t$ and a short-term average cost frontier as $SAC^t(y^t, w_v^t, x_f^t, w_f^t) = [c_v^t(y^t, w_v^t, x_f^t) + w_f^{tT} x_f^t]/Y^t$ respectively, and we define Y^t as in the aggregate context, as the value of a aggregate output quantity index in period t. In both cases "average" cost incorporates both y^t and Y^t.[14]

8.3.4 Incorporating capacity utilization into a duPont triangle

We have surveyed three concepts of capacity output. Two are output-oriented and the third input-oriented. Two pairs of the output-oriented

---

[14] Segerson and Squires (1990, 1995) consider primal and dual measures of capacity utilization for multiple-product firms that do not require the construction of an aggregate output quantity index. For the primal measure they consider two options: homothetic separability, so that $c(y, w) = h(y)g(w)$ and/or $c_v(y, w_v, x_f) = h_v(y)g_v(w_v, x_f)$, and a radial measure similar to those of Gold and Johansen that ignores a non-radial component of CU associated with differences in the output mixes in y and y^c. For the dual measure they derive CU measures from the shadow value of a single fixed input. They also allow for multiple fixed inputs, and note that non-unitary ratios of shadow values to market prices generate non-unitary partial capacity utilization measures that can be offsetting and generate CU = 1.

definitions are radial, and so independent of prices. The other two pairs are price-based solutions to economic optimization problems. Both direct and indirect measures provide managerial interpretations of a primal production model with binding fixed input or fixed input budget constraints and no limit to the employment of variable inputs. The input-oriented definitions are price-based models based on short-term and long-term average cost frontiers, the former conditioned on fixed input quantities and prices and variable input prices. What we lack is an analytical framework that links capacity utilization, however modeled, with financial performance. Developing such a linkage is the subject of this section.

We are now prepared to introduce the four output-oriented capacity utilization measures into a duPont triangle. For the output maximization problem we have, from Figure 8.2 in which $y^{GJ} = y/D_o(x_f, y)$ and expression (8.7),

$$\pi/A = \pi/R \times p^T y/[p^T y/D_o(x_f, y)] \times [p^T y/D_o(x_f, y)]/A, \tag{8.10}$$

in which CU^{GJ} is $p^T y/[p^T y/D_o(x_f, y)] = p^T y/p^T y^{GJ} = R/R^{GJ} = D_o(x_f, y)$, and potential asset turnover becomes $[p^T y/D_o(x_f, y)]/A = p^T y^{GJ}/A = R^{GJ}/A$. Although CU^{GJ} appears to be price-dependent, prices appear in CU^{GJ} to implement the division operator, and to maintain a revenue-based numerator in the potential asset turnover term, but they drop out, leaving $CU^{GJ} = D_o(x_f, y)$. As in Section 8.3.2, CU^{GJ} decomposes into wasted capacity and excess capacity components, and so expression (8.10) contains four drivers of ROA.

For the revenue maximization problem we have

$$\pi/A = \pi/R \times p^T y/p^T y^r \times p^T y^r/A, \tag{8.11}$$

in which CU^r is $p^T y/p^T y^r = R/R^r$ and potential asset turnover is $p^T y^r/A = R^r/A$. In this case CU^r is price-dependent, and decomposes into wasted capacity, excess capacity, and misallocated capacity. Consequently, expression (8.11) contains five drivers of ROA.

For the variable profit maximization problem we have

$$\pi_v/A = \pi_v/R \times p^T y/p^T y^{v\pi} \times p^T y^{v\pi}/A, \tag{8.12}$$

in which $p^T y/p^T y^{v\pi} = CU^{v\pi}$ and $p^T y^{v\pi}/A$ is potential asset turnover. $CU^{v\pi}$ is also price-dependent, and decomposes into wasted capacity, excess capacity, and misallocated capacity. Expression (8.12) also contains five drivers of ROA.

For the ray economic variable profit maximization problem we have

$$\pi_v/A = \pi_v/R \times p^T y/p^T y^{rec} \times p^T y^{rec}/A, \tag{8.13}$$

in which $p^T y/p^T y^{rec} = CU^{rec}$ and $p^T y^{rec}/A$ is potential asset turnover. The main difference between expressions (8.12) and (8.13) concerns the CU components. $CU^{v\pi}$ compares output vectors y and $y^{v\pi}$, and consists of wasted capacity, excess capacity, and misallocated capacity. CU^{rec} compares output vectors y and y^{rec}, leaving no room for misallocated capacity, and no need of an output price vector because y^{rec} is a radial expansion of y, although prices are used to implement the division operator, and to maintain a revenue-based numerator in the potential asset turnover term.

We turn to the four fixed cost indirect maximization problems. The problems themselves are structurally identical to the corresponding direct problems, replacing x_f with w_f/C_f in the respective output sets. Consequently, the four fixed cost indirect ROA decompositions mirror those in expressions (8.10) to (8.13), with the proviso that x_f is replaced with w_f/C_f in the various components of the ROA decompositions. In the output maximization problem (8.10) $IQ(x_f)$ expands to $IQ(w_f/C_f)$, and so $D_o(w_f/C_f, y) \leq D_o(x_f, y) \leq 1$, which reduces the rate of capacity utilization and expands the magnitude of potential asset turnover. The results are qualitatively unchanged for the three remaining problems because $IQ(x_f)$ expands to $IQ(w_f/C_f)$, $IQ(x_f, x_v^{v\pi})$ expands to $IQ(w_f/C_f, x_v^{v\pi})$, and $IQ(x_f, x_v^{rec})$ expands to $IQ(w_f/C_f, x_v^{rec})$. Regardless of the optimization problem, replacing x_f with w_f/C_f reduces the rate of capacity utilization and increases potential asset turnover.

Any of the four input-oriented definitions of capacity output in Section 8.3.3 can be used in the preliminary decomposition of ROA in expression (8.7), but not in expression (8.6) unless $y^c = \lambda y$, $\lambda > 0$, Gold's "stipulated patterns of product proportions." Since both y and y^c are on the same average cost frontier, any deviation of y from y^c is attributable exclusively to CU $\neq 1$, variation in cost efficiency having been eliminated.

We have eight output-oriented capacity output vectors, four direct and four indirect, and four input-oriented capacity output vectors to insert into the ROA decomposition expressions (8.6) and (8.7). All twelve can be used in expression (8.7), but if $M > 1$ only four output-oriented capacity output vectors, the direct and fixed cost indirect solutions to the corresponding output maximization and ray economic variable profit maximization problems, can be inserted into expression (8.6) without Gold's "stipulated patterns of product proportions."

We conclude this section by offering some observations on the introduction of capacity utilization into a duPont triangle.

(i) The introduction of CU into a duPont triangle creates not one but three new drivers of ROA: wasted capacity (technical inefficiency), excess capacity (radial under-utilization of capacity after accounting for technical inefficiency), and, in the revenue maximization and variable profit maximization problems only, misallocated capacity (an inappropriate output mix). Each is likely to be under management control;

(ii) In each triangle CU influences ROA through its influence on asset turnover; it does not influence ROA through its influence on productivity, which does not appear explicitly in any triangle;

(iii) The four direct optimization problems generate four different full capacity output vectors ($y^{GJ}, y^r, y^{v\pi}$, and y^{rec}) and so four different measures of $CU \leq 1$;

(iv) In the output maximization and revenue maximization problems the introduction of CU leaves π/R unchanged, and converts asset turnover to potential asset turnover $p^T y^{GJ}/A$ or $p^T y^r/A$, the asset turnover that full capacity utilization at y^{GJ} or y^r would generate;

(v) In the variable profit maximization and the ray economic variable profit maximization problems the introduction of CU converts the profit margin to a variable profit margin π_v/R, and also converts asset turnover to potential asset turnover $R^{v\pi}/A$ or R^{rec}/A, the asset turnover that full capacity utilization at $y^{v\pi}$ or y^{rec} would generate;

(vi) In the output maximization and revenue maximization problems debate about whether economic capacity exceeds or falls short of engineering capacity is pointless. Both full capacity output vectors y^{GJ} and y^r belong to $IQ(x_f)$; the only meaningful difference between them is that y^r features a different product mix that generates more revenue than y^{GJ} does;

(vii) In the variable profit maximization and ray economic variable profit maximization problems economic capacity must fall short of engineering capacity since the former problems have more constraints than the latter, and so $Q(x_f, x_v^{v\pi}) \subseteq Q(x_f)$ and $Q(x_f, x_v^{rec}) \subseteq Q(x_f)$. The difference between them creates what Coelli et al. (2002) call the optimal amount of capacity idleness, and Rodriguez-Álvarez, Roibás-Alonso, and Wall (2013) call "reserve service capacity to deal with demand uncertainty," the cost of which is $(p^T y' - p^T y^{v\pi})$ or $(p^T y^{GJ} - p^T y^{rec})$. However, any combination of an increase in p and a reduction in w_v causes $Q(x_f, x_v^{v\pi})$ and $Q(x_f, x_v^{rec})$ to converge toward $Q(x_f)$, and so excess capacity shrinks; and

(viii) It is worth mentioning, if not pursuing further, that capacity can be constrained by more than a firm's fixed inputs x_f or its fixed input budget C_f. External capacity constraints are common, and include regulatory constraints, financing constraints, and inadequate infrastructure. The combination of internal and external capacity constraints can cause CU to be volatile, and volatility of CU causes volatility of ROA, as GM experienced a century ago. A current mining illustration is available at http://au.advfn.com.

8.3.5 Incorporating productivity into a duPont triangle

In Sections 8.3.2 and 8.3.3 we introduced a dozen definitions of capacity output y^c and its rate of utilization y/y^c generated by alternative orientations and behavioral assumptions. We then introduced these definitions of CU into a duPont triangle; this exercise shows how CU influences ROA, regardless of how y^c is defined. Having succeeded in introducing alternative definitions of capacity utilization into a duPont triangle, we now attempt to introduce productivity into a duPont triangle.

We write the duPont triangle (without a capacity utilization component) as

$$\pi/A = \pi/R \times R/A$$
$$= (1 - \Pi^{-1}) \times R/A, \tag{8.14}$$

and, following Gold, we argue that Π must be positively related to productivity, and so the profit margin, and thus ROA, must be positively related to productivity, regardless of its orientation. This argument is plausible, but analytically unconvincing. The components of the duPont triangle are absolute variables describing levels, but unless $M = N = 1$, Y/X is a relative variable comparing one situation (e.g., time period) to another. An analytically satisfying demonstration requires an intertemporal framework in which productivity *change* influences ROA *change*. We develop such a framework in Section 8.4.

8.4 DRIVERS OF CHANGE IN RETURN ON ASSETS IN A DUPONT TRIANGLE FRAMEWORK

We begin by converting an atemporal duPont triangle to an intertemporal (or interfirm) duPont triangle change. We then show how change in the rate of capacity utilization, productivity change, and price change affect ROA change.

The ratio of comparison period to base period duPont triangles is

$$\frac{\pi^1/A^1}{\pi^0/A^0} = \frac{\pi^1/R^1}{\pi^0/R^0} \times \frac{R^1/A^1}{R^0/A^0}. \tag{8.15}$$

We introduce change in the rate of capacity utilization first. Converting the second equality in expression (8.7) to an intertemporal context and defining $CU = p^T y / p^T y^c$, with y^c the solution vector to any of the output-oriented direct and indirect optimization problems in Section 8.3.2 or any of the input-oriented optimization problems in Section 8.3.3, we have

$$\frac{\pi^1/A^1}{\pi^0/A^0} = \frac{\pi^1/R^1}{\pi^0/R^0} \times \frac{CU^1}{CU^0} \times \frac{p^{1T}y^{c1}/A^1}{p^{0T}y^{c0}/A^0}, \tag{8.16}$$

which attributes ROA change to profit margin change, change in the rate of capacity utilization, and change in potential asset turnover. Change in the rate of capacity utilization influences ROA change through its impact on asset turnover change, presumably because increases in CU bring actual turnover closer to its potential. Neither productivity change nor price recovery change appears in expression (8.16).

We next consider how price change and productivity change influence ROA change. The key is to acknowledge that change in the profit margin derives from both price changes and quantity changes, and we write

$$\frac{\pi^1/R^1}{\pi^0/R^0} = \frac{\pi^1/R^1}{\pi_0^1/R_0^1} \times \frac{\pi_0^1/R_0^1}{\pi^0/R^0}$$
$$= \frac{\pi_1^0/R_1^0}{\pi^0/R^0} \times \frac{\pi^1/R^1}{\pi_1^0/R_1^0}, \tag{8.17}$$

in which $R_0^1 = p^{0T}y^1$ and $\pi_0^1 = p^{0T}y^1 - w^{0T}x^1$ in the first equality are comparison period revenue and profit evaluated at base period prices, and $R_1^0 = p^{1T}y^0$ and $\pi_1^0 = p^{1T}y^0 - w^{1T}x^0$ in the second equality are base period revenue and profit evaluated at comparison period prices. In the first equality the first term on the right side is that part of the margin change that can be attributed solely to price change, since it is the ratio of comparison period margins evaluated at comparison period and base period prices. The second term on the right side is that part of the margin change attributable solely to quantity change, since it is the ratio of comparison period margin evaluated at base period prices and the nominal base period margin. We call these two terms a price effect and a quantity effect, respectively. The first term in the second equality is also a price effect since it is the ratio of the base period profit margin evaluated at comparison period prices and base period prices. The second term is also a quantity effect because it is the ratio of comparison period and base period profit margins evaluated at comparison period prices. The first equality pairs a Paasche price effect with a Laspeyres quantity effect, and the second pairs a Laspeyres price effect with a Paasche quantity effect. The first pairing is more widely used, but the second has its adherents, including Frankel (1963), to whom we referred in Chapter 3.

We develop two strategies for decomposing the profit margin change component of ROA change. In Section 8.4.1 we express the quantity effects in expression (8.17) in terms of augmented (by a size change term) versions of the theoretical Malmquist productivity index proposed by Caves, Christensen, and Diewert (1982) (CCD), and we leave the price effects unchanged. In Section 8.4.2 we express both the quantity effects and the price effects in terms of empirical Laspeyres and Paasche quantity indexes. This enables us to prove that the price and quantity effects in expression (8.17) are price recovery and productivity effects. Both strategies decompose the quantity effect, but in different ways that provide complementary information.

8.4.1 The theoretical CCD Malmquist productivity index strategy

We begin with the quantity effect $(\pi_0^1/R_0^1)/(\pi^0/R^0)$ in the first equality in expression (8.17). The analysis requires cost allocation, which we introduced in Section 4.3.2 of Chapter 4 and revisited in Chapter 6. Assuming that cost allocation is feasible, we write

$$
\begin{aligned}
\pi^0 &= p^{0T}y^0 - w^{0T}x^0 \\
&= (p^0 - c^0)^T y^0,
\end{aligned}
\tag{8.18}
$$

since $w^{0T}x^0 = c^{0T}y^0$, c^0 being a vector of base period unit costs of producing each output. Writing base period profit in this way enables us to rewrite the base period profit margin as

$$\pi^0/R^0 = [(p^0-c^0)^T y^0]/R^0$$
$$= [(p^0-c^0)/R^0]^T y^0 \qquad (8.19)$$
$$= \rho^{0T} y^0,$$

in which $\rho_m^0 = (p_m^0 - c_m^0)/R^0$, $m = 1, \ldots, M$. Similarly, we can rewrite the real comparison period profit margin as

$$\pi_0^1/R_0^1 = [(p^0 - c_0^1)^T y^1]/R_0^1$$
$$= [(p^0 - c_0^1)/R_0^1]^T y^1 \qquad (8.20)$$
$$= \rho_0^{1T} y^1,$$

in which $c_0^{1T} y^1 = w^{0T} x^1$ and $\rho_0^1 = (p^0 - c_0^1)/R_0^1$. Consequently, the quantity effect in the first equality in expression (8.17) can be rewritten as[15]

$$\frac{\pi_0^1/R_0^1}{\pi^0/R^0} = \frac{\rho_0^{1T} y^1}{\rho^{0T} y^0}. \qquad (8.21)$$

The next step is to interpret expression (8.21), which we do with the assistance of Figure 8.4, which adds output $y^D \in T^0$ to Figure 6.2 in

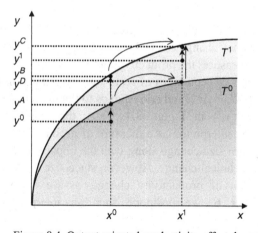

Figure 8.4 Output-oriented productivity effect decomposition

---

[15] The weight vector ρ^0 in expression (8.19) and in the denominator of expression (8.21) is a base period weight vector. However, the weight vector ρ_0^1 in expression (8.20) and in the numerator of expression (8.21) combines base period prices and comparison period quantities. Balk (2008; 68) associates such "hybrid" weights with Lowe indexes.

Chapter 6, and in which T^0 and T^1 are base period and comparison period production frontiers analogous to $IQ^0(x^0)$ and $IQ^1(x^1)$. We have

$$\frac{\pi_0^1/R_0^1}{\pi^0/R^0} = \frac{\rho_0^{1T}y^1/\rho_0^{1T}y^C}{\rho^{0T}y^0/\rho^{0T}y^A} \times \frac{\rho_0^{1T}y^C}{\rho_0^{1T}y^D} \times \frac{\rho_0^{1T}y^D}{\rho^{0T}y^A}, \tag{8.22}$$

in which $y^A = y^0/D_o^0(x^0,y^0)$, $y^B = y^0/D_o^1(x^0,y^0)$, $y^C = y^1/D_o^1(x^1,y^1)$, and $y^D = y^1/D_o^0(x^1,y^1)$. We rewrite expression (8.22) as

$$\begin{aligned}
\frac{\pi_0^1/R_0^1}{\pi^0/R^0} &= \frac{D_o^1(x^1,y^1)}{D_o^0(x^0,y^0)} \times \frac{D_o^0(x^1,y^1)}{D_o^1(x^1,y^1)} \times \frac{\rho_0^{1T}y^D}{\rho^{0T}y^A} \\
&= \frac{D_o^0(x^1,y^1)}{D_o^0(x^0,y^0)} \times \frac{\rho_0^{1T}y^D}{\rho^{0T}y^A},
\end{aligned} \tag{8.23}$$

in which $D_o^0(x^1,y^1)/D_o^0(x^0,y^0) = [D_o^1(x^1,y^1)/D_o^0(x^0,y^0)] \times [D_o^0(x^1,y^1)/D_o^1(x^1,y^1)]$ is an output-oriented base period CCD Malmquist productivity index. The two components $D_o^1(x^1,y^1)/D_o^0(x^0,y^0)$ and $D_o^0(x^1,y^1)/D_o^1(x^1,y^1)$ measure technical efficiency change and technical change (at x^1), respectively, as is apparent from Figure 8.4. Consequently,

$$\frac{\pi_0^1/R_0^1}{\pi^0/R^0} = M_{o\,CCD}^0(x^1,x^0,y^1,y^0) \times \frac{\rho_0^{1T}y^D}{\rho^{0T}y^A}. \tag{8.24}$$

The term $M_{o\,CCD}^0(x^1,x^0,y^1,y^0)$ captures the productivity impacts of output-oriented technical efficiency change and technical change, and nothing else. The term $\rho_0^{1T}y^D/\rho^{0T}y^A$ measures the productivity impact of size change that captures the joint impacts of economies of scale and diversification that is absent from $M_{o\,CCD}^0(x^1,x^0,y^1,y^0)$, and corresponds to the movement along T^0 from (x^0,y^A) to (x^1,y^D) in Figure 8.4. Thus, the quantity effect $(\pi_0^1/R_0^1)/(\pi^0/R^0)$ can be interpreted as a measure of productivity change that includes the impact of size change along with the impacts of technical efficiency change and technical change. However, since size change is not necessarily a component of productivity change, as we discussed in Section 6.5 of Chapter 6, we postpone such an interpretation to Section 8.4.2.[16]

---

[16] Grifell-Tatjé and Lovell (1995) showed that the two components $D_o^1(x^1,y^1)/D_o^0(x^0,y^0)$ and $D_o^0(x^1,y^1)/D_o^1(x^1,y^1)$ measure technical efficiency change and technical change when the best practice technologies are allowed to satisfy variable returns to scale. They asserted that "the Malmquist productivity index does not accurately measure productivity change. The bias is

Substituting expression (8.24) into the first equality in expression (8.17), and substituting the resulting profit margin decomposition into expression (8.16), yields the following decomposition of ROA change incorporating (and decomposing and augmenting) an output-oriented base period CCD Malmquist productivity index

$$\frac{\pi^1/A^1}{\pi^0/A^0} = \frac{\pi^1/R^1}{\pi_0^1/R_0^1} \times \left\{ \frac{D_o^1(x^1,y^1)}{D_o^0(x^0,y^0)} \times \frac{D_o^0(x^1,y^1)}{D_o^1(x^1,y^1)} \times \frac{\rho_0^{1T}y^D}{\rho^{0T}y^A} \right\} \times \frac{CU^1}{CU^0} \times \frac{R^{c1}/A^1}{R^{c0}/A^0},$$

(8.25)

in which $CU^1/CU^0 = (p^{1T}y^1/p^{1T}y^{c1}) / (p^{0T}y^0/p^{0T}y^{c0})$ and $R^c = p^T y^c$. Expression (8.25) attributes ROA change to price change, three components of productivity change, change in capacity utilization, and change in potential asset turnover.

Starting with the first equality in expression (8.17) leads to a decomposition of ROA change in expression (8.25) built on a base period CCD Malmquist productivity index and a size change term calculated along base period technology. Starting with the second equality in expression (8.17) and following the same procedures generates a decomposition of ROA change built on a comparison period CCD Malmquist productivity index and a size change term calculated along comparison period technology. Taking the geometric mean of the two decompositions generates the following decomposition of ROA change incorporating a geometric mean CCD Malmquist productivity index

$$\frac{\pi^1/A^1}{\pi^0/A^0} = \left[\frac{\pi^1/R^1}{\pi_o^1/R_o^1} \times \frac{\pi_1^0/R_1^0}{\pi^0/R^0} \right]^{1/2}$$

$$\times \left\{ \frac{D_o^1(x^1,y^1)}{D_o^0(x^0,y^0)} \times \left[\frac{D_o^0(x^1,y^1)}{D_o^1(x^1,y^1)} \times \frac{D_o^0(x^0,y^0)}{D_o^1(x^0,y^0)} \right]^{1/2} \right.$$

$$\times \left. \left[\frac{\rho_0^{1T}y^D}{\rho^{0T}y^A} \times \frac{\rho^{1T}y^C}{\rho_1^{0T}y^B} \right]^{1/2} \right\} \times \frac{CU^1}{CU^0} \times \frac{R^{c1}/A^1}{R^{c0}/A^0}, \quad (8.26)$$

systematic, and depends on the magnitude of scale economies." Our effort to augment $M_{o\,CCD}^0(x^1,x^0,y^1,y^0)$ with a size change effect intended to capture the joint impacts of economies of scale and diversification has antecedents; Ray and Desli (1997) and Grifell-Tatjé and Lovell (1999a) augment the CCD productivity index with a size change term, although these terms differ.

in which $\rho_1^0 = [(p^1 - c_1^0)/R_1^0]^T y^0$, $c_1^0 = w^{1T} x^0$, and $R_1^0 = p^{1T} y^0$. The vectors y^C and y^B are located on T^1 in Figure 8.4. Expression (8.26) mimics expression (8.15) by expressing ROA change as the product of margin change (the first two rows) and asset turnover change (the third row). Margin change is the product of price change (the first row) and productivity change (the second row). Price change is the geometric mean of the two price effects in expression (8.17). Productivity change is the product of a geometric mean CCD Malmquist productivity index and a geometric mean size change term. Finally, asset turnover change is the product of change in capacity utilization and change in potential asset turnover.

Expression (8.26) incorporates CU change as a driver of ROA change, but CU change has no direct impact on productivity change. However, Schultze (1963), former chairman of the US Council of Economic Advisors and former director of the US Bureau of the Budget, has argued, and provided supporting empirical evidence, that change in the rate of capacity utilization exerts a positive influence on productivity change at the aggregate level. Many subsequent writers, including Kendrick and Grossman (1980), concur. Another literature, smaller perhaps, suggests that profit margins vary directly with the rate of capacity utilization, although the mechanism through which capacity utilization change influences margin change is unspecified. Both literatures enjoy empirical support. Accordingly we next introduce CU change as a driver of productivity change, and so margin change, in an expression for ROA change. This framework does not prejudge the sign of the relationship.

We incorporate CU change as a driver of productivity change by exploiting expression (8.9), which states that technical efficiency change can be expressed as the product of change in capacity utilization and change in available capacity. Expression (8.26) contains a technical efficiency change component $D_o^1(x^1, y^1)/D_o^0(x^0, y^0)$ as a driver of productivity change. Replacing the technical efficiency change component with the right side of expression (8.9), and merging the final two terms in expression (8.26) to avoid double counting CU change, generates an alternative decomposition of ROA change also based on an augmented (by a size change term) geometric mean CCD Malmquist productivity index given by

$$\frac{\pi^1/A^1}{\pi^0/A^0} = \left[\frac{\pi^1/R^1}{\pi_o^1/R_o^1} \times \frac{\pi_1^0/R_1^0}{\pi^0/R^0}\right]^{1/2}$$

$$\times \left\{\frac{CU^{c1}}{CU^{c0}} \times \frac{p^T y^{c1}/p^T y^{a1}}{p^T y^{c0}/p^T y^{a0}} \times \left[\frac{D_o^0(x^1,y^1)}{D_o^1(x^1,y^1)} \times \frac{D_o^0(x^0,y^0)}{D_o^1(x^0,y^0)}\right]^{1/2}\right.$$

$$\left. \times \left[\frac{\rho_0^{1T}y^D}{\rho^{0T}y^A} \times \frac{\rho^{1T}y^C}{\rho_1^{0T}y^B}\right]^{1/2}\right\} \times \frac{R^1/A^1}{R^0/A^0}, \qquad (8.27)$$

which decomposes ROA change into the product of margin change and asset turnover change. Margin change is the product of price change and productivity change. Productivity change is the product of CU change, change in available capacity, technical change, and size change. The cost of introducing CU change as a driver of productivity change is that, rather than entering as an additional driver, it replaces a conventional driver, change in technical efficiency. The offsetting benefit is that it is consistent with the arguments of Schultze and others, without prejudging the direction of its impact on productivity change.

Expressions (8.26) and (8.27) provide alternative decompositions of ROA change incorporating productivity change and change in capacity utilization. The difference between them is the placement of CU change as a driver of ROA change. In expression (8.26) CU change is a component of asset turnover change, the idea being that increases in CU bring actual turnover closer to its potential. In expression (8.27) CU change is a component of productivity change, which in turn is a driver of margin change.[17]

Summarizing Section 8.4.1, we set out to decompose ROA change from one time period to the next. Our strategy is based on the CCD Malmquist productivity index, which is known to decompose into the product of technical efficiency change and technical change. It is also known to lack a size change component, and we have introduced what we believe is a new size change term. The key insights contained in expressions (8.9) and (8.17) have led us to a pair of decompositions of ROA change in expressions (8.26)

---

[17] It is possible to combine the two approaches in expressions (8.26) and (8.27), giving CU change a two-fold role, as a component of asset turnover change and as an influence on productivity change, simply by not merging the final two terms in expression (8.26), although this approach may be accused of double counting the contribution of CU change to ROA change.

and (8.27). These expressions are devoid of financial ratios (with the partial exception of the actual and potential asset turnover terms), and contain relevant economic drivers of ROA change. Change in capacity utilization plays one role in expression (8.26) and a different role in expression (8.27). Both decompositions are based on the assumption that cost allocation is feasible, although both would go through under a weaker feasibility condition of variable cost allocation with only minor terminological and notational changes. However, neither decomposition expresses the price effect in terms of change in price recovery. The index number strategy we introduce in Section 8.4.2 does express the price effect in terms of a price recovery index.

8.4.2 The empirical index number strategy

The analysis in Section 8.4.1 is based on expression (8.17), which decomposes change in the profit margin π/R into two products of a quantity effect and a price effect. We then use an augmented (by a size change component) output-oriented CCD productivity index to propose an interpretation of the geometric mean of the two quantity effects as a productivity effect, on the assumptions that cost allocation is feasible and size change is a driver of productivity change. However, we are unable to provide an analogous interpretation of the geometric mean of the two price effects as a price recovery effect. Such an interpretation appears to require empirical quantity- and price-based indexes, which we develop in this section. Thus, both Sections 8.4.1 and 8.4.2 share a common heritage in expression (8.17).

A few mathematical manipulations enable us to write the price effect in the first equality of expression (8.17) as

$$\frac{\pi^1/R^1}{\pi_0^1/R_0^1} = \frac{\pi^1}{R^1 - \left(\dfrac{P_P}{W_P}\right) w^{1T}x^1}, \tag{8.28}$$

in which P_P/W_P is a Paasche price recovery index, with $P_P/W_P \gtreqless 1 \Leftrightarrow (\pi^1/R^1)/(\pi_0^1/R_0^1) \gtreqless 1$. Expression (8.28) contains comparison period and base period prices, but only comparison period quantities, and shows the contribution of price recovery to profit margin change from a Paasche perspective.

We follow the same strategy to write the quantity effect in the first equality of expression (8.17) as

$$\frac{\pi_0^1/R_0^1}{\pi^0/R^0} = \frac{\pi_0^1}{R_0^1 - \left(\dfrac{Y_L}{X_L}\right)w^{0T}x^1}, \qquad (8.29)$$

in which Y_L/X_L is a Laspeyres productivity index, with $Y_L/X_L \gtrless 1 \Leftrightarrow (\pi_0^1/R_0^1)/(\pi^0/R^0) \gtrless 1$. Expression (8.29) contains comparison period and base period quantities, but only base period prices, and shows the contribution of productivity change to profit margin change from a Laspeyres perspective. In addition, since $(\pi_0^1/R_0^1)/(\pi^0/R^0)$ is a productivity effect, it follows that $\rho_0^{1T}y^D/\rho^{0T}y^A$ in expression (8.24) in Section 8.4.1 correctly measures the productivity impact of size change, and so expression (8.24) provides a decomposition of expression (8.29) into the product of a base period CCD Malmquist productivity index and a measure of size change calculated along base period technology.

Substituting expressions (8.28) and (8.29) into the first equality in expression (8.17) and substituting the resulting expression into expression (8.16) yields the following decomposition of ROA change based on empirical price and quantity indexes

$$\frac{\pi^1/A^1}{\pi^0/A^0} = \left[\frac{\pi^1}{R^1 - \left(\dfrac{P_P}{W_P}\right)w^{1T}x^1} \times \frac{\pi_0^1}{R_0^1 - \left(\dfrac{Y_L}{X_L}\right)w^{0T}x^1} \right] \times \frac{CU^1}{CU^0} \times \frac{R^{c1}/A^1}{R^{c0}/A^0},$$

$$(8.30)$$

which attributes ROA change to price recovery change, productivity change, change in capacity utilization, and change in potential asset turnover. One difference between expressions (8.25) and (8.30) is that the price effect in expression (8.30) contains a Paasche price recovery index. Another difference is that the augmented CCD productivity index in expression (8.25) decomposes by economic driver, while the Laspeyres productivity index in expression (8.30) decomposes by variable. Change in the rate of capacity utilization is not a driver of productivity change in either expression.

Following the same procedures with the second line of expression (8.17) generates a similar decomposition of ROA change, with Laspeyres price recovery component and Paasche productivity component. Taking the geometric mean of the two yields

$$
\frac{\pi^1/A^1}{\pi^0/A^0} = \left[\frac{\pi^1}{R^1 - \left(\dfrac{P_P}{W_P}\right) w^{1T}x^1} \times \frac{\pi_1^0}{R_1^0 - \left(\dfrac{P_L}{W_L}\right) w^{1T}x^0} \right]^{1/2}
$$

$$
\times \left[\frac{\pi_0^1}{R_0^1 - \left(\dfrac{Y_L}{X_L}\right) w^{0T}x^1} \times \frac{\pi^1}{R^1 - \left(\dfrac{Y_P}{X_P}\right) w^{1T}x^1} \right]^{1/2}
$$

$$
\times \frac{CU^1}{CU^0} \times \frac{R^{c1}/A^1}{R^{c0}/A^0}. \tag{8.31}
$$

Expression (8.31) decomposes ROA change into a price recovery index that is the geometric mean of Paasche and Laspeyres price recovery indexes, a productivity index that is the geometric mean of Laspeyres and Paasche productivity indexes, capacity utilization change, and change in potential asset turnover.

The similarity of the profit margin change in expression (8.31) to the profitability decomposition $\Pi^1/\Pi^0 = (P/W) \times (Y/X)$ in expression (2.19) in Chapter 2 is apparent. Here the two components of profit margin change measure the respective contributions of (P/W) and (Y/X) to ROA change.

Recalling the relationship between base period expressions (8.25) and (8.30), and an analogous relationship equating the Paasche productivity component of expression (8.31) with the product of a comparison period CCD Malmquist productivity index and a measure of size change calculated along comparison period technology, enables us to exploit the second row of expression (8.26) to rewrite expression (8.31) as

$$
\frac{\pi^1/A^1}{\pi^0/A^0} = \left[\frac{\pi^1}{R^1 - \left(\dfrac{P_P}{W_P}\right) w^{1T}x^1} \times \frac{\pi_1^0}{R_1^0 - \left(\dfrac{P_L}{W_L}\right) w^{1T}x^0} \right]^{1/2}
$$

$$
\times [M_o^0{}_{\text{CCD}}(x^1,x^0,y^1,y^0) \times M_o^1{}_{\text{CCD}}(x^1,x^0,y^1,y^0)]^{1/2}
$$

$$
\times \left[\frac{\rho_0^{1T}y^D}{\rho^{0T}y^A} \times \frac{\rho^{1T}y^C}{\rho_1^{0T}y^B} \right]^{1/2} \times \frac{CU^1}{CU^0} \times \frac{R^{c1}/A^1}{R^{c0}/A^0}. \tag{8.32}
$$

Expression (8.32) decomposes ROA change using an empirical price recovery index and a theoretical productivity index consisting of a geometric mean CCD Malmquist index augmented with a geometric mean size effect. The final two components, CU change and change in potential asset turnover, can be merged into change in asset turnover.

In expressions (8.31) and (8.32) CU change influences ROA change through its impact on change in asset turnover. An alternative strategy is to substitute price recovery and productivity indexes into expression (8.15) rather than expression (8.16), and make use of Gold's expression (8.5), which states that productivity change is the product of potential productivity change Y^c/X and capacity utilization change Y/Y^c. Alternatively assigning Laspeyres and Paasche structure to Y, Y^c, and X yields the ROA decomposition

$$\frac{\pi^1/A^1}{\pi^0/A^0} = \left[\frac{\pi^1}{R^1 - \left(\frac{P_P}{W_P}\right)w^{1T}x^1} \times \frac{\pi^0_1}{R^0_1 - \left(\frac{P_L}{W_L}\right)w^{1T}x^0} \right]^{1/2}$$

$$\times \left[\frac{\pi^1_0}{R^1_0 - \left(\frac{Y_L}{Y^c_L}\right)\left(\frac{Y^c_L}{X_L}\right)w^{0T}x^1} \times \frac{\pi^0_1}{R^1 - \left(\frac{Y_P}{Y^c_P}\right)\left(\frac{Y^c_P}{X_P}\right)w^{1T}x^1} \right]^{1/2} \times \frac{R^1/A^1}{R^0/A^0}.$$

$$(8.33)$$

In expression (8.33), change in capacity utilization influences ROA change through its impact on productivity change, which drives change in the profit margin, which drives ROA change.

Expressions (8.31) to (8.33) provide three alternative empirical price-based decompositions of ROA change. Expressions (8.31) and (8.33) are exclusively price-based, and differ in the role they assign to CU change. Expression (8.32) replaces a price-based productivity term with a theoretical productivity term.

The quantity vectors needed to implement the ROA change decompositions in price-based expressions (8.31) to (8.33) (and technology-based expressions (8.26) and (8.27) in Section 8.4.1) are either observed $(y^1, y^0,$ $x^1, x^0)$ or solutions to optimization problems specified in Section 8.3 $(y^{c0},$ $y^{c1})$, or radial expansions or contractions of observed quantity vectors as in Section 8.4.1. The two sets of decompositions are interpreted in exactly the same way; the only difference is that one uses distance functions and the other uses prices to decompose productivity change and to measure change in capacity utilization.

The objective and structure of Section 8.4.2 replicate those of Section 8.4.1, replacing a theoretical technology-based framework with an empirical price-based framework. Our final decompositions of ROA change in expressions (8.31) to (8.33) have the same structure as the two final decompositions in expressions (8.26) and (8.27) in Section 8.4.1, but decompositions (8.31) to (8.33) express the price and quantity effects of expression (8.17) explicitly in terms of Paasche and Laspeyres price recovery and productivity indexes. We call the price and quantity effects Fisher effects because they are geometric means of Paasche and Laspeyres price and quantity effects, although these effects do not contain explicit Fisher price recovery and productivity indexes. However, it is important to note that the price effects in expressions (8.26), (8.27), and (8.31) to (8.33) are all geometric means of the two price effects in expression (8.17), and so they have the same value. All four productivity effects have the same value, for the same reason, and this opens up the possibility of decomposing the productivity effect by economic driver *and* by individual quantity variable.[18]

Sections 8.4.1 and 8.4.2 each take two approaches to the treatment of change in capacity utilization, the first treating it as a driver of asset turnover change (expressions (8.26), and (8.31) and (8.32)), and the second treating it as a driver of productivity change, which drives ROA change through its impact on profit margin change (expressions (8.27) and (8.33)). The first approach is simpler and easier to implement, but it will not satisfy those with theory and evidence to support capacity utilization change as a driver of productivity change. The second approach will receive their support, but it comes at the cost of replacing rather than complementing technical efficiency change as a driver of productivity change.

We conclude by viewing Sections 8.4.1 and 8.4.2 as providing complementary decompositions of ROA change, in two respects. First, the empirical approach can clarify issues raised by the theoretical approach, and vice

---

[18] The ROA change decomposition in expressions (8.31) and (8.33) is based on Laspeyres and Paasche price recovery and productivity indexes. It does not appear possible to generate similar decompositions based on Edgeworth-Marshall arithmetic mean price recovery and productivity indexes because all ROA change decompositions derive from expression (8.17), which does not decompose using Edgeworth-Marshall price and quantity vectors because this introduces a third pair $(\bar{p}, \bar{w})$ and $(\bar{y}, \bar{x})$ into the analysis.

versa; this occurs throughout the book. An example concerns the size effect in expression (8.24), the interpretation of which is reinforced beneath expression (8.29). Second, both approaches provide complementary analyses of the placement of change in capacity utilization as a driver of ROA change. Most significantly, the theme of this book is the relationship between productivity and financial performance, and both approaches provide a framework within which to conduct an empirical exploration into the relationship when financial performance is measured by ROA change.

8.5 SUMMARY AND CONCLUSIONS

The financial health of a business is typically characterized in terms of various financial ratios. The duPont triangle formalizes the characterization, measuring financial health with return on assets, which is expressed as the product of two driving financial ratios, the profit margin and asset turnover. Gold and subsequent writers have hypothesized that the rate of capacity utilization also influences return on assets, and so in Section 8.3 we express return on assets as the product of the profit margin, the rate of capacity utilization, and potential asset turnover. This is the first step toward meeting our objective of introducing economic variables into the duPont triangle. We then propose a series of output-oriented and input-oriented measures of capacity output, from which alternative measures of the rate of capacity utilization are derived.

The second step toward meeting our objective is the introduction of productivity and price recovery as drivers of return on assets. However, since these two variables are change variables, describing change from one period to the next, in Section 8.4 we convert the duPont triangle, expressed as the product of three level variables, to an intertemporal ratio of duPont triangles in which ROA change is the product of change in the profit margin and change in asset turnover. In some contexts we decompose change in asset turnover into the product of change in the rate of capacity utilization and change in potential asset turnover.

We develop two analytical frameworks within which to create an economic decomposition of ROA change in terms of its economic drivers. The first, in Section 8.4.1, is technology-based, and exploits a theoretical productivity index, and the second, in Section 8.4.2, is based on empirical price and quantity indexes. Both frameworks provide valuable information to management concerning the likely sources of changes in its financial performance.

Our preferred technology-based decomposition appears in expression (8.26), which attributes ROA change to four drivers: price recovery change (although not in explicit form), productivity change (itself the product of three drivers), capacity utilization change, and change in potential asset turnover. In expression (8.27) change in capacity utilization plays a different role, as a driver of productivity change. However, its role as a driver of productivity change comes at a cost, since it replaces a conventional driver, technical efficiency change.

Our preferred decomposition based on empirical price and quantity indexes appears in expressions (8.31) and (8.32), which decompose ROA change into the product of the same four drivers as our preferred technology-based decomposition. In expression (8.33) change in capacity utilization plays the same role as in expression (8.27), as a driver of productivity change.

The two frameworks have offsetting strengths. The impacts of change in capacity utilization and change in potential asset turnover are the same in both decompositions, so the offsetting strengths must appear in the price recovery change and productivity change expressions. The technology-based framework does not require price information, and decomposes the productivity change term into the product of three economic drivers. However, it requires cost allocation, and it does not introduce an explicit expression for price recovery change. The price- and quantity-based framework generates explicit expressions for both price recovery change and productivity change, which in turn provide information on the contributions of individual quantity changes and price changes to ROA change. The price- and quantity-based framework does not require cost allocation, and it is calculated rather than estimated, so it does not face a degrees of freedom constraint, but it does require complete price information (or the replacement of output prices with allocated unit costs).

It is noteworthy that in both frameworks our preferred specification is one in which change in capacity utilization appears as a component of asset turnover change, but not again as a driver of productivity change. This double role of capacity utilization was proposed many years ago by Schultze. His suggestion that change in capacity utilization exerts a positive influence on productivity change was not new, but he explained the complexity of the relationship, concluding that "through influences on *prices and productivity*, cyclical changes in capacity-utilization rates affect the share of income going to profits" (emphasis added). This also suggests yet another role for change in capacity utilization, as a driver of price recovery change, and hence as an influence on income distribution. His suggestion that change in capacity utilization exerts a positive influence on ROA change was not new either, but he illustrated the relationship empirically, using aggregate US data.

Summarizing, the duPont triangle measures financial performance with ROA, and decomposes ROA into the product of a pair of managerially informative financial ratios. We begin by converting this atemporal relationship to an intertemporal one, and we assert that the two financial ratios must have economic drivers. We then develop a pair of analytical frameworks containing change in a modified financial ratio, change in capacity utilization, price recovery change, and productivity change as drivers of ROA change.

Bibliography

Abb, F. (1961), "Productivity Measurement for the Small Business," *Productivity Measurement Review* 26 (August), 47–65.

Aigner, D. J., C. A. K. Lovell, and P. Schmidt (1977), "Formulation and Estimation of Stochastic Frontier Production Function Models," *Journal of Econometrics* 6:1 (July), 21–37.

Albuquerque, A. (2009), "Peer Firms in Relative Performance Evaluation," *Journal of Accounting and Economics* 48:1 (October), 69–89.

Alsyouf, I. (2007), "The Role of Maintenance in Improving Companies' Productivity and Profitability," *International Journal of Production Economics* 105:1 (January), 70–78.

Alvarez, A., and P. Schmidt (2006), "Is Skill More Important than Luck in Explaining Fish Catches?" *Journal of Productivity Analysis* 26:1 (August), 15–25.

American Engineering Council (1921), *Waste in Industry*. Washington, DC: Federated American Engineering Societies.

Amey, L. R. (1960), "Business Efficiency: An Interfirm Comparison," *Productivity Measurement Review* 21 (May), 32–45.

Amey, L. R. (1969), *The Efficiency of Business Enterprises*. London: George Allen and Unwin Ltd.

Amir, E., I. Kama, and J. Livnat (2011), "Conditional versus Unconditional Persistence of RNOA Components: Implications for Valuation," *Review of Accounting Studies* 16:2 (June), 302–27.

Amiti, M., and S.-J. Wei (2009), "Service Offshoring and Productivity: Evidence from the US," *The World Economy* 33:2 (February), 203–20.

Andersson, M., and H. Lööf (2011), "Agglomeration and Productivity: Evidence from Firm-Level Data," *Annals of Regional Science* 46:3 (June), 601–20.

Anonymous (1955), "Productivity in Italian Industry," *Productivity Measurement Review* 3 (November), 27–29.

Applebaum, E. (1979), "Testing Price Taking Behavior," *Journal of Econometrics* 9:3 (February), 283–94.

359

Arocena, P., L. Blázquez, and E. Grifell-Tatjé (2011), "Assessing the Consequences of Industry Restructuring on Firms' Performance," *Journal of Economic Policy Reform* 14:1 (March), 21–39.

Arruñada Sanchez, B. (1987), "Los Excedentes de Productividad de la Banca Privada," *Investigaciones Económicas*, segunda época, 11:1, 151–78.

Arthur D. Little (2008), *Five Habits of Highly Efficient Banks*. www.adl.com/uploads/tx_extthoughtleadership/ADL_Five_Habits_of_Highly_Efficient_Banks.pdf

Asaftei, G. (2008), "The Contribution of Product Mix versus Efficiency and Technical Change in US Banking," *Journal of Banking & Finance* 32:11 (November), 2336–45.

Atkinson, T. (2005), *Atkinson Review: Final Report; Measurement of Government Output and Productivity for the National Accounts*. New York: Palgrave Macmillan.

Aw, B. Y., S. Chung, and M. J. Roberts (2003), "Productivity, Output, and Failure: A Comparison of Taiwanese and Korean Manufacturers," *Economic Journal* 113 (November), F485–510.

Bahiri, S., and H. W. Martin (1970), "Productivity Costing and Management," *Management International Review* 10:1, 55–77.

Balk, B. M. (1998), *Industrial Price, Quantity and Productivity Indexes*. Boston: Kluwer Academic Publishers.

Balk, B. M. (2003), "The Residual: On Monitoring and Benchmarking Firms, Industries, and Economies with Respect to Productivity," *Journal of Productivity Analysis* 20:1 (July), 5–47.

Balk, B. M. (2004), "Decompositions of Fisher Indexes," *Economics Letters* 82:1 (January), 107–13.

Balk, B. M. (2008), *Price and Quantity Index Numbers: Models for Measuring Aggregate Change and Difference*. New York: Cambridge University Press.

Balk, B. M. (2009), "On the Relation Between Gross Output- and Value Added-Based Productivity Measures: The Importance of the Domar Factor," *Macroeconomic Dynamics* 13 (Supplement 2), 241–67.

Balk, B. M. (2010), "An Assumption-free Framework for Measuring Productivity Change," *Review of Income and Wealth* 56:1 (June), S224–56.

Banker, R. D., H.-H. Chang, and S. K. Majumdar (1993), "Analyzing the Underlying Dimensions of Firm Profitability," *Managerial and Decision Economics* 14:1 (January–February), 25–36.

Banker, R. D., H.-H. Chang, and S. K. Majumdar (1995), "The Consequences of Evolving Competition on the Components of Firms' Profits: Recent Evidence from the U.S. Telecommunications Industry," *Information Economics and Policy* 7:1 (April), 37–56.

Banker, R. D., H.-H. Chang, and S. K. Majumdar (1996a), "Profitability, Productivity and Price Recovery Patterns in the U.S. Telecommunications Industry," *Review of Industrial Organization* 11:1 (February), 1–17.

Banker, R. D., H.-H. Chang, and S. K. Majumdar (1996b), "A Framework for Analyzing Changes in Strategic Performance," *Strategic Management Journal* 17:9 (November), 693–712.

Banker, R. D., S. M. Datar, and R. S. Kaplan (1989), "Productivity Measurement and Management Accounting," *Journal of Accounting, Auditing and Finance* 4:4 (Fall), 528–54.

Baños-Caballero, S., P. J. García-Teruel, and P. Martínez-Solano (2012), "How does Working Capital Management Affect the Profitability of Spanish SMEs?" *Small Business Economics* 39:2 (September), 517–29.

Barnes, P. (2011), "Multifactor Productivity Growth Cycles at the Industry Level," Australian Productivity Commission Staff Working Paper. http://www.pc.gov.au/research/staff-working/industry-multifactor-productivity

Bartelsman, E., J. Haltiwanger, and S. Scarpetta (2013), "Cross-Country Differences in Productivity: The Role of Allocation and Selection," *American Economic Review* 103:1 (February), 305–34.

Bashan, O., Y. Goldschmidt, G. Levkowitz, and L. Shashua (1973), "Laspeyres Indexes for Variance Analysis in Cost Accounting," *Accounting Review* 48:4 (October), 790–93.

Basu, S., and J. Fernald (2001), "Why Is Productivity Procyclical? Why Do We Care," Chapter 7 in C. R. Hulten, E. R. Dean, and M. J. Harper, eds., *New Developments in Productivity Analysis*. Chicago: University of Chicago Press, pp. 225–96.

BEA (United States Department of Commerce, Bureau of Economic Analysis) (2011), "Returns for Domestic Nonfinancial Business," *Survey of Current Business* 91: 6 (June), 24–28. bea.gov/scb/pdf/2011/06June/0611_domestic.pdf

Belcher, J. G., Jr (1987), *Productivity Plus +*. Houston: Gulf Publishing Co.

Bell, S. (1940), *Productivity, Wages, and National Income*. Washington, DC: The Brookings Institution.

Benner, M. J., and F. M. Veloso (2008), "ISO 9000 Practices and Financial Performance: A Technology Coherence Perspective," *Journal of Operations Management* 26:5 (September), 611–29.

Bennet, T. L. (1920), "The Theory of Measurement of Changes in Cost of Living," *Journal of the Royal Statistical Society* 83:3 (May), 455–62.

Bernard, A. B., S. J. Redding, and P. K. Schott (2010), "Multiple-Product Firms and Product Switching," *American Economic Review* 100:1 (January), 70–97.

Berndt, E. R., and C. J. Morrison (1981), "Capacity Utilization Measures: Underlying Economic Theory and an Alternative Approach," *American Economic Review* 71:2 (May), 48–52.

Bjurek, H. (1996), "The Malmquist Total Factor Productivity Index," *Scandinavian Journal of Economics* 98:2, 303–13.

Black, S. E., and L. M. Lynch (2004), "What's Driving the New Economy? The Benefits of Workplace Innovation," *Economic Journal* 114 (February), F97–116.

Blázquez Gómez, L. and E. Grifell-Tatjé (2008), "Multi-Output Compensation System in Electricity Distribution: The Case of Spain," *Hacienda Pública Española / Revista de Economía Pública* 185:2, 115–49.

Bliss, J. H. (1923), *Financial and Operating Ratios in Management*. New York: The Ronald Press Co.

Bloom, N., B. Eifert, A. Mahajan, D. McKenzie, and J. Roberts (2013), "Does Management Matter? Evidence from India," *Quarterly Journal of Economics* 128:1 (February), 1–51.

Bloom, N., C. Genakos, R. Sadun, and J. Van Reenen (2012), "Management Practices Across Firms and Countries," *Academy of Management Perspectives* 26:1 (February), 12–33.

Bloom, N., R. Sadun, and J. Van Reenen (2012), "Americans Do It Better: US Multinationals and the Productivity Miracle," *American Economic Review* 102:1 (February), 167–201.

Bloom, N., and J. Van Reenen (2007), "Measuring and Explaining Management Practices Across Firms and Countries," *Quarterly Journal of Economics* 122:4 (November), 1351–408.

Bloom, N., and J. Van Reenen (2010), "Why Do Management Practices Differ Across Firms and Countries?" *Journal of Economic Perspectives* 24:1 (Winter), 203–24.

Bloom, N., and J. Van Reenen (2011), "Human Resource Management and Productivity," Chapter 19 in D. Card and O. Ashenfelter, eds., *Handbook of Labor Economics, Volume IV*. Amsterdam: Elsevier, pp. 1697–767.

BLS (United States Department of Labor, Bureau of Labor Statistics), *Productivity Page*. www.bls.gov/bls/productivity.htm

Boel, B. (2003), *The European Productivity Agency and Transatlantic Relations, 1953–1961*. Copenhagen: The University of Copenhagen Museum Tusculanum Press.

Bonini, S., T. M. Koller, and P. H. Mirvis (2009), "Valuing Social Responsibility Programs," *McKinsey Quarterly* (July).

Borenstein, S., and J. Farrell (2000), "Is Cost-Cutting Evidence of X-Inefficiency?" *American Economic Review* 90:2 (May), 224–27.

Bowley, A. L. (1928), "Notes on Index Numbers," *Economic Journal* 38:150 (June), 216–37.

Brayton, G. N. (1985), "Productivity Measure Aids in Profit Analysis," *Management Accounting* (January), 54–58.

Brea, H., E. Grifell-Tatjé, and C. A. K. Lovell (2011), "Testing the Product Test," *Economics Letters* 113:2 (November), 157–59.

Brea-Solís, H., R. Casadesus-Masanell, and E. Grifell-Tatjé (in press), "Business Model Evaluation: Quantifying Wal-Mart's Sources of Advantage," *Strategic Entrepreneurship Journal, Special Issue on Business Models*.

Cahen, L. (1960), "Évolution de la Productivité Globale dans l'Extraction Française de Charbon," *Études et Conjoncture*, November, 886–991.

Callen, J. L. (1988), "An Index Number Theory of Accounting Cost Variances," *Journal of Accounting, Auditing and Finance* (Summer), 87–112.

Castellani, D., and F. Pieri (2013), "R&D Offshoring and the Productivity Growth of European Regions," *Research Policy* 42:9 (November), 1581–94.

Casu, B., A. Ferrari, and T. Zhao (2013), "Regulatory Reform and Productivity Change in Indian Banking," *Review of Economics and Statistics* 95:3 (July), 1066–77.

Caves, D. W., L. R. Christensen, and W. E. Diewert (1982), "The Economic Theory of Index Numbers and the Measurement of Input, Output, and Productivity," *Econometrica* 50:6 (November), 1393–414.

Caves, D. W., L. R. Christensen, and J. A. Swanson (1980), "Productivity in U.S. Railroads, 1951–1974," *Bell Journal of Economics* 11:1 (Spring), 166–81.

CERC (Centre d'Étude des Revenus et des Coûts) (1969a), "'Surplus de Productivité Globale' et 'Comptes de Surplus'," Documents du Centre d'Étude des Revenus et des Coûts, n° 1, 1ᵉʳ trimestre. Paris: CERC.

CERC (Centre d'Étude des Revenus et des Coûts) (1969b), "Productivité Globale et Comptes de Surplus de la SNCF," Documents du Centre d'Étude des Revenus et des Coûts, n° 3/4, 3ᵉ et 4ᵉ trimestres. Paris: CERC.

CERC (Centre d'Étude des Revenus et des Coûts) (1970), "Productivité Globale et Comptes de Surplus du Gaz de France," Documents du Centre d'Étude des Revenus et des Coûts, n° 8, 4ᵉ trimestre. Paris: CERC.

CERC (Centre d'Étude des Revenus et des Coûts) (1971), "Productivité Globale et Comptes de Surplus des Charbonnages de France," Documents du Centre d'Étude des Revenus et des Coûts, n° 11, 3ᵉ trimestre. Paris: CERC.

CERC (Centre d'Étude des Revenus et des Coûts) (1972), "Productivité Globale et Comptes de Surplus d'Électricité de France," Documents du Centre d'Étude des Revenus et des Coûts, n° 13, 1ᵉʳ trimestre. Paris: CERC.

CERC (Centre d'Étude des Revenus et des Coûts) (1980), "Productivité Globale et Comptes de Surplus," Documents du Centre d'Étude des Revenus et des Coûts, n ° 55/56, 3ᵉ et 4ᵉ trimestre. Paris: CERC.

Chandler, A. D. (1962), *Strategy and Structure: Chapters on the History of the Industrial Enterprise.* Cambridge, MA: The MIT Press.

Chapron, J.-E., and Y. Geffroy (1984), "Répartition des Gains de Productivité et Inflation," in E. Archambault and O. Arkhipoff, eds., *Études de Comptabilité Nationale.* Paris: Economica.

Charnes, A., W. W. Cooper, and E. Rhodes (1978), "Measuring the Efficiency of Decision-Making Units," *European Journal of Operational Research* 2:6 (November), 429–44.

Chaudry, M. A. (1982), "Projecting Productivity to the Bottom Line," *Productivity Brief* 18 (October),1–8.

Chaudry, M. A., M. Burnside, and D. Eldor (1985), "NIPA: A Model for Net Income and Productivity Analysis," Chapter 4 in A. Dogramaci and N. R. Adam, eds., *Managerial Issues in Productivity Analysis.* Boston: Kluwer-Nijhoff Publishing, pp. 81–108.

Cobb, C., and P. H. Douglas (1928), "A Theory of Production," *American Economic Review* Supplement, 18, 139–65.

Coelli, T., E. Grifell-Tatjé, and S. Perelman (2002), "Capacity Utilisation and Profitability: A Decomposition of Short-Run Profitability," *International Journal of Production Economics* 79:3 (October), 261–78.

Cohen, J. P. (2010), "The Broader Effects of Transportation Infrastructure: Spatial Econometrics and Productivity Approaches," *Transportation Research Part E* 46:3 (May), 317–26.

Collard-Wexler, A., and J. De Loecker (in press), "Reallocation and Technology: Evidence from the U.S. Steel Industry," *American Economic Review.*

Cooper, W. W., L. M. Seiford, and K. Tone (2000), *Data Envelopment Analysis: A Comprehensive Text with Models, Applications, References and DEA-Solver Software.* Boston: Kluwer Academic Publishers.

Copeland, M. A. (1937), "Concepts of National Income," *Studies in Income and Wealth, Volume 1*. New York: National Bureau of Economic Research.

Copeland, M. A., and E. M. Martin (1938), "The Correction of Wealth and Income Estimates for Price Changes," *Studies in Income and Wealth, Volume 2*. New York: National Bureau of Economic Research.

Corbett, C. J., M. J. Montes-Sancho, and D. A. Kirsch (2005), "The Financial Impact of ISO 9000 Certification in the United States: An Empirical Analysis," *Management Science* 51:7 (July), 1046–59.

Corrado, C., and J. Mattey (1997), "Capacity Utilization," *Journal of Economic Perspectives* 11:1 (Winter), 151–67.

Corredor, P., and S. Goñi (2011), "TQM and Performance: Is the Relationship So Obvious?" *Journal of Business Research* 64:8 (August), 830–38.

Costanza, A. (1955), "Osservazioni sul concetto e sulla misura della produttivita," *Produttivita*, 317–22.

Courbis, R., and P. Templé (1975), "La Méthode des 'Comptes de Surplus' et ses Applications Macroéconomiques," *Collections de l'NSEE* 160, Série C, n° 35, Juillet, 1–100.

Crafts, N. (2004), "Steam as a General Purpose Technology: A Growth Accounting Perspective," *Economic Journal* 114 (April), 338–51.

Cruz-Cázares, C., C. Bayona-Sáez, and T. García-Marco (2013), "You Can't Manage Right What You Can't Measure Well: Technological Innovation Efficiency," *Research Policy* 42:6–7 (July-August), 1239–50.

Darrough, M. N. (1988), "Variance Analysis: A Unifying Cost Function Approach," *Contemporary Accounting Research* 5:1, 199–221.

David, P. A. (1990), "The Dynamo and the Computer: An Historical Perspective on the Modern Productivity Paradox," *American Economic Review* 80:2 (May), 355–61.

Davis, E., and J. Kay (1990), "Assessing Corporate Performance," *Business Strategy Review* 1:2 (June), 1–16.

Davis, H. S. (1947), *The Industrial Study of Economic Progress*. Philadelphia: University of Pennsylvania Press.

Davis, H. S. (1955), *Productivity Accounting*. Philadelphia: University of Pennsylvania Press.

Davis, I. (2005), "The Biggest Contract," *The Economist*, May 26.

Davis, J. J. (1927), "The Problem of the Worker Displaced by Machinery," *Monthly Labor Review* 25:3 (September), 32–34.

Dean, J. (1941), *The Relation of Cost to Output for a Leather Belt Shop*. New York: National Bureau of Economic Research. http://www.nber.org/books/dean41-1

De Borger, B., and K. Kerstens (2000), "The Malmquist Productivity Index and Plant Capacity Utilization," *Scandinavian Journal of Economics* 102:2 (June), 303–10.

Dehning, B., V. J. Richardson, and R. W. Zmud (2007), "The Financial Performance Effects of IT-Based Supply Chain Management Systems in Manufacturing Firms," *Journal of Operations Management* 25:4 (June), 806–24.

Denison, E. F. (1962), *The Sources of Economic Growth in the United States and the Alternatives Before Us*. Supplementary Paper 13, Committee for Economic Development.

Denison, E. F. (1974), *Accounting for United States Economic Growth 1929–1969.* Washington, DC: The Brookings Institution.

Denny, M., M. Fuss, and L. Waverman (1981), "The Measurement and Interpretation of Total Factor Productivity in Regulated Industries, with an Application to Canadian Telecommunications," Chapter 8 in T. G. Cowing and R. Stevenson, eds., *Productivity Measurement in Regulated Industries.* New York: Academic Press, pp. 179–218.

De Witte, K., and D. S. Saal (2010), "Is a Little Sunshine All We Need? On the Impact of Sunshine Regulation on Profits, Productivity and Prices in the Dutch Drinking Water Sector," *Journal of Regulatory Economics* 37:3 (June), 219–42.

Diebold, J. (1952), "The Significance of Productivity Data," *Harvard Business Review* 30:4 (July/August), 53–63.

Diewert, W. E. (1981), "The Economic Theory of Index Numbers: A Survey," Chapter 7 in A. Deaton, ed., *Essays in the Theory and Measurement of Consumer Behaviour in Honour of Sir Richard Stone.* Cambridge: Cambridge University Press, pp. 163–208.

Diewert, W. E. (1992), "The Measurement of Productivity," *Bulletin of Economic Research* 44:3, 163–98.

Diewert, W. E. (2005), "Index Number Theory Using Differences Rather than Ratios," *American Journal of Economics and Sociology* 64:1 (January), 311–60.

Diewert, W. E. (2008), "Index Numbers," *The New Palgrave Dictionary of Economics Online.* www.dictionaryofeconomics.com/dictionary

Diewert, W. E. (2011), "Measuring Productivity in the Public Sector: Some Conceptual Problems," *Journal of Productivity Analysis* 36:2 (October), 177–91.

Diewert, W. E. (2012), "The Measurement of Productivity in the Nonmarket Sector," *Journal of Productivity Analysis* 37:3 (June), 217–29.

Diewert, W. E. (2014), "Decompositions of Profitability Change Using Cost Functions," *Journal of Econometrics.* DOI: 10.1016/j.jeconom.2014.06.009.

Diewert, W. E., and A. O. Nakamura (2007), "The Measurement of Productivity for Nations," Chapter 66 in J. Heckman and E. Leamer, eds., *Handbook of Econometrics, Volume 6A.* Amsterdam: Elsevier BV, pp. 4501–86.

Dohrmann, T., and G. Pinshaw (2009), "The Road to Improved Tax Compliance: A McKinsey Benchmarking Study of Tax Administrations – 2008–2009," www.mckinsey.com

Domar, E. D. (1961), "On the Measurement of Technological Change," *Economic Journal* 71:284 (December), 709–29.

Domar, E. D. (1966), "The Soviet Collective Farm as a Producer Cooperative," *American Economic Review* 56:4 (September), 734–57.

Downie, J. (1958), *The Competitive Process.* London: Gerald Duckworth & Co.

Draca, M., R. Sadun, and J. Van Reenen (2007), "Productivity and ICTs: A Review of the Evidence," Chapter 5 in R. Mansell, C. Avgerou, D. Quah, and R. Silverstone, eds., *The Oxford Handbook of Information and Communication Technologies.* Oxford: Oxford University Press, pp. 100–47.

Drucker, P. F. (1954), *The Practice of Management.* New York: Harper & Row.

Drucker, P. F. (1955), "'Management Science' and the Manager," *Management Science* 1:2 (January), 115–26.

Duan, J.-C., J. Sun, and T. Wang (2012), "Multiperiod Corporate Default Prediction – A Forward Intensity Approach," *Journal of Econometrics* 170:1 (September), 191–209.

Eakin, B. K., A. T. Bozzo, M. E. Meitzen, and P. E. Schoech (2010), "Railroad Performance Under the Staggers Act," *Regulation* 33:4 (Winter), 32–38.

Edgeworth, F. Y. (1925), *Papers Relating to Political Economy, Volume I*. London: Macmillan and Co., Ltd.

Eichhorn, W. and J. Voeller (1976), *Theory of the Price Index*. Lecture Notes in Economics and Mathematical Systems 140. Berlin: Springer-Verlag.

Eilon, S. (1984), *The Art of Reckoning – Analysis of Performance Criteria*. London: Academic Press.

Eilon, S., B. Gold, and J. Soesan (1975), "A Productivity Study in a Chemical Plant," *Omega* 3:3, 329–43.

Eilon, S,. B. Gold, and J. Soesan (1976), *Applied Productivity Analysis for Industry*. Oxford: Pergamon Press.

Eilon, S., and J. Teague (1973), "On Measures of Productivity," *Omega* 1:5, 505–11.

Eldor, D., and E. Sudit (1981), "Productivity-based Financial Net Income Analysis," *Omega* 9:6, 605–11.

Eslava, M., J. Haltiwanger, A. Kugler, and M. Kugler (2004), "The Effects of Structural Reforms on Productivity and Profitability Enhancing Reallocation: Evidence from Colombia," *Journal of Development Economics* 75:2 (December), 333–71.

Eslava, M., J. Haltiwanger, A. Kugler, and M. Kugler (2010), "Factor Adjustments After Deregulation: Panel Evidence from Colombian Plants," *Review of Economics and Statistics* 92:2 (May), 378–91.

Estache, A., and E. Grifell-Tatjé (2013), "How (un)even Was the Distribution of the Impacts of Mali's Water Privatization across Stakeholders?" *Journal of Development Studies* 49:4 (April), 483–99.

European Productivity Agency (1955–1966), *Productivity Measurement Review*.

European Productivity Agency (1955), *Productivity Measurement I. Concepts*. Paris: Organisation for European Economic Cooperation.

European Productivity Agency (1956), *Productivity Measurement II. Plant Level Measurements Methods and Results*. Paris: Organisation for European Economic Cooperation.

Evans, W. D. (1947), "Recent Productivity Trends and Their Implications," *Journal of the American Statistical Association* 42:238 (June), 211–23.

Executive Office of the President (2013), "The Economic Benefits of Fixing Our Broken Immigration System," report prepared by the National Economic Council, the Domestic Policy Council, the President's Council of Economic Advisors and the Office of Management and Budget, July. http://www.whitehouse.gov/sites/default/files/docs/report.pdf

Fabricant, S. (1940), *The Output of Manufacturing Industries, 1899–1937*. New York: National Bureau of Economic Research.

Fabricant, S. (1961), "Basic Facts on Productivity Change," pp. xxxv–lii in Kendrick (1961), also issued as National Bureau of Economic Research Occasional Paper 63, New York, National Bureau of Economic Research, 1959.

FAO (United Nations Food and Agriculture Organization) (2000), "Report of the Technical Consultation on the Measurement of Fishing Capacity," FAO Fisheries Report No. 615, Rome.

Färe, R., S. Grosskopf, and J. Kirkley (2000), "Multi-Output Capacity Measures and Their Relevance for Productivity," *Bulletin of Economic Research* 52:2 (April), 101–12.

Färe, R., S. Grosskopf, and E. C. Kokkelenberg (1989), "Measuring Plant Capacity, Utilization and Technical Change: A Nonparametric Approach," *International Economic Review* 30:3 (August), 655–66.

Färe, R., S. Grosskopf, and P. Roos (1996), "On Two Definitions of Productivity," *Economics Letters* 53:3 (December), 269–74.

Färe, R., and D. Primont (1995), *Multi-Output Production and Duality: Theory and Applications*. Boston: Kluwer Academic Publishers.

Farrell, M. J. (1957), "The Measurement of Productive Efficiency," *Journal of the Royal Statistical Society, Series A, General*, 120:3, 253–82.

Fernald, J., and B. Neiman (2011), "Growth Accounting with Misallocation: Or, Doing Less with More in Singapore," *American Economic Journal: Macroeconomics* 3:2 (April), 29–74.

Feyrer, J. (2011), "The US Productivity Slowdown, the Baby Boom, and Management Quality," *Journal of Population Economics* 24:1 (January), 267–84.

Field, A. J. (2003), "The Most Technologically Progressive Decade of the Century," *American Economic Review* 93:4 (September), 1399–413.

Fisher, I. (1922), *The Making of Index Numbers*. Boston: Houghton Mifflin.

Fisher, T. J. (1990), "Business Productivity Measurement using Standard Cost Accounting Information," *International Journal of Operations & Production Management* 10:8, 61–69.

Fluet, C., and P. Lefebvre (1987), "The Sharing of Total Factor Productivity Gains in Canadian Manufacturing: A Price Accounting Approach 1965–1980," *Applied Economics* 19:2 (February), 245–57.

Foster, L., J. Haltiwanger, and C. Syverson (2008), "Reallocation, Firm Turnover, and Efficiency: Selection on Productivity or Profitability?" *American Economic Review* 98:1 (March), 394–425.

Fourastié, J. (1957), *Productivity, Prices and Wages*. Paris: European Productivity Agency.

Fox, J. T., and V. Smeets (2011), "Does Input Quality Drive Measured Differences in Firm Productivity?" *International Economic Review* 52:4 (November), 961–89.

Frankel, M. (1963), "Review of Kendrick & Creamer (1961)," *Journal of the American Statistical Association* 58:301 (March), 258–59.

Fraquelli, G., and D. Vannoni (2000), "Multidimensional Performance in Telecommunications, Regulation and Competition: Analysing the European Major Players," *Information Economics and Policy* 12:1 (March), 27–46.

Freeman, R. B., and M. M. Kleiner (2005), "The Last American Shoe Manufacturers: Decreasing Productivity and Increasing Profits in the Shift from Piece Rates to Continuous Flow Production," *Industrial Relations* 44:2 (April), 307–30.

Fried, H., C. A. K. Lovell, and S. S. Schmidt, eds. (2008), *The Measurement of Productive Efficiency and Productivity Growth*. New York: Oxford University Press.

Friedman, M. (1970), "The Social Responsibility of Business Is to Increase Its Profits," *New York Times Magazine* September 13.

Fuglie, K. O., J. M. MacDonald, and E. Ball (2007), "Productivity Growth in U.S. Agriculture," *EB-9,* Economic Research Service, U.S. Department of Agriculture. www.ers.usda.gov/publications/EB9/eb9.pdf

Gadsby, M. (1921), "Engineers' Report on Industrial Waste," *Monthly Labor Review* 13:3 (September), 493–503.

García Marín, Á., and N. Voigtländer (2013), "Exporting and Plant-Level Efficiency Gains: It's in the Measure," NBER Working Paper No. 19033, May. www.nber.org/papers/w19033

Geels, T. (1988), "Analyse de la Productivité Globale et de la Répartition des Avantages dan les Six Societes Belges de Transports Urbains par la Méthode des Comptes de Surplus," Chapter 5 in B. Thiry and H. Tulkens, eds., *La Performance "Économique des Societés Belges de Transports Urbains.* Liège, Belgium: CIRIEC.

Genescà Garrigosa, E., and E. Grifell-Tatjé (1992), "Profits and Total Factor Productivity: A Comparative Analysis," *Omega* 20:5/6, 553–68.

Georgescu-Roegen, N. (1951), "The Aggregate Linear Production Function and Its Applications to von Neumann's Economic Model," Chapter IV in T. C. Koopmans, ed., *Activity Analysis of Production and Allocation.* New York: John Wiley & Sons, Inc.

Gilchrist, R. R. (1971), *Managing for Profit: The Value Added Concept.* London: George Allen and Unwin.

Gold, B. (1955), *Foundations of Productivity Analysis.* Pittsburgh, PA: University of Pittsburgh Press.

Gold, B. (1971), *Explorations in Managerial Economics: Productivity, Costs, Technology and Growth.* New York: Basic Books.

Gold, B., and R. M. Kraus (1964), "Integrating Physical with Financial Measures for Managerial Controls," *Academy of Management Journal* (June), 109–27.

Greenstone, M., J. A. List, and C. Syverson (2012), "The Effects of Environmental Regulation on the Competitiveness of U.S. Manufacturing," NBER Working Paper No. 18392, September. www.nber.org/papers/w18392

Grifell-Tatjé, E. (2011), "Profit, Productivity and Distribution: Differences Across Organizational Form," *Socio-Economic Planning Sciences* 45:2 (June), 72–83.

Grifell-Tatjé, E., and C. A. K. Lovell (1995), "A Note on the Malmquist Productivity Index," *Economics Letters* 47:2 (February), 169–75.

Grifell-Tatjé, E., and C. A. K. Lovell (1999a), "A Generalized Malmquist Productivity Index," *Top* 7:1, 81–101.

Grifell-Tatjé, E., and C. A. K. Lovell (1999b), "Profits and Productivity," *Management Science* 45:9 (September), 1177–93.

Grifell-Tatjé, E., and C. A. K. Lovell (2000), "Cost and Productivity," *Managerial and Decision Economics* 21:1 (January/February), 19–30.

Grifell-Tatjé, E., and C. A. K. Lovell (2003), "The Managers versus the Consultants," *Scandinavian Journal of Economics* 105:1, 119–38.

Grifell-Tatjé, E., and C. A. K. Lovell (2004), "Decomposing the Dividend," *Journal of Comparative Economics* 32:3 (September), 500–18.

Grifell-Tatjé, E., and C. A. K. Lovell (2008), "Productivity at the Post: Its Drivers and Its Distribution," *Journal of Regulatory Economics* 33:2 (April), 133–58.

Griliches, Z. (2000), *R&D, Education, and Productivity*. Cambridge, MA: Harvard University Press.

Grosskopf, S., K. J. Hayes, L. L. Taylor, and W. L. Weber (1997), "Budget-Constrained Frontier Measures of Fiscal Equality and Efficiency in Schooling," *Review of Economics & Statistics* 79:1 (February), 116–24.

Grosskopf, S. K. J. Hayes, L. L. Taylor, and W. L. Weber (1999), "Anticipating the Consequences of School Reform: A New Use of DEA," *Management Science* 45:4 (April), 608–20.

Grossman, E. S. (1984a), "Company Productivity Measurement," *Business Economics* 19:3 (July), 18–23.

Grossman, E. S. (1984b), "Company Productivity Measurement," Papers in Applied Business Economics, National Association of Business Economists.

Gruen, D. (2012), "The Importance of Productivity," *Productivity Perspectives 2012*. http://www.pc.gov.au/research/conferences/productivity-perspectives/2012

Hadley, D., and X. Irz (2008), "Productivity and Farm Profit: A Microeconomic Analysis of the Cereal Sector in England and Wales," *Applied Economics* 40:5, 613–24.

Hall, R. E., and C. I. Jones (1997), "Levels of Economic Activity Across Countries," *American Economic Review* 87:2 (May), 173–77.

Hansen, D. R., M. M. Mowen, and L. H. Hammer (1992), "Profit-Linked Productivity Measurement," *Journal of Management Accounting Research* 4 (Fall), 79–98.

Hansmann, H. (1988), "Ownership of the Firm," *Journal of Law, Economics and Organization* 4:2 (Fall), 267–304.

Harper, J. (1984), *Measuring Business Performance: A Manager's Guide*. Aldershot, UK: Gower Publishing.

Hayzen, A. J., and J. M. Reeve (2000), "Examining the Relationships in Productivity Accounting," *Management Accounting Quarterly* (Summer), 33–39.

Hendrickson, K. (1961), "Inter-Firm Comparisons at Equal Levels of Utilisation: New Ways of Increasing Efficiency," *Productivity Measurement Review* 24 (February), 31–59.

Hickman, B. G. (1964), "On a New Method of Capacity Estimation," *Journal of the American Statistical Association* 59:306 (June), 529–49.

Hicks, J. R. (1935), "Annual Survey of Economic Theory: The Theory of Monopoly," *Econometrica* 3:1 (January), 1–20.

Hill, R. J. (2006), "Superlative Index Numbers: Not All of Them Are Super," *Journal of Econometrics* 130:1 (January), 25–43.

Hilmola, O.-P. (2006), "As Currency Changes Matter: Improving the Control of Profitability and Productivity in Manufacturing Companies," *International Journal of Productivity and Quality Management* 1:4, 321–38.

Hoch, I. (1955), "Estimation of Production Function Parameters and Testing for Efficiency," *Econometrica* 23:3 (July), 325–26.

Hopper, W. D. (1965), "Allocation Efficiency in Traditional Indian Agriculture," *Journal of Farm Economics* 47:3 (August), 611–24.

Horrigan, J. O. (1968), "A Short History of Financial Ratio Analysis," *Accounting Review* 43:2 (April), 284–94.

Horváthová, E. (2012), "The Impact of Environmental Performance on Firm Performance: Short-term Costs and Long-term Benefits?" *Ecological Economics* 84 (December), 91–97.

Hotelling, H. (1932), "Edgeworth's Taxation Paradox and the Nature of Demand and Supply Functions," *Journal of Political Economy* 40:5 (October), 577–616.

Houéry, N. (1977), *Mesurer la Productivité: Les Comptes de Surplus.* Paris: Dunod.

Hsieh, C.-T. (2002), "What Explains the Industrial Revolution in East Asia? Evidence from the Factor Markets," *American Economic Review* 92:3 (June), 502–26.

Huselid, M. A. (1995), "The Impact of Human Resource Management Practices on Turnover, Productivity, and Corporate Financial Performance," *Academy of Management Journal* 38:3 (June), 635–72.

Ichniowski, C., K. Shaw, and G. Prennushi (1997), "The Effects of Human Resource Management Practices on Productivity: A Study of Steel Finishing Lines," *American Economic Review* 87:3 (June), 291–313.

Ingham, H. (1961), "Inter-Firm Comparison for Management," *Productivity Measurement Review* 26 (August), 5–19.

Ingham, H. (1965), "International Inter-Firm Comparisons: A Discussion on Methods," *Productivity Measurement Review* 41 (May), 81–89.

Ingham, H., and L. T. Harrington (1958), *Interfirm Comparison for Management.* Southampton: The Millbrook Press Ltd.

Iwata, H., and K. Okada (2011), "How Does Environmental Performance Affect Financial Performance? Evidence from Japanese Manufacturing Firms," *Ecological Economics* 70:9 (July), 1691–700.

Jensen, M. C. (2010), "Value Maximization, Stakeholder Theory, and the Corporate Objective Function," *Journal of Applied Corporate Finance* 22:1 (Winter), 32–42.

Jerome, H. (1932), "The Measurement of Productivity Changes and the Displacement of Labor," *American Economic Review* 22:1 (March), 32–40.

Jerome, H. (1934), *Mechanization in Industry.* New York: National Bureau of Economic Research. http://papers.nber.org/books/jero34-1

Johansen, L. (1968), "Production Functions and the Concept of Capacity," in *Recherches Récent sur la Function de Production. Collection Économie Mathématique et Économétrie 2*, Centre d'Études et de la Recherche, Université de Namur, Belgium. [Reprinted as Chapter 19 in F. R. Førsund, ed., *Collected Works of Leif Johansen, Vol 1.* Amsterdam: North-Holland (1987), pp. 359–82.].

Johnson, H. T. (1972), "Early Cost Accounting for Internal Management Control: Lyman Mills in the 1850s," *Business History Review* 46:4 (Winter), 466–74.

Johnson, H. T. (1975), "Management Accounting in an Early Integrated Industrial: E. I. duPont de Nemours Powder Company, 1903–1912," *Business History Review* 49:2 (Summer), 184–204.

Johnson, H. T. (1978), "Management Accounting in an Early Multidivisional Organization: General Motors in the 1920s," *Business History Review* 52:4 (Winter), 490–517.

Johnson, R. C., and G. Noguera (2012), "Proximity and Production Fragmentation," *American Economic Review* 102:3 (May), 407–11.

Jones, G. T. (1933), *Increasing Return.* Cambridge: Cambridge University Press.

Jorgenson, D. W., and Z. Griliches (1967), "The Explanation of Productivity Change," *Review of Economic Studies* 34:3 (July), 249–83.

Kaplan, R. S. (1983), "Measuring Manufacturing Performance: A New Challenge for Managerial Accounting Research," *Accounting Review* 58:4 (October), 686–705.

Kaplan, R. S. (1984), "The Evolution of Management Accounting," *Accounting Review* 59:3 (July), 390–418.

Kaplan, R. S., and D. P. Norton (1992), "The Balanced Scorecard – Measures That Drive Performance," *Harvard Business Review* 70:1 (January–February), 71–79.

Kendrick, J. W. (1961), *Productivity Trends in the United States*. Princeton, NJ: Princeton University Press.

Kendrick, J. W. (1984), *Improving Company Productivity: Handbook with Case Studies*. Baltimore: Johns Hopkins University Press.

Kendrick, J. W., and D. Creamer (1961), *Measuring Company Productivity: Handbook with Case Studies*. Studies in Business Economics 74. New York: The Conference Board.

Kendrick, J. W., and E. S. Grossman (1980), *Productivity in the United States: Trends and Cycles*. Baltimore: Johns Hopkins University Press.

Kilby, P. (1962), "Organization and Productivity in Backward Economies," *Quarterly Journal of Economics* 76:2 (May), 303–10.

Kinney, M. R., and W. F. Wempe (2002), "Further Evidence on the Extent and Origins of JIT's Profitability Effects," *Accounting Review* 77:1 (January), 203–25.

Kitzmuller, M., and J. Shimshack (2012), "Economic Perspectives on Corporate Social Responsibility," *Journal of Economic Literature* 50:1 (March), 51–84.

Klein, L. R. (1960), "Some Theoretical Issues in the Measurement of Capacity," *Econometrica* 28:2 (April), 272–86.

Klein. P. G., and H. Luu (2003), "Politics and Productivity," *Economic Inquiry* 41:3 (July), 433–47.

Kline, C. A., Jr., and H. L. Hessler (1952), "The du Pont Chart System for Appraising Operating Performance," *N. A. C. A. Bulletin* (August, Section 3), 1595–619.

Konüs, A. (1939), "The Problem of the True Index of the Cost of Living," *Econometrica* 7:1 (January), 10–29.

Koopmans, T. C. (1951), "Analysis of Production as an Efficient Combination of Activities," Chapter III in T. C. Koopmans, ed., *Activity Analysis of Production and Allocation*. New York: John Wiley & Sons, Inc., pp. 33–97.

Kraus, J. (1978), "Productivity and Profit Models of the Firm," *Business Economics*, 13:4 (September), 10–14.

Kumbhakar, S. C., and C. A. K. Lovell (2000), *Stochastic Frontier Analysis*. New York: Cambridge University Press.

Kuosmanen, T., and T. Sipiläinen (2009), "Exact Decomposition of the Fisher Ideal Total Factor Productivity Index," *Journal of Productivity Analysis* 31:3 (June), 137–50.

Kurosawa, K. (1975), "An Aggregate Index for the Analysis of Productivity and Profitability," *Omega* 3:2, 157–68.

Kurosawa, K. (1991), *Productivity Measurement and Management at the Company Level: The Japanese Experience*. Amsterdam: Elsevier.

Kutlu, L., and R. C. Sickles (2012), "Estimation of Market Power in the Presence of Firm Level Inefficiencies," *Journal of Econometrics* 168:1 (May), 141–55.

Landes, D. S. (1990), "Why Are We So Rich and They So Poor?" *American Economic Review* 80:2 (May), 1–13.

Laspeyres, E. (1871), "Die Berechnung einer mittleren Waarenpreissteigerung," *Jahrbücher für Nationalökonomie und Statistik* 16, 296–314.

Lawrence, D., W. E. Diewert, and K. Fox (2006), "The Contributions of Productivity, Price Changes and Firm Size to Profitability," *Journal of Productivity Analysis* 26:1 (August), 1–13.

Lee, J.-D., S.-B. Park, and T.-Y. Kim (1999), "Profit, Productivity, and Price Differential: An International Performance Comparison of the Natural Gas Transportation Industry," *Energy Policy* 27:11 (October), 679–89.

de Leeuw, F. (1962), "The Concept of Capacity," *Journal of the American Statistical Association* 57:300 (December), 826–40.

Lehmann, E., S. Warning, and J. Weigand (2004), "Governance Structures, Multidimensional Efficiency and Firm Profitability," *Journal of Management and Governance* 8:3, 279–304.

Lewis, W. W. (2004), *The Power of Productivity*. Chicago: The University of Chicago Press.

Lim, S. H., and C. A. K. Lovell (2008), "Short-run Total Cost Change and Productivity of U.S. Class I Railroads," *Journal of Transport Economics and Policy* 42:1 (January), 155–88.

Lim, S. H., and C. A. K. Lovell (2009), "Profit and Productivity of U.S. Class I Railroads," *Managerial and Decision Economics* 30:7 (October), 423–42.

Lindebo, E., A. Hoff, and N. Vestergaard (2007), "Revenue-based Capacity Utilisation Measures and Decomposition: The Case of Danish North Sea Trawlers," *European Journal of Operational Research* 180:1 (July), 215–27.

Lioui, A., and Z. Sharma (2012), "Environmental Corporate Social Responsibility and Financial Performance: Disentangling Direct and Indirect Effects," *Ecological Economics* 78 (June), 100–11.

Lo, C. K. Y., A. C. L. Yeung, and T. C. E. Cheng (2012), "The Impact of Environmental Management Systems on Financial Performance in Fashion and Textiles Industries," *International Journal of Production Economics* 135:2 (February), 561–67.

van Loggerenberg, B. J., and S. J. Cucchiaro (1981–82), "Productivity Measurement and the Bottom Line," *National Productivity Review* (Winter), 87–99.

Lovell, C. A. K. (2003), "The Decomposition of Malmquist Productivity Indexes," *Journal of Productivity Analysis* 20:3 (November), 437–58.

Lovell, C. A. K., and J. E. Lovell (2013), "Productivity Decline in Australian Coal Mining," *Journal of Productivity Analysis* 40:3 (December), 443–55.

Lückerath-Rovers, M. (2013), "Women on Boards and Firm Performance," *Journal of Management and Governance* 17:2 (May), 491–509.

Machlup, F. (1952), *The Economics of Sellers' Competition*. Baltimore: The Johns Hopkins Press.

Malmquist, S. (1953), "Index Numbers and Indifference Surfaces," *Trabajos de Estadística* 4, 209–42.

Marshall, A. (1887), "Remedies for Fluctuations of General Prices," *Contemporary Review* 51 (March), 355–75. Reprinted as Chapter 8 in A. C. Pigou, ed., *Memorials of Alfred Marshall*. London: Macmillan, 1925.

Marshall, A. (1892), *Elements of Economics of Industry*. London: Macmillan.

Mason, E. S. (1941), "Preface" to Dean (1941).

Maxwell, W. D. (1965), "Short-Run Returns to Scale and the Production of Services," *Southern Economic Journal* 32:1 (July), 1–14.

McKinsey & Company, *McKinsey Quarterly*. www.mckinsey.com

McKinsey & Company, McKinsey Global Institute. www.mckinsey.com

Mensah, Y. M. (1982), "A Dynamic Approach to the Evaluation of Input-Variable Cost Center Performance," *Accounting Review* 57:4 (October), 681–700.

Méraud, J. (1966), "Introduction a la Journée d'Études du 14 Décembre 1966." [Published as an appendix to CERC (1969a)]

Mevellec, P. (1977), "La Méthode des Surplus Appliquée aux Coopératives Agricoles," *Revue des Études Coopératives* 187, 23–59.

Miller, D. M. (1984), "Profitability = Productivity + Price Recovery," *Harvard Business Review* 62:3 (May/June), 145–53.

Miller, D. M., and P. M. Rao (1989), "Analysis of Profit-Linked Total-Factor Productivity Measurement Models at the Firm Level," *Management Science* 35:6 (June), 757–67.

Mills, F. C. (1937), "Industrial Productivity and Prices," *Journal of the American Statistical Association* 32:198 (June), 247–62.

Moorsteen, R. H. (1961), "On Measuring Productive Potential and Relative Efficiency," *Quarterly Journal of Economics* 75:3 (August), 451–67.

Mundlak, Y. (1961), "Empirical Production Function Free of Management Bias," *Journal of Farm Economics* 43:1 (February), 44–56.

Nerlove, M. (1963), "Returns to Scale in Electricity Supply," in C. Crist et al., eds., *Measurement in Economics: Studies in Mathematical Economics and Econometrics in Memory of Yehuda Grunfeld*. Stanford: Stanford University Press, pp. 167–98.

von Neumann, J. (1945–46), "A Model of General Economic Equilibrium," *Review of Economic Studies* 13, 1–9.

New South Wales Treasury (1999), "Profit Composition Analysis: A Technique for Linking Productivity Measurement & Financial Performance," Office of Financial Management Research & Information Paper TRP 99-5, New South Wales Treasury, Sydney, Australia. www.treasury.nsw.gov.au/indexes/trpindex.html

Nickell, S. (1995), *The Performance of Companies*. Oxford, UK and Cambridge, USA: Blackwell.

Norman, R. G., and S. Bahiri (1972), *Productivity Measurement and Incentives*. London: Butterworths.

North, D. C. (1990), *Institutions, Institutional Change and Economic Performance*. Cambridge: Cambridge University Press.

O'Donnell, A. T., and J. K. Swales (1982), "A Note on Profitability as a Measure of Company Efficiency," *Managerial and Decision Economics* 3:4 (December), 188–93.

374   Bibliography

O'Donnell, C. J. (2012a), "Nonparametric Estimates of the Components of Productivity and Profitability Change in U.S. Agriculture," *American Journal of Agricultural Economics* 94:4 (July), 873–90.

O'Donnell, C. J. (2012b), "An Aggregate Quantity Framework for Measuring and Decomposing Productivity Change," *Journal of Productivity Analysis* 38:3 (December), 255–72.

OECD (Organization for Economic Co-operation and Development), *Economy Page.* www.oecd.org/economy/

Ohanian, L. E. (2001), "Why Did Productivity Fall So Much During the Great Depression?" *American Economic Review* 91:2 (May), 34–38.

Paasche, H. (1874), "Ueber die Preisentwicklung der letzten Jahre nach den Hamburger Börsennotierungen," *Jahrbücher für Nationalökonomie und Statistik* 23, 168–78.

Palepu, K. G., and P. M. Healy (2008), *Business Analysis & Valuation,* Fourth Edition, *Text & Cases.* Mason OH: South-Western Cengage Learning.

Paul, C. J. M. (1999), *Cost Structure and the Measurement of Economic Performance.* Boston: Kluwer Academic Publishers.

PC (Australian Productivity Commission) (2001), *Cost Recovery by Government Agencies.* www.pc.gov.au/projects/inquiry/costrecovery/docs/finalreport

PC (Australian Productivity Commission) (2008), *Financial Performance of Government Trading Enterprises, 2004–05 to 2006–07.* www.pc.gov.au/research/commission/gte0607

Penrose, E. T. (1959), *The Theory of the Growth of the Firm.* Oxford: Basil Blackwell.

Peri, G. (2012), "The Effect of Immigration on Productivity: Evidence from US States," *Review of Economics & Statistics* 94:1 (February), 348–58.

Perrin, J. (1975), "Comptes de Surplus Pour Un Nouveau Tableau de Bord de l'Entreprise," *Revue Française de Gestion* 2 (Novembre–Décembre), 35–40.

Poschke, M. (2010), "The Regulation of Entry and Aggregate Productivity," *Economic Journal* 120:549 (December), 1175–200.

Premachandra, I. M., Y. Chen, and J. Watson (2011), "DEA as a Tool for Predicting Corporate Failure and Success: A Case of Bankruptcy Assessment," *Omega* 39:6 (December), 620–26.

Puiseux, L., and P. Bernard (1965), "Les Progrès de Productivité et Leur Utilisation a l'Électricité de France de 1952 a 1962," *Études et Conjoncture* (Janvier), 77–98.

Puiseux, L., and P. Bernard (1966), "Essai de Mesure de la Productivité Globale des Facteurs a l'Électricité de France de 1954 a 1962," *Revue Française de L'Energie* 180 (Mai), 421–40.

Quirk, J. P., and R. D. Fort (1997), *Pay Dirt: The Business of Professional Team Sports.* Princeton: Princeton University Press.

Rao, M. P. (2000), "A Simple Method to Link Productivity to Profitability," *Management Accounting Quarterly* (Summer), 12–17.

Rao, M. P. (2002), "Evaluating the Impact of IT Investments Using the PPP Model," *Decision Sciences Institute 2002 Annual Meeting Proceedings* 1192–97.

Rao, M. P. (2006), "A Performance Measurement System Using a Profit-Linked Multi-Factor Measurement Model," *Industrial Management & Data Systems* 106:3, 362–79.

Ray, S. C., and E. Desli (1997), "Productivity Growth, Technical Progress, and Efficiency Change in Industrialized Countries: Comment," *American Economic Review* 87:5 (December), 1033–39.

Ray, S. C., and K. Mukherjee (1996), "Decomposition of the Fisher Ideal Index of Productivity: A Nonparametric Dual Analysis of U.S. Airlines Data," *Economic Journal* 106:439 (November), 1659–78.

Rodriguez-Álvarez, A., D. Roibás-Alonso, and A. Wall (2013), "The Response of Decentralized Health Services to Demand Uncertainty and the Role of Political Parties in the Spanish Public Health System," *Journal of Productivity Analysis* 40:3 (December), 357–65.

Roger-Machart, J. (1969), "Progrès de Globale et Politique de Répartition des Surplus a l'Électricité de France de 1954 a 1966," *Revue Française de l'Énergie* 20:211 (Mai), 351–70.

Rostas, L. (1943), "Industrial Production, Productivity and Distribution in Britain, Germany and the United States," *Economic Journal* 53:209 (April), 39–54.

Rowan, D. C., and J. H. Dunning (1968), "Inter-Firm Efficiency Comparisons: U.S. and U.K. Manufacturing Enterprises in Britain," *Banca Nazionale del Lavoro* 21, 132–82.

Saal, D. S., and D. Parker (2001), "Productivity and Price Performance in the Privatized Water and Sewerage Companies of England and Wales," *Journal of Regulatory Economics* 20:1 (July), 61–90.

Sahoo, B. K., and K. Tone (2009), "Radial and Non-Radial Decompositions of Profit Change: With an Application to Indian Banking," *European Journal of Operational Research* 196:3 (August), 1130–46.

Salerian, J. (2003), "Analysing the Performance of Firms Using a Decomposable Ideal Index Number to Link Profit, Prices and Productivity," *Australian Economic Review* 36:2 (June), 143–55.

Salter, W. E. G. (1966), *Productivity and Technical Change*, Second Edition. Cambridge: Cambridge University Press.

Schaible, S. (1981), "A Survey of Fractional Programming," in S. Schaible and W. T. Ziemba, eds., *Generalized Concavity in Optimization and Economics*. New York: Academic Press, pp. 417–39.

Schmitt, A., and J. Van Biesebroeck (2013), "Proximity Strategies in Outsourcing Relations: The Role of Geographical, Cultural and Relational Proximity in the European Automotive Industry," *Journal of International Business Studies* 44:5 (June/July), 475–503.

Schmitz, J. A., Jr. (2005), "What Determines Productivity? Lessons from the Dramatic Recovery of the U.S. and Canadian Iron Ore Industries Following Their Early 1980s Crisis," *Journal of Political Economy* 113:3 (June), 582–625.

Schoar, A. (2002), "Effects of Corporate Diversification on Productivity," *Journal of Finance* 57:6 (December), 2379–403.

Schultz, T. W. (1964), *Transforming Traditional Agriculture*. New Haven, CT: Yale University Press.

Schultze, C. L. (1963), "Uses of Capacity Measures for Short-Run Economic Analysis," *American Economic Review* 53:2 (May), 293–308.

Scott, J. A. (1950), *The Measurement of Industrial Efficiency.* London: Sir Isaac Pittman & Sons.

Scully, G. W. (1995), *The Market Structure of Sports.* Chicago: University of Chicago Press.

Segerson, K., and D. Squires (1990), "On the Measurement of Economic Capacity Utilization for Multi-Product Industries," *Journal of Econometrics* 44:3 (June), 347–61.

Segerson, K., and D. Squires (1995), "Measurement of Capacity Utilization for Revenue-Maximizing Firms," *Bulletin of Economic Research* 47:1 (January), 77–84.

Sharma, D. S. (2005), "The Association between ISO 9000 Certification and Financial Performance," *International Journal of Accounting* 40:2 (Summer), 151–72.

Shephard, R. W. (1974), *Indirect Production Functions.* Mathematical Systems in Economics, No. 10. Meisenheim Am Glan, Germany: Verlag Anton Hain.

Shubik, M. (2011), "A Note on Accounting and Economic Theory: Past, Present and Future," *Accounting, Economics, and Law* 1:1 www.bepress.com/ael/vol1iss1/1

Siegel, I. H. (1952), *Concepts and Measurement of Production and Productivity.* Washington, DC: US Bureau of Labor Statistics.

Siegel, I. H. (1955), "Aspects of Productivity Measurement and Meaning," Chapter III in European Productivity Agency (1955), pp. 43–59.

Siegel, I. H. (1961), "On the Design of Consistent Output and Input Indexes for Productivity Measurement," in *Output, Input and Productivity Measurement,* National Bureau of Economic Research Studies in Income and Wealth, Volume 25. Princeton, NJ: Princeton University Press, pp. 23–41.

Siegel, I. H. (1980), *Company Productivity: Measurement for Improvement.* Kalamazoo, MI: W. E. Upjohn Institute.

Siegel, I. H. (1986), *Productivity Measurement in Organizations: Private Firms and Public Agencies.* New York: Pergammon Press.

Sink, D. S., T. C. Tuttle, and S. J. DeVries (1984), "Productivity Measurement and Evaluation: What Is Available?" *National Productivity Review* (Summer), 265–87.

Smith, I. G. (1973), *The Measurement of Productivity: A Systems Approach in the Context of Productivity Agreements.* Epping, UK: Gower Press.

Smithies, A. (1957), "Economic Fluctuations and Growth," *Econometrica* 25:1 (January), 1–52.

Soliman, M. T. (2008), "The Use of DuPont Analysis by Market Participants," *The Accounting Review* 83:3 (May), 823–53.

Solow, R. M. (1987), "We'd Better Watch Out," *New York Times* July 12.

Squires, B. M. (1917), "Productivity and Cost of Labor in the Lumber Industry," *Monthly Labor Review* 5:4 (October), 66–79.

Stern, B. (1939), "Labor Productivity in the Boot and Shoe Industry," *Monthly Labor Review* 48:2 (February), 271–92.

Stewart, E. (1922), "Efficiency of American Labor," *Monthly Labor Review* 15:1 (July), 1–12.

Stigler, G. J. (1966), *The Theory of Price,* Third Edition. New York: Macmillan.

Sudit, E. F. (1984), *Productivity Based Management.* Boston: Kluwer-Nijhoff.

Syverson, C. (2004a), "Product Substitutability and Productivity Dispersion," *Review of Economics and Statistics* 86:2 (May), 534–50.

Syverson, C. (2004b), "Market Structure and Productivity: A Concrete Example," *Journal of Political Economy* 112:6 (December), 1181–222.

Syverson, C. (2011), "What Determines Productivity?" *Journal of Economic Literature* 49:2 (June), 326–65.

Taussig, R. A., and W. L. Shaw (1985), "Accounting for Productivity: A Practical Approach," *Management Accounting* (May), 48–52.

Tax, S. (1953), *Penny Capitalism*. Chicago: University of Chicago Press.

Temin, P., ed. (1991), *Inside the Business Enterprise: Historical Perspectives on the Use of Information*. Chicago: University of Chicago Press.

Templé, P. (1971), "La Méthode des Surplus. Un Essai d'Application aux Comptes des Entreprises (1959–1967)," *Économie et Statistique* 29 (Décembre), 33–50.

Templé, P. (1976), "Déformations des Prix Relatifs et Gains de Productivité," *Economie et Statistique* 78 (May), 29–39.

Thouin, M. F., J. J. Hoffman, and E. W. Ford (2009), "IT Outsourcing and Firm-Level Performance : A Transaction Cost Perspective," *Information & Management* 46:8 (December), 463–69.

Törnqvist, L. (1936), "The Bank of Finland's Consumption Price Index," *Bank of Finland Monthly Bulletin* 10, 1–8.

Van Reenen, J. (2011), "Does Competition Raise Productivity Through Improving Management Quality?" *International Journal of Industrial Organization* 29:3 (May), 306–16.

Vincent, L. A. (1961), "The Main Formulae for Productivity Measurement in a National Economy or Sector," *Productivity Measurement Review* 25 (May), 5–17.

Vincent, L.-A. (1965), "De La Mesure de la Productivité aux Problemes Generaux de Gestion Economique," *Revue Economique* 6 (November), 879–924.

Vincent, A. L. A. (1968), *La Mesure de la Productivité*. Paris: Dunod.

Vincent, L. A. (1969), "La Productivité Globale Cle de L'Étude de la Repartition," *Revue Economique* 20:5 (Septembre), 783–829.

Wait, D. J. (1980), "Productivity Measurement: A Management Accounting Challenge," *Management Accounting* (May), 24–30.

Walsh, C. M. (1924), "Professor Edgeworth's Views on Index-Numbers," *Quarterly Journal of Economics* 38:3 (May), 500–19.

Wang, S. L., P. W. Heisey, W. E. Huffman, and K. O. Fuglie (2013), "Public R&D, Private R&D, and U.S. Agricultural Productivity Growth: Dynamic and Long-Run Relationships," *American Journal of Agricultural Economics* 95:5 (October), 1287–93.

Ward, B. (1958), "The Firm in Illyria: Market Syndicalism," *American Economic Review* 48:4 (September), 566–89.

Waters II, W. G., and J. Street (1998), "Monitoring the Performance of Government Trading Enterprises," *Australian Economic Review* 31:4 (December), 357–71.

Waters II, W. G., and M. W. Tretheway (1999), "Comparing Total Factor Productivity and Price Performance – Concepts and Application to Canadian Railways," *Journal of Transport Economics and Policy* 33:2, 209–20.

Weber, C. (1963), "The Mathematics of Variance Analysis," *Accounting Review* 38:3 (July), 534–39.

West, D. M. (2011), "Creating a 'Brain Gain' for U.S. Employers: The Role of Immigration," Brookings Policy Brief No. 178, January. http://www.brookings. edu/~/media/research/files/papers/2011/1/immigration%20west/01_immigration_west.pdf

Wolff, F.-C., D. Squires and P. Guillotreau (2013), "The Firm's Management in Production: Management, Firm, and Time Effects in an Indian Ocean Tuna Fishery," *American Journal of Agricultural Economics* 95:3 (April), 547–67.

"Donaldson Brown" http://www2.dupont.com/Phoenix_Heritage/en_US/1918_detail. html#more

The Economist (2013), "Here, There and Everywhere." http://www.economist.com/ search/apachesolr_search/outsourcing%20and%20offshoring

Review of Economic Dynamics 16:1 (January 2013), Special Issue: Misallocation and Productivity.

Author index

Subject index

Printed in the United States
By Bookmasters